THE
COUNTRY WOMEN'S
ASSOCIATION
COOK
BOOK

THE
COUNTRY WOMEN'S
ASSOCIATION

COOK
BOOK

Seventy Years in the Kitchen

These recipes have been compiled by members of the
Country Women's Association of NSW.

MURDOCH BOOKS

Published in 2009 by Murdoch Books Pty Limited

Murdoch Books Australia
Pier 8/9, 23 Hickson Road
Millers Point NSW 2000
Phone: +61 (0) 2 8220 2000
Fax: +61 (0) 2 8220 2558
www.murdochbooks.com.au

Murdoch Books UK Limited
Erico House, 6th Floor
93–99 Upper Richmond Road
Putney, London SW15 2TG
Phone: +44 (0) 20 8785 5995
Fax: +44 (0) 20 8785 5985
www.murdochbooks.co.uk

Chief Executive: Juliet Rogers
Publishing Director: Kay Scarlett

© Text, design and photography copyright
2009 Murdoch Books

Commissioning Editor: Jane Lawson
Project Manager and Editor:
    Jacqueline Blanchard
Food Editor: Leanne Kitchen
Food Consultant: Morna Wilson
Concept and Design: Sarah Odgers
Production: Alexandra Gonzalez

National Library of Australia
    Cataloguing-in-Publication Data:
Title: The Country Women's Association
    Cook Book: Seventy Years in the
    Kitchen.
Edition: 17th revised.
ISBN: 9781741963595 (hardback).
Subjects: Cookery.
Other Authors/Contributors:
Country Women's Association of
    New South Wales.
Dewey Number: 641.5

Photographs courtesy of the Country
    Women's Association of NSW.
Colour separation: Colour Chiefs
Printed by 1010 Printing International
    Limited in 2009. PRINTED IN
    CHINA. Reprinted 2009.

First published in 1937
and in print ever since.

Contents

Beverages

Ambrosia

*110 g (¹/₂ cup) sugar, juice of 3 oranges, juice of 1 grapefruit,
juice of 1 lemon, 4 cups pineapple juice, 1 slice chopped pineapple,
30 g (¹/₂ cup) shredded coconut, 5 chopped maraschino cherries*

Put the sugar and 750 ml (3 cups) water in a saucepan and simmer for 5 minutes, then allow to cool. Mix in the orange, grapefruit, lemon and pineapple juices, then add the chopped pineapple, coconut and cherries, stirring well. Serve chilled.

Boston Cream

*900 g (4 cups) sugar, 4 tablespoons cream of tartar,
1¹/₂ tablespoons lemon essence, 3 teaspoons tartaric acid, 1 egg white*

Put the sugar and cream of tartar in a bowl and pour over 2.4 litres of boiling water, stirring to combine and dissolve. When cold, add the lemon essence and tartaric acid. Whisk the egg white until stiff peaks form and gently stir through to combine. Serve chilled.

Caramel (For Flavouring)

900 g (4 cups) sugar, 500 ml (2 cups) boiling water

This water gives to many drinks a distinctive flavour. Put the sugar and 250 ml (1 cup) water into a saucepan and boil rather fast until the mixture begins to turn brown. Be very careful to take it off the heat at once, because it burns easily, which ruins the flavour. Pour in the boiling water, stand over gentle heat, and stir until all dissolved. More water can be added if liked. It may be used at once or poured into sterilised bottles for future use.

Cherry Cocktail

400 g (2 cups) pitted cherries, 160 g (1 cup) chopped pineapple, juice of 1 lemon,
125 ml (¹/₂ cup) pineapple juice, sugar, mint leaves

Put the cherries and pineapple in a jug. Pour in the lemon juice and pineapple juice. Chill thoroughly. Grind some sugar and mint leaves together and sprinkle into the cherry cocktail. Refrigerate for 1 hour before serving.

Cider Cup

600 ml cider, 750 ml (3 cups) soda water, 250 ml (1 cup) sherry,
1 tablespoon sugar, a pinch of grated nutmeg, 6 drops lemon essence,
juice of ¹/₂ lemon, 1 strip lemon rind

Mix together the cider, soda water and sherry. Stir in the sugar, nutmeg, lemon essence, lemon juice and lemon rind. Refrigerate until ready to serve.

Claret Cup

Lemon, sugar, ground nutmeg, lemonade, soda water, claret

Allow six 750 ml bottles of lemonade and three 750 ml bottles of soda water for every two 750 ml bottles of claret. Thinly slice the lemon, removing the seeds, and put into a large bowl. Sprinkle with sugar and a little ground nutmeg. When ready to serve, pour over first the lemonade, then the soda water and lastly the claret. Mix well and drop into it some crushed ice, to serve.

When picnicking and you wish to take a bottle of milk, add a pinch of bicarbonate of soda and it will keep fresh all day corked.

Hot Cocoa

The perfect cup of cocoa, like any other quality food,
requires a little extra care and attention in its preparation.
To make the perfect cup, the cocoa is first mixed with the required
quantity of sugar to a smooth paste, by adding a small quantity of
warm milk, then it is added to the remainder of the milk. It is then
transferred to a saucepan, just brought to the boil, and tipped into
a jug for whisking. It is then ready to serve.

Currant Cocktail

*150 g (1 cup) currants, 220 g (1 cup) sugar, juice of 2 oranges,
juice of 2 lemons, 2.4 litres (9²/₃ cups) soda water, orange slices*

Put the currants in a saucepan with 500 ml (2 cups) water and bring to the boil.
Reduce the heat and simmer gently until the currants are soft and broken. Add the
sugar and simmer for 10 minutes; strain. For every 500 ml (2 cups) currant syrup
add the strained juice of 2 oranges and 2 lemons. Chill and add the soda water. Serve
with orange slices to garnish.

Eden Cocktail

9 passionfruit, juice of 8 oranges, 600 ml cider, 2 tablespoons ginger ale

Strain juice from the passionfruit pulp and orange juice into a bowl and add the cider
and ginger ale. Chill and serve in cocktail glasses.

Fiji Fruit Cocktail

1 banana, 250 ml (1 cup) pineapple juice, 2 oranges, 750 ml (3 cups) ginger ale

Dice the banana. Mix the banana, pineapple juice and orange juice together. Just
before serving add the chilled ginger ale and serve at once.

Fruit Cocktail 1

1 grapefruit, crushed pineapple, banana, strawberries, 80 ml (¹/₃ cup) sherry,
3 tablespoons apricot brandy, 110 g (¹/₂ cup) sugar, a pinch of salt, cherries

Remove the pulp from the grapefruit, put into a bowl with the pineapple, banana and strawberries. Pour over the sherry, apricot brandy, sugar and salt, and stir to combine. Chill thoroughly. Serve in cocktail glasses, garnished with cherries.

Fruit Cocktail 2

juice of 1 lemon, juice of 1 orange, mint leaves, strawberry

Half-fill a shaker with ice and add the lemon and orange juices. Add several leaves of mint. Shake well, strain, and serve in small glasses. Decorate with a strawberry.

Fruit Cocktail 3

125 ml (¹/₂ cup) fruit syrup, 2 tablespoons freshly squeezed lemon juice,
2 tablespoons freshly squeezed orange juice, 1 tablespoon sugar,
300 ml soda water, strawberries

Shake all of the ingredients, except the strawberries, together in a shaker. Serve in tall glasses with some shaved ice. Place a strawberry in each glass and serve.

If sugar is added to mint while chopping on the board, mint will be easier to chop and finer, and sugar will not drop to bottom of jug when served.

Fruit Cup

440 g (2 cups) sugar, 600 ml strong tea, 12 oranges, 6 lemons, 800 g (3 cups)
tinned crushed pineapple, 1 fresh pineapple, two 750 ml bottles soda water

Boil the sugar in 250 ml (1 cup) water for 10 minutes. Pour the tea in as soon as it
has infused (strain any leaves). Squeeze and strain the juice from the oranges and
lemons and add to the mixture with the pineapple. Cut the skin from the fresh
pineapple and remove the core, finely chop and add to the mixture. Pour into a large
bowl and add the soda water and sufficient cold water to make 4 litres, or to taste.

Variation If not using pineapple add the juice of 6–9 lemons instead. You
can adjust this recipe to serve up to 200 people, using 12 dozen oranges, 9 dozen
lemons, 2.4 g (12 cups) tinned crushed pineapple, 3.6 litres strong tea, 3.6 kg sugar
melted into a syrup, 6 litres soda water and enough cold water to make up to
15–18 litres.

Fruit Punch 1

300 ml strong tea, 4 tablespoons sugar, 185 ml (3/4 cup) freshly squeezed orange
juice, 3 tablespoons freshly squeezed lemon juice, 4 tablespoons sugar,
300 ml ginger ale, 300 ml soda water, 3 tablespoons sherry

Pour the tea over the sugar and as soon as it dissolves add the orange and lemon
juice. Strain over a large piece of ice. Just before serving, add the ginger ale, soda
water and sherry. Garnish with slices of orange or lemon.

Fruit Punch 2

1/2 pineapple, 220 g (1 cup) sugar, 250 ml (1 cup) freshly squeezed orange juice,
125 ml (1/2 cup) freshly squeezed lemon juice

Remove the pineapple skin and chop the flesh. Boil 1.2 litres water and add the
sugar and pineapple. Add the orange and lemon juice, then allow to cool. Strain and
refrigerate until ready to serve. Serve with crushed ice.

Fruit Punch 3

440 g (2 cups) sugar, juice of 6 oranges, juice of 6 lemons,
160 g (1 cup) chopped pineapple, 175 g (1 cup) chopped strawberries,
1 chopped banana, 200 g (1 cup) maraschino cherries

Combine 500 ml (2 cups) water and the sugar in a saucepan over medium heat and stir until the sugar dissolves. Remove from heat and allow to cool, then stir in the lemon and orange juice and refrigerate until chilled. Stir the fruit into the water just before serving. Sufficient for 25 people.

Fruit Punch 4

1 tablespoon freshly squeezed lemon juice, 375 ml (1½ cups) freshly squeezed
orange juice, 220 g (1 cup) sugar, 1.2 litres ginger ale, 1.2 litres soda water,
1 handful pitted cherries

Mix the lemon and orange juice together and stir in the sugar. Refrigerate for 4 hours. Fill a jug with ice and pour over it the fruit juice, ginger ale and soda water. Add the cherries and serve at once.

Ginger Beer

140 g finely sliced ginger, 2.25 kg (10¼ cups) sugar, 300 ml freshly squeezed
lemon juice, 115 g (⅓ cup) honey, 1 egg white, 1 tablespoon lemon essence

Boil the ginger in 3.6 litres of water for 30 minutes, then add the sugar, lemon juice, honey and another 3 litres of water. Strain through a fine sieve. Lightly whisk the egg white and add to the liquid when cold. Stir through the essence of lemon. Allow to stand for 4 days, then pour into sterilised bottles and seal securely. The ginger beer will be ready 3 days after bottling.

Grapefruit Cocktail

250 ml (1 cup) grapefruit juice, 250 ml (1 cup) freshly squeezed orange juice, sugar, 150 g (1 cup) strawberries, 190 g (1 cup) chopped pineapple, extra strawberries for garnish

Mix the juice from the grapefruit and oranges in a bowl, sweeten to taste with sugar, and chill. Wash the strawberries, cut in halves and mix into the cocktail with the diced pineapple. Serve in cocktail glasses or in the grapefruit shells. Garnish with whole strawberries.

Half and Half

1 orange, 1 lemon, 50 g (¹/₃ cup) sugar cubes, 1.2 litres boiling water

Wash and dry the fruit. Rub the sugar cubes over the skin of the lemon to extract the oil. Put the sugar into a jug and squeeze in the juice from the orange and lemon. Pour in the boiling water and allow to cool. Strain and chill the juice, then serve with shaved ice. The juice of 12 passionfruit can be substituted for the orange and lemon.

Iced Tea

*2 teaspoons tea leaves, 125 ml (¹/₂ cup) freshly squeezed orange juice,
125 ml (¹/₂ cup) freshly squeezed lemon juice,
600 ml boiling water, 1 teaspoon sugar, lemon slices*

Make the tea with 600 ml freshly boiled water and allow to infuse for 4 minutes. Strain carefully into a jug containing crushed ice. Mix in the orange juice, lemon juices and sugar. Chill and serve with sugar and thin lemon slices. This is a delicious summer beverage and may be served with tea or supper.

Lemonade

Lemons, sugar, boiling water

Allow the juice of 1 lemon for each person. For each lemon used, melt 1 tablespoon sugar with 2 tablespoons boiling water and stir well. Serve in tall glasses and fill with chilled, plain or aerated water.

Lemon Egg Cream Flip

1 egg white, sugar, juice of 1 lemon

Whisk the egg white and sugar to a stiff froth, then add the lemon juice. Whisk again, then add 500 ml (2 cups) water and serve. This is a refreshing drink for summer.

Lemon Ice Cream Soda

juice of 1 lemon, sugar, ice cream, orange or vanilla essence, soda water

Put into a large tumbler the lemon juice and add a little sugar. Add a portion of ice cream, which may be flavoured with orange or vanilla essence; fill up with soda water and serve at once with straws.

Lemon Syrup

2 lemons, 1.3 kg (6 cups) sugar, 1.8 litres boiling water,
1½ tablespoons tartaric acid, 1 teaspoon lemon essence

Peel the lemons and remove any white pith. Cut into quarters and remove the seeds. Put the sugar and a little water in a saucepan and boil until the sugar is slightly browned, then add remainder of water and the lemons. Let boil until the sugar is dissolved, and just before removing from the heat, add the tartaric acid and lemon essence. Strain, pour into sterilised bottles and seal securely when cold.

Lemon Tea

½ lemon to each person, 300 ml boiling water, 1 teaspoon tea leaves, lemon slices

Squeeze the lemon into a jug and add the boiling water. Pour this onto the tea in the teapot and stand for 2 minutes; strain into glasses. Serve cut slices of lemon separately. Lemon tea can be served with ice. Allow tea to become quite cold. Put a lump of ice into each glass. Pour tea over. Serve with lemon slices.

Limeade

juice of 2 limes, sugar, soda water

Place some crushed ice in a glass. Pour over the lime juice and sugar. Fill with water or soda water. Serve at once.

Mint Julep

1 bunch mint, 220 g (1 cup) sugar, juice of 5 lemons, two 750 ml bottles ginger ale

Wash the mint, then place it in a bowl and cover it with the sugar. Strain the lemon juice over the top. Leave for 2 hours, then transfer the liquid to a glass jug. Add a large lump of ice and stir through the ginger ale. Garnish with extra mint sprigs.

Mint Tea

3.6 litres strong tea, 660 g (3 cups) caster sugar, 450 ml freshly squeezed lemon juice, 2.25 litres soda water, fresh mint sprigs

Make tea in the usual way (allow 4 teaspoons tea leaves for every 1.2 litres of boiling water). Strain the tea. Add sugar, then cool. Stir in the lemon juice, add soda water and serve in a jug with ice. Place sprigs of mint in the jug. A few berries, green grapes, or a slice of lemon and orange may be added to each jug.

A delicious and beneficial orange cordial

Finely grate the zest of 6–8 oranges and 2 lemons. Juice all the citrus fruit. Pour 1.8 litres boiling water over the juice and zest and stir in 2.25 kg sugar, 3 tablespoons tartaric acid, 1½ tablespoons citric acid and 375 g epsom salts. Cool, then pour into sterilised bottles.

Pineapple Ambrosia

110 g (½ cup) sugar, 500 ml (2 cups) tinned pineapple syrup, 600 ml ginger ale

Put 500 ml (2 cups) water in a saucepan with the sugar and bring to the boil. Boil for 5 minutes, then add the pineapple syrup and chill. Before serving, add the ginger ale and stir well.

Pineapple Cup

520 g (2 cups) tinned crushed pineapple, juice of 1 grapefruit, juice of 2 oranges, juice of 1 lemon, 160 g (½ cup) red currant jelly, maraschino cherries, mint sprigs

Mix together the pineapple pulp and grapefruit, orange and lemon juices. Melt the red currant jelly and add to juice with 2.1 litres water. Chill thoroughly. Serve in goblets garnished with maraschino cherries and sprigs of mint.

Pineapple Syrup

Pineapple, sugar, tartaric acid

Peel, core, and cut up as much pineapple as required, cover with water for 24 hours (less in summer), then bring to the boil slowly and simmer for 1 hour, or a little longer. Strain and allow 220 g (1 cup) sugar for every 250 ml (1 cup) syrup. Return to the boil, reduce the heat and simmer for 20 minutes. Allow to cool, then add 3 tablespoons tartaric acid and bottle as soon as the acid has dissolved. A little in a glass of iced water or soda water makes a delicious drink.

Sherbert

2 teaspoons lemon essence, 225 g (1³/₄ cups) icing sugar,
115 g (¹/₂ cup) tartaric acid, 115 g (¹/₂ cup) bicarbonate of soda

Put the essence of lemon onto the sugar and leave to dry. Mix in the tartaric acid and bicarbonate of soda. Pass all the ingredients through a fine sieve. Put the powder into a bottle and seal securely. It is important that dampness be excluded. Used in the preparation of 1 teaspoon to a tumbler of water it makes a very refreshing drink.

Strawberry Cocktail

Strawberries, sugar, maraschino cherries, whipped cream

Mash the strawberries, sweeten with the sugar and press through a sieve. Place on ice until required. Mix equal quantities of the strawberry pulp and maraschino cherries and serve with shaved ice and a spoonful of whipped cream on each glass.

Strawberry Lemonade

12 strawberries, juice of ¹/₂ lemon, 2 teaspoons sugar, 1 stiffly beaten egg white

Press the strawberries through a sieve into a shaker. Add the lemon juice to the shaker with the sugar and 185 ml (³/₄ cup) crushed ice and water. Shake vigorously and strain into a glass. Stir in the egg white and garnish with a strawberry.

Sugar Syrup

Boil 880 g (4 cups) sugar in 1 litre (4 cups) water for 10 minutes.
This syrup gives a smooth texture to drinks and is easily mixed
through. The syrup can be kept on hand and used as needed.

Sugar Syrup for Summer Drinks

1.3 kg (6 cups) sugar

Boil 1.25 litres (5 cups) water and the sugar together for 5 minutes. Pour into a sterilised jar and seal securely. Allow 1 tablespoon of this syrup to each glass.

Summer Punch

440 g (2 cups) sugar, 1 large handful mint leaves,
625 ml (1½ cups) boiling water, 250 ml (1 cup) cranberry juice,
250 ml (1 cup) freshly squeezed orange juice, 250 ml (1 cup) freshly squeezed
lemon juice, 600 ml claret, soda water, caster sugar

Make a syrup by boiling 1.2 litres water and the sugar for 20 minutes. Pour the boiling water over the mint. Cover, allow to stand for 5 minutes; strain. Add to the syrup. When cool, add the cranberry juice, the strained orange and lemon juices and claret. Dilute to taste with soda water. Garnish with fresh sprigs of mint dusted with caster sugar.

Tea Punch

4 tablespoons sugar, 250 ml (1 cup) hot tea,
185 ml (¾ cup) freshly squeezed orange juice, 80 ml (⅓ cup) freshly squeezed
lemon juice, 600 ml ginger ale, 600 ml soda water,
3 tablespoons sherry, mint sprigs, orange slices

Stir the sugar into the hot tea. When dissolved, add the orange and lemon juices. When cold, add ginger ale, soda water and sherry; then some shaved ice. Serve in glasses garnished with sprigs of mint or thin slices of orange.

Tempting Iced Coffee

Iced coffee, which has been flavoured with vanilla, makes a delicious drink if served with a 'topping' of partially whipped cream, or again, iced coffee can be mixed with soda water, and if liked, a little cream added. To make an iced coffee, put 1 litre (4 cups) milk and 2 tablespoons coffee syrup into a jug and stir well, or better still, pour from one jug to another until well mixed. Chill thoroughly, and pour into tall glasses and serve with whipped cream on top, also a little powdered cinnamon. To make the coffee syrup put 3 heaped tablespoons coffee, a pinch of salt and 250 ml (1 cup) water into a saucepan and simmer slowly for 2 minutes. Remove from the heat and allow to stand for 5 minutes. Strain carefully into a saucepan, add 220 g (1 cup) sugar, and stir until the sugar is dissolved. Bring to the boil and boil without stirring for about 5 minutes. Cool, pour into a jar, and keep in the ice-chest until needed.

Tennis Cup

1 small pineapple, juice of 2 oranges, 3 lemons, 220 g (1 cup) sugar,
2.4 litres iced water

Remove the skin of the pineapple and thinly slice the flesh. Place in a bowl with the orange juice. Finely grate a little of the lemon zest and juice the lemons. Add the juice and zest to the bowl with the sugar. Cover the bowl and let it stand for 1 hour. Strain the juice and stir in 2.4 litres iced water. Return a few pieces of pineapple to the drink and serve.

Tomato Juice Cocktail 1

250 ml (1 cup) tomato juice, 1 tablespoonful vinegar, a pinch of salt,
½ bay leaf, 1 teaspoon grated onion,
1 tablespoonful freshly squeezed lemon juice, celery stick

Mix the tomato juice with the vinegar, salt, bay leaf, onion, lemon juice and a bruised celery stick. Allow to stand for 15 minutes and strain and serve.

Tomato Juice Cocktail 2

500 ml (2 cups) tomato juice, ½ teaspoon salt, ½ teaspoon grated onion,
½ bay leaf, 1 teaspoon vinegar

Combine all the ingredients in a saucepan and simmer for 10 minutes. Strain the cocktail and chill thoroughly before serving.

Tomato Juice Cocktail 3

500 ml (2 cups) tomato juice, 2 teaspoons onion juice, ½ bay leaf,
1 teaspoon salt, ½ teaspoon sugar, 2 teaspoons chopped parsley,
2 tablespoons freshly squeezed lemon juice, 2 tablespoons Worcestershire sauce,
2 teaspoons chilli sauce, 2 celery sticks

Combine the tomato juice, onion juice, bay leaf, salt, sugar, parsley, lemon juice, Worcestershire sauce and chilli sauce, mixing well. Chill and strain the liquid, then serve in glasses with the bruised celery sticks.

Waikiki Punch

Heat 500 ml (2 cups) pineapple juice in a saucepan and stir
in 110 g (½ cup) sugar until dissolved. Allow to cool,
then stir in 500 ml (2 cups) cold water and 500 ml (2 cups)
grape juice. Serve chilled with crushed ice.

CWA of New South Wales, Gunnedah — the younger set.

STARTERS

Canapés

A canapé is a small piece of bread of suitable size and shape, either fried or toasted. Modern substitutes for the bread include a variety of intriguing wafers and crackers, which can be transformed with the whisk of a pastry brush dipped in beaten egg and a moment's browning under the grill. But, whatever the foundation, it is the spread or filling that gives a canapé its individuality. The majority of fillings are improved by early mixing and rest in the refrigerator before serving.

Browned Bread Cubes

Cut fresh bread in slices a bit over 1 cm thick; remove crusts and cut each slice into nine cubes. Dip in melted butter and then in finely grated Parmesan cheese. Bake in a 240°C oven until lightly browned.

Bubble Bread

This bread is similar to a Thin Captain biscuit, being dry, very thin, but delicious for savouries, cheese, or just butter. Take 280 g (1¾ cups) plain flour, 1 teaspoon salt, 2 teaspoons butter, and rub into flour and salt. Mix into a stiff paste with a little milk. Knead a little. Take small pieces of dough and roll out as thinly as possible. Prick all over with a fork. Cut into strips and bake in 220°C oven until lightly browned. Will keep for weeks in an airtight container.

Caviar Canapés

For the red (dyed) roe, flank the caviar with a border of finely chopped green pepper and hard-cooked egg white. For the real Russian caviar add 1 tablespoon sour cream to 55 g caviar. Chill. Finely chop ½ white onion and 3 parsley sprigs and add to the caviar. Fill wafer cups or toast cases with caviar and place a bit of the chopped onion and parsley in the centre.

Christmas Canapés

Cut bread in star-shaped pieces; toast on one side. Spread the untoasted side with sardine paste and cover with pimento that has been cut to the same size and shape as the toast. Cream some butter and flavour to taste with sardine paste. With a tiny paper tube, make a border of the sardine butter around the edge of the canapé. Cover with finely chopped parsley. Put a mound of caviar in the centre, sprinkle with a few drops of freshly squeezed lemon juice and a little more parsley. Sifted egg yolks may replace the caviar. These canapés may be made in bell shapes if desired.

Cinnamon Toast

Toast thin slices of bread and spread with butter. Sprinkle with equal quantities of cinnamon and sugar. Put in the oven for a few minutes and serve hot.

Cottage Cheese

Heat 1.2 litres milk to lukewarm, dissolve 4 teaspoons liquid rennet in a little hot water and add to the milk. Let set undisturbed for 12 hours in a cool place. Turn into a large square piece of muslin, tie in ball formation, and let all liquid drip out. Leave 12 hours. Put into bowl, add salt and form into pats. Nice with bread and butter, or salad.

Creole Canapés

Take some chicken livers, mushrooms, lemon juice, onion juice, salt and pepper to taste, strips of pimento, buttered toast. Allow one chicken liver for each savoury required, and one croute of buttered toast. Sauté the livers in a little hot bacon fat, with 1 teaspoon onion juice, until tender, then crush and smooth to a paste with a wooden spoon. Season to taste with salt, lemon juice and pepper. Spread on the croutes, sprinkle with chopped, cooked mushrooms (using fresh or tinned ones), and garnish each savoury with a strip of pimento.

Croutons Anglais

Mix 3 hard-boiled egg yolks with 1 teaspoon chopped capers and a pinch of curry powder. Add cream until it forms a smooth paste. Arrange this in patterns on squares of toast and garnish with slices of tomato and gherkin.

Croutons Marine

Mix to a paste 2 hard-boiled egg yolks, a pinch of mustard, salt, 1 tablespoon parsley and a little butter. Spread heart-shaped croutons with this mixture and arrange an anchovy fillet on each, surrounded by chopped gherkins.

Gruyére Spread

Blend to a smooth paste 50 g grated Gruyére cheese with 1 teaspoon cream and 2 teaspoons sherry. Place in wafer cups and serve.

Liverwurst Spread

Mash 115 g liverwurst; mix with 3 tablespoons mayonnaise, 4 tablespoons boiled rice (you will need 2 tablespoons uncooked rice), and ½ teaspoon celery salt. Mound slightly on rounds of bread and top with a little Indian Chutney (see recipes, pages 193–4).

Lobster Spread

Chop some fresh lobster meat. For every 85 g (½ cup) lobster meat mix in 2 teaspoons sherry and 2 tablespoons freshly grated cheese. (Preserve fingertips by pressing the cheese through a wire strainer). Butter thin slices of bread and cut into triangles. Cover with the spread, mounding it slightly. Sprinkle with buttered crumbs. Lightly brown under the grill.

Olive Spread

Chop 12 small pitted olives. Finely chop or grind 40 g (¼ cup) raw almonds. Cut 4 slices crisply cooked bacon into fine pieces. Then mix all together with 90 g (⅓ cup) mayonnaise and salt, to taste. Decorate with a round of olive.

Prawn and Egg Mayonnaise Spread

Put an equal quantity of freshly shelled prawns and hard-boiled eggs (cut into dice) together in a glass soufflé dish. Mix lightly with a good mayonnaise sauce. Chill well and serve on top of sliced brown bread and butter.

Sardine Canapés

Use squares of toast. Spread the toast thickly with Anchovy Butter (see recipe, page 119) and arrange a sardine over each. Garnish with a cucumber, gherkins and capers.

Sausage Canapés

Use chicken and ham sausage. Cut the bread in rounds of the same size. Spread with butter and cover with a thinly sliced round of sausage. Decorate with rounds of sliced gherkins and radishes.

Savoury Cream Spread

Whip 125 g (½ cup) cream and mix in cayenne pepper, to taste. Add a few drops of white vinegar, a pinch of salt and a little mustard. Use for topping any savouries or garnishing canapés.

Appetisers

Angels on Horseback

Prawns, cleaned and marinated for a time in French Dressing (see recipe, page 100), are placed on toothpicks and arranged on a large pale yellow grapefruit.

Asparagus Cups

Drain 425 g tinned asparagus spears and cut the stems into small pieces, keeping a few nice tips for garnishing. Add a little cream and a few drops lemon juice to 1 cup white sauce (see recipe, page 118) and stir through the asparagus. Fill pastry cups with this mixture and serve hot.

Asparagus Logs

Roll out Puff Pastry (see recipe, page 286) to about 5 mm thick. Cut into small squares as for sausage rolls. Put an asparagus spear on each square, roll pastry over and glaze with beaten egg. Bake in a 180°C oven for 30 minutes. Serve hot. You can use slices of bacon, rolled neatly, instead of asparagus.

Bacon Eggs

Halve 4 hard-boiled eggs lengthways; remove and mash the yolks. Grill 4 slices of bacon and cut into fine pieces. Mix the yolks and bacon with 2 tablespoons finely chopped parsley and 4 tablespoons mayonnaise. Fill the egg whites with the filling and run a pastry wheel across the top. Dot with paprika.

Bacon Roll-up

Bacon, of course, is a part of our daily fare, but given this simple style it steps into the canapé class. Cut slices of bacon in half, spread each with 1 teaspoon freshly grated cheese and ¼ teaspoon chutney or Indian Chutney (see recipes, pages 193–4). Or, just spread the bacon with mustard. Roll up tightly and spear with a toothpick. Grill the bacon for 2 minutes on each side. Drain on paper towel and serve hot.

Bendigo Savoury Rolls

Roll out some Puff Pastry (see recipe, page 286) and smear with a little mustard, sprinkle thickly with dry grated cheese and season with salt and pepper. Roll up like a roly-poly and flatten the roll lightly with a rolling pin. Cut into small oblongs. Put half a blanched almond on each and bake in a 220°C oven.

Caviar Baskets

Peel some hard-boiled eggs and chill. Cut a slice from the larger end of each egg so the basket will stand, then cut away part of the white, leaving a handle. Remove the yolks and mash to a paste. Mix with enough highly seasoned mayonnaise to flavour and moisten well. Season with red lumpfish roe, a few drops of onion juice and some lemon juice. Finely chop the leftover egg whites and add to the filling. Fill the baskets and top with the mayonnaise mixture, piping it with a rose or star nozzle. Dot the centre of the rosette with a fleck of pimento. Serve on a circle of watercress.

Chaud-froid

A chaud-froid of egg is easily done, and very pretty when finished. The eggs
are usually hard-boiled, then shelled and halved lengthways. The yolks are then
removed, rubbed through a sieve and mixed with finely minced ham or tongue,
a bit of minced pickle, a little French Dressing (see recipe, page 100) to moisten,
and a few chopped capers. They are seasoned and replaced in the egg white.
The halves are then put together again and dipped in the chaud-froid sauce.
While this is stiffening, the decorations are arranged.

In the same way you may prepare meat slices and breasts of chicken or turkey,
or braised veal cutlets, lamb chops, or even slices of salmon, halibut and tuna fish,
which have been neatly prepared and made into attractive pieces for serving.

Chaud-froid of Chicken

Allow a whole roast chicken to cool, remove the skin and cut neat joints; lay
on a flat dish. Dissolve 2 teaspoons powdered gelatine in a little water and add
to a bowl with 1 tablespoon cream and 250 ml (1 cup) White Sauce (see recipe,
page 118). When cool, coat each piece of chicken with the sauce and allow to
set. Pile the chicken pieces in the centre of a dish and garnish with crisp salad
vegetables and hard-boiled eggs.

Chaud-froid of Eggs

Poach 6–8 eggs. Drain and place them on a flat dish. Allow to get quite cold, then
neatly trim the edges with a sharp knife. Into a large cake tin pour some Savoury
Jelly (Aspic) (see recipe, page 149) to a depth of 4 cm. Set it firmly. Mix together
225 ml Béchamel Sauce (see recipe, page 105) and 225 ml Savoury Jelly. Garnish
the tops of the eggs with strips of chilli, gherkin and some capers. Pour a thin layer
of jelly over each egg to glaze them. Allow to set firm, then trim the edges again.
Gently invert the jelly from the tin, without breaking, onto a flat dish. Arrange the
eggs on the jelly. Garnish with shredded lettuce leaves, curled celery and sliced
tomatoes. Serve with a suitable dressing.

Chaud-froid of Eggs and Asparagus

Poach 6–8 eggs. Drain and place them on a flat dish. Allow to get quite cold, then
neatly trim the edges with a sharp knife. Mix together 150 ml White Sauce (see
recipe, page 118) and 150 ml Savoury Jelly (Aspic) (see recipe, page 149). Drain
and purée 425 g tinned asparagus spears and add to the sauce mixture. Stir the
mixture until it is cold, but not setting. Brush this mixture over each egg and allow
to set firm. Pour a little jelly over each to give a glossy appearance. Trim edges with
a knife. When all is set, arrange on a flat dish on on a bed of lettuce leaves and
place any leftover asparagus on top. Serve with a suitable dressing.

Celery Sticks

Use tender white inner celery sticks and allow the white leaves to remain on the top. Wash them in cold water and dry thoroughly. Mix 2 tablespoons of cream cheese with 1 tablespoon softened butter and 2 tablespoons cream. Season to taste with a little chopped parsley, some salt, pepper, mustard and paprika. Fill the celery with the cheese mixture. Serve standing upright in the centre of a plate of canapés or hors-d'oeuvres.

Cheese Cubes

Cut 115 g cheese into cubes. Spear a tiny pickle or onion onto a toothpick, then the cheese cube. Sprinkle with a little paprika and add a walnut-half on the other end.

Cheese Dreams

Cut circles into sliced white bread, so they have a diameter of 4 cm each. Spread thickly with Welsh Rarebit mixture (see recipe, page 48); top with a round of bacon that has been cut to fit and bake in a 220°C oven for 5–7 minutes. Garnish with a circle of capers around the base and a slice of stuffed olive on top.

Cheese Éclairs

Make 150 ml thick White Sauce (see recipe, page 118), using a little cream if you have it to spare, and stir into the sauce 2–3 tablespoons of grated cheese. Season with a little mustard, salt and cayenne pepper and beat to a smooth cream. It must be firm and heated through. Fill éclair cases with the sauce and put in the oven to warm before serving.

Cheese Rolls

Cut slices of thin bread and spread with butter. Spread with a thick layer of cream cheese or Neufchâtel cheese and roll up into a log. Toast under a hot grill and serve very hot.

Cheese Straws 1

Rub 55 g butter into 85 g flour; mix with 175 g (1¾ cups) finely-grated parmesan cheese, 55 g (½ cup) breadcrumbs, ½ teaspoon salt and a pinch of cayenne pepper. Add enough water to form a rather dry paste. Roll out thinly and cut into strips. Bake on greased baking trays in a 180°C oven for 5–10 minutes, or until golden and crisp.

Cheese Straws 2

Rub 150 g (1 cup) plain flour together with 2 tablespoons butter and 3 tablespoons cheese. Mix with a little cold water, to moisten, then stir through some cayenne pepper and salt, to taste. Roll the dough out to 1 cm thick and cut into long, thin strips. Bake in a 220°C oven for 15–20 minutes, or until golden and crisp.

Cheese Straws 3

Rub 55 g butter into 55 g (½ cup) plain flour. Add 55 g (½ cup) grated cheese, cayenne pepper and salt, to taste. Mix all the ingredients together well. Roll out the dough to 1 cm thick and cut into strips. Bake in a 180°C oven for 5–10 minutes, or until golden and crisp.

Cheese Straws — Special

Mix 55 g (½ cup) plain flour with 55 g (½ cup) breadcrumbs and 55 g (½ cup) grated cheese. Rub in 55 g butter and add cayenne pepper and salt, to taste. Moisten with 1 egg, stirring thoroughly to combine. Roll the dough out to 1 cm thick and cut into long, thin strips. Bake in a 220°C oven for 15–20 minutes, or until golden and crisp.

Cheese Toast

Remove the crusts from 2 slices of bread and toast under the grill on one side only. When cool, butter the untoasted side. Meanwhile, whip 2 egg whites to a stiff froth. Stir in 55 g (½ cup) grated cheese, ½ teaspoon finely chopped chives and season to taste. Pile the mixture on the buttered side of the toast. Bake in a 180°C oven for 10–15 minutes, or until golden brown.

Cheese Turnovers

Sift 150 g (1 cup) self-raising flour into a bowl and rub in 2 tablespoons butter and 1 heaped tablespoon cream cheese. Add 1 beaten egg (keeping back a little to use for brushing), then add sufficient cold water to make a stiff dough. Roll out the dough very thinly, cut with a small fluted pastry cutter, and spread Anchovy Butter (see recipe, page 119) on one half of the biscuit. Brush the edge with cold water and fold over the other half of the biscuit to cover (like you do turnovers). Brush the top of each turnover with the remaining egg. Bake in a 180°C oven for 10–20 minutes, or until golden.

Crabmeat Puffs

Mix 175 g (1 cup) tinned chopped crabmeat with 2 tablespoons cream and 125 ml (½ cup) White Sauce (see recipe, page 118). Add a few drops of pink food colouring and stir to combine. Fill puff pastry cases with the crabmeat mixture and serve hot. Whitebait puffs are made in the same way by substituting whitebait for crabmeat.

Devilled Chicken Livers

Halve the livers and brush with mustard, then sprinkle with salt and paprika. Wrap the livers in bacon slices and grill or toast in a 220°C oven. Serve with gherkin pickles sliced thinly almost to the end, then spread out in fan shape.

Devilled Oysters

Mix tomato sauce, Worcestershire sauce, melted butter, juice of 1 lemon, mustard, cayenne pepper and a pinch of salt together in a bowl. Pour over cleaned oysters on the half-shell and sprinkle a few breadcrumbs on top. Bake in a 240°C oven for 6 minutes.

Grilled Oysters

Place the unopened oysters under a hot grill. As soon as they are open they will be cooked. Open them. Melt some butter in a saucepan over low heat and stir in some salt, cayenne pepper and a squeeze of lemon juice. Put a little on each oyster. Serve at once, garnished with sprigs of parsley

Ham Toast

Mince 115 g ham and put in a saucepan with 2 teaspoons butter, 2 tablespoons cream, 2 beaten egg yolks, some chopped capers and little cayenne pepper. Stir over low heat until thick. Spread on hot buttered toast that has been cut into circles with a 2.5 cm diameter pastry cutter. Dust with paprika and serve at once.

Hors-d'oeuvres Allemandes

Cook frankfurter sausages for 5 minutes in boiling water to which enough malt vinegar has been added to make it slightly acid. Drain, peel, cool and cut the sausages into 2.5 cm pieces. Marinate these in French Dressing (see recipe, page 100) for 1 hour, then roll in finely chopped parsley to coat. Cut small peeled tomatoes into thin slices; on these place slices of hard-boiled egg, then stand the sausage sections upright on the egg slices. Top each with a disc of pimento.

Liptauer Cheese

Mix together 450 g cream cheese and 115 g softened butter. Rinse about 5 anchovy fillets and chop into fine pieces. Stir into the cheese, together with a little grated onion, capers and plenty of cayenne pepper. Season with salt, to taste, and pile up on a dish. Serve surrounded by radishes and parsley.

Liverwurst Tidbits

Mash 225 g liverwurst to a paste, then mix in 1 egg yolk, 80 g (1 cup) breadcrumbs and 80 g (½ cup) chopped green capsicums. Add enough tomato sauce to the mixture so it is soft enough to roll. Add salt, to taste, and fold in 1 stiffly beaten egg white. Deep-fry teaspoonfuls of the mixture, in batches, for 3–5 minutes, or until golden brown. Drain on paper towel and serve hot.

Mock Whitebait Pastries

Make 225 g Puff Pastry (see recipe, page 286) and line small patty tins with it. Soak 1 set lamb's brains in warm water with some salt, then peel and put into a saucepan with enough cold water to cover. Bring to the boil, then reduce the heat and simmer gently for 8 minutes. Drain the brains, put in a bowl and add 1 teaspoon Anchovy Sauce (see recipe, page 109) and beat to a paste with a fork. Fill the pastry cases with the anchovy mixture and cover with a round of pastry to make a lid, sealing to enclose. Brush over with a little milk or beaten egg and bake in a 180°C oven until the pastries are cooked through. May be served hot or cold, garnished with sprigs of parsley.

Mushroom and Ham Savouries

Cook 115 g (1¼ cups) sliced mushrooms in a little butter. Add 3 tablespoons finely chopped ham and 2 teaspoons plain flour. Stir in 125 ml (½ cup) milk and season with salt and pepper. Fry some sliced bread slowly in a little butter until crisp on both sides and spread over the mushroom mixture. Sprinkle grated cheese over the top and brown slightly under a hot grill.

Mushroom Savouries

Cook the mushrooms in a frying pan with a little butter for a few minutes. Drain off and reserve 125 ml (½ cup) of the liquid and finely chop the mushrooms. Put the mushrooms in a bowl with the reserved cooking liquid, 1 tablespoon cream and 1 tablespoon White Sauce (see recipe, page 118), stirring to combine well. Fill small choux pastry cases with the mixture and garnish with chopped parsley.

Olives in Blankets

Cut strips of bacon into thin, short strips, about 6 cm long. Wrap each piece of bacon around an olive, pierce with a wooden toothpick and cook under a hot grill to crisp the bacon. Serve hot.

Oyster Cocktail

Combine 1 tablespoon Worcestershire sauce, 2 tablespoons tomato sauce, 1 tablespoon lemon juice and 2 tablespoons whipped cream. Place shucked and cleaned oysters in cocktail glasses and top with the sauce. Garnish with a slice of lemon. Alternatively, you can serve the oysters in the shell and place a small container, such as an egg cup, in centre of the plate and fill it with sauce.

Oyster Fritters

Take 12 oysters on the half-shell and sprinkle with salt, cayenne pepper and a little lemon juice. To make the batter, sift 75 g (½ cup) plain flour into a bowl and make a well in the centre. Pour in 1 tablespoon of oil or melted butter and 150 ml tepid water, and stir gradually until smooth. Gently fold through 2 stiffly beaten egg whites. Dip the oysters into the batter and deep-fry until golden brown. Drain and serve immediately, garnished with slices of lemon and sprigs of parsley.

Oysters in Bacon

Remove the rind of 115 g bacon slices and cut each into 10 cm lengths. Remove the oysters from the half-shell and wash in their own liquor. Place an oyster on each piece of bacon. Squeeze a drop of lemon juice over and add a sprinkle of cayenne pepper. Roll up the bacon and skewer in position. Cook the rolls in a 220°C oven for 8–10 minutes.

Oyster Pastries

Make some Puff Pastry (see recipe, page 286). Cut into rounds with a pastry cutter. Cut halfway through each round with a smaller pastry cutter. Bake in a 220°C oven for 15 minutes. Make a white sauce with 150 ml milk, 2 teaspoons plain flour, 2 teaspoons butter and 150 ml reserved oyster liquor. Add some salt, cayenne pepper, lemon juice and Anchovy Sauce (see recipe, page 109), to taste, then the shucked oysters. Remove the centres from the pastries, fill with the oyster mixture, and replace the lid, to serve.

Oyster Puffs

In a saucepan, make a thin White Sauce (see recipe, page 118) and add also the oyster liquor from 12 oysters on the half-shell. Stir in 2 teaspoons Anchovy Sauce (see recipe, page 109) and at the last minute add the oysters. Put one oyster and a little sauce into each case and serve immediately.

Oyster Tidbits

Take 8–10 shucked oysters and the same amount of fried bread pieces (about 5 cm squares). Warm the oysters between two plates in the oven. Spread each piece of bread with Anchovy Butter (see recipe, page 119), cover with some fried bacon that has been cut to size and place an oyster on top. Season, and serve hot.

Parmesan Beignets

Heat 55 g butter and 250 ml (1 cup) water in a saucepan; when boiling, remove from the heat, stir in 75 g (1/2 cup) plain flour, and beat until smooth. Return to heat; stir until mixture cooks, leaving the saucepan sides cleanly, and forms a smooth ball. Remove from the heat; stir in 1 tablespoon grated parmesan cheese and 2 tablespoons grated cheese. Season with salt, cayenne pepper and a little mustard, to taste. Add 2 egg yolks to the pan, stirring to combine, and whisk the egg whites to a stiff froth; fold in lightly. Take tablespoonfuls at a time and deep-fry until golden brown — do not cook too quickly or they will brown too much. Drain on paper towel, sprinkle with parmesan cheese and serve on a hot dish, garnished with a sliced lemon and parsley sprigs.

Petite Bouchée de Crevettes

Hollow out small baked puff pastry shapes and stuff with a mixture of small prawns and champignons (mushrooms) mixed with mayonnaise sauce.

Prawn Baskets

Spear the ends of a prawn closely together with a toothpick. Chop 4 sprigs of parsley or watercress, 1 very small onion and a bit of bay leaf. Mix with 2 tablespoons mayonnaise, 1/4 teaspoon lemon juice and 1/4 teaspoon black pepper. Place a little in the centre of each prawn, and serve.

Prawn Cocktail

Mix together 1 tablespoon strained lemon juice, 1 tablespoon tomato sauce, 1/2 teaspoon Tabasco and 1/2 teaspoon grated horseradish, stirring well. Add 9 peeled prawns and season with a few drops of Tabasco sauce. Serve very cold in a cocktail glass, garnished with a slice of lemon.

Prawn Cups

Chill the hard-boiled eggs several hours before serving. Peel and cut in half lengthways; cut a slice from the end of each half and remove the yolks. Mash tinned prawn meat into small pieces and marinate in lemon juice and tarragon vinegar for 30 minutes. Drain and mix with a little mayonnaise. Pipe a rosette on each egg cup. Serve on thin slices of pickled beets cut with a small scalloped pastry cutter.

Prawns in Savoury Jelly (Aspic)

Use small moulds. Decorate with a slice of lemon, cut into quarters. Arrange an anchovy fillet in the middle. Cover with Savoury Jelly (Aspic) (see recipe, page 149) to set. Shell the prawns, removing the heads and tails, and arrange these around the sides of the moulds. Fill up with jelly. Place on individual plates surrounded with watercress or lettuce and serve with Anchovy Sauce (see recipe, page 109).

Prunes in Bacon

Pit the prunes, and replace the pit with a rinsed blanched almond. Roll each prune in a thin slice of rindless bacon. Stick a toothpick through to keep rolled and bake in a 200°C oven until golden brown. Serve at once.

Salted Almonds

Put 115 g (¾ cup) raw almonds in a small saucepan; cover with boiling water and heat to boiling point. Drain, skin, and dry the almonds in a tea towel. Melt 1 tablespoon of butter or oil in small frying pan; add the prepared almonds; turn and stir them until lightly browned. Drain on paper towel. Sprinkle salt to coat.

Sardine Cigarettes

Scrape skins from sardines. Make a Short Pastry (see recipe, page 287) and roll out very thin. Cut into rectangles, about 4 cm wide and 7.5 cm long. Roll up each sardine in a piece of pastry. Wet edges with milk to join edges nicely. Brush with egg. Roll in dry breadcrumbs. Bake until golden and sprinkle with grated cheese.

Savoury Supreme

Mix some finely chopped ham with finely chopped walnuts, some mango chutney, mustard and a little butter and a dash of salt and pepper. Once combined, spread on toast and top with a slice of cheese. Melt the cheese under a hot grill, then serve.

Tomato Toast Savoury

Peel 3 tomatoes and slice. Put in a frying pan with some butter; add salt and pepper to taste. Simmer for 10 minutes, add 3 beaten eggs and when it thickens serve at once on buttered toast.

Savoury Boats

To make the savoury boat pastry cases put 115 g (¾ cup) plain flour in a bowl with ¼ teaspoon baking powder and a pinch each of salt and cayenne pepper. Rub 55 g butter lightly into the dry ingredients and add 1½ teaspoons water to make a dry dough. Turn out and roll thinly. Cut to shape and line boat-shaped moulds. Prick the centres or line with baking paper and fill with rice. Bake in a 180°C oven for about 10 minutes. Remove rice and return to the oven for another 5 minutes to dry the pastry. Fill with a savoury mixture of your choice:

- Whipped cream, flavoured with cream cheese, salt and cayenne pepper. Garnish with watercress.
- Asparagus stems mashed with seasoned, thick, rich White Sauce (see recipe, page 118). Garnish with parsley.
- Whipped cream, flavoured with Anchovy Sauce (see recipe, page 109) and coloured pale pink. Garnish with anchovy fillets and slices of stuffed olives.
- Chopped ham, tongue and a gherkin mixed with seasoned White Sauce (see recipe, page 118). Garnish with olives and gherkins.
- Oysters, prawns, lobster or crabmeat, chopped, and mixed with rich White Sauce (see recipe, page 118) seasoned with salt, cayenne pepper and a few drops of lemon juice. Garnish with slices of lemon and parsley.

Looking Back in Time...

HOMEMADE SOAP

Put 2.25 kg fat and 450 g resin into a clean kerosene tin, half-fill with water (9.5 litres). Boil for 30 minutes, stirring well. Remove from the heat and put in 3 tablespoons of borax and slowly shake in 450 g caustic soda. Add the caustic soda 1 tablespoon at a time, as it bubbles up if put in too quickly. Add 125 ml (½ cup) kerosene. Boil gently for 2 hours, or just enough to keep it moving. When done, put into two long flat tins. Let it stand for 2 days, then cut into bars and put up to dry. Add citronella, if liked.

Entrées

Anchovy Squares

Cut some squares of toast, butter and spread with a thick layer of Anchovy Butter (see recipe, page 119). Blanch some almonds and cut them thinly on the diagonal, so as to obtain as large a piece as possible. Arrange them on top of the plate and place under a hot grill for a few moments to roast the almonds.

Asparagus Pudding

Beat 15 g butter to a cream, add 75 g (½ cup) flour, 1 tablespoon finely chopped bacon, 2 well-beaten eggs, 1 bunch asparagus spears cut into small pieces, and enough milk to form a stiff batter. Season with salt and pepper. Place in buttered pudding basin and steam for 2 hours. Pour butter over the top to serve.

Bananas and Bacon

Fry about 8 bacon slices. When crisp, set aside and keep hot; peel 4 bananas, cut each in half lengthways, season with salt and pepper, and fry in the bacon fat over high heat for a few minutes. Have ready toasted pieces of bread and spread these with paprika or Green Butter (see recipe, page 119). Place a slice of fried bacon on each toast and top with half a banana. Garnish with sprigs of parsley; serve hot.

Beef Croquettes

Put 1 cup finely chopped cold roast beef in a bowl and mix well with 2 cups hot mashed potatoes. Work in 1 well-beaten egg and shape the mixture into little cakes. Roll in flour, or egg and dry breadcrumbs, and deep-fry for 3 minutes each. For a variation, serve these in heated halves of peaches.

Brain Savoury

Make some Shortcrust Pastry (see recipe, page 287), roll out thinly and line some boat-shaped moulds. Prick the centres or place a piece of baking paper in each and fill with rice. Bake in a 180°C oven for about 10 minutes. Remove the paper and rice, return the pastry cases to the oven for another 5 minutes to dry. Soak, skin and cook 1 set lamb's brains. Chop the brains and add 125 ml (½ cup) White Sauce (see recipe, page 118), mixing to combine. Spoon into the pastry cases and serve.

Cawnpore Cutlets

Put 185 g (1 cup) cold boiled rice, 225 g (1 cup) cooked minced meat, 2 teaspoons curry powder, 2 teaspoons Worcestershire sauce, 1 well-beaten egg, 1 teaspoon finely chopped parsley, 1 teaspoon finely chopped onion and 1 teaspoon butter in a saucepan. Season with salt and pepper and cook for 5 minutes, stirring all the time. Remove from the heat and allow to cool. Form the mixture into cutlet shapes, glaze with egg, roll in dry breadcrumbs, to coat, and deep-fry until golden brown.

Cheese Croquettes

Mix together 250 g (2 cups) grated cheese, 100 g (1 cup) dry breadcrumbs, some salt and cayenne pepper in a bowl. Form into small balls; dip into a bowl with 1 well-beaten egg and extra breadcrumbs, and deep-fry until golden. Serve hot.

Chicken Croquettes

Mix 450 g (2 cups) cooked chicken, 4 tablespoons chopped mushrooms, 1 teaspoon parsley, ½ teaspoon onion juice and 1 tablespoon lemon juice. Put 1 cup White Sauce (see recipe, page 118) in a saucepan and add the chicken mixture. Cook for 3 minutes, then stir in 2 well-beaten eggs. Pour the mixture into a greased dish and refrigerate for 1 hour. Shape the mixture into balls and roll in dry breadcrumbs, to coat. Dip into egg wash and then again in breadcrumbs and deep-fry for 3 minutes. Serve hot.

Chicken Dormers

Cut the hard-boiled eggs in half lengthways. Mix a little minced chicken with 1 tablespoon finely chopped ham, parsley, salt and cayenne pepper in a bowl. Add a squeeze of lemon juice and the yolks eggs, keeping out just a small portion of one yolk. Fill the whites of the eggs with the mixture and press the two halves together. Roll the eggs in flour, egg wash and breadcrumbs. Deep-fry until golden. Serve each egg in a crisp lettuce leaf with the reserved egg yolk grated over the top.

Corn Fritters

Chop 400 g (2 cups) drained tinned corn kernels very fine and put in a bowl with 1 well-beaten egg. Add 1 teaspoon melted butter, 300 g (2 cups) plain flour, 2 teaspoons baking powder and 125 ml (½ cup) milk. Season with salt and pepper and mix to combine; shape into patties. Deep-fry for 2–3 minutes. Serve hot.

Curried Tomatoes

Peel and slice 900 g tomatoes and put a layer of slices in the bottom of a baking dish. Sprinkle with salt and dust with curry powder. Cover with a thin layer of boiled rice and a piece of butter. Continue layering until the dish is full, having a layer of tomatoes on top. Sprinkle with dry breadcrumbs and dot with pieces of butter. Bake in a 220°C oven for 30 minutes and serve hot. An onion added to the above improves the flavour.

Devilled Corn on Toast

Put 2 teaspoons butter, 3 tablespoons grated cheese and 1 tablespoon cream or milk into a saucepan, and stir over low heat until smooth. Add 4 tablespoons cooked sweet corn, 1 tablespoon Worcestershire sauce and 1 lightly beaten egg. Season with salt and cayenne pepper, and continue stirring over low heat until the mixture sets. Arrange a slice of grilled bacon on each slice of toast, and top each with the corn mixture. Garnish with small sprigs of parsley; serve hot.

Eggs in a Savoury Jelly

Hard-boil 4–6 eggs and cool under running water. Peel and slice the eggs and place in a thin layer of Savoury Jelly (Aspic) (see recipe, page 109) in the bottom of individual moulds and allow to set. Add a slice of egg, with a little jelly poured onto it. When this is set arrange slices of egg around the sides and set with jelly. Then fill up with jelly and place slices of tomato and cucumber lightly around. Garnish with curls of celery and radishes and serve with a suitable dressing.

When poaching eggs, use the very freshest, and when boiling for savoury eggs or salads, stale eggs will be found much easier to peel.

English Monkey

Soak 80 g (1 cup) breadcrumbs in 250 ml (1 cup) milk for 15 minutes. Melt 1 tablespoon butter in a saucepan and add 90 g (3/4 cup) grated cheese, stirring well. When the cheese has melted, add the soaked breadcrumbs to the pan and season with salt and cayenne pepper. Mix together well, add 1 well-beaten egg, and cook for 3 minutes. Serve on buttered toast.

Fish Croquettes

Mince 450–500 g cooked fish (about 2 cups), and season to taste. Moisten with 125 ml (1/2 cup) White Sauce (see recipe, page 118). Chill the mixture and mould into croquettes. Roll in dry breadcrumbs, then in egg wash and again in breadcrumbs. Deep-fry for 3 minutes, or until golden. You can substitute the fish with the same amount of crab or lobster meat.

Ham Oysters

Mix together 200 g (1 cup) finely chopped or minced ham, 160 g (2 cups) breadcrumbs, 2 well-beaten eggs and 250 ml (1 cup) hot milk. Combine well and season with a dash of pepper. Drop spoonfuls of the mixture into a hot oil in a pan, about the size of a fried oyster, and cook for 1–2 minutes on each side. This is delicious when served with fried bananas.

Mustard mixed with milk to which has been added a pinch of salt will not harden in the pot.

Ham Pyramids

Chop 55 g ham and 2 gherkins very finely. Skin 1 tomato and chop the flesh. Mix together in a bowl and stir in 1 teaspoon chutney. Season with salt and pepper, to taste. Mix to a paste with 2 tablespoons mayonnaise. Pile the mixture in pyramids over diamonds of toast. Serve each piece, cold, on a small crisp lettuce leaf.

Macaroni and Ham

Break up 115 g (¾ cup) macaroni into bits and bring to the boil in a saucepan of lightly salted water. Reduce the heat and simmer for about 20 minutes, or until cooked. Drain and place the macaroni in the dish it is to be served in. Put 2 teaspoons of butter into a saucepan with 2 teaspoons plain flour and 450 ml milk. Bring to the boil; when smooth add 1 well-beaten egg. Season with ½ teaspoon pepper and 1 teaspoon mustard. Lastly, add 200 g (1 cup) finely chopped or minced ham. Mix the ham, macaroni and sauce, then cover with breadcrumbs and brown the top in oven.

Mushrooms on Savoury Toast

Melt 1½ tablespoons butter in a small saucepan. Wash 4 large field mushrooms, add to the melted butter, and when it is hot, sprinkle with pepper. Cover, and simmer for 10 minutes, or until well cooked. Take about 1 tablespoon of mashed potato, and beat it to a smooth paste with 1 tablespoon cream. Season with salt and pepper. Toast the squares of bread lightly. Drain the butter off the mushrooms and mix the butter with ½ teaspoon Anchovy Butter (see recipe, page 119), and spread it on the hot toast. Place a hot mushroom on each piece of toast and pipe some creamed potatoes around the edge. Serve hot.

Oysters and Bacon

Put tomatoes into boiling water and then remove the skin. Cut into thin slices. Put slices of tomato in the bottom of a greased baking dish. Cover with oysters, then a layer of tomatoes, and sprinkle with salt and cayenne pepper. Lay slices of bacon over the top and bake in a 180°C oven for 10–15 minutes. Serve at once.

Potato Balls

Peel and boil 625 g potatoes and dry them off. Mash the potatoes with 2 teaspoons butter, 4 tablespoon finely grated cheese and 1 egg yolk. Season with salt and pepper and allow to cool. Take small portions of the potato mixture and roll into balls. Dip into egg wash, then coat with dry breadcrumbs. Deep-fry until golden brown. Do not attempt to fry too many at one time, or the temperature of the oil will be reduced. Drain on paper towel and serve hot.

Tomato Cheese

Butter a baking dish and sprinkle with dry breadcrumbs. Slice 625 g tomatoes and arrange a layer in the dish. Grate 55 g (1/2 cup) Gouda or Edam cheese, sprinkle a little on the tomatoes, followed by some breadcrumbs. Continue layering the tomatoes, cheese and breadcrumbs until the dish is full. Finish with a layer of breadcrumbs and a few dots of butter. Season with salt and pepper and bake in a 180°C oven for 30 minutes.

Tomato Cream Toast

Peel 225 g tomatoes and roughly chop them. Place in a saucepan with salt and pepper. Cover the pan and cook slowly for 5 minutes. Beat 1 egg and stir into 125 ml (1/2 cup) cream. Add this to the tomatoes in the pan and mix through. Serve at once on slices of buttered toast.

Welsh Rarebit

Mix 1 tablespoon mustard with 1 tablespoon of wine or beer. Heat another 2 tablespoons of wine or beer, then add the mustard mixture and 125 g (1 cup) grated cheese. Stir until the cheese is melted and season with salt and pepper. Butter a few slices of hot toast and spread with the cheese mixture. Serve at once.

Worcestershire Loaf

Put 550 g steak and 225 g streaky bacon through a mincing machine, add 1/2 teaspoon salt, 1/4 teaspoon pepper, 100 g (1 cup) dry breadcrumbs, 1 well-beaten egg, 1 tablespoon Worcestershire sauce, mixing together well. Turn out onto a well-floured surface and press together into a neat loaf. Tie up in a piece of muslin dusted with flour and boil for 2 hours. When cooked, remove from the cloth and lightly roll the loaf in dry breadcrumbs to coat. Cut the loaf in slices and serve with lettuce and potato salad.

Savouries

Croutons of bread can be used as a foundation for savouries with various toppings. To make the bases, cut slices of stale bread about 1 cm thick and cut with biscuit cutters of various shapes. For example, you can cut the bread into diamonds, hearts, spades, half-moon, triangles, rounds, etc. Deep-fry in a saucepan of vegetable oil until crisp and golden. Drain well on paper towels. These may be served either hot or cold with your favourite toppings:

- Spread base with cream cheese, then top with a slice of hard-boiled egg, a slice of gherkin and sprinkle with grated cheese.
- Spread base with thick mayonnaise, then top with a slice of frankfurter and garnish with beetroot and parsley.
- Spread base with ham paste, then top with a slice of hard-boiled egg. Garnish with capers and thin strips of gherkin.
- Spread base with thick mayonnaise, arrange four slices of olive in the centre to form a daisy shape, adding a small piece of yellow yolk for centre.
- Spread base thickly with cream cheese and stand olive in the centre. Garnish with strips of red chilli.
- Spread base with gherkin paste and arrange thin strips of olive, gherkin and chilli over the top. Garnish with yolk of egg and parsley.
- Spread base with cheese paste, make mound in centre and garnish with thin strips of beetroot.
- Spread base with asparagus paste or mashed asparagus. Garnish with asparagus tips and parsley.
- Spread base with cream cheese, make into mound and top with half a walnut.
- Spread base with cream cheese and sliced pickled walnut. Garnish with thin strips of red chilli.

Sandwiches

If you always keep a stock of savoury pastes, boxes of cheese, mixed shelled nuts and a few bottles each of bottled meats and prawns in your cupboard or larder, you can always make up a filling for sandwiches at a moment's notice. If you prefer to have your fillings already prepared, there are a variety of delicious pastes on the market that are most useful for the summer store cupboard. The following list gives examples of some of the best sandwich breads and fillings:

- BROWN BREAD: sliced fried champignons, seasoned with pepper, salt and ground mace; cream cheese, flavoured to taste with Worcestershire sauce and chopped onion; moistened cream of mayonnaise mixed with chopped walnuts or brazil nuts.
- WHITE BREAD: thinly sliced tongue, mayonnaise and shredded lettuce; liver sausage paste and watercress; salmon, prawns and cucumber.
- HALF-FRIED BREAD: shrimp or prawn mayonnaise; anchovy paste mixed to taste with grated cheese, lemon juice, chopped parsley and diced cucumber. Put filling on un-fried sides.
- DINNER OR SMALL BREAD ROLLS: ham and watercress; scotch eggs, sliced with lettuce and mayonnaise.
- ROUNDS OF BAKED PASTRY: cold creamed champignons; tongue, mayonnaise and watercress; shrimp and green pea mayonnaise.
- CHEESE BISCUITS OR CREAM CRACKERS: peanut butter and chopped stuffed olives; cream cheese, mixed to taste with chopped tinned pimento, walnuts, parsley, and seasoning, to taste.
- OATCAKES: Roquefort cheese, creamed with French dressing and used with shredded lettuce; honey and devonshire cream.
- ROUNDS OF SPONGE CAKES OR SPONGE FINGERS OR DROPS: strawberry jam and devonshire cream; sliced bananas and ginger in syrup, moistened whipped cream.

Be sure and label your plates of sandwiches and cut into fancy shapes.

Popular Sandwich Ideas

When making sandwiches, lettuce should be cut quite finely before being laced in a sandwich, and cucumbers should be soaked after slicing in oil and vinegar. The sandwich becomes daintier if cold meat is minced first. All salad sandwiches are improved by this treatment. The following fillings make excellent sandwiches:

- Scrambled eggs with or without tomato; a little cream makes it richer.
- Raisins, sultanas and mixed nuts all well minced and spread on bread and butter are delicious. If weather is cold, use cream cheese instead of butter.
- Anchovy or meat paste can be mixed with butter and spread fairly thickly on thin bread. Add sliced hard-boiled eggs.
- Spread butter and jam on bread, then add grated chocolate and a little whipped cream.
- Finely chop chicken, ham and sweet pickle, then lightly moisten with mayonnaise dressing.
- Cream cheese, topped with chopped olives and mayonnaise.
- Grated carrot mixed with well-seasoned mayonnaise dressing to moisten, taking care not to make too wet.
- Finely chopped prawns, celery and tinned crushed pineapple, moistened with mayonnaise.
- Very finely chopped watercress, seasoned, then blended with softened butter.
- Finely chopped hard-boiled eggs with tomato sauce.
- Minced cooked steak, moistened with horseradish sauce.
- Minced cooked liver and bacon with tomato and Worcestershire sauces.
- Lobster paste mixed with mayonnaise.
- Chopped prawns and gherkins in mayonnaise or sauce.
- Chopped preserved ginger and nuts.
- Minced tongue and pickle.
- Mashed banana with lemon juice and sugar.
- Grated apple mixed with honey and nuts.
- Grated cheese mixed with marmalade.

Anchovy Butter Sandwiches

125 g (¹/₂ cup) butter, 55 g anchovy fillets, bread

Beat the butter to a cream and add the very finely chopped anchovies. Use to spread over bread. This anchovy butter can also be made into a green butter by adding a little parsley. Simply boil the parsley for 5 minutes, then rinse under cold running water. Drain and strip the parsley from the stalks and finely chop. Work this into the creamed anchovy butter.

Cucumber Sandwiches

Cucumber, salad dressing, bread, butter

Pare and slice the cucumbers, stand them in cold water for 1 hour. Spread some salad dressing on the bread and butter, and fill with slices of cucumber.

Ham Butter Sandwiches

125 g (¹/₂ cup) butter, 2 hard-boiled egg yolks,
115 g (¹/₂ cup) finely chopped ham, bread

Cream the butter. Rub the yolks through a sieve and mix into the butter with the minced ham. Season with pepper and spread over bread to make sandwiches.

Mint Sandwiches

90 (¹/₃ cup) cream cheese, cream, 1 tablespoon finely chopped mint, brown bread

Soften the cream cheese and mix together with a little cream to make a good consistency for spreading. Season with salt and a little pepper and stir through the mint. Spread over brown bread to make sandwiches.

Mock Chicken Sandwiches

1 small onion, 1 large tomato, 2 teaspoons butter, ½ teaspoon chopped thyme,
80 g (½ cup) diced cheese,1 well-beaten egg

Finely chop the onion and tomato. Put in a saucepan with the butter, thyme and cheese. Simmer gently for about 10 minutes. Add the beaten egg and continue simmering until the mixture thickens — don't let it boil. Remove from the heat and keep stirring until quite thick. Pour into sterilised jars and seal securely when cool. Store in the refrigerator and spread over slices of bread as required.

Mock Oyster Sandwiches

2 set of lamb's brains, 1 teaspoon Anchovy Sauce (see recipe, page 109),
1 teaspoon thick cream, cayenne pepper, a dash of lemon juice, bread

Skin and cook the brains, then cool and chop finely. Carefully mix in the Anchovy Sauce and cream. Add a sprinkle of cayenne pepper and a squeeze of lemon juice. Handle carefully, or it will be mushy when made up. Use as a sandwich filling between slices of bread.

Prune and Nut Sandwiches

125 g (½ cup) pitted prunes, 2 tablespoons chopped walnuts,
mayonnaise, bread

Chop the prunes and mix with the walnuts. Moisten with mayonnaise and spread between slices of bread. Cut into fancy shapes.

Club Sandwiches

A classic club sandwich uses three slices of bread for each sandwich and layers different fillings between. The fillings can be varied to your liking. For example, you can make a club sandwich by spreading a slice of toast with mayonnaise and topping with a lettuce leaf and slices of cooked chicken. Cover with a second piece of toast and lay slices of crisp bacon and another lettuce leaf on top. Cover with remaining toast and lay on top a big slice of tomato, spread with mayonnaise. Sprinkle with a little finely shredded lettuce, and serve with 2 olives and a gherkin on the plate beside the sandwich.

Some of the more popular club sandwiches are listed below:

- **CHICKEN**: an upper layer of chicken, a lower layer of well-flavoured scrambled egg and sliced gherkins, and a middle layer of green salad.
- **MISTLETOE**: chicken Salad, sliced tomatoes, lettuce, salad dressing
- **ACACIA**: devilled egg, cheese and celery, salad dressing.
- **KURRAJONG**: asparagus, sliced tomato, lettuce, mayonnaise.
- **WILGA**: grilled ham, grilled pork sausage, lettuce.
- **WHITEWOOD**: salmon, gherkin, sliced tomato, lettuce, mayonnaise.
- **BOONERY**: grilled Sausage, grilled bacon, tomato, mayonnaise.
- **COOLABAH**: white chicken, grilled ham, tomato, lettuce, mayonnaise
- **NEEDLEWOOD**: fried egg, grilled ham, lettuce, salad dressing.
- **LILLI PILLI**: 1 grilled sausage cut in half lengthways, spread with mustard; place on this 2 squares of grilled bacon, on this a slice of tomato, pepper, salt; place under grill with a piece of toast on top. Garnish with shredded lettuce and mayonnaise.
- **LOBSTER CLUB SANDWICH**: spread slices of toast with lobster salad, pour over sandwich a sauce made by melting 225 g processed cheese over a very low heat and gradually adding 125 ml (½ cup) hot milk. Season to taste and cool.
- **HAM AND EGG CLUB SANDWICH**: take 3 slices of buttered toast, spread a little horseradish on one. On this lay slices of fried ham. Add another slice of toast, hard-boiled egg, then a little mayonnaise mixed with chopped gherkins. Cover with another slice of toast.
- **CRAB CLUB SANDWICH**: cover a piece of toast with tender young lettuce leaves. Spread with mayonnaise, then place 2 slices of tomato on top. Mix the crab meat with mayonnaise and spread it over the tomato. Cover with another slice of buttered toast and serve.

Salad Sandwich Loaf

1 loaf bread, mayonnaise, thinly sliced tomato, piccalilli, shredded lettuce,
cream cheese, cream

Remove all the crusts from a loaf of sandwich bread and cut lengthways into four even-sized slices. Spread one slice with mayonnaise and sliced tomatoes. Cover with another slice of bread and spread with mayonnaise and gherkin relish. Cover with a third slice of bread and spread with mayonnaise and lettuce. Cover with the final slice of bread. Soften the cream cheese with fresh cream and cover the entire loaf with the cream cheese mixture. Refrigerate for 1 hour before serving. Cut across the loaf and serve. A cheese mixture may be used instead of the gherkin relish.

Savoury Cheese Sandwich

1 loaf unsliced brown bread, butter, 60 g (1/2 cup) grated cheese,
mayonnaise, 3 tablespoons finely chopped parsley or mint,
a squeeze of lemon juice, 250 g (1 cup) cream cheese,
sliced gherkins or olives

Remove the crust from the bread and cut the whole loaf into three horizontal slices. Butter one slice of bread. Mix together half the grated cheese and moisten with salad dressing; spread thickly over one slice. Mix together the finely chopped parsley or mint, lemon juice and melted butter. When set, spread over the second slice. Butter the final slice of bread and sprinkle with the rest of the grated cheese flavoured with paprika. Press the slices together firmly, and cover with the top and sides with cream cheese. Decorate with sliced gherkins or stuffed olives, slice and serve.

Savoury Rolled Sandwiches

Asparagus rolls lead the way for a new sandwich shape,
and now we can roll any type of sandwich. Ribbon sandwiches
are a delight to the eye, for they mix the various colours of bread.
Cut a whole unsliced loaf of bread the long way of the loaf,
allowing for a long roll, which can be cut in round slices
afterwards like a miniature Swiss roll.

Take some very fresh brown bread and spread lightly with
slightly warmed and stirred butter (this prevents the new bread
from crumbling). Cut into fairly thin slices with a serrated knife.
Place a length of tinned asparagus in the middle of each slice
(the same length as the bread), season, and roll into a little sausage.
Arrange daintily on plates.

As a change from asparagus for a rolled sandwich, you can use
a variety of other fillings. Try a stalk of cleaned crisp celery that has
been spread with cream cheese and sprinkled with cayenne pepper,
then roll. You can also skin and boil some sardines and roll one
in each piece of bread after adding a squeeze of lemon juice and
cayenne pepper. Another option is to top, tail and shell some large
prawns and roll out one in each piece of bread.

Savoury Sandwich Filling

1 tablespoon butter, 1 tablespoon grated cheese, 1 thyme sprig,
1 large peeled tomato, 1 teaspoon grated onion, bread

Melt the butter in a saucepan and add the grated cheese, thyme sprig, tomato and
onion. Season with salt and pepper and boil for 5 minutes. Pour into a sterilised
jar; seal securely when cool. Use as a filling for sandwiches. These sandwiches are
particularly good for school lunches.

Toasted Lobster Sandwich

Lobster, butter, a dash of lemon juice, bread,
Mushroom Sauce (see recipe, page 113)

Remove the tail meat from the lobster and cut into thick slices. Melt the butter in a saucepan and sauté the lobster meat. Squeeze in a little lemon juice. Place the lobster meat on a slice of buttered toast and cover with another slice of toast. Pour the mushroom sauce over and serve hot.

Treble Sandwiches

3 slices bread, potted meat, sliced pickled onions,
cream cheese, cayenne pepper

Allow 3 slices buttered bread for each sandwich. Between the bottom 2 slices spread potted meat and the pickles. Spread cream cheese over the second slice and season with salt and cayenne pepper. Cover with the third slice of bread. Press well, and cut through into suitable sections.

It is a change to have small crusty bread rolls instead of sliced bread. Scoop the centres out of the rolls and stuff them with either asparagus in white sauce, crab or lobster in white sauce, oysters in white sauce, or cooked minced chicken and ham in white sauce — delicious!

CWA of New South Wales refreshment kiosk at Trangie cattle sales, 1956.

LIGHT
MEALS
AND SIDES

Eggs and Omelettes

It is absolutely necessary to make omelettes using fresh eggs; it would be impossible to make a light omelette with stale eggs. A strong round pan is needed and kept specially for omelettes.

Allow 2 eggs for one person, but if making for a number of people, fewer eggs may be used for the larger quantity, say 8 eggs for five people. Place all whites in one bowl and all yolks in another bowl and beat very well separately. If using one egg beater be sure to wash it when taking it from the yolks to beat the whites.

Melt in your omelette pan 30 g butter until it sizzles. Pour in the beaten yolks, adding salt and pepper to taste. Just as the yolks begin to set, add a heaped tablespoon of whipped cream and then the stiffly beaten egg whites. Mix thoroughly over heat. If not set on top, place under a grill for a few minutes. Never wash your pan, wipe it with paper towel instead.

Another method is to beat the yolks of two eggs and the whites of same in separate bowls — the yolks to a thick cream and the whites to a stiff froth. Add herbs and seasoning for a savoury omelette, or sugar and milk for sweet. Fold the beaten whites into the beaten yolks. Melt 30 g butter in a pan and add the egg mixture. Brown under a grill for a few minutes.

Asparagus Eggs

First make a sauce by heating 55 g butter and 2 tablespoons vinegar in saucepan, until the butter is melted and stir quickly. Add 425 g drained tinned asparagus and heat through. Serve with 6 poached eggs and rounds of buttered toast. Grate over a little nutmeg and then add 2 tablespoons grated cheese and garnish with parsley.

Asparagus Omelette

Allow for 1 tablespoon finely chopped cooked asparagus spears for every 2 eggs. Separate the eggs into yolks and whites. Add the asparagus to the yolks; fold in the stiffly-beaten egg whites. Turn into the greased pan and cook as before. Fold and serve with 2–3 asparagus spears per omelette as a garnish.

Cheese Omelette

Separate 3 eggs into yolks and whites. Beat each separately; the whites must be perfectly stiff. Have a hot pan ready with butter melted in it. Put the eggs in a bowl with 1 tablespoon water, 2 tablespoons grated cheese, $\frac{1}{2}$ teaspoon salt and a pinch of pepper, stirring well. Pour into pan and when nicely set and brown, turn and brown the other side. Fold over, sprinkle with grated cheese and grill for 1 minute to melt the cheese. Serve immediately.

Coddled Eggs

Put eggs into a saucepan of boiling water and turn off the heat. Put a lid on tightly and allow the eggs to remain in the water for 6 minutes. Serve hot.

Eggs à la Milanaise

Poach the required number of eggs in vinegar-flavoured water, take out, and strain. Have ready White Sauce (see recipe, page 118) and add some grated cheese to it, then place in a baking dish. Place eggs on top of sauce and sprinkle with grated cheese. Put into oven to reheat. Serve at once.

Egg and Nut Cutlets

Place 85 g butter in saucepan, crack 6 eggs in with butter, beat up like scrambled eggs; place eggs with 350 g (2 cups) crushed nuts, add 1 teaspoon salt, $\frac{1}{2}$ teaspoon pepper and 400 g (4 cups) dry breadcrumbs. Place 4 tablespoons flour in 125 ml ($\frac{1}{2}$ cup) water to make a paste to cover 42 lamb cutlets. Fry lightly and serve hot.

Eggs and Spinach

Chop spinach finely. Add salt and cayenne pepper. Grease some ramekins and three-quarters fill with spinach. Break an egg in carefully on top of the spinach. Sprinkle with grated cheese. Stand in a dish. Bake in a 180°C oven until the eggs are set. Serve at once in the ramekins.

Egg Envelopes

Make a Shortcrust Pastry (see recipe, page 287). Roll out thinly and cut into squares. With floured hands take a small portion of sausage meat, roll into a ball, then flatten into a round. Lay in the centre of the pastry. Cut a hard-boiled egg into thick slices and lay a slice over the meat. Sprinkle with salt and cayenne pepper. Wet the edges of the pastry and bring the four corners to centre. Repeat with the remaining pastry, sausage meat and egg. Glaze all with egg. Bake in 220°C oven until the pastry is brown, then lessen heat and cook slowly another 20 minutes. Serve hot or cold.

Eggs Lyonnaise

Boil 6 eggs until hard. Grate 2 onions. Melt 30 g butter in a saucepan, add onions, fry until brown. Add 225 ml chicken or vegetable stock, season to taste with salt and pepper, then simmer until creamy. Remove shells from eggs, then remove yolks from whites. Mince whites and add to onion sauce. Bring to the boil. Heat 6 croutons of fried bread with the sauce, place a yolk on top of each croute, and dab each yolk with a little of the sauce.

To remove egg stains from spoons and forks, stand in separated milk in an aluminium saucepan until clean

Eggs Poached in Milk

Put into a clean pan sufficient milk to poach eggs required. When eggs are set, place them on toast. Thicken the milk with flour, stir in 2 teaspoons butter, salt, pepper and parsley. Pour sauce over eggs.

Eggs with Macaroni

Boil some eggs until hard, cut them lengthways into 8 pieces. Have ready about 155 g (1 cup) boiled macaroni and 85 g (2/3 cup) grated cheese. Mix together and put into a buttered dish. Pour over 250 ml (1 cup) White Sauce (see recipe, page 118); season with salt and pepper. Cover with breadcrumbs and a little butter and bake in a 180°C oven for 20 minutes.

French Omelette

Separate 3 eggs into yolks and whites. Whisk each separately; the whites must be perfectly stiff. To well-beaten yolks add 1 teaspoon chopped parsley, 2 tablespoons milk or cream, 1 teaspoon grated onion or French shallot. Fold in stiffly beaten whites. Pour into hot well-buttered pan. Cook until beginning to set, then place under grill to set. Fold one side across the other. Serve at once with quarters of lemon. This omelette can be made with 2 eggs and 1 tablespoon milk. A little grated cheese and cayenne pepper may be used instead of parsley or herbs.

Fried Eggs and Bacon

Remove rind from some bacon slices. Place the bacon in a cold frying pan and cook slowly until the fat is clear. Place a little clarified fat in the frying pan and make it just warm, break 1 egg into a saucer, remove the white speck and slide carefully into the warm fat. Cook slowly, pouring spoonfuls of fat over the egg while cooking. When set, lift out with an egg slice. Drain well and place on the slices of bacon.

Omelette à la Valois

Break 4 eggs into a bowl and add 1 tablespoon of milk or cream, ½ teaspoon salt and pepper; beat for 2 minutes. Melt 30 g butter in omelette pan, add 1 tablespoon breadcrumbs and toss until light brown. Drop in the egg mixture and stir for 2 minutes. Then let the mixture rest 1 minute before serving.

Omelette For One

Beat 1 egg, add 1 tablespoon of milk and a little salt and pepper. Chop together 1 teaspoon of parsley, 1 tablespoon grated onion, 1 tablespoon grated cheese. Add to egg and milk. Put teaspoon butter in pan; when hot add egg mixture. Cook slowly until set.

Omelette Macédoine

Beat 4 eggs, add 2 tablespoons caster sugar, 2 teaspoons rum and 115 g (½ cup) glacé fruit, which should be finely chopped. Cook slowly in butter in the usual way, fold over, and serve with the following sauce: Heat 1 tablespoon of strong black coffee; add 1 tablespoon sugar and stir in the beaten yolks of 3 eggs. Cook until it thickens, but do not allow to boil. Pour over the omelette and serve.

Omelette Soufflé

Boil 1 tablespoon water with ½ teaspoon vanilla essence and 1 tablespoon sugar until reduced by half. Allow to cool, then add 2 eggs yolks, beating well. Whisk 3 egg whites very well and stir them into the yolk mixture a little at a time. Very carefully melt about 1 tablespoon butter in a pan, pour egg mixture in and cook over heat until set. Put pan under the grill or into the oven for a little while to brown slightly. Slip omelette on to a plate, leaving the butter in the pan. Put 1 tablespoon hot jam on omelette, and fold over. Sprinkle with caster sugar, to serve.

Oyster Omelette

Allow 3 oysters to each egg. Heat the oysters in their liquor; finely chop them and add to the egg yolks. Fold in the stiffly beaten egg white; turn into a hot buttered frying pan. Cook gently until brown on the bottom. To set the top, place under the grill or in the oven. Serve immediately on a warm plate.

Poached Egg

Take a small frying pan, fill to three-quarters full with water and bring to the boil. Add salt and 6 drops vinegar. Break the egg carefully into a saucer. Drop the egg into the water, allow to cook slowly until set. Make the toast and butter. Cut into a round. Lift the egg out carefully with an egg slice. Drain, place on the toast. Sprinkle with very finely chopped parsley. Serve at once, very hot.

Omelettes must be served as soon as they are done. Never try to keep an omelette hot in the oven; the best very soon become leathery if kept waiting.

Rice Breakfast Omelette

Separate 2 eggs into yolks and whites. Beat each separately; the whites must be perfectly stiff. Add the yolks to 60 ml (¼ cup) milk, 95 g (½ cup) boiled white rice, 1 tablespoon melted butter and a little finely chopped parsley; season with salt and pepper. Then add the egg whites. Fold lightly; cook over slow heat. Season with salt and when set, fold over. Serve with sauce, chopped spring onion or parsley.

Rum Omelette

A rum omelette is a plain omelette mixture. When cooked, fold over, sprinkle with caster sugar and place under grill until glazed. Pour over it 1 teaspoon rum. Set a match to it and send to the table alight.

Savoury Eggs

Melt 2 tablespoons butter in a saucepan and add 2 teaspoons tomato sauce, 2 teaspoons Worcestershire sauce, 2–3 finely chopped anchovy fillets and 1 teaspoon mustard; heat through. Slice 5 hard-boiled eggs and add to the sauce. Serve on toast.

Savoury Fried Eggs

Put into frying pan 1 tablespoon butter, 1 tablespoon cream, 2 tablespoons tomato sauce, salt and pepper. Stir well and break into it the number of eggs required (this amount does for 4 eggs). Cook until set, then put the pan in oven to brown the tops. Put each egg on a piece of toast and pour the sauce over the top.

Savoury Scrambled Eggs

Place in a saucepan 1 tablespoon butter, 1 teaspoon curry powder, 1 tablespoon Anchovy Sauce (see recipe, page 109). Mix eggs as for scrambled eggs. Pour into mixture in saucepan (which has been melted on stove), set in usual way. Serve on toast.

A good omelette should not be overcooked —
the centre should not be as well set
as the outside.

Scotch Eggs

Heat 125 ml (½ cup) milk in a saucepan and add 80 g (1 cup) breadcrumbs; simmer for 5 minutes. Add 155 g (1 cup) coarsely chopped ham, ½ teaspoon mustard, ¼ teaspoon salt, a pinch of cayenne pepper and 1 lightly beaten egg. Cook until thickened. Remove from the heat and divide into six portions. Roll a portion of mixture around 6 hard-boiled eggs. Brush with a lightly beaten raw egg, dip in dried breadcrumbs and deep-fry until brown. May be halved and served hot with brown gravy or tomato sauce, or served cold with a salad or packed into a picnic basket.

Sweet Omelette

Take 5 eggs, separate yolks from whites, beat whites stiffly. Add to the yolks 1 tablespoon caster sugar and a tiny pinch of salt. Beat well, then mix lightly with the whites. Pour into a frying pan in which 1 teaspoon of butter has been melted. Watch that it does not cook too quickly and burn. When it has set, fold one side across. Lift onto a dish, sprinkle with sugar and put under a hot grill for a few seconds. Serve with plum jam sauce. Makes enough for 3–4 people.

Tomato Omelette

Roughly chop 2 small onions and 4 large tomatoes and fry well in 1 tablespoon of butter or dripping until the onions are cooked. Beat 1 egg well with 125 ml (½ cup) milk, add salt to taste, then pour into the pan over the tomatoes and onions. Serve on slices of brown toast.

Soups

Stocks form the foundation of soups and can be made from most meats (except pork, corned or smoked meat), bones, fish or vegetables by bringing them slowly to the boil and simmering for some hours. The ingredients are chopped up and placed in cold water. When cooking has to be hurried, do not add salt until near the end. For clear stock, leave vegetables whole or in large pieces. To clarify the soup, stir in one lightly beaten egg white and the crushed shell 30 minutes before serving. Stir until it boils and then simmer. Strain through wet muslin or a fine sieve before serving.

Soup Accompaniments

Croutons: Cut stale bread into small squares, about 1 cm square. Deep-fry in hot oil or sauté in just enough oil to prevent them from burning. Drain and cool.

Melba Toast: Cut bread in wafer-thin slices and bake in a 150°C oven until golden.

Mornay Toast: Cut bread into thin slices, sprinkle with grated cheese and dust with cayenne pepper and paprika. Bake in a 150°C oven until golden.

Cheese Rolls: Butter wafer-thin slices of bread and spread with grated cheese. Roll, fasten with a toothpick, and bake in a 150°C oven until golden.

Artichoke Soup

Peel and cut 1.3 kg jerusalem artichokes and put in a stockpot. Slice 1 onion, 1 turnip and 5 celery sticks and add to the pot. Add 2.4 litres stock and bring to the boil. Reduce the heat and simmer until tender. Blend the vegetables in a food processor until smooth, then add 300 ml milk or cream. Return to the boil, add salt and pepper, and serve with fried croutons.

Asparagus Soup

Make a white sauce by melting 2 teaspoons butter in a saucepan. Add 2 teaspoons flour and 600 ml milk very slowly. Add the liquid from 425 g tinned asparagus and simmer for a few minutes. Then, after keeping out a few asparagus stems to use as a garnish, add the asparagus to the mixture. Simmer again for a few minutes, then strain and press through a sieve. Season with salt and pepper, to taste. (A mixture of half milk and half stock may be used instead of the milk.)

Beef Tea

Cut 450 g gravy beef into small pieces and barely cover with cold water. Bring very slowly to the boil, stirring briskly the whole time. As soon as it comes to the boil, remove from the heat, strain, season and serve with fingers of toast.

Brown Stock

Chop 1.3 kg shin beef (or 900 g shin beef and a knuckle of veal) into small pieces and fry a quarter of the meat in butter until well browned. Cover the rest with 3.6 litres water and 2 teaspoons salt. Stand for 1 hour, then add the fried meat and bring to the boil. Reduce the heat and simmer. When the scum has ceased to rise, add 2 onions with their skins, 1 carrot and 1 turnip. Wrap 3 cloves and 1 teaspoon mixed dried herbs in muslin and secure; add to the soup. Simmer for 4–5 hours. Cool; skim off fat before using.

Brown Vegetable Soup

Roughly chop 1 onion, 1 carrot, 1 celery stick and 1 tomato. Heat 2 teaspoons oil in a frying pan and cook the vegetables until golden brown. Add 2 teaspoons plain flour to the pan and cook for 3 minutes, then add 1.2 litres stock and stir until boiling. Simmer for 1 hour 30 minutes, skimming occasionally, then push the vegetables through a sieve. Stir through 2 teaspoons Worcestershire sauce and season to taste with salt and pepper.

Carrot Soup

Melt 30 g butter in a saucepan and slice and fry 1 large onion. When slightly coloured, add a few sticks of celery and 3 peeled and chopped carrots. Season with salt and pepper, a pinch of sugar and 1 litre stock. Simmer for 1 hour 30 minutes, then purée in a food processor and skim any fat from the top. Return to the saucepan and add 1 teaspoon of cornflour with a little milk. Simmer again until the thickening is well cooked. Serve hot with small squares of toast.

Celery Soup

Wash 1 head celery and cut into 2 cm pieces. Put into a saucepan with 2.4 litres stock and cook until tender. Purée in a food processor. Melt 55 g butter in a saucepan and add 55 g (1/3 cup) plain flour. Stir for a few seconds over heat, add the celery purée and stir until it boils and thickens. Gradually add 1 litre milk and just bring to the boil. Add salt and cayenne pepper. Serve with fried croutons.

Chicken Broth

Joint a 1/2 chicken and chop the bones. Put the chicken in a saucepan with 1 onion and 1.2 litres water. Add a pinch each of salt, pepper and mace. Bring slowly to the boil. Remove the scum as it rises. Simmer for 3 hours. Strain. Remove any fat from the surface, reheat the broth and stir through 1 teaspoon finely chopped parsley, to serve.

Chicken Soup

Cut 1 whole chicken into quarters and place in a pan with 1 onion, 2 slices lean ham and 2.4 litres water. Let simmer until very tender; strain. The meat may be used in any way desired. Remove all fat. Add 45 g (¼ cup) rinsed rice, a little chopped parsley and salt and pepper, to taste. Simmer until the rice is tender. Add 250 ml (1 cup) milk and a roux made from 1 tablespoon each of plain flour and chicken fat. Cook for about 5 minutes, or until the soup thickens.

Consommés

Add 80 g (½ cup) grated carrot, 70 g (½ cup) grated celery and 65 g (½ cup) green peas to 1.2 litres clear white stock. Simmer for 45 minutes. Flavour with 1 tablespoon sherry just before serving.

For a PRINCESS CONSOMMÉ, add diced cooked chicken and 65 g (½ cup) cooked green peas to clear white stock. Stir through 2 tablespoons dry white wine just before serving.

To make an ICED COMSOMMÉ, cut up 625 g shin beef. Put into saucepan with 1.2 litres cold water. Add 1 level teaspoon salt and bring to the boil very slowly. Remove the scum from the broth, add 1 parsley sprig, 1 celery stick, 1 small carrot and ½ small turnip. Simmer gently for 2–3 hours. Strain the soup through a piece of muslin or a fine sieve. With careful simmering the soup should be quite clear. When cold, remove the fat, reheat the soup, pour into serving cups, and leave on ice until required. Before serving, sprinkle some very finely chopped parsley into the soup. Allow a good cupful of soup for each person.

Consommé Noodle

Make some noodle paste in the following manner: put 115 g (¾ cup) plain flour in a bowl with ¼ teaspoon salt. Make a well in the centre and add 1–2 egg yolks. Mix these into the flour until a smooth paste forms. Knead well until it feels velvety. Turn out onto a floured board. Roll very thinly, until you can almost see through it. Flour it well and fold it over and over, like a pancake. Take a sharp knife and cut it across in very narrow strips. Then shake them loosely apart. Have ready a large saucepan of boiling water, slightly salted. Throw in the strips. Boil for 5–6 minutes, stirring occasionally. Drain off all the water. Put the strips into about 2.4 litres of Consommé (see recipe, page 71) and serve.

Cottage Soup

Slice 2 small onions and put them into a saucepan with 2 tablespoons pearl barley and 1.5 litres (6 cups) stock. Simmer gently for 1 hour, then strain. Melt 30 g butter in a saucepan and fry 1 finely chopped bacon slice. Gradually stir in enough oatmeal to form a paste, then add 1.5 litres stock and simmer for another 40 minutes. Add the sauce and season to taste with salt and pepper.

Cream of Oyster Soup

Remove 12 oysters from the half shell and reserve any liquid. Boil the oyster liquor and strain. Melt 30 g butter in a saucepan, then add 40 g (¼ cup) plain flour and cook for 3 minutes. Stir in 450 ml milk. Add the strained oyster liquor, a dash of lemon juice, a pinch of cayenne pepper and a little Anchovy Sauce (see recipe, page 109). Bring to the boil. Remove from the heat and add 80 ml (⅓ cup) cream. Put 2–3 oysters in a shallow bowl and pour the soup over them. Do not garnish oyster soup.

Fish Purée

Scald 1 small chopped onion in 1.2 litres milk. Make a white sauce of the milk, 4 tablespoons plain flour and 4 tablespoons butter. Rub 2 cups flaked and cooked fish through a sieve and combine with the sauce. Season with salt and pepper, to taste, and serve hot.

Giblet Soup

Wash 1 set giblets well. Put into a saucepan with 1.2 litres water and a pinch each of salt and cayenne pepper. Bring slowly to the boil. Add 1 chopped onion. Simmer for 1 hour 30 minutes, or until the giblets are tender. Strain, return the liquid to the saucepan and add 1 tablespoon sago. Cook until it is clear. Chop the giblets finely and return to the soup. Reheat and serve at once.

Invalid Soup

Cut 85 g veal fillet into very small pieces. Rinse 2 tablespoons rice under cold running water. Put into a saucepan with 600 ml milk, a little chopped onion and a pinch of salt. Allow to simmer for 3 hours. Strain and reheat without boiling, otherwise the soup is apt to curdle. The soup should be the consistency of thick cream. Serve in a small bowl with fingers of toast.

Lentil Soup

Rinse 250 g (1 cup) red lentils, then soak in cold water for a few hours. Drain the lentils. Roughly chop 1 onion, 2 carrots and 2 parsnips and place in a saucepan with 1.2 litres stock and the lentils. Add a pinch of salt and pepper; cook until the lentils are soft. Blend the lentils in a food processor until smooth. Mix 1 tablespoon plain flour with a little cold water and add to the purée; stir until boiling, then cook for a few minutes more. Serve with finely chopped parsley and small squares of toast.

Milk Soup

Cut 1 onion into quarters. Boil the onion in 600 ml milk until soft. Strain. Melt 2 teaspoons butter in a saucepan and add 2 teaspoons plain flour. Cook for 1 minute. Add the strained milk and stir over low heat until the soup boils and thickens. Season with salt and pepper, and serve very hot with croutons of fried or toasted bread.

Mulligatawny

Cut 1 onion into rings. Dice 2 ham slices. Heat 30 g butter in a saucepan. Add the onion and ham and fry until brown. Add 1 peeled, sliced apple, 1 small peeled carrot and 1 peeled turnip. Stir in 2 teaspoons curry powder, 1/2 teaspoon curry paste and 1.2 litres stock. Cover and bring to the boil, then simmer gently for 1 hour. Blend in a food processor. Mix in 1 tablespoon plain flour with a little water and stir through the soup to thicken. Bring to the boil, boil for a few minutes, and serve at once.

Mutton Broth

Cut the meat off 625 g lamb neck chops and finely chop, removing any fat. Put the meat and bones into a saucepan with 2.4 litres water, a pinch each of salt and cayenne pepper, and 55 g (1/4 cup) well washed pearl barley. Bring slowly to the boil, then reduce the heat and simmer for 30 minutes. Roughly chop 1 carrot, 1 turnip, 1 onion and 1 celery stick and add to the pan. Simmer for 1 hour 30 minutes, skimming any scum from the surface. Remove and discard the bones. Stir through a little chopped parsley, season to taste, and serve hot.

Pea Soup

Place 1 ham bone in large saucepan with 1 carrot, 1 onion and 2 whole potatoes. Add 3.6 litres boiling water and 220 g (1 cup) dried green split peas which have been soaked overnight. Cook gently until tender. Strain through a colander and season with salt, pepper and fresh mint. Serve with croutons or melba toast.

Potato Soup

Thinly slice 3 potatoes and ½ onion. Put into a saucepan with 450 ml stock or water. Boil until the potato is soft, then press through a coarse strainer. Return to saucepan. Blend 2 teaspoons flour with 125 ml (½ cup) milk and stir into soup. Bring to the boil and season with salt and pepper, to taste. Serve hot with croutons.

Pumpkin Soup

Cut 900 g peeled pumpkin into dice and put in a pan with 85 g butter, 1 teaspoon salt and 1 teaspoon sugar. Stir for a few minutes, add 600 ml stock and simmer until the pumpkin is tender. Blend in a food processor, return to the pan and add 1.8 litres milk or stock. Blend 1 tablespoon plain flour with a little milk to make a paste, then stir through the soup to thicken. Bring to the boil, then reduce the heat and simmer for 15 minutes. Serve hot.

Scotch Broth

Trim 625 g lamb neck chops, removing all the fat, and chop into pieces. Put into a stewing pan with 2.4 litres water. Bring to the boil, skim well, then reduce the heat and simmer for 2 hours. Meanwhile, slice 3 large onions and chop 2 carrots and 4 turnips. Add to the meat. Rinse 110 g (½ cup) pearl barley and add to the pan. Simmer again for 1 hour. Season with salt and pepper and, just before serving, mix in 2 teaspoons finely chopped parsley.

Tomato Soup

Stew and strain 1.2 kg tomatoes and add 1 teaspoon each of salt and pepper. Boil 1.2 litres milk; smooth together 1 tablespoon plain flour and 1 tablespoon butter, add to the boiling milk, but do not put in the tomatoes until wanted. Add a pinch of bicarbonate of soda to the tomatoes and stir through, then pour into the milk mixture. Serve at once.

Tomato Soup to Keep

Put 900 g tomatoes, 1 onion, 1 teaspoon peppercorns, 1/2 teaspoon salt and 1 tablespoon brown sugar into a stockpot with 1.5 litres (6 cups) water. Boil rapidly for 30 minutes, then rub through a colander. Bottle and securely seal the tomatoes in sterilised jars while hot. When needed, heat desired quantity, add a pinch of bicarbonate of soda, 500 ml (2 cups) milk. Thicken with flour and a fair-sized piece of butter, or if preferred 125 ml (1/2 cup) cream just before serving.

Veal Broth

Put a knuckle of veal into a saucepan with 1.8 litres water and a pinch of salt. Bring to the boil. Roughly chop 1 onion, 1 turnip, 4 celery sticks and 1 parsnip. Add to the pan with 1 blade mace (or 1 large pinch ground mace) and return to the boil. Reduce the heat and simmer for 1 hour 30 minutes. Take meat out; remove any meat from the bone and return to the pan (discard the bones, fat and gristle). Add 55 g (1/4 cup) washed rice and continue cooking for 30 minutes longer. Add 1 tablespoon finely chopped parsley and season with salt and pepper, to taste. Serve hot.

Vermicelli Soup

Remove the fat from 1.2 litres White Stock (see below) and bring to the boil. Add 40 g vermicelli noodles, broken into small pieces. Cook for about 15 minutes in the stock, or until the vermicelli is soft. Add 3 tablespoons cream and season, to taste. Add a pinch of cayenne pepper. Serve with fingers of toast and grated cheese.

White Stock

For white stock, use a knuckle of veal, veal bones, fowl or mutton instead
of beef as for brown stock. Put the meat in a stockpot with
1 onion, 1 celery stick, 1 carrot and 1 bunch fresh herbs. Cover with
3.6 litres water and 2 teaspoons salt. Bring to the boil, then reduce the heat
and simmer for 4–5 hours. Strain and skim off any fat before using.

HOME-CURED BACON

For every 45 kg of meat use 3.6 kg salt, 450 g soft brown sugar, 85 g saltpetre or 'Cure-it' (available from the deli section in most large supermarkets) and 40 g allspice. If the pig is old and tough, more dry salt may be added with advantage. After cutting up and cooling the carcase, the meat must be placed on a sloping surface and a portion of the salt rubbed into the skin with the aid of a stone, until the skin becomes quite soft. The flesh should then be rubbed with salt and the meat piled up and allowed to drain for 48 hours; all liquid which drains from the meat at this period must be discarded.

After the flesh has drained, half of the remaining salt is to be mixed with half of the saltpetre and rubbed thoroughly into the meat. The remainder of the salt and the saltpetre should be mixed with the brown sugar and spice and thoroughly rubbed into the flesh. Pile the meat up again and allow to drain. All the liquid that drains at this stage should be collected and poured liberally over the flesh on alternate days. At the end of three weeks the meat should be soaked in cold water for 12 hours, then hung up and dried and smoked for 7 days.

It should always be remembered that climatic conditions have much to do with the success of bacon curing; apart from that and the quality of the meat, the care of the operator is the most important factor.

Vegetables

Care must be taken to thoroughly wash and prepare vegetables. Root vegetables are put in boiling water and are boiled very slowly with the lid on the saucepan — the exception to this rule is old potatoes, which should be put into cold salted water.

Boiling Vegetables

Green vegetables are put in boiling water and boiled hard with the lid off to allow the gases to escape and preserve their colour. If the green vegetables are very young and tender, do not cook so fast. All green vegetables may have a tiny pinch of bicarbonate of soda added to the water, and salt to taste. For root vegetables, allow 2 teaspoons salt to every 1.2 litres water. For green vegetables, allow 1 teaspoon salt to every 1.2 litres water.

Cabbage and lettuce contain alkalis and need acid condiments, such as vinegar or lemon juice. Beets, turnips, squash, beans and peas need sugar added to make up for the sweetness lost in cooking.

When cooking greens, a ham bone will impart a very nice flavour to the vegetable; a bacon bone may be used. Onion or spring onion used discreetly is a tasty addition to vegetable dishes.

To test when vegetables are done, pass a fork through the stalk or stem; if soft, they are ready. See the table on page 79 for further cooking times.

A most important thing to do when boiling vegetables is to free them from the water in which they have been cooked. There are five ways in which this may be done:

- Drain in a colander; for example, parsnips, carrots, turnips and onions.
- Draining and pressing with a saucer; for example, cabbage or spinach.
- Draining on toast; for example, vegetable marrow, asparagus, celery, cauliflower. Vegetables drained with toast on the bottom of the vegetable dish should have melted butter poured over them.
- Draining in colander, then shaking well and returning to the saucepan and shaking over the heat with a little butter and pepper added; for example, peas, beans, new potatoes.
- Old potatoes should be strained when a little more than half-cooked — test by piercing a potato with a skewer. If there is a hard ball in the centre they are at the right stage, then strain off water and place a clean cloth on the potatoes. Stand off the heat with the lid on for about 10 minutes, then remove the lid to allow the steam to escape; leave with the cloth on until ready to serve or mash. Potatoes cooked in this way will always be floury and white. You can add ½ teaspoon baking powder to the potatoes when creaming them.

TIMETABLE FOR COOKING VEGETABLES

Artichokes (jerusalem)	30–35 minutes
Artichoke (globe)	40–50 minutes; boil until leaves draw out easily
Asparagus	15–20 minutes
Broad Beans	15–30 minutes, depending on age
French Beans	15–25 minutes
Beetroot	1 hour 30 minutes–2 hours
Cabbage	30–35 minutes
Carrots	30 minutes
Cauliflower	15 minutes, longer if large
Celery	Simmer 2 hours
Onions	Simmer 1–2 hours
Peas	Boil fast, 10–12 minutes, if old a little longer
Potatoes (old)	25 minutes (old); 20 minutes (young)
Pumpkin	Bake 1 hour, boil 30 minutes
Spinach	15–20 minutes
Turnips	30–35 minutes
Vegetable Marrow	15–30 minutes; steam longer

Steaming Vegetables

Alternatively, vegetables that are steamed instead of boiled retain much more of their valuable salts, and any that are leftover can be reheated and taste as good as when first cooked. Salt may be sprinkled over them in the steamer during the cooking process. New potatoes are best steamed; add salt and mint to the water. Peel after cooking and put in a hot saucepan with 30 g butter to every 450 g potatoes. Serve in hot dish with very finely chopped parsley sprinkled over them.

Roasting Root Vegetables and Pumpkin

Peel vegetables and cut into uniform size pieces. Vegetables may be roasted in a frying pan with meat or separately. Melt the oil in a hot frying pan. Place the vegetables in and dredge lightly with flour and salt. Return to a 200°C oven, turn when half cooked. If not sufficiently crisp, advance the heat for 5–10 minutes after removing meat from the pan.

A second method is to parboil vegetables in salted water until half cooked, then drain well and while hot, place in a baking tray with hot oil and roast in a 220°C oven until browned.

Asparagus with Cheese Sauce

Blend 4 tablespoons plain flour with 2 tablespoons melted butter. Season with salt and pepper and add 500 ml (2 cups) milk. Cook until thick, then add 110 g (^{2}/$_3$ cup) chopped cheese. Cook until the cheese melts, stirring well. Place tinned asparagus stems on buttered toast and pour the cheese sauce over the asparagus. Garnish with crisp bacon and parsley.

Baked Potatoes

Boil, then mash about 450 g boiled potatoes very smoothly. Beat in 2 egg yolks, 3 tablespoons milk and 1 tablespoon butter. Season with salt and pepper, to taste. Add 1 stiffly beaten egg white, place in a buttered dish and bake in a 180°C oven for 20 minutes.

Baked Potatoes and Cheese

Bake 6 large peeled potatoes in the oven, without butter or oil. Halve them and scoop out the centre. Mash this thoroughly. Mix together 185 g (1½ cups) grated cheese and 80 ml (⅓ cup) hot milk and beat until smooth. Mix this with the mashed potato and add 2 teaspoons salt and a pinch of paprika; whip until creamy. Re-fill the potato cases with this mixture and cook in a 220°C oven. Bake until golden brown on top.

Boiled Asparagus

Scrape fresh asparagus spears so they are quite clean and then let them soak in salt and water for 1 hour. Trim them into equal lengths and tie them up in small bundles with kitchen string. Stand in a saucepan of water with the tips uncovered and boil gently for about 30 minutes, or until the stalks are tender. Dip slices of toast, about 1 cm thick, with the crust cut off, into the asparagus liquor. Untie the bundles, lay the asparagus upon the toast and serve with melted butter in a sauce boat.

Boiled Beetroot

Peel and thinly slice 1 large or 2 small beetroot. Put into a saucepan with 1 teaspoon sugar, 1 teaspoon salt and enough water to cover. Put the lid on the saucepan and bring to the boil. Reduce the heat and simmer for 20 minutes, or until tender. Pour off the cooking liquid, add a similar quantity of vinegar. Put the cooked beetroot into a sterilised jar and cover with liquid. It is then ready for use.

Brussels Sprouts Lyonnaise

Lightly cook 450 g Brussels sprouts. Melt 2½ tablespoons bacon fat in a frying pan. Add 1 chopped onion and cook until yellow, then stir in 4 tablespoons stock; season with salt and paprika. Add the sprouts and cook, stirring frequently until the stock is absorbed. Sprinkle with chopped parsley to serve.

Candied Parsnips

Cut each peeled parsnip into 8 pieces lengthways and cook until tender in salted water. Drain and sprinkle thickly with brown sugar and bits of butter. Dust over with nutmeg and place in the oven until the sugar begins to caramelise. Serve very hot.

Candied Sweet Potatoes

Parboil 4 sweet potatoes and slice them lengthways. Place a layer of potatoes in a greased baking dish, sprinkle generously with desiccated coconut, alternating layers of coconut and potatoes — you will need about 90 g (1 cup) coconut in total. Pour 250 ml (1 cup) milk over the potatoes and coconut, add 170 g (¾ cup) sugar and ½ teaspoon cinnamon. Bake in a 220°C oven for 20 minutes.

Carrot Moulds

Mix 310 g (2 cups) grated carrot and 40 g (½ cup) breadcrumbs. Add 2 beaten eggs, a pinch of salt, 2 tablespoons melted fat or oil and 250 ml (½ cup) milk. Fill a greased ring mould and set in a pan of hot water. Bake in 150°C oven until firm. Fill with any hot savoury mixture; for example, salmon à la king.

Carrot Purée

Peel 6 large carrots, cut each into eight pieces; heat 1½ tablespoons butter, then add the carrots and fry gently for 5 minutes, but do not brown them. Add 2.4 litres stock, and simmer for about 1 hour, or until tender. Rub the carrots through a sieve, reheat, and add 300 ml milk. Blend 1½ tablespoons flour with a little cold milk, add to the carrots. Cook gently for 5 minutes; season with salt and cayenne pepper, to taste.

Cauliflower

Divide the cauliflower into nicely shaped pieces and cook in boiling salted water until tender, but not too soft. Drain well. Sprinkle with a little plain flour seasoned with salt and pepper, roll each piece of cauliflower in the flour, dip in beaten egg, and deep-fry for a few minutes until golden brown. Drain on paper towel and serve.

Cauliflower Boiled in Milk

A delicious way to cook cauliflower is to boil it in milk instead of water; when cooked, drain, using the milk to make a White Sauce (or see recipe, page 118) by simply adding it to the usual ingredients of flour, butter and pepper (salt having already been used when boiling the vegetable).

Corn

Cook the corn on the cob in boiling salted water for 10 minutes. Do not leave in water, remove immediately. If liked, grill. Serve with melted butter.

Corn Soufflé

Make a white sauce, using 1 tablespoon flour, 1 tablespoon butter, 125 ml (½ cup) milk, seasoning to taste (or see recipe, page 118). Add 400 g (2 cups) cooked corn kernels to the mixture, cool slightly, then fold in 2 well-beaten eggs. Turn into a greased pie dish and bake in a 180°C oven for 30 minutes. Other vegetables, such as green peas, chopped carrots, cauliflower or spinach, may be used with equal success.

Creamed Celery

Cover 250 g (2 cups) celery pieces with boiling water and boil until tender. Make a sauce with 125 ml (½ cup) celery water, 125 ml (½ cup) milk, 2 tablespoons flour and butter. Add the cooked celery and season with salt and pepper, to taste.

Creamed Leeks

Trim and wash 3 leeks. Place in boiling salted water with 1 teaspoon freshly squeezed lemon juice and boil rapidly without a lid for 10 minutes. Drain. Make a sauce as follows: put 500 ml (2 cups) milk into a saucepan with 2.5 cm piece lemon rind, salt, 6 whole peppercorns, 1 blade mace (or 1 large pinch ground mace) and 1 parsley sprig. Bring slowly to simmering point. Simmer for 10 minutes. Strain. Melt 1 tablespoon butter in a saucepan and add 1 tablespoon flour, stirring to form a paste. Then add the strained milk, a little a time, stirring constantly until it boils. Reduce the heat and simmer for 5 minutes. Add 1 teaspoon lemon juice and the drained leeks. Return to the heat and simmer until the leeks are cooked.

Creamed Mushrooms

Wash mushrooms but do not peel; trim stalks. Cut into quarters and lightly flour by shaking in a paper bag with flour and salt. Fry the mushrooms quickly in butter until very lightly browned, shaking constantly. Add enough milk to cover them and simmer gently for 10 minutes. Drain and serve.

French Fried Onions

Peel 4 white onions and cut into 5 mm slices. Separate into rings. Beat 1 egg lightly in a bowl and add 3 tablespoons milk, 3 tablespoons water, 150 g (1 cup) plain flour and ½ teaspoon salt. Beat well. Dip rings into batter one at a time and deep-fry until golden brown. Drain and serve hot.

Fried Eggplant

Cut the eggplant into 1 cm slices and sprinkle with salt. Let stand for 2 hours. About 30 minutes before you intend to serve them, wipe each slice dry with paper towel, dip into a bowl with 1 well-beaten egg and coat in breadcrumbs. Sauté in hot oil until cooked.

Fried Parsley

Wash the curly parsley well, pick off the stalks, leaving large heads. Dry well — if damp, it will not be crisp. When a slight smoke is rising from a pan of frying oil, put the parsley in a frying basket and lower into the oil. Shake it gently and leave in the oil until the noise stops and it has nearly left off bubbling — it will take about 6 seconds. Drain on paper towel and serve at once. The parsley should be crisp and quite green; if brown, the fat is too hot, or it was cooked for too long.

Fried Tomatoes

Cut some firm ripe tomatoes into 1 cm slices. Season a bowl of dry breadcrumbs with salt and pepper and dip the tomatoes into the breadcrumbs, making sure both sides are coated. Sauté in hot oil until cooked and golden.

Glazed Carrots

Wash and peel 3 carrots and cut into thin slices. Cook in a pan of 750 ml (3 cups) boiling salted water. When nearly cooked, strain off the liquid, reserving 185 ml (3/4 cup). Return the liquid to the pan; add 3 tablespoons sugar and 125 g butter. Cook without a lid until the liquid thickens and darkens. Lift out the carrots carefully, keeping the glazed side uppermost, to serve.

Green Peas in Turnip Cups

Put the required number of small white turnips into a saucepan with well-seasoned stock to which 1 teaspoon sugar has been added. Bring to the boil and cook until tender. Hollow out the centres of each turnip to form cups — the pulp can be used to flavour vegetable salads, soups or stews. Have ready a quantity of fresh peas, which have been cooked until tender. Add salt, to taste, and mix with 1 tablespoon diced ham to every 450 g (3 cups) peas; add a small knob of butter. Season the peas with pepper and pile them up in the turnip cups. Serve with grilled chops or steaks, or as a separate vegetable course.

Mushrooms au Gratin

Soak the mushrooms in salted water for 5 minutes. Wash well, peel and trim the stalks. Put the mushrooms into a greased baking dish, sprinkle with grated cheese, salt, cayenne pepper and finally with dry breadcrumbs; dot with a knob of butter. Bake in a 180°C oven for 20–30 minutes. Garnish with parsley, to serve.

Mushroom Soufflé

Melt 2 teaspoons butter in a saucepan. Remove from the heat and stir in 1 tablespoon plain flour, then return to the heat and cook for 1 minute. Add 185 ml (³⁄₄ cup) milk, stir until it boils and thickens. Cool slightly, then add 3 egg yolks, salt and cayenne pepper. Add 6 large, finely chopped mushrooms and toss to combine. Whisk the whites from 3 eggs until stiffly peaks form, then incorporate into the mushroom mixture. Pour into buttered soufflé dishes and bake in a 220°C oven for 30–35 minutes. Serve at once.

Noisette Potatoes

Peel 900 g potatoes or 450 g very small new potatoes. If using large boiling potatoes, hollow out with small ball cutter, into marbles. Peel the new potatoes if using. Place in a saucepan and cover with cold water; bring to the boil and cook until just tender. Drain and dry. Heat 3 tablespoons butter in a heavy-based frying pan and add the potatoes, salt and pepper. Cover with a lid and shake over low heat until brown all over.

Potatoes with Bacon

Roast large potatoes in their jackets. When cooked, slice each potato in half and cover the cut surface with chopped bacon fried in its own fat. These potatoes are great served with barbecued meats.

Potato Nests

Scrub 3 large potatoes, then bake them in the oven until they are soft. Using a teaspoon, make a hole in the top of each and scoop out the inside. Mash this finely — for each tablespoon of potato pulp allow 1 tablespoon minced meat or fish, ¹⁄₂ teaspoon chopped parsley, 15 g butter, and salt and pepper, to taste. Refill the skins carefully with the mixture; sprinkle a little grated cheese on top of each, and put them back in the oven until the cheese is melted and the potatoes are piping hot.

Puffed Potatoes

Wash and peel the required number of potatoes and cut them into slices about the thickness of a twenty cent coin. Put them into cold water and then dry well in a cloth. Have a deep saucepan of hot oil ready, put the potatoes into a frying basket, plunge into the hot oil and shake occasionally. Take them out of the oil just before they colour, and let the oil get hot again. Again plunge the potatoes into the oil and shake well. Repeat the process once more, drain well, and serve very hot with salt sprinkled over. The potatoes should be well puffed out, crisp, golden and free from grease.

Scalloped Potatoes

Peel potatoes, slice very thinly. Alternate layers of potatoes in a casserole dish with a sprinkling of flour, chunks of butter or margarine, salt, pepper and a slice or two of onion. Fill casserole almost to top, dotting the top generously with butter. Put the dish in a 180°C oven and bake for 15 minutes. Add hot milk to the dish. Return to the oven with the lid on, until the potatoes are tender, then remove lid and allow the top to brown.

Spinach Supreme

Drain and chop the leaves of 1 large bunch of spinach (more if needed for large number). Add 250 ml (1 cup) milk and 125 g (1 cup) grated cheese. Mix well and place all in a baking dish. Cover with 125 g (1 cup) grated cheese and bake in a 180°C oven until the cheese is melted and slightly browned; before taking from oven, cover top with thin strips of bacon and allow bacon to cook until crisp.

Stuffed Cucumber

To make the forcemeat filling, mix 250 g minced beef or pork meat, ¼ teaspoon finely chopped onion, ½ teaspoon finely chopped parsley and 2 teaspoons dry breadcrumbs and bind together with 1 well-beaten egg. Set aside until needed. Cut 2 short cucumbers into 5 cm lengths and peel them. Scoop out the seeds without spoiling the shape of the cucumber. This is best done with a round pastry cutter. Fill the holes with forcemeat — do not press too tightly or the cucumber will crack during cooking. Stand these stuffed pieces of cucumber on their ends in a greased baking dish and sprinkle a few buttered breadcrumbs over the top of each. Place a greased sheet of baking paper over them, greased side down, and then stand the tin in a large roasting tin half-filled with water. Bake in a 180°C oven for 20 minutes, or until the cucumber is tender. Cut as many round croutons of bread as you have pieces of cucumber and let the croutons be a little larger than the cucumber. Fry them a pale golden brown, then drain thoroughly. Lift the pieces of cucumber with an egg slice and stand one on the centre of each crouton. Arrange neatly on a dish, pour tomato sauce round and serve. These cucumber cups may also be filled with any creamed savoury dish, such as chicken or fish.

Stuffed Potatoes

Scrub 3 large potatoes and bake them slowly until tender. Cut them in half lengthways and scoop out the potato. Put the flesh into a saucepan with 30 g butter, 60 g (½ cup) finely grated cheese, and salt and pepper, to taste. Stir until melted and moisten with milk as required. Melt 40 g butter in another pan, drain 1 cup of bottled macédoine vegetables, and toss in the butter until hot. Return the potato to the shells, leaving a hollow in the centre. Fill with the vegetables and serve hot.

When mashing potatoes, use hot milk instead of cold and add a little baking powder — about a teaspoon to a large pot — and beat well. It will make them fluffy, and they will go further.

Stuffed Vegetable Marrow

Choose 1 large vegetable marrow. Halve the marrow lengthways, then cut in two pieces widthways. Scoop out the seeds and cook in boiling water for about 8 minutes. Mix 200 g (2 cups) dry breadcrumbs with 1 small grated onion, 1 teaspoon finely chopped parsley and a pinch of dried Italian herbs. Add 60 g (²/₃ cup) chopped mushrooms. Season with salt and pepper and moisten with 2 tablespoons melted butter, 1 beaten egg and a little stock, if needed. When the marrow is tender turn into a colander to drain. Arrange one complete half in the bottom of a greased casserole dish. Pack the seasoning on top and flatten with a fork. Cover with remaining half of marrow. Cover and cook for 1 hour. Serve hot, garnished with parsley.

Tomato Soufflé

Scald and skin 450 g tomatoes. Remove the hard centres and heat the remainder of the fruit to a pulp. Season with salt, pepper and cayenne pepper, and add a little lemon juice (or tarragon vinegar), to taste. Pour into a non-metallic saucepan, add 2 teaspoons cornflour, stir over heat until it boils, then reduce the heat and continue to stir until it is perfectly smooth. Place in a bowl, and when cool, mix in the whisked yolks of 2 eggs. Beat the egg whites from 2 eggs to a stiff froth and stir through. Pour into a small baking dish and bake for 5–10 minutes in a 200°C oven. Serve immediately.

Salads

A perfect salad looks cool and inviting when the ingredients are blended with skill, making a salad that is delicious to eat and full of nutritional value. During hot weather, salads are invaluable. To make a perfect salad, the fruit and vegetables used must be of the freshest and best quality. A salad is indigestible when the ingredients are of poor quality, not crisp, and are soft and discoloured.

Thoroughly wash and look well over all greens. Put in cold water without salt. Then put in a sieve to drain and dry in a clean cloth. Do not add dressing to salad until required, or the salad will lose its crispness. Mix salads with a silver or wooden spoon and cut fruit and vegetables with a rustless or stainless steel knife.

To give flavour to a salad, rub a clove of garlic around the inside of the bowl. Alternatively, you can place a piece of garlic in a ball of bread and drop it in the salad while mixing the ingredients. Be sure to remove the garlic before serving — this ensures the aroma of the garlic is added to the salad.

Apple, Carrot and Orange Salad

Dice 1 apple, 1 celery stick and grate 1 carrot. Remove the pulp of 1 orange and finely chop the flesh. Combine the ingredients with a little mayonnaise and allow to stand for 20 minutes. Serve on crisp lettuce leaves, masked with more mayonnaise.

Apple Celery Salad

Trim 1 head celery, removing the tough outer stalks and reserve for another use. Let the inner celery stalks lie in cold water for 30 minutes, then drain and dry well. Cut the celery into julienne. Peel and core 2–3 apples and cut them into very fine slices. Put celery and apples in a bowl and pour over enough salad dressing to moisten them. Mix together very lightly. Line a salad dish with crisp leaves of lettuce, arrange apples and celery on top. Garnish with 2–3 chopped gherkins and a few chopped nuts, if desired. Serve before the apples have time to discolour.

Asparagus Salad

Drain 425 g tinned asparagus spears and add to a saucepan with enough water to make 750 ml (3 cups) in total. Add 1 teaspoon salt, 2 cups chopped celery (from the heart), the juice of 1 lemon and a pinch of pepper. Bring to the boil. Add 1½ tablespoons gelatine powder and stir until dissolved. Line a soufflé dish or mould with the asparagus spears and a little celery. Mix the rest of the celery with the liquid, pour into the mould and allow to set. Arrange on lettuce, either the whole mould or cut up into dice.

Australian Salad

Wipe 6 tomatoes, cut off the tops and scoop out the centres, taking care not to break the cases. Sprinkle the insides of each with salt, pepper and a little sugar. Mash the tomato pulp and mix it with 3 teaspoons of grated cheese and 2 teaspoons each of finely chopped pineapple and chopped nuts, 4 tablespoons finely shredded lettuce and 1 teaspoon of finely chopped parsley (if liked, add 1 teaspoon chopped spring onion). Fill the tomato cases with mixture, sprinkle the top with a little cayenne pepper, then mask with a thick mayonnaise. Set each tomato on a crisp lettuce leaf and serve chilled. This is a delicious dish for summer tea.

Beetroot Salad

Peel and slice 2 large whole cooked beetroot. Line a mould or glass dish with the slices, filling the centre with the smaller slices of beetroot. Dissolve 1 tablespoon powdered gelatine in 310 ml (1¼ cups) hot water, add 125 ml (½ cup) vinegar and salt, pepper and sugar, to taste. Leave to thicken slightly, then pour over the beetroot; allow to set. Serve garnished with shredded lettuce and sliced tomato. Serve with Mayonnaise Dressing (see recipe, page 101). This amount serves 6 people. If liked, more vinegar and less water in proportion may be used in this recipe, which also may be varied by using other vegetables to replace some of the beetroot.

Carrot Salad

Peel, dice and cook 2 large carrots. Cool and place in a serving dish. Sprinkle with salt, cayenne pepper, sugar, oil, finely grated lemon zest, and a little grated horseradish. Mix well. Arrange a border of shredded lettuce around.

Chicken and Celery Salad

Take the white meat of a chicken (either roasted, boiled or fricasséed), cut it small or mince it fine. Take the same quantity or more of white tender celery and cut into small pieces. Mix the celery and chicken together 1–2 hours before serving, then add the dressing. To make the dressing, mash the yolk of 1 hard-boiled egg very fine with a fork and add it to the yolk of 1 raw egg, with 1 teaspoon each of salt and pepper and ½ teaspoon mustard powder. Stir until smooth before gradually adding 60 ml (¼ cup) olive oil and 1 tablespoon white wine vinegar. Mix the chicken with the dressing, pile it up on the dish and spread some of the dressing over the outside. Garnish with the delicate leaves of celery, the white of the egg cut into rings, green pickles cut into thin slices and pickled beetroot cut into slices and stars. Garnish alternately with rings of eggs and the celery leaves.

Egg Salad

Remove the coarse outside leaves from 1 lettuce. Wash, drain, and dry the inner leaves without bruising them. Shred very finely. Wash and dry 2 celery sticks, removing the strings. Cut into fine dice. Peel, wash, dry and slice 3 French shallots. Mix lightly together and arrange the lettuce, shallots and celery in layers in a serving dish. Remove the shells from 3 hard-boiled eggs and cut 2 eggs into quarters lengthways. Arrange over the prepared lettuce. Chop the remaining egg yolk and sprinkle over the lettuce and egg quarters. Garnish with curled celery and watercress. Serve mayonnaise or salad dressing separately.

Hard-boiled eggs will not discolour if put in boiling water and boiled for just 12 minutes. Remove the shell and plunge the egg into cold water before using.

Grapefruit and Apple Salad

Wash, drain, and dry the leaves of 1 lettuce in a cloth, being careful not to bruise the leaves. Peel 1 grapefruit and 1 orange, carefully removing all the pith and seeds, and separate each fruit segment. Peel, core, and dice 2 apples and mix with enough dressing or mayonnaise to bind together. Arrange the prepared citrus segments like flower petals on crisp lettuce leaves and fill the centre of each with apple mixture. Garnish with stuffed or stoned olives and serve very cold.

Indian Salad

Indian salad is appetising in hot weather. It consists of 1 lettuce with a dressing made of 1 tablespoon chutney, a good pinch of allspice, 2 tablespoons vinegar and, if preferred, 1 tablespoon claret. The lettuce is put into the middle of the salad bowl and around it are placed thin slices of hard-boiled egg, a few prawns and slices or quarters of lemon.

Jellied Chicken Salad

Heat 600 ml stock in a saucepan. Soak 1½ tablespoons powdered gelatine in a little cold stock. Add the gelatine to the stock and stir until dissolved; leave to cool. When it begins to thicken add 125 ml (½ cup) mayonnaise, 70 g (½ cup) diced celery and 1 cup cold, cooked chopped chicken. Mix well and pour into wet individual ramekins. Leave until firmly set. When ready to serve, dip each mould into warm water for a few seconds to loosen the jelly and turn out onto a crisp, curled lettuce leaf. Garnish with tomato rings and capers, or sliced gherkins. Serve very cold.

Jellied Fruit Salad

Soak 2 tablespoons powdered gelatine in 3 tablespoons cold water for a few minutes. Add 625 ml (2½ cups) boiling water, 250 ml (1 cup) orange juice, 125 ml (½ cup) lemon juice, 110 g (½ cup) sugar and a pinch of salt. When the mixture begins to stiffen, add 1 cup drained tinned pineapple pieces and 1 cup diced banana. Turn into a wet mould and allow to set. When ready to serve, turn out and arrange on lettuce leaves. Serve with mayonnaise or salad dressing.

Jellied Vegetable Salad

Take some cooked vegetables, such as carrots, turnips, beetroot, peas or beans and dice evenly. Dissolve 1 tablespoon powdered gelatine in 500 ml (2 cups) boiling water, and flavour with salt, pepper and a little sugar. Stir in 1 tablespoon vinegar and some finely chopped mint leaves. Put the vegetables into a fancy mould or into small individual moulds. Cover with Savoury Jelly (Aspic) (see recipe, page 149), refrigerate, and when set, serve with lettuce and mayonnaise.

Kamilaroi Potato Salad

Peel and boil 6 potatoes, then mash with 1 tablespoon butter, 1 teaspoon salt, 2 tablespoons milk; beat to a cream. Add a little pepper, 1 finely chopped onion or French shallot, 2 teaspoons finely chopped parsley, 2 teaspoons olive oil and 2 teaspoons vinegar. The amount of oil and vinegar must be left to the individual taste of the cook. Mix in 2 teaspoons sugar and beat until quite light. Turn out onto a rather flat dish and shape into a smooth oblong. Flute up the sides with a knife, decorate with capers and circles of hard-boiled eggs, or with grated carrot and eggs cut into quarters lengthways. Finely cut lettuce looks nice, or a few leaves from the heart of a lettuce may be used. Prepare this just before serving.

Lobster Salad

Prepare a simple salad with 1 lettuce, 2 sliced or chopped tomatoes and 1 sliced cucumber. Mix 150 ml melted Savoury Jelly (Aspic) (see recipe, page 149) in 125 ml (1/2 cup) mayonnaise. Brush 1 cooked lobster with this mixture and serve with the salad and a little Mayonnaise Dressing (see recipe, page 101). Decorate with diced jelly. Chicken may be used in this salad instead of lobster.

Oyster Salad

Take 24 oysters from their shells and cut in halves. Mix together with 2 cups finely chopped celery and 1 finely chopped red capsicum. Cut up 4 gherkins. Mix all the ingredients together and chill until needed, then serve on crisp lettuce leaves with Mayonnaise Dressing (see recipe, page 101).

Paw Paw or Rockmelon Salad

To make a delicious paw paw or rockmelon salad, cut the rind off the fruit and chop the flesh into slices. Sprinkle with sugar and add a dash of sherry to improve the flavour. Serve in glass dishes.

Pear and Cheese Salad

Take 825 g tinned pear halves or peel, halve and core the same weight of fresh pears. Mix 125 g (1 cup) grated cheese with 125 ml (1/2 cup) cream. To serve, place the pear halves on lettuce leaves and put a ball of the cheese mixture into the hollow of each pear half. Cover with mayonnaise and sprinkle with 90 g (3/4 cup) chopped walnuts (or the nuts may be mixed with the cream and cheese earlier, if liked).

Pineapple Salad

Wash, dry and chill the lettuce leaves. Thoroughly mix some finely chopped parsley and a little salt with cottage cheese and roll into small balls; set aside in the refrigerator. Drain the tinned sliced pineapple. Line a salad bowl with the lettuce leaves and arrange sliced pineapple on top. Pour over Russian Dressing (see recipe, page 102). Cheese balls should be placed on pineapple.

This salad may also be served garnished with pimento and covered with French Dressing (see recipe, page 100) and biscuits.

Potato Salad

Wash and dry 1 lettuce and shred into a salad bowl. Add 2 chopped pickled onions, 2 chopped gherkins and a little chopped parsley to 4 tablespoons mayonnaise; mixing well to combine. Peel and dice 450 g cold, boiled potatoes and stir through the mayonnaise mixture. Arrange on a bed of lettuce and garnish with sliced hard-boiled eggs.

Russian Salad

Pour a little melted Savoury Jelly (Aspic) (see recipe, page 149) into a border mould and put a circle of peas all round it, using a hatpin to put them in place. Pour a little jelly over to set them. Meanwhile, make a design around the edge, using fancy pieces of carrot, cauliflower and turnips, arranging in a design. If desired, the vegetables can be mixed up just before the jelly is about to set. Stir in some powdered egg yolk on top of the peas as they are setting.

Salad De Luxe

Cut 3 hard-boiled eggs into slices, remove the yolks and marinate the white in a little French Dressing (see recipe, page 100) in which a little chopped parsley has been added. Drain the juice from 425 g tinned asparagus spears (fresh asparagus may be used instead). Drain the egg rings and insert a stick of asparagus into each ring. Arrange crisp lettuce leaves on a large serving dish and place the prepared asparagus around the edge to form a border. Arrange a border inside of cooked peas. Add another row of cooked carrots cut into portions — the centre of the carrots should be scooped out and filled with chopped apples, nuts and celery mixed with mayonnaise. In the centre of the dish place a mixture of a chicken and lean ham that has been cut into dice and mixed with mayonnaise; pile into a pyramid. Pass the egg yolks through a sieve and sprinkle over the top. Serve at once.

Never use salt in the water when you freshen a lettuce, and never sprinkle salt on the lettuce after you have cut it up as it will lose its crispness. Dry the lettuce before adding to a salad by shaking in a cloth or salad basket before cutting it up.

Salmon Mayonnaise with Salad Dressing

Blend the yolks of 2 hard-boiled eggs, 1 teaspoon mustard, 1 tablespoon oil (if liked), 3–4 tablespoons vinegar and 3–4 tablespoons cream or condensed milk. Strain and set aside — it will keep for 24 hours if kept in a cool place. Cut 450 g of cold boiled fish into slices (or use 415 g tinned salmon). Place in a glass or silver dish with half of the above dressing stirred in with it, the remainder being spread on top. Serve on lettuce leaves. This mayonnaise can be also used for green or asparagus salad.

Salmon Salad

Take 370 g (2 cups) cooked rice and 210 g tinned salmon and mix with a fork. Season with ½ teaspoon salt and a little pepper. Mix together 1 tablespoon olive oil, 2 tablespoons vinegar, 1 teaspoon French mustard and pour over the rice and salmon. Refrigerate until ready to eat. Serve on washed and dried lettuce leaves.

Cucumbers will keep fresh if they are placed in a jug with a little water, stem end down, and are most digestible if cut up and sprinkled with salt 15 minutes before needed. Pour off any liquid that forms before adding to a salad. English people do not remove the rind of a cucumber. It is served on a dish whole and thick slices cut off as required, and the rind is eaten as well, the reason being that it is more digestible with the rind on and does not repeat.

Stuffed Celery Salad

Mash your favourite cheese to a paste with olive oil, then add pepper and chopped French shallots. Select well-shaped pieces of celery and fill each piece with the mixture. Chill before serving.

Stuffed Egg Salad

Peel and halve 6 hard-boiled eggs; remove the yolks. Mash the yolks with 1 teaspoon salt, ¼ teaspoon paprika and ½ teaspoon finely snipped chives. Moisten with mayonnaise, to taste, and pile up in the egg whites; stand in a cool place until cold. Take a small slice from the bottom of each egg to make the egg halves stand flat and place two halves on a plate lined with crisp lettuce or endive leaves. Serve with ham or tongue, or any other cold meat.

Stuffed Tomato Salad

Remove a slice from the top of 6 tomatoes, then scoop out the insides carefully and set aside while you prepare the stuffing. Mince 2 slices ham, 1 tablespoon capers and 1 hard-boiled egg. Add 1 tablespoon finely chopped onion, 2 tablespoons peas and salt, to taste. Stuff the tomatoes, cover with another grated hard-boiled egg, then with a spoonful of mayonnaise (alternatively you can moisten the stuffing with mayonnaise). Serve these on a plate lined with lettuce leaves.

Sweet Corn Salad

Mix together 270 g (1⅓ cups) tinned corn kernels, a little chopped onion, 3–4 chopped olives and 1 chopped gherkin. Place in a bowl with watercress and lettuce and serve with dressing.

Tomato and Cream Cheese Salad

Peel tomatoes and refrigerate until very cold, allowing 1 tomato for each person. Cut into 8 pieces without severing the portions at the base. Pull each portion out without breaking it, to form a flower. Sprinkle with salt and pepper. Add 1 teaspoon finely chopped chives, a little salt and cayenne pepper to some cream cheese and mix well. Form into a round ball or place in a piping bag with a star nozzle, and force out cheese into the centre of each tomato. Place on a bed of crisp lettuce, garnish with slices of hard-boiled eggs and serve with mayonnaise.

Tomato Jelly Salad

Dissolve 1 tablespoon powdered gelatine in a little water. Warm 500 ml (2 cups) tomato juice and pour onto the gelatine. Stir well. Set in a deep sandwich tin. Turn out, cut into rounds and serve on a bed of shredded lettuce. Garnish with tomato and serve at once.

Dressings and Sauces

Salad Dressings

Dressing for Tomatoes

1 chopped spring onion, finely chopped walnuts,
a pinch of mustard powder, mayonnaise

Add the spring onion, chopped walnuts and a pinch of mustard to the mayonnaise and mix well. Drizzle over thick slices of tomatoes, and serve.

French Dressing

1½ tablespoons vinegar, ¼ teaspoon French mustard,
a pinch of paprika, 4 tablespoons olive oil, ½ teaspoon onion juice

Mix 1 teaspoon salt, vinegar, mustard and paprika together in a small bowl, then stir in the olive oil and onion juice. Refrigerate the dressing and serve cold with any green salad. If liked, ½ teaspoon of sugar can be added to this recipe.

Genoese Dressing

2–3 tablespoons lemon juice, paprika, 80 ml (⅓ cup) olive oil,
3 tablespoons cream

Mix the lemon juice and paprika together with a pinch of pepper. Stir in the oil, then cream, by degrees. The ingredients should all be as cold as possible before mixing; season with ½ teaspoon salt, if desired, and use at once.

Golden Salad Dressing

250 ml (1 cup) pineapple juice, 2 tablespoons flour,
2 teaspoons mustard powder, 55 g (¼ cup) caster sugar,
2 well-beaten egg yolks, 2 tablespoons lemon juice,
250 ml (1 cup) whipped cream

Put the pineapple juice in a bowl and sit over a saucepan of simmering water. Add the combined flour, mustard powder and sugar to the pineapple juice and stir until the mixture thickens. Add the egg yolks and lemon juice and cook for 3 minutes more. Remove from the heat and when cold stir in the whipped cream.

Mayonnaise Dressing

3 egg yolks, 1 teaspoon mustard, 150 ml olive oil,
1 teaspoon lemon juice, 1 tablespoon vinegar

Beat the egg yolks and add the mustard with a pinch each of salt and pepper. Add the oil, drop by drop, stirring the mixture briskly. When all the oil is added, stir in the lemon juice and vinegar, mixing to combine. Keep in a cool place until required.

Mayonnaise (Sweet)

2 tablespoons sugar, 1 teaspoon mustard powder, a pinch of cayenne pepper or
white pepper, 2 tablespoons thick cream or condensed milk,
1 teaspoon olive oil, 1 tablespoon vinegar

Mix all of the dry ingredients together with 1 teaspoon salt, then add the cream and oil, stirring to combine. Finally, add the vinegar, a little at a time. The sweet mayonnaise is ready for use.

Mint Vinegar (Sweet)

600 ml malt vinegar, 230 g (1 cup) brown sugar, 2 tablespoons chopped mint

Put the vinegar, sugar and mint in a jar with a lid and shake thoroughly to combine. Make sure it is sealed securely and leave for at lease 6 days before using. Will keep indefinitely.

Oil and Vinegar Dressing

2 tablespoons olive oil, 3 teaspoons vinegar

Add ¼ teaspoon salt and ¼ teaspoon pepper to the oil and add the vinegar. Mix well before using. The best way to make this dressing is to put all of the ingredients in a bottle and shake well. Lemon juice may be substituted for vinegar.

Roquefort Dressing

2 tablespoons Roquefort cheese, French Dressing

Mash the cheese with a fork and moisten with French Dressing (see recipe, page 100) until you get a creamy liquid. Refrigerate until chilled and then use for masking crisp heart of lettuce leaves.

Russian Dressing

250 ml (1 cup) mayonnaise, 2 tablespoons finely chopped parsley,
1 tablespoon finely chopped gherkin, 2 teaspoons caviar,
125 ml (½ cup) chilli sauce or tomato sauce

Put all of the ingredients in a bowl and mix thoroughly to combine. Refrigerate the dressing and serve cold.

Salad Dressing 1

3 teaspoons cornflour, 150 ml milk, 1 teaspoon mustard powder,
1 teaspoon sugar, 1 tablespoon vinegar, olive oil

Mix the cornflour with a little cold water until smooth. Heat the milk in a saucepan and add the cornflour paste. Cook for 3 minutes, stirring all the time. Remove from the heat and allow to cool. Mix the mustard, sugar and vinegar in a separate bowl and add ½ teaspoon salt; add to the sauce. A few drops of olive oil added when blending in the vinegar gives a smoother, richer mixture.

Salad Dressing 2

1 tablespoon condensed milk, ½ teaspoon mustard powder,
1 teaspoon salt, a pinch of pepper, vinegar or freshly squeezed lemon juice

Mix the condensed milk, mustard, salt and pepper thoroughly. Add enough vinegar or lemon juice to make it of a pouring consistency.

Salad Dressing 3

1 tablespoon flour, 1½ tablespoons sugar, 1 tablespoon mustard,
1½ tablespoons butter, 2 eggs, 185 ml (¾ cup) milk, 60 ml (¼ cup) vinegar

Combine the flour and sugar in a bowl, then add the melted butter and mustard, stirring to combine. Beat the eggs and add to the sauce, gradually smoothing any lumps. Add the milk, stir well, then slowly add the vinegar, stirring constantly. Boil in the top of a double boiler until thick, being careful to stir well to avoid any lumps forming. Remove from the heat, cool, and when required, thin to the desired consistency with milk or vinegar. This dressing may be made with water instead of milk, and will keep indefinitely, cream being added to thin.

Sour Cream Dressing

250 g (1 cup) sour cream, 2 tablespoons lemon juice, 2 tablespoons vinegar,
2 teaspoons sugar, ½ teaspoon mustard powder, paprika

Beat the sour cream until smooth, then add the lemon juice and vinegar, stirring well to combine. Add ½ teaspoon salt, sugar, mustard and a dash each of pepper and paprika. Chill in the refrigerator before serving.

Tarragon Dressing

2 tablespoons olive oil, 2 teaspoon vinegar, 1 teaspoon tarragon vinegar

Put all of the ingredients into a jar with a tight-fitting lid and shake well to combine. Season with salt and pepper, to taste and refrigerate before using.

Thousand Island Dressing

250 g (1 cup) mayonnaise, 4 tablespoons chopped pimentos, 2 tablespoons
chopped pitted olives, cayenne pepper

Put the mayonnaise in a bowl and stir through the pimentos and olives. Season with salt and cayenne pepper, to taste, and serve at once.

Vinaigrette Sauce

300 ml tarragon vinegar, ½ teaspoon mustard powder, 150 ml olive oil,
½ teaspoon chopped French shallots, 1 teaspoon chopped capers,
½ teaspoon chopped parsley, ½ teaspoon snipped chives

Put the vinegar into a bowl and add the mustard powder and a pinch of salt. Stir in the oil and remaining ingredients. Mix together, and serve.

Savoury Sauces

White sauces, drawn butter sauces and brown sauces are the three basic sauces from which many other sauces are made by using variations.

It is important to cook the sauces to a very smooth consistency, and then season, to taste. Mix the flour and water or stock together first and then add this to the simmering liquid, stirring constantly to prevent it becoming lumpy. Once the flour is added, simmer for a few minutes to 'cook' out the flour. If the sauce has been made in advance, be sure to keep the lid on the saucepan to avoid a skin forming on the surface.

If egg is to be added to sauce (a whole egg or an egg yolk) it is best to put the slightly beaten egg in a bowl and add a little hot sauce to it (heating the egg gradually). Then pour this portion of sauce back into the saucepan and heat only for a minute. Do not allow the sauce to boil once the egg has been added or it will curdle.

Apple Sauce

450 g apples, 1 tablespoon sugar, 2 teaspoons butter

Peel, core and cut up the apples. Place in a stewing pan or saucepan with 2 tablespoons water. Simmer gently until they turn into a soft pulp, stirring to prevent burning. Stir in the sugar until it dissolves. Rub the pulp through a sieve, return to the pan and stir in the butter.

Béchamel Sauce

70 g butter, 2 tablespoons plain flour, 600 ml chicken or veal stock in which a few mushrooms have been simmering

Melt the butter in a saucepan and stir in the flour until smooth. Cook the mixture for 2 minutes, stirring constantly, without browning. Gradually add the strained stock and bring the mixture to a simmer before adding more. Continue adding stock, stirring constantly, then cook the sauce over low heat for 8–10 minutes. Season with salt and pepper, to taste. Strain the sauce through a fine sieve, reheat, and serve.

Bread Sauce 1

300 ml milk, 1 tablespoon finely chopped onion, 1 blade mace,
60 g (³/4 cup) fresh white breadcrumbs, 1 teaspoon butter

Put the milk in a saucepan with the onion and mace. Bring to the boil, then strain the liquid into a clean pan and add the breadcrumbs and butter. Season with salt and pepper and cook for a few minutes. This bread sauce is excellent served with roast chicken.

Bread Sauce 2

225 g (2³/4 cups) fresh breadcrumbs, 600 ml milk, 1 sliced onion, 6 peppercorns,
1¹/2 tablespoons butter or 2 tablespoons cream, cayenne pepper

Put the breadcrumbs in a saucepan and cover with the milk, onion, peppercorns and a pinch of salt and leave for 20 minutes. Bring to the boil. Lift out the onion and peppercorns; add the butter and cayenne pepper. Serve immediately.

Brown Sauce

1¹/2 tablespoons butter, 3 tablespoons flour, 250 ml (1 cup) stock

Melt the butter in frying pan, then add the flour and cook without stirring until mixture is browned (the darker the better), but do not burn. Add salt and pepper, then remove from the heat and slowly add 250 ml (1 cup) water and the stock, stirring to prevent lumps forming. Cook until thickened, stirring constantly; serve hot.

Variations There are many variations to this brown sauce:
- MUSHROOM SAUCE: add ¹/2 cup tinned mushrooms to the brown sauce.
- OLIVE SAUCE: finely chop 6 stuffed olives and simmer in the brown sauce.
- RED CURRANT SAUCE: add 80 g (¹/4 cup) red currant jelly and 2 teaspoons lemon juice.
- SAUCE PIQUANT: add 1 tablespoon vinegar, 1 tablespoon finely chopped capers, 1 finely chopped green capsicum and 1 tablespoon chopped onion.

Brown Vegetable Sauce

½ small carrot, ½ onion, small handful parsley, 1½ tablespoons butter,
1 teaspoon flour, 300 ml stock, cayenne pepper, juice of 1 lemon

Finely chop the carrot, onion and parsley. Heat the butter in a saucepan and add the carrot, onion and parsley. Cook until brown, then add the flour, and fry for a few seconds, before adding the stock. Season with the salt, pepper and cayenne pepper and simmer for about 30 minutes. You can either strain the sauce or serve with the vegetables. Add the lemon juice and stir through just before serving.

Caper Sauce

300 ml Béchamel Sauce (see recipe, page 105), 2½ tablespoons rinsed capers,
1 tablespoon vinegar

Make the béchamel sauce in the usual way, then add the capers and bring to the boil. Add the vinegar and stir through before serving.

Chasseur Sauce

250 ml (1 cup) Brown Sauce (see recipe, opposite),
1 tablespoon finely chopped ham, 2 tablespoons sherry

Make the brown sauce in the usual way. Strain, pour the sauce back into a clean pan and add the ham and sherry, stirring to combine. Serve the very hot with cutlets.

Celery Sauce

celery stalks, 55 g butter, 2 tablespoons plain flour, 600 ml milk,
2 teaspoons cream, 2 egg yolks, ground nutmeg

Peel the celery stalks to remove any stringy bits and cut into small dice. Place in a bowl of cold water and soak for about 20 minutes. Pour off the water, cover with boiling water and set aside until tender; strain. Melt the butter in a small saucepan and add the flour. Gradually stir in the milk and cream, and cook until very hot. Add the cooked celery. Beat the egg yolks with a little salt, pepper and nutmeg in a bowl, then add a little of the hot sauce, stirring well. Pour this mixture into the sauce in the pan, stirring constantly. Cook for a few minutes without boiling, then serve.

Cheese Sauce

250 ml (1 cup) White Sauce (see recipe, page 118), 40 g (1/3 cup) grated cheese

Make the white sauce in the usual way and add the grated cheese. Stir thoroughly until the cheese is melted and the sauce is smooth, then serve immediately.

Cold Cucumber Sauce

*1 short cucumber, 80 ml (1/3 cup) Béchamel Sauce (see recipe, page 105),
80 ml (1/3 cup) cream, 150 ml mayonnaise, cayenne pepper,
a few drops of green food colouring*

Peel the cucumber and cut into thick slices. Put in a saucepan and bring to the boil in lightly salted water; cook until tender. Drain the cucumber and rub through a fine sieve. Return the cucumber pulp to a clean saucepan with the Béchamel Sauce, stirring well. Bring to the boil and, if too thick, add a little milk to thin it. Remove from the heat and allow to cool. Whip the cream and add to the mayonnaise. Stir through the cooled sauce and add the seasonings, to taste, then the green food colouring. This cold cucumber sauce is delicious served with asparagus.

Damson Sauce

450 g damsons (plums), sugar, 125 ml (1/2 cup) port wine, 1 teaspoon butter

Pick and wash the damsons. Place in a saucepan with 250 ml (1 cup) water and bring to the boil. Reduce the heat and cook until soft. Rub the fruit through a sieve after removing the stone, and add sugar to taste. Reheat, then add the port and butter, stirring through just before serving. Serve hot or cold.

Drawn Butter Sauce

1½ tablespoon butter, 2 tablespoons plain flour, 250 ml (1 cup) hot water

Melt the butter in a saucepan and add flour, mixing until well blended. Season with salt and pepper. Remove from the heat and slowly add the boiling water, stirring constantly to keep smooth. Cook until the sauce has thickened, stirring constantly, to prevent any lumps forming. Serve immediately.

Variations There are many variations to this drawn butter sauce:
- ANCHOVY SAUCE: add ½ teaspoon anchovy paste to the drawn butter sauce and blend well.
- CAPER SAUCE: add 50 g (¼ cup) rinsed and drained capers to the sauce and heat for a few minutes before serving.
- EGG SAUCE: cut a cold hard-boiled egg lengthways and add to the drawn butter sauce. Stir in carefully so that the egg will not break up.
- PARSLEY SAUCE: add some finely chopped parsley to the drawn butter sauce and stir well to combine.
- VELOUTÉ SAUCE: replace the boiling water in the drawn butter sauce recipe with stock and prepare as usual.

Espagnole Sauce

1 onion, ½ carrot, 55 g butter, whole peppercorns, 2 tablespoons plain flour, 600 ml water or beef stock, 1 tomato, 125 ml (½ cup) sherry

Finely chop the onion and carrot. Melt the butter in a saucepan, and when hot, add the onion, carrot and a few peppercorns. Fry until light brown, stir in the flour and a few herbs. Add the water or stock and stir until boiling. Slice the tomato and add to the pan with the sherry. Season with salt and cook gently for 30 minutes. Strain through a fine sieve and use immediately.

French Plum Sauce

2 large ripe tomatoes, 4 plums, sugar, 2 teaspoons powdered gelatine,
1 tablespoon claret, red food colouring, 2 teaspoons vinegar,
1 teaspoon finely grated onion

Before you start, measure the weight of the tomatoes and plums — this will give you the amount of sugar required. Rub the tomatoes and plums together through a sieve to remove the skins and extract the pulp. Place the fruit pulp in a large pan and add the sugar. Dissolve the powdered gelatine in a small bowl with the claret and a few drops of red food colouring. Stir into the fruit pulp and add the vinegar, salt, pepper and onion. Serve with entrées.

Genoese Sauce

300 ml Brown Sauce (see recipe, page 106), 1 chopped French shallot,
2 teaspoons mushroom catsup, a pinch of sugar, 250 ml (1 cup) claret,
1 teaspoon chopped parsley, 2 tablespoons butter

Put the Brown Sauce into a saucepan with the French shallot, the mushroom catsup, sugar and a little pepper. Add the claret and boil together for 10 minutes, then strain. Add the parsley and whisk in the butter. Serve warm.

Gherkin Sauce

1 large gherkin, 2 tablespoons butter,
1 tablespoon plain flour, 1 tablespoon vinegar

Finely chop the gherkin. Melt the butter in a saucepan, add the flour, mix well, then add 185 ml (^{3}/4 cup) water and stir the mixture until it boils. Add the gherkin, 1 teaspoon salt, ^{1}/2 teaspoon pepper and vinegar. Reduce the heat and simmer for 10 minutes. Serve with fish.

Hollandaise Sauce 1

1½ tablespoons butter, 1½ tablespoons plain flour, 4 egg yolks,
2 teaspoons lemon juice, cayenne pepper

Melt the butter in a saucepan and add the flour; fry gently without browning for a few minutes. Slowly add 300 ml water and stir until the mixture boils. Continue boiling for 5 minutes, then remove from the heat and stir in the egg yolks one by one, until smooth. Add the lemon juice and season with salt and cayenne pepper, to taste.

Hollandaise Sauce 2

250 ml (1 cup) White Sauce (see recipe, page 118), 2 egg yolks,
1 tablespoon lemon juice, cayenne pepper

Prepare the White Sauce as usual. Beat the egg yolks and stir into the sauce over low heat, until combined and smooth. Add the lemon juice and a little cayenne pepper, to serve.

Horseradish Sauce

Horseradish, 1 teaspoon plain flour, cayenne pepper,
150 ml cream, 1 teaspoon vinegar

Grate a stick of horseradish very finely, or use prepared horseradish, and mix it in a bowl with the flour, a little salt and cayenne pepper. Add the cream and slowly drizzle in the vinegar, stirring all the time, until smooth and combined.

Indian Sauce/Curry Sauce

1 small onion, 1 tablespoon butter, 1 tablespoon plain flour,
1 tablespoon curry powder, 300 ml stock, 1 chopped tomato,
a dash of lemon juice, 6 sultanas, ½ teaspoon grated coconut

Finely chop the onion. Melt the butter in a saucepan and add the onion, frying for a few minutes. Add the flour and curry powder, stirring well. Add the stock, tomato, lemon juice, sultanas and coconut. Season with salt and pepper and simmer for 30 minutes, then strain and use.

Mint Jelly

1 cup mint leaves, 250 ml (1 cup) boiling water, 1 tablespoon powdered gelatine,
250 ml (1 cup) vinegar, 110 g (½ cup) sugar, 1 teaspoon lemon juice

Remove the stalks from the mint, wash and dry the leaves, and finely chop. Soak the gelatine in vinegar. Dissolve the sugar and ½ teaspoon salt in the boiling water. Add the vinegar and gelatine to the water and stir until thoroughly dissolved. Add the mint and strained lemon juice. Stir occasionally as the mixture cools and thickens, to prevent the mint sinking, and pour into a wet mould. Turn the set jelly from the mould, and cut into cubes or fancy shapes with a wet knife. Serve in place of mint sauce with cold lamb roast, or use as a base for jellying cold cooked lamb with green peas. If green jelly is preferred, add a few drops green food colouring before pouring the jelly into the wet mould. See also Mint Chutney on page 196.

Mint Sauce 1

55 g butter, 3 tablespoons sugar, 2 tablespoons mustard powder,
250 ml (1 cup) vinegar, 2 eggs, pan juices from meat

Melt the butter in a saucepan and add the sugar, mustard and vinegar. Beat the eggs and add to the pan. Add enough of the pan juices in which beef has been cooked to make a sauce the consistency of warm honey. This makes quite a lot. Serve with hot corned beef, and use any leftover sauce as a salad dressing for cold beef.

Mint Sauce 2

1 tablespoon finely chopped mint leaves, 1 tablespoon sugar,
1 tablespoon boiling water, 4 tablespoons vinegar

Put the mint in a bowl and add the sugar. Pour the boiling water into the bowl and allow to stand until cold. Stir in the vinegar. Serve with roast lamb.

Variation Another way to make mint sauce is to sprinkle a good pinch of salt into a mortar and pestle with some mint leaves, and grind to a paste. Add to every tablespoon of water, one of white vinegar and a tablespoon of caster sugar. (Allow for 1 tablespoon water for 1 tablespoon mint.)

Mint Sauce Jelly

10 mint sprigs, 1 tablespoon powdered gelatine, 250 ml (1 cup) vinegar,
250 ml (1 cup) boiling water

Remove the stalks from the mint, wash and dry the leaves, and finely chop. Soak the gelatine in the vinegar, stirring to dissolve the gelatine. Add 1 teaspoon salt and the boiling water and stir in the mint. Stand in a shallow mould and set.

Mushroom Sauce

Brown Sauce (see recipe, page 106), 24 small finely sliced mushrooms

Make the brown sauce in the usual way and add the washed mushrooms to the pan. Simmer for 20 minutes. Leave the mushrooms whole, or chop finely. Serve very hot.

Orange Mint Sauce for Lamb

1/4 cup finely chopped mint leaves, 60 ml (1/4 cup) orange juice,
1 tablespoon caster sugar

Put the mint in a bowl and add the orange juice and sugar, stirring well. Allow to stand in a warm place for 30 minutes, then serve.

Orange Sauce

3 tablespoons butter, 4 tablespoons plain flour, 170 ml (2/3 cup) orange juice,
finely grated zest of 1/2 orange, 1 tablespoon sherry

Melt the butter in a saucepan and stir in the flour to make a smooth paste. Gradually add 330 ml (1 1/3 cups) water, stirring until smooth. Season with salt and pepper, to taste. Just before serving, add the orange juice, orange zest and 1 tablespoon sherry. Serve with roast duck.

Oyster Sauce

12 oysters, 300 ml chicken or fish stock, 1 tablespoon plain flour,
2 tablespoons cream, 55 g butter, lemon juice

Wash the oysters. Put them in hot stock for a few minutes until just cooked through, strain this liquid and add to any of the reserved juices from the oysters; bring to the boil. Stir in the combined flour and cream, until nicely thickened. Add the butter and a little pepper, then put the oysters into the sauce, and stir in a few drops of lemon juice. Let the sauce stand in the saucepan for 5 minutes, before using.

Plum Sauce

4.5 kg plums, 1.2 litres vinegar, 900 g (4 cups) sugar, 2 tablespoons ground cloves,
2 teaspoons cayenne pepper, 150 g (1 heaped cup) salt, 6 garlic cloves or
2 large onions, 2 tablespoons allspice, 2 tablespoons peppercorns,
2 teaspoons ground ginger

Put all of the ingredients together in a large saucepan and bring to the boil. Reduce the heat and simmer for 4 hours, or until thickened. Strain through a colander, and if not using immediately, pour into sterilised jars and seal securely when cool.

Prawn Sauce

6–8 cooked prawns, 1 large anchovy,
2 finely chopped French shallots, 2 teaspoons capers,
1 finely chopped garlic clove, 2 tablespoons lemon juice,
150 ml stock, 1 blade mace, 50 g butter, plain flour, 150 ml thick cream

Take the shells off the prawns and put them into a saucepan. Add the anchovy to the pan with the French shallots, capers, garlic and 1½ tablespoons of the lemon juice, and heat for 6 minutes. Pour in the stock and add a shake of pepper and the mace. Simmer slowly for 15 minutes. Roll the butter in the flour and add to the pan, simmering for 10 minutes, or until the sauce has thickened. Strain the sauce, add the remaining lemon juice and stir in the cream.

If a sauce has been kept, say, for a day,
it should be well beaten and made smooth
again before reheating.

Raisin Sauce for Ham

125 g (1 cup) seedless raisins, 110 g (½ cup) sugar,
2 tablespoons lemon juice, 125 ml (½ cup) orange juice

Simmer the raisins in a saucepan with 250 ml (1 cup) water until soft. Add the sugar and boil gently for 15 minutes. Add the lemon and orange juices and stir in, then serve.

Sauce Nouvelle

600 ml cream, 3 egg yolks, 1 tablespoon butter,
1 tablespoon white vinegar

Whip 300 ml of the cream and set aside. Put the egg yolks in a saucepan with the butter and a pinch each of salt and pepper. Add the unwhipped cream and cook slowly, without boiling, whisking continuously. Remove from the heat and allow to cool. Add the whipped cream and vinegar just before serving. Serve with cold asparagus.

Sherry Sauce

1½ tablespoons butter, 1 tablespoon plain flour,
1 tablespoon finely chopped onion, 2 teaspoons finely chopped French shallots,
4 finely chopped anchovies, cayenne pepper, 1 tablespoon vinegar,
125 ml (½ cup) sherry, Parisisan essence

Melt the butter in a saucepan and add the flour, stirring to a smooth paste. Add the onion, French shallot, anchovy and a pinch of cayenne pepper. Add 300 ml water and bring to the boil. Reduce the heat and simmer until the onion is tender. Add the vinegar, sherry and Parisian essence. Serve with steamed chicken.

Tomato Sauce 1

2–3 tomatoes, 1 teaspoon finely chopped onion, thyme or mint leaves,
1½ tablespoons butter, 2 tablespoons plain flour

Finely chop the tomatoes and place in a saucepan with the onion and 125 ml (½ cup) water. Add the thyme or mint and season with salt and pepper. Cook until tender, and put through a sieve. Melt the butter in a separate saucepan and stir in the flour to make a smooth paste. Add the butter mixture to the tomatoes and stir well. Bring to the boil, remove from the heat and serve.

Tomato Sauce 2

4.5 kg tomatoes, 500 ml (2 cups) vinegar, 900 g (4 cups) sugar, 1 tablespoon
cloves, ½ teaspoon cayenne pepper, 4 large apples, 2 large onions,
3 finely chopped garlic cloves

Put all ingredients into a preserving pan and cook over medium heat until reduced and thickened. Season to taste. Pour into sterilised jars and seal securely when cool.

Tomato Sauce 3

7.2 kg tomatoes, 900 g (4 cups) brown sugar, 900 g pumpkin, 2 large onions,
1 tablespoon mixed spice, 1 tablespoon white pepper, 1 teaspoon cayenne pepper,
1.2 litres vinegar, 6 garlic cloves

Put all of the ingredients together in a large stockpot with 200 g (1½ cups) salt and let stand all night (12 hours). The next day, put the saucepan over high heat and bring to the boil. Reduce the heat and simmer for about 3 hours, or until well cooked. Strain and boil for a further 30 minutes. Pour into sterilised jars and seal securely when cool.

Tomato Sauce 4

18 kg tomatoes, 2.7 kg apples, 6 garlic cloves, 2.7 kg (12 cups) sugar,
1 tablespoon white pepper, 2 tablespoons cloves,
2 tablespoons mixed spice, 2 tablespoons peppercorns,
2 tablespoons ground ginger, 1.5 litres vinegar, cayenne pepper

Roughly chop the tomatoes and peel and core the apples. Put the tomatoes, apples, garlic, sugar, white pepper, cloves, mixed spice, peppercorns and ginger in a large stockpot with 225 g (1³/4 cups) salt and boil together until the tomatoes and apples are pulpy. Strain through a colander, return to the warm pot and add the vinegar and cayenne pepper, to taste. Boil for 4 hours (to test the sauce, put a little on a saucer — if there is no liquid on top when the sauce has cooled then it is ready for bottling). Pour into sterilised jars and seal securely when cool.

When making white sauce and milk is scarce, save the water the potatoes have been boiled in and add some butter in half quantity milk and proceed as usual.

White Sauce

1¹/2 tablespoons butter, 2 tablespoons flour, 250 ml (1 cup) milk

Melt butter in a saucepan, then add the flour, mixing well to form a smooth paste. Season with ¹/2 teaspoon each of salt and pepper, then remove from the heat and slowly add the milk, stirring constantly to keep the mixture very smooth. Return to the heat and continue stirring until the sauce thickens.

Variation To make a white vegetable sauce, use 125 ml (¹/2 cup) milk and 125 ml (¹/2 cup) vegetable stock in place of the milk, and finish the sauce as for white sauce. Vegetables may be added to vegetable sauce.

Butters

Anchovy Butter

If using salted anchovies, soak them in a bowl of milk for 3 hours. Bone 3 anchovies, if necessary, and add them to a bowl with 3 hard-boiled egg yolks. Mix in 3 tablespoons softened butter, a little lemon juice and onion juice, and season with paprika. Mix well and rub through a sieve. This mixture will keep for some weeks in a sterilised airtight jar.

Green Butter

Finely chop 1 handful chervil, 1 handful tarragon and 1 handful parsley and place in a saucepan. Add 75 g (1/3 cup) green pitted olives with add just enough water to cover; blanch. Drain well and pound in a mortar using a pestle. Finely chop 2 French shallots. Heat 1 teaspoon butter in a saucepan and cook the French shallots until golden. Remove from the heat and cool. Stir into the herbs. Work in the remaining softened butter and rub through a sieve. Season with salt and pepper. The butter is now ready to use.

Granadilla Butter

Cut 3 small granadillas (purple passionfruit) in half, scoop out the seeds and pulp and place in a bowl. Cover with 220 g (1 cup) sugar, stir, and allow to stand for 30 minutes, then strain well, reserving the juice. Beat 2 eggs, then add 1 tablespoon butter and the granadilla juice. Pour into a double boiler, or into a jug standing in boiling water, and cook for 15 minutes, or until the mixture begins to thicken. Pour into sterilised jars and seal securely when cool. This butter will keep for months.

Montpellier Butter

Soften 115 g butter a little, before mixing in a bowl with 2 teaspoons finely chopped parsley, 1 teaspoon finely chopped capers, 1 chopped gherkin and a little cayenne pepper. Add 1 teaspoon olive oil, 1 teaspoon lemon juice and some finely chopped French shallots. Season with salt and pepper, to taste.

Variation To make ravigot butter, prepare it in the same way as for Montpellier butter, but leave out the gherkins, capers and oil.

Sweet Sauces

Brandy Sauce

1 tablespoon cornflour, 2 tablespoons sugar, 80 ml (¹/₃ cup) brandy

Stir the cornflour into 300 ml water. Place in a saucepan with the sugar and bring to the boil. Boil for 5 minutes, stirring all the time. Add the brandy, then remove from the heat and use immediately.

Butterscotch Fudge Sauce

230 g (1 cup) brown sugar, 1 tablespoon butter, 2 tablespoons milk,
1 teaspoon vanilla essence

Put the sugar, butter and milk in a saucepan and bring to the boil. Boil for 6 minutes, then add the vanilla essence and stand in warm water to keep hot until ready for use.

Butterscotch Sauce 1

230 g (1 cup) brown sugar, 175 g (¹/₂ cup) honey,
2 teaspoons cornflour, 1 tablespoon butter

Put the sugar, honey and a pinch of salt in a saucepan and add 250 ml (1 cup) water. Bring to the boil and boil for 5 minutes. Mix the cornflour with a little water to form a paste and stir into the sugar syrup. Reduce the heat and simmer for about 5 minutes, or until the mixture thickens. Stir in the butter. Serve with boiled, steamed or baked puddings.

Butterscotch Sauce 2

230 g (1 cup) brown sugar, 350 g (1 cup) honey,
125 ml (½ cup) cream or unsweetened condensed or evaporated milk

Put the sugar and honey in a saucepan and add 250 ml (1 cup) water. Heat the liquid until it reaches 110°C on a sugar thermometer. Cool slightly, stir in the cream and serve with ice cream.

Chocolate Fudge Sauce

125 g (1 cup) grated chocolate, 2 tablespoons icing sugar, 300 ml cream

Put the grated chocolate and sugar in a saucepan over low heat. Add 1 tablespoon water and stir until the chocolate has melted. Add the cream and stir until hot enough to serve.

Chocolate Sauce

1 teaspoon cornflour, 1 teaspoon cocoa powder,
300 ml milk, 2 tablespoons sugar, ½ teaspoon vanilla essence

Mix the cornflour and cocoa together and a little of the cold milk, stirring to combine. Put the remaining milk in a saucepan and bring to the boil. Add the cocoa mixture and boil for 10 minutes. Stir in the sugar and vanilla essence before serving.

Foamy Sauce

1 tablespoon butter, 2 tablespoons sugar, 2 egg whites,
125 ml (¹/₂ cup) boiling water, 2 tablespoons brandy or sherry

Beat the butter and sugar together until light, then add the well-beaten egg whites. Stir in the water and sherry, mixing until smooth. Pour this mixture into a heatproof bowl, sit over a saucepan of boiling water and whisk contents over mild heat, until foamy and light. Serve with steamed puddings.

Hard Sauce

125 g butter, 450 g (3²/₃ cups) icing sugar, 1 egg white,
pink food colouring, green food colouring

Cream the butter and add gradually beat in the icing sugar. When light and fluffy and almost white, work in the stiffly beaten egg white and flavour as desired. Sauce may be divided into three portions, leaving one white, colouring another with pink food colouring and another with green food colouring.

Jam Sauce

160 g (¹/₂ cup) jam, 1 teaspoon freshly squeezed lemon juice

Put the jam and 250 ml (1 cup) water in a saucepan and bring to the boil. Reduce the heat and simmer until a heavy fruit syrup forms. Add the lemon juice and serve with steamed or baked puddings.

Sherry Sauce

2 egg yolks, 2 tablespoons caster sugar, 150 ml sherry

Lightly beat the egg yolks in a bowl and stir in the sugar. Add the sherry, and pour all into a heatproof bowl. Stand in a saucepan of boiling water and whisk until thick and creamy, being careful not to let it get too hot or it will curdle. Serve immediately.

Velvet Sauce

125 g butter, 110 g (1/2 cup) sugar, 2 eggs, 125 ml (1/2 cup) cream, brandy or sherry

Beat together the butter and sugar. Separate the eggs and add the beaten yolks. Beat the egg whites separately until stiff peaks form, then add to the butter mixture. Stir in the cream, and add enough brandy or sherry to flavour to your liking.

Whipped Butter Sauce

40 g butter, 125 g (1 cup) icing sugar, 125 g (1/2 cup) whipped cream, vanilla essence

Cream the butter and icing sugar and stir in the whipped cream. Add vanilla essence to taste and refrigerate before serving.

CWA of New South Wales Royal Agricultural Society Kiosk, circa 1950s.

MAINS

Fish and Seafood

Selecting and Preparing Fish and Seafood

Always select firm fish with red gills, bulging bright eyes and very little odour. Wash well in salted water, but do not leave in the water. Remove the fins and tails with scissors and scale the fish by drawing the back of a knife over the fish, starting at the tail end.

To bone and fillet fish insert a sharp knife close to the backbone at the tail end, and cut the flesh from the bone, working toward the head and keeping the knife as close as possible to the bone. Small bones may be removed with the fingers. To skin fish, slit the skin along the fins and draw gently away from the flesh, starting at the tail, with fingers dipped in salt.

CRUMBING FISH: Dust fish fillets lightly in flour, brush with egg wash and roll in dry breadcrumbs. Heat vegetable oil in a deep frying pan and when a blue haze appears, lower the fish into the pan and cook until golden.

BATTERING FISH: Gradually add 125 ml (½ cup) water to 120 g (¾ cup) flour and a pinch of salt, beating until quite smooth. Add 1½ tablespoons melted butter and allow to stand. When ready to use, beat 1 egg white until stiff peaks form, then fold into the batter. Dip the fish fillets in the batter, draining off any excess. Heat vegetable oil in a deep frying pan and when a blue haze appears, lower the fish into the pan and cook until golden.

POACHING OR STEAMING FISH: Fish that are thick in the shoulder, such as bream, are best for poaching. Cook in sea water or water as salty as the sea. Add a little parsley and freshly squeezed lemon juice to the water. Sprinkle with salt, place a bed of parsley in a steamer and lay the fish over the top before steaming.

To prepare a fish for poaching, trim the fins and leave the eyes in. Rub all over the fish with lemon juice. A medium-sized fish requires about 20 minutes. To test if the fish is cooked, insert a skewer into the thickest part of the fish (just behind the head) — the flesh should come away from the bone.

GRILLING FISH: Do not skin fish when grilling, as this allows all moisture to escape. Trim the fish, split open and sprinkle with lemon juice, salt and pepper. Melt about 1½ tablespoons butter or use olive oil to baste the fish while grilling slowly. Serve with rounds of lemon.

COOKING LOBSTERS: To cook lobsters, experts recommend plunging the lobsters alive into boiling water. Some people, however, prefer to place the live lobster in the freezer for 20–30 minutes before cooking. This puts the lobster to 'sleep'. The lobsters are cooked for about 30 minutes, depending on size — an easy way to check is when the tails curl and are firm when you pull on them. If overdone, the flesh becomes stringy. When cold, cut the lobsters in halves from head to tail and remove the flesh.

COOKING CRABS: Crabs, too, are usually bought in the shops, already cooked, but if obtained fresh the same method of cooking applies as for lobsters, except that crabs require only 15–20 minutes cooking. When cooked, remove the crabs from the water and drain. To remove the flesh, place the crab with the hard shell facing down. Bend back the underside; a soft, spongy substance will be exposed. Remove and discard this, then wash and dry the crab. Break the body in half and pick out the meat.

COOKING PRAWNS: Add the prawns to a saucepan of boiling sea water or salted water (if the latter, use 105 g (⅓ cup) salt to 1.5 litres water), and cook for 6–8 minutes. Wash well and drain. Remove the shell carefully, also the vein that runs the length of the body.

Baked Fish with Stuffing

Select fish of medium size; wash, wipe dry and salt. Mix together 80 g (1 cup) stale day-old breadcrumbs and 1 tablespoon melted butter. Season with ½ teaspoon salt and ¼ teaspoon pepper. Stuff the fish with this mixture (a little very finely powdered sage and a couple of eggs could be added if liked). Wrap the fish with fine string to keep the seasoning in the fish. Place in a well-buttered baking tray with baking paper under it, dredge in seasoned flour and add 250 ml (1 cup) boiling water to the pan. Bake in 220°C oven — you will need to cook for 15 minutes for each 450 g fish. Baste with the gravy that forms in the pan. When cooked, carefully slide the fish onto a serving dish and garnish with lemon and parsley. Some people add tomato sauce to the dressing, others like fish covered with layers of tomatoes.

Creamed Fish

Steam 450 g fish fillets. Melt 2 tablespoons butter in a saucepan and stir in 1 heaped tablespoon flour. Cook for 3 minutes, then gradually add 600 ml milk, stirring continuously. Stir until the sauce thickens and boils, then remove from the heat. Stir in 2 tablespoons cream and season to taste. Use a fork to coarsely break up the fish and add to the pan, stirring through. Spoon the mixture into ramekins until three-quarters full and sprinkle stale, day-old breadcrumbs on top. Dot with small pieces of butter and bake in a 220°C oven for 10 minutes. If more convenient, the dish may be browned under the grill. Garnish with slices of lemon, to serve.

Curried Prawns

Melt 55 g butter in a frying pan and cook 1 finely chopped onion for 15 minutes over very low heat without colouring it. Add 2 teaspoons curry powder and fry for a few minutes, then add ½ teaspoon curry paste and cook for a further 3–4 minutes. Add ½ finely chopped apple, 1½ tablespoons rice flour, ½ teaspoon sugar and a pinch of salt. Add 450 ml stock, 2 teaspoons chutney and 1 tablespoon desiccated coconut, stirring well. Cook for about 30 minutes, then add 450 g peeled, cleaned prawns. Cook for 6–10 minutes. Before serving, add 2 tablespoons cream and a squeeze of lemon juice and bring mixture just back to the boil. Serve in a border of boiled rice and decorate with a few whole prawns.

Fish Fillets Bonne Femme

Put 450 g fish fillets in a saucepan with 185 ml (¾ cup) fish stock and poach in a 180°C oven for 15 minutes. Melt 2 tablespoons butter in a frying pan and cook 45 g (½ cup) sliced mushrooms for 5 minutes. Remove the mushrooms from the pan and keep warm. Add 1½ tablespoons flour to the pan and stir until smooth, then add 185 ml (¾ cup) liquid from the fish. Add 60 ml (¼ cup) milk, 125 ml (½ cup) white wine and 1 tablespoon cream. Arrange the poached fish fillets on a serving dish and pour over the sauce. Scatter the mushrooms on top.

Fish Mornay

Place 450 g fish fillets in a baking dish which has been greased with butter. Sprinkle a little chopped onion over the fish and enough freshly squeezed lemon juice to cover. Season with salt and pepper. Pour over 600 ml White Sauce (see recipe, page 118) and finish with a layer of grated cheese. Cook in a 180°C oven for 30 minutes. Serve immediately.

Fish Soufflé

Put 450 g (about 1 cup) cooked cold fish fillets in a bowl with 230 g (1 cup) mashed potato and 125 ml (½ cup) milk; stir well. Add 1 well-beaten egg and mix well. Place in a greased baking dish and cook in a 180°C oven until hot. Separate an egg. Beat the egg white until stiff, then stir into the beaten yolk, and season with salt and pepper. Pour over the fish, return to the oven and cook until brown. Serve immediately.

Fricasseed Fish

Fillet a fish, such as whiting or bream. Put the fish bones in a saucepan with 300 ml water. Simmer for about 5 minutes, then strain. Make a Drawn Butter Sauce (see recipe, page 109), using the fish stock and 300 ml milk instead of water. Add a little finely chopped parsley and stir through. Chop the fish into small pieces and add to the sauce. Cook gently without stirring for about 10 minutes.

Lobster Newburg

Sauté 3 cups chopped lobster meat in butter for about 2 minutes. Season, to taste. Moisten with 100 ml sherry. Stir in 250 ml (1 cup) cream and bring to boil. Thicken with 3 beaten egg yolks and 1 tablespoon brandy. Stir well until the mixture thickens, but do not boil. Add another 100 ml sherry and stir through before serving.

Poached Fish Fillets with Seafood Sauce

Chop the meat from 1 lobster into small pieces and add 450 g peeled, cleaned prawns. Stir through 1 teaspoon paprika and 1.2 litres White Sauce (see recipe, page 118); keep warm in the top of a double boiler. Meanwhile, roll up 8 long, thin fish fillets and fasten with a toothpick. Place in a frying pan with 375 ml (1½ cups) milk and 375 ml (1½ cups) water. Season with salt and pepper and simmer gently for about 10 minutes, or until the fish is white and cooked through. Take the rolls out and arrange on a serving dish. Pour the hot sauce over, to serve.

Prawn Jelly

Take some prawns, remove the shells, heads and tails. Place the prawns in a saucepan with a little water and salt and cook until the prawns turn pink and start to curl. Transfer the prawns to the base of a jelly mould. Stir 2 teaspoons gelatine through 300 ml stock until completely dissolved. Allow to cool, then pour over the prawns. Refrigerate until set. Turn the prawn jelly out and serve on a bed of shredded lettuce.

Salmon Balls

Boil and mash 4 potatoes. Strain the liquid from 450 g tinned salmon (reserving the liquid) and break into small pieces with a fork. Mix the salmon through the potatoes and add 2 teaspoons finely chopped parsley, salt, cayenne pepper and a squeeze of lemon juice; moisten with the salmon liquid if necessary. Roll the mixture into balls, using a little flour for shaping. Dip into egg wash, then toss in dry breadcrumbs. Deep-fry until golden brown. Drain on paper towels and serve hot.

Salmon Jelly

Take 450 g tinned of salmon and break into small pieces with a fork. Dissolve 1½ tablespoons powdered gelatine in 60 ml (¼ cup) hot water, then add 185 ml (¾ cup) vinegar or freshly squeezed lemon juice, salt, pepper and 250 ml (1 cup) water. Pour a little of this mixture into a round mould. When firm, arrange slices of hard-boiled egg in the base, then pour over a little liquid. When the jelly liquid is thickening, stir the salmon into the remaining gelatine mixture and pour into the mould. When set, garnish with shredded lettuce and slices of lemon. Vinegar or lemon may be omitted from ingredients and 250 ml (1 cup) water used instead.

Salmon Loaf

Take 450 g tinned salmon and break into small pieces with a fork. Add 4 tablespoons melted butter, 80 g (1 cup) breadcrumbs, 2 tablespoons self-raising flour, ½ teaspoon salt and 4 well-beaten eggs. Put into a well-greased pudding basin (mould), cover with a tight-fitting lid and steam in a saucepan of boiling water for 1 hour. Serve hot with diced potatoes and a cream gravy, or serve cold, cut into slices, with lettuce, parsley and lemon to garnish.

Salmon Mould

Soften 1 tablespoon powdered gelatine in 60 ml (¼ cup) water. In the top of a double boiler, combine 1 tablespoon salt, 1 teaspoon mustard powder, a pinch of cayenne pepper, 2 lightly beaten egg yolks and 185 ml (¾ cup) milk, and cook over boiling water until thickened, stirring constantly. Add 4 tablespoons freshly squeezed lemon juice, 1½ tablespoons melted butter and the gelatine water, stirring until the gelatine dissolves. Remove from the heat and add 175 g (1 cup) tinned salmon, stirring well. Turn into a decorative fish mould and refrigerate until firm.

Smoked Fish

Use a whole smoked fish or fish fillets. If the fish is very salty, soak for a while before cooking. Put the fish into a saucepan of warm water or milk, bring to the boil over medium heat. Reduce the heat and simmer gently 20–30 minutes, according to the thickness of the fish. Serve with 300 ml Drawn Butter Sauce (see recipe, page 109) that has been flavoured with lemon, salt and pepper. A little Anchovy Sauce (see recipe, page 109) can be added, if desired. Garnish with chopped parsley.

Soused Fish

Scale 900 g whole fish. Slice a little more than halfway through, to butterfly, so that you can place it flat on a baking dish. Place 1 sliced onion on top and sprinkle with some peppercorns, cloves, 1 chopped chilli, ½ teaspoon allspice, ½ teaspoon salt and a bunch of herbs, such as parsely, tarragon, bay leaf and thyme. Pour over 450 ml vinegar and cover with baking paper. Bake in a 180°C oven for about 20 minutes, or until soft and cooked through. Carefully transfer the whole fish to a serving dish. Strain the stock over the top and garnish with slices of lemon, cucumber and tomato.

Stuffed Whole Snapper

Scale 1 large whole snapper and remove the bones, leaving the head attached. Flavour 160 g (2 cups) stale day-old breadcrumbs with a little finely chopped onion, parsley and celery, and put the stuffing between the two halves of the fish in a greased ovenproof dish. Scatter dry breadcrumbs over the fish with a few knobs of butter. Add 225 g peeled, cleaned prawns and 2 dozen shucked oysters to 600 ml White Sauce (see recipe, page 118). Pour the sauce and seafood around the fish in the dish. Cook in a 180°C oven until the fish is cooked through.

Tuna Shortcake

Sift together 300 g (2 cups) plain flour, 3 teaspoons baking powder and ½ teaspoon salt. Cut in 250 g butter using two knives and add 185 ml (¾ cup) milk to make a soft dough. Pat out half of the dough in a greased 20 cm round cake tin; brush with melted butter or margarine. Pat out the remaining dough and place on top. Bake the shortcake in a 220°C oven for 15–20 minutes. Meanwhile, put 400 g (1¼ cups) condensed mushroom soup in a saucepan with 225 g tinned tuna, 80 g (½ cup) peas and 95 g (½ cup) sliced olives, stirring until combined and the mixture is hot. Pile the hot filling between shortcake layers and on top of shortcake.

Whiting Fillets with Cream Sauce

Scale, clean, fillet, wash and dry 3 whole whiting. Melt 1 tablespoon butter in a small saucepan. Add 1 tablespoon flour and stir until smooth. Cook for 1 minute, then add 185 ml (¾ cup) milk or fish stock and stir until the mixture boils and thickens. Slice 300 g peeled, cleaned prawns and add to the sauce with 2 tablespoons cream. Season with salt, cayenne pepper and 1 teaspoon freshly squeezed lemon juice. Put the prepared fish fillets in a greased baking dish, skin side down. Spread half of each fillet with the prawn mixture and fold over. Add 60 ml (¼ cup) boiling water; cover with baking paper and bake slowly in a 170°C oven until tender. Prepare 375 ml (1½ cups) White Sauce (see recipe, page 118) and stir in 250 ml (1 cup) cream, seasoning to taste. Transfer the cooked fish to a hot serving dish. Coat each fillet with sauce, sprinkle with chopped parsley or chopped pistachio nuts. Garnish with slices of lemon.

Garnish for Cold Fish

Decorate whole cooked, cold white fish with cut lemons and parsley, sprinkle it with lobster coral, surround with lettuce leaves and a little mayonnaise. Alternatively, flake cold fish and toss in mayonnaise, place on a dish and surround with potato salad. Slice a hard-boiled egg into rings and arrange the white of the egg over the fish with a star of beetroot on each. Rub the yolk through a sieve and sprinkle over the top.

Poultry and Game

Choosing Poultry

When young the feet will be pliable, the tip of the breast bone soft; they will be plump in appearance and the skin moist and smooth. Poultry is better dry plucked as scalding impairs the flavour.

Trussing a Fowl

Pluck it while warm; if the fowl is allowed to get cold it will have to be scalded before plucking. Singe all the hairs off with a lighted taper or sheet of lighted white paper, scale the legs and chop off the claws or feet. To truss a fowl for roasting, cut neck skin round leaving it 1–2 centimetres long, open neck-skin down the back of the neck and cut the neck off quite close to the body. Remove the crop and tie with a piece of cotton before cutting off. Then put the fingers in and loosen everything inside the fowl, being careful not to break the gall bladder. Make an opening in the apron right under the tail, put the hand in and catch the gizzard firmly and draw everything (entrails) out, press everything back from the opening and tie entrails with a piece of cotton. Save the liver, heart, gizzard; cut everything that looks greenish away from the liver and also the gall bag, open the gizzard without breaking the inside bag. Wash inside of fowl carefully with warm water. The fowl is now ready for stuffing and roasting.

To truss a fowl for boiling, proceed in exactly the same way as for roasting, except cut off the legs at the joints; the skin on the breast and thighs should be loosened so as to push the legs right inside. Boiled fowls are never stuffed. Serve with egg or parsley sauce (see recipe for Drawn Butter Sauce, page 109). When ready to cook, rub the fowl all over with lemon juice, and wrap in buttered baking paper or a white cloth.

Choosing a Turkey

Select a young gobbler, as it has the best flavour. If dry-plucked it will retain its rich flavour. Do not wash it with water if it can be helped, as washing extracts the delicate juices. If the gobbler is not too young, it is better to steam it, or parboil it before roasting.

Turkeys should be bought with white meat and black legs; as they get old their legs become red. Turkey chickens are delicious boiled or steamed and served with celery sauce. Season not too tightly at the breast, rub the bird with butter and sprinkle lightly with flour.

Boning a Turkey

Choose the turkey untrussed, as it will then be firmer and easier to work on. First singe it and pick out the feathers. Remove the legs at the knee joints, at the same time withdrawing the sinews. Cut off the neck close to the body, leaving a flap of skin to turn over as in ordinary trussing, then lay the turkey on a board with the back uppermost and make a cut through the skin right down the middle of the back. With the point of the boning knife work down one side, raising the flesh as cleanly as possible, being careful not to break through the skin. Disjoint both the legs and the wings from the body and continue removing the flesh from the carcase, until the centre of the breastbone is reached. Then proceed with the other side of the bird in the same way and lift the carcase out.

Next bone the legs. Take hold of the first bone where it is disjointed from the body and scrape the flesh off it until the next joint is reached. Crack the joint and remove the first part of the bone. Remove the flesh from the other part of the bone in the same way, turning the leg outside in. Bone the second leg and then remove as much from the wing-bone as possible, cutting off the lower joint entirely.

Now spread out the turkey on the table, remove any pieces of sinew or gristle, trim off any discoloured parts at the neck or tail and the job is done.

Boning a Fowl

To bone a fowl it should be plump and must only be plucked while still warm. Take off the head, open the neck-skin at the back, remove the neck in the usual way, sever the wing joints, work the flesh off the 'merry thought' (wishbone) and take the bone out, remove the 'step-mothers' wing bones, then work the flesh off gradually with a sharp knife or using your fingers, turning the fowl inside out. Tie the entrails before cutting off. Use 625 g minced pork and 625 g minced veal for seasoning. Add salt and pepper, some chopped truffles or mushrooms and the yolk of 4 hard-boiled eggs. Sprinkle the fowl with salt and pepper, fill with the seasoning mixture, making the breast high, sew it up carefully and into good shape, turn the neck skin back, twist the wings over it and cook and serve as for a turkey. Rub the bird with lemon juice, wrap in muslin and steam or boil for about 2 hours, or until tender. Take out of muslin and wrap in fresh muslin and place under a weight until cold.

Giblet Gravy

Boil turkey giblets in water. Add a pinch of salt. When the stock is ready, make a gravy in the pan using the giblet stock instead of water to brown the flour. Chop the gizzard into very small pieces and add to the strained gravy. Stir in 1 teaspoon of freshly squeezed lemon juice and serve with roast turkey.

Goose

After cleaning the goose, fill with seasoning. Press the legs into the body to give a plump appearance. Pass the trussing needle through the bottom of the wing, through the neck and through the other wing. Pass the needle through the back of the leg near the knee joint, through the body of the bird and back of the other leg, and tie firmly with kitchen string. Heat a little olive oil or vegetable oil in a baking dish and place goose in after wrapping in baking paper. Baste frequently. About 30 minutes before cooking is finished, remove paper so that goose will brown.

Place goose on hot serving dish and remove the string. Strain away all but about 1 tablespoon of the fat. Add flour, salt and pepper, and brown well. Add stock and bring to the boil. The gravy should be a little thicker than that served with fowl.

Garnishes for Goose

Peel and core 12 small apples. Make a syrup by boiling 660 g (3 cups) sugar and 500 ml (2 cups) water until fairly thick. Tint the syrup with red food colouring. Cook the apples in the syrup until soft, but not broken, turning them so they will be evenly tinted. Sprinkle with sugar and glaze under a hot grill. Serve with goose that has been stuffed with a mixture of chopped prunes and nuts (not peanuts), stale day-old breadcrumbs and some herbs, such as sage, thyme or marjoram. You can also serve the goose with red cabbage that has been stewed with chopped onion and apple and plenty of butter, or a sweet compote of fruits with cranberry sauce.

Choosing Game

To test if game is young, hold the bird by the lower beak; when young it will snap off. The legs will look almost smooth and the quill feathers soft. When it is in good condition, the breast of the bird will be hard and firm and well covered with flesh. Hen birds are usually the tenderest. They should never be washed inside, but should be wiped out with a clean cloth.

Game requires careful cooking, though it should never be overdone as it dries and toughens very quickly. Wild duck, teal duck and pigeons are exceptions, and should be basted frequently to prevent dryness. Slices of streaky bacon placed over the breast of game while roasting help to prevent this.

Roasting Game

Pheasants require 45 minutes; grouse and partridges require 30 minutes; wild duck and quail require 20 minutes; teal, snipe, and plovers require 15 minutes.

All dark-fleshed birds, such as duck, should be cooked about as rare as you cook roast beef. Birds with white flesh should be done as well as fowl. Allow 20 minutes roasting for black duck, 15 minutes for teal, 10 minutes for plover and 15 minutes for quail. These times are allowed for game that has been 'hung', which will age it, make it tender and develop the flavour. Longer time must be allowed for cooking game that is still very fresh.

Serve all game, except turkey, with red currant jelly or spiced plums; turkey should be served with cranberry jelly. Celery Sauce (see recipe, page 107) is preferred to bread sauce with game.

Garnishes for Game

Garnishes depend on the individual taste for game. A garnish of watercress and cut lemon is best and looks attractive. Fried breadcrumbs and potato chips or straws should be served separately. A green salad is a modern accompaniment and should be served with a French dressing, not a mayonnaise. Wild duck or teak duck can be served with Damson Sauce (see recipe, page 108) — if cranberries not obtainable, then serve with orange or celery salad. You can also serve game with fried breadcrumbs. Simply melt 1½ tablespoons butter in a frying pan and add 80 g (1 cup) fresh breadcrumbs. Stir until the butter is absorbed. Drain on paper towel and serve as a garnish. Grilled orange slices are also great with game dishes. Wash and dry seedless oranges and cut into 1 cm thick slices. Dip the orange slices in sugar, then cook in a saucepan of melted butter until the edges are slightly brown.

Braised Wild Duck (Black Duck or Teal)

Prepare ducks carefully for cooking and wipe out the inside with a clean cloth. Stuff the ducks with seasoning. Truss them into shape and tie with fine twine.

Melt a little butter in a large saucepan and add chopped onions; fry until brown, but do not burn. Drain off any excess butter, leaving the onion in the pan. Add stock — if you have none at hand, water will do — sufficient to cover the saucepan to a depth of 5 cm. Add bacon cut in cubes, a little finely grated lemon zest and the juice of half a lemon. Season with herbs, salt and pepper. If you have the liver, heart and gizzard of the duck, add these also to the stock. Place the ducks in the saucepan and allow the whole to simmer for 1–2 hours, according to the age of the birds.

When cooked, take the ducks out and strain the stock. Add wine and sugar to the stock and thicken with arrowroot — the mixture should be a clear dark brown. Arrange the ducks on a serving dish and pour the gravy over and around the ducks. Garnish with grilled curls of bacon, sliced lemon and heaps of freshly cooked green peas. The gizzard may also be used as a garnish.

Chicken à la King

Melt 2 tablespoons butter in a saucepan and sauté 90 g (1 cup) sliced mushrooms and 1 chopped green capsicum. Remove the mushroom and pepper from the pan and set aside. Add 2 tablespoons flour to the pan with 250 ml (1 cup) chicken stock and stir until thickened. Add 450 g (2 cups) diced cooked chicken and when hot, add 250 g (1 cup) sour cream and 2 beaten egg yolks. Return the mushrooms and pepper to the pan and stir through 1 tablespoon sherry. Serve immediately.

Chicken Cream

Mix together 225 g (1 cup) chopped chicken and 50 g (⅓ cp) chopped ham and beat in a mortar until quite smooth. Place in a bowl, season with salt and cayenne pepper and add 1 beaten egg yolk. Gradually stir in 150 ml White Sauce (see recipe, page 118). Whip 150 ml cream in one bowl and 1 egg white in another. Slowly stir both through the sauce. Pour the mixture into a greased mould and steam lightly for 30 minutes, or until set. Serve with Béchamel Sauce (see recipe, page 105), to which has been added 2 tablespoons cream. Fry about 12 mushrooms to use as garnish.

Chicken Croquettes

Melt 1½ tablespoons butter in a saucepan and stir in 1½ tablespoons plain flour to make a smooth paste. Add 150 ml stock and stir to combine. Add 80 ml (⅓ cup) cream, bring to the boil and season with salt, pepper and a squeeze of lemon juice. Add 85 g (⅓ cup) chopped cooked chicken and 50 g (⅓ cup) chopped cooked ham and stir to combine and heat through. Remove from the heat.

Cut sheets of Puff Pastry (see recipe, page 286) into 10 cm squares. Place some of the chicken mixture in the centre of each, brush the edges with a little water and fold over, pressing to seal the edges. Brush with egg wash and roll in dry breadcrumbs, shaking off any excess. Deep-fry until golden, drain on paper towel and garnish with fried parsley.

Chicken Curry

Joint a chicken and put in a saucepan with sufficient water to just cover it; simmer until tender. Remove the chicken from the pan and set aside, reserving the stock. Melt 2 tablespoons butter in a clean saucepan and sauté 2 finely chopped onions until brown. Return the chicken to the pan and cook for 3–4 minutes, then sprinkle over 1–2 tablespoons curry powder. Add the chicken stock back to the pan and stir in 1 tablespoon plain flour mixed with a little cold water. Stir until the stock thickens. Add a little of the stock to 1 well-beaten egg yolk and then add to the pan, mixing well. Serve the curry with steamed rice.

Chicken in Milk (Italian Nun's Recipe)

Place 1 whole chicken in a saucepan with 300 ml milk. Simmer very gently for 20 minutes, then remove the chicken and discard the milk. Place a knob of butter inside the chicken, put in a roasting tin and place a piece of greased baking paper over the breast. Cook in the oven for 1 hour, basting liberally with butter as it cooks.

Chicken Marengo

Cut 1 whole chicken into pieces and fry until golden brown in 3 tablespoons butter. Add 125 ml (½ cup) white wine to the pan and cook slowly for 30 minutes. Add 2 finely chopped onions, 6 sliced mushrooms and 2 chopped tomatoes, from which the skin and seeds have been removed. Add 2 teaspoons chopped parsley and season. Cook for a further 15 minutes. The sauce may be slightly thickened if preferred.

Chicken Maryland

Clean and joint a young chicken, leaving the breasts whole. Simmer neck and giblets to obtain 250 ml (1 cup) of stock. Dip pieces of chicken first into a bowl of seasoned flour, then into 1 beaten egg and finally into a bowl of dry breadcrumbs. Place in a greased roasting pan and bake in a hot oven for 30–40 minutes, basting frequently with a mixture of 60 ml (¼ cup) melted butter and 60 ml (¼ cup) hot water. When cooked, remove the chicken pieces and make a gravy from the pan juices together with 1½ tablespoons flour, 250 ml (1 cup) milk and the stock.

Chicken Patties

Make at least 250 ml (1 cup) Béchamel Sauce in the usual way (see recipe, page 105) and add 225 g (1 cup) chopped cooked chicken. Stir to combine, then pour the mixture into paper cases, to serve. Serve hot or cold. Rub hard-boiled egg yolks through a sieve and sprinkle over the chicken patty cases to garnish.

Chicken Pie (Large)

Cut 1 whole chicken into neat joints. Finely cut 85 g ham or bacon into dice. Layer the chicken and ham alternately into a round baking dish. Slice 2 hard-boiled eggs and add a layer to the dish. Season with salt and cayenne pepper, to taste. Pour in 300 ml hot stock and stir well. Roll out enough puff pastry to cover the dish and press the edges to seal. Bake in a 220°C oven until the pastry is brown. Cover with baking paper or foil, reduce the heat, and cook slowly for 1 hour 15 minutes. Serve hot.

Chicken Pies

Roll 450 g Puff Pastry (see recipe, page 286) out to 3 mm thick. Cut out the pie bases using a plain pastry cutter. Using a smaller cutter, mark the centre and cut separate rounds for the pie lids. Brush with egg wash. Blind bake the pastry in a hot oven 15–20 minutes, or until light golden. Melt 55 g butter in saucepan. Add 3½ tablespoons flour and stir until smooth. Cook for 1 minute, then add 375 ml (1½ cups) milk; stir until the liquid boils and thickens. Add 125 ml (½ cup) cream and season with salt and cayenne pepper. Add 450 g (2 cups) chopped cooked chicken and combine. Push out the centres that make the pastry lids and fill the pastry cases. Place the lids on top and heat in the oven for 10–15 minutes. Serve the pies garnished with parsley.

Chicken Supreme

Divide 1 chicken into neat joints, put into a saucepan with 1 small whole onion and 875 ml (3½ cups) chicken stock. Cook slowly until tender. Remove the chicken from the stock and keep warm. Reserve the stock. Melt 40 g butter in a saucepan add 2½ tablespoons plain flour. Stir for 1 minute, then slowly add the reserved stock, stirring over gentle heat until the stock boils and thickens. Pour a little of the sauce gradually into a bowl with 1 beaten egg yolk and stir in 1 tablespoon cream. Return this egg mixture to the pan and cook for 1 minute without boiling; season with salt and cayenne pepper. Return the chicken to the pan and reheat. Garnish with chopped parsley, to serve.

Fricassée Chicken

Joint 1 whole chicken and put into a saucepan with sufficient water to just cover. Add 1 chopped onion, 1 chopped carrot, salt, peppercorns and a piece of lemon zest. Bring to the boil, then reduce the heat and simmer until tender. Remove the chicken from the pan. Strain the liquid back into the clean pan, then add 250 ml (1 cup) milk for every 310 ml (1¼ cups) stock. Blend 2 tablespoons flour with a little milk to make a paste; then add to the stock and milk in the pan. Bring to the boil and simmer for 5 minutes, stirring constantly. Return the chicken to the pan, stir through a little chopped parsley and 1 tablespoon lemon juice. Serve immediately.

Fried Chicken

Cut chicken into pieces. Place in a paper bag with 75 g (½ cup) plain flour and 1 teaspoon salt. Shake to coat the chicken. Heat 4 tablespoons butter or margarine in a heavy-based frying pan and fry the chicken on each side until brown. Cover the pan and cook slowly for about 30 minutes, or until the chicken is tender. Make a rich cream gravy from 2 tablespoons of pan juices, 2 tablespoons flour and 310 ml (1¼ cups) milk.

Grilled Duckling

Cut the duckling down the back to open it up and use a skewer to keep it flat. Sprinkle with salt and pepper and a little melted butter. Grill on a barbecue hotplate for 10 minutes, brush again with melted butter, and continue cooking, turning often, until cooked. Serve with Orange Sauce (see recipe, page 114).

Roast Chicken

The size of the chicken depends on the number of guests. From a good-sized bird at least 6 helpings may be carved, with the seasoning to help. Make the seasoning with 200 g (2 cups) breadcrumbs, 115 g chopped suet or 50 g butter, the finely grated zest of 1 lemon and a little parsley. Season the stuffing with salt and pepper and stir through 1 beaten egg and a little milk (if necessary) to combine. Stuff the bird, then place in a roasting tray. Cover the breast with a slathering of softened butter and place a sheet of baking paper over the top. Cook in a 180°C oven for 20 minutes. Turn over and cook for a further 20 minutes. Turn again and cook for a 20 minutes longer, re-covering with paper before returning to the oven each time.

Variation You can also make a crumbed roast chicken. Prepare in the same way and place a slice of streaky bacon over the breast. Roast the chicken in the oven, basting frequently. Cook for 30 minutes. Remove from the oven and take off the bacon. Brush the bird over with egg wash using a pastry brush. Coat it thickly with dry breadcrumbs. Return to the oven and roast for a further 20 minutes.

Roast Duck

Choose a duck weighing 1.3–2.25 kg. If tender, the windpipe will give easily when pressed. Wipe inside the duck with a slightly damp cloth; sprinkle the inside well with salt and pepper and dredge with flour. Put the grated zest of ½ orange into the baking dish with butter. Stuff the duck with sage and onion stuffing. Cover the breast of the duck with thin slices of orange, then a greased sheet of baking paper, and place in a 220°C oven for 15 minutes. Reduce the temperature to 180°C and cook for 30 minutes, basting every 10 minutes or so. Remove the paper from the bird and baste well; allow to brown. For cooking, allow 20 minutes for every 450 g duck.

Spiced Apples

These spiced apples are perfect for serving with roast duck. Core, but do not peel, as many tart apples as needed. Insert 2–3 cloves in each apple. Make a syrup of equal parts of sugar and water and add a little ground cinnamon. Add a few drops of red food colouring to help give the apple a red glaze. Cook the apples in the syrup until almost tender, being careful not to allow them to become soft. Cook slowly and baste apples with syrup, which should coat the apples nicely.

Roast Duck with Mushroom Stuffing

Wash the duck inside and out. Wipe dry. Rub with salt and pepper. Melt 55 g butter in a saucepan. Add 1 chopped onion and a pinch of salt, and fry until the onion is transparent. Add 450 g chopped mushrooms. Cover and cook until tender. Remove from the heat and stuff the duck with the mushroom mixture. Truss the bird in usual way. Place in a roasting tin. Melt 2 tablespoons butter and brush over. Cover and cook for about 1 hour. Uncover and brown before serving.

Roast Fowl with Veal Stuffing

First, make a veal stuffing. Mix together 25 g beef suet or butter and 50 g (1/3 cup) chopped ham in a bowl. Add 2 teaspoons chopped parsley, 1–2 teaspoons mixed dried herbs and the finely grated zest of 1/2 lemon. Blend in a food processor until well combined. Add 120 g (1 1/2 cups) breadcrumbs and season with a little grated nutmeg, salt, pepper and cayenne pepper. Stir all the ingredients to thoroughly combine. Beat 2 eggs in a separate bowl and stir well. Stuff the bird and place in a baking dish with some dripping or butter, cover with baking paper and roast gently for 1 1/2–2 hours, basting regularly. Remove the paper when the fowl is almost cooked and allow it to brown. Serve with baked or chip potatoes, rolls of bacon, bread sauce or gravy.

Summer Day Chicken

Prepare salad vegetables and have them thoroughly cold.
Cut cold cooked chicken fillets into neat shapes. Season with
salt and pepper, and mask each with mayonnaise and
Savoury Jelly (Aspic) (see recipe, page 149). Decorate with strips
of gherkin and chilli, or stuffed olive slices, then sprinkle
with paprika. Chill in the refrigerator. When ready to serve,
garnish with salad vegetables.

Steamed Chicken

Rub the breast of chicken with freshly squeezed lemon juice. Wrap the chicken in greased baking paper. Place in a saucepan, add a little milk, water, 1 blade mace, a sprig of parsley, salt and cayenne pepper. Cover and steam for about 30 minutes. Remove the chicken from saucepan and discard the paper. Keep warm. Strain the pan juices back into a clean pan and stir in a little flour. Bring to the boil and cook for 1 minute. Pour over the chicken and serve immediately.

Stuffed Turkey

After cleaning, stuff the turkey with seasoning. Twist the upper wing bones back over the skin of the neck. Press the legs into the body to give a plump appearance. Pass the trussing needle through the bottom of the wing through the skin of the neck and through the other wing. Pass the needle to the back of the other leg and tie string firmly. Make oil hot and place turkey in, covering with greased baking paper. Place in a 220°C oven for 10 minutes, then reduce the heat. Cook for 2 –2½ hours, according to size. Baste frequently. About 20 minutes before bird is cooked, remove paper and allow turkey to brown. Garnish with lemon.

Turkey Cream

Melt 1½ tablespoons butter and stir in 225 g (1 cup) chopped cooked turkey and 50 g (⅓ cup) chopped ham. Add 80 g (1 cup) breadcrumbs and 30 g (⅓ cup) chopped turkey stuffing. Season with salt and pepper and bind together with 1 well-beaten egg. Pour the mixture into a greased mould and cover with baking paper. Steam for 45 minutes. Let the cream stand for a few minutes, so that it will turn out easily. Transfer to a serving dish and serve with Béchamel Sauce (see recipe, page 105) with fingers of bread around the turkey cream.

Turkey Pastries

Mix 225 g (1 cup) chopped cooked turkey in a saucepan with 2 tablespoons finely chopped mushrooms and 80 ml (⅓ cup) White Sauce (see recipe, page 118). Cook for 1 minute, remove from the heat and allow to cool. Roll out some Puff Pastry very thinly (see recipe, page 286) and cut into twelve 10 cm rounds. Divide the mushroom sauce between the pastry rounds. Wet the rim of the pastry with a little water and fold each round over to form a half-moon shape. In a separate bowl mix together 1 egg and 1 tablespoon milk. Brush the pastries with the egg wash and roll in dry breadcrumbs to coat. Deep-fry the pastries until golden. Drain on paper towel and serve at once.

Meat

Cooking Meat

When cooking meat, the two chief points are preserving the juices and making the meat tender. To preserve the juices, the meat should be exposed to great heat for the first few minutes to seal the outside. Never stick in forks or skewers, as the perforations allow the meat juices to escape. The meat should be frequently basted to prevent it drying and to help make it crisp and brown, but the chief thing is to keep the meat tender by cooking it very slowly after the first few minutes.

Selecting Meat

Beef should have a bright red colour and moist juicy surface when cut, firm muscle and thick edge of straw-coloured fat. Veal should be faintly pink in colour with little or no fat. When selecting pork, the skin should be pale and cool to touch, the lean finely grained, and the fat quite white and firm. Choose it with a moderate amount of fat. Very lean pork is poor in flavour; very fat pork is wasteful. Beware of pork with very thick skin; it will be old and tough. Lamb and mutton should have deep pink flesh, an edge of pinkish white fat and firm white fibres.

Roasting Beef

Before roasting, wipe and weigh the meat. Then allow 10–15 minutes per 500 grams for cooking. The exact time allowed will vary to the thickness of the joint, and whether the meat is preferred well done or underdone. The joint should be cooked in a very hot oven until browned, the heat should then be moderated, and the joint cooked slowly and basted often until done. Long, slow cooking makes the meat more tender. Mutton should not be served underdone; neither should veal or pork. The two latter meats require thorough cooking.

For example, to roast a sirloin of beef, select a nice sirloin, the weight of which should not exceed 5 kilograms as otherwise the outside would be too much done, whilst the inside would not be done enough. The mode is to bake it in the oven, basting it often. Sprinkle a little salt over the cooked joint, and then empty the dripping-pan of all the dripping. Pour in some boiling water, slightly salted, stir it about and strain over the meat. Garnish with tufts of horseradish, and take horseradish sauce to table with it. It will take about 2½ hours to roast a sirloin of 5 kilograms.

Roasting Pork

Pork leg or loin is generally chosen for roasting, and the skin must be well scored. A leg is scored in a spiral pattern from the knuckle, while a loin is scored in the direction of the chop bones. The crackling should be brushed over well with vegetable oil before putting it into the oven. It will then be deliciously crisp, but not tough.

The joint must be put into a 220°C oven, for 10 minutes, then reduced to 180°C until the meat is thoroughly cooked, basting it occasionally to keep it moist. Allow 25 minutes for every 450 g, plus an extra 20 minutes.

To make the gravy, slowly pour off the fat from the pan, leaving just the brown sediment at the bottom. Add ½ teaspoon salt and 300 ml boiling water and stand the pan over gentle heat. Stir while it boils, for 1 minute, scraping the residue from the bottom of the pan. Strain before serving. Serve roast pork with sage and onion and Apple Sauce (see recipe, page 105).

Gravy

When making gravy and using flour, stir or rub the dry flour into the butter or dripping. Brown the flour and add salt, pepper, and either water or stock. Allow the stock to boil a minute, being careful not to let it get lumpy. If not dark enough add a little caramel or parisian essence; just one drop should be sufficient. Strain and serve quite hot and never send greasy gravy to the table. Every particle of fat should be removed before serving.

Stewing

The most economical of all ways of cooking is stewing because all the cheap parts of meat may be used and there is no waste — the goodness that comes out of the meat is in the gravy — and it also requires very little fuel and very little time in preparation.

For stewing, allow 1 teaspoon salt, ½ teaspoon pepper, 3 teaspoons flour and 450 ml water for each 500 g meat. The meat should first be fried to harden the outside and keep the juice in the meat — frying also improves the colour and flavour. Exceptions to this are for Irish stew and stewed tripe.

Stews must never be allowed to boil, just barely simmer. The fat that may arise must always be removed before dishing, first by skimming, and afterwards by using paper towel to take off any fat that is left after skimming.

As a rule, stews are garnished with chopped parsley and decorated with vegetables cut in fancy shapes; the exception being Irish stew.

Frying

Frying is the quickest and most effective, but the least wholesome, of all the ways of cooking food. There are two kinds of frying. Wet frying is cooking the meat in the saucepan nearly full of oil, just like boiling in a saucepan of water. It is used to cook things that need very little cooking or that cook quickly. For example, fritters and rissoles made of cooked meat, filleted fish or small fish, potato chips and doughnuts. The oil is only hot enough for wet frying when a bluish smoke rises from it. About 1–2 litres vegetable oil will be required and the same oil can be used over and over again if carefully strained after cooling. The great heat of the oil purifies it and kills flavours. An old iron saucepan is best, but the frying baskets that are supplied with saucepans to fit are excellent.

Dry-frying is the other way to fry meat and involves cooking in a pan with about 2 tablespoons of oil or less. It is ready for frying when it smokes, and is used for things that cook slowly; for example, whole fish (unless very small), cutlets, sausages, liver, bacon, pancakes and omelettes.

Grilling

The meat is cooked over or under or in front of an open fire or other direct heat so that there is a distance of about 12 cm between the meat and the source of heat. Chops and tender steaks such as sirloin, porterhouse, rump and fillet are best for grilling. If the steak is lean, moisten the meat during grilling with a little melted butter or other fat. To keep the juices held in, the meat is turned after the first minute and then allowed to cook evenly on both sides.

TIMETABLE FOR GRILLING MEATS

Rump Steak (2 cm thick)	8 minutes (underdone), 10 minutes (well done) and 2 minutes for gravy
Mutton Chop	10 minutes (lightly done), 12 minutes (well done)
Sheep's Kidney	9 minutes
Spring Chicken	35 minutes
Split Bloater	6 minutes

Pan Broiling

To pan broil, meat is browned quickly by placing on a sizzling hot skillet, heavy frying pan or similar utensil, and then cooked more slowly on both sides.

TIMETABLE FOR BAKING AND PAN BOILING MEATS

Beef and Mutton	15 minutes per 500 g and 15 minutes over
Beef and Mutton (without bone)	20 minutes per 500 g and 15 minutes over
Veal	25 minutes per 500 g and 25 minutes over
Lamb (Hindquarter)	2 hours
Lamb (Forequarter)	1½ hours
Corned Beef	20 minutes per 500 g and 20 minutes over
Pork	25 minutes per 500 g and 25 minutes over
Suckling Pig	2½ to 3 hours
Ham	25 minutes per 500 g and 25 minutes over
Tongue	3–4 hours, according to size. Soak overnight if dry-salted.

Savoury Jelly (Aspic)

Savoury jelly is used as a garnish and also used with cold sauces to mask cold dished. Many luncheon dishes are served chilled in savoury jelly, and are delicious. A good clear stock, free from every particle of fat, is needed as a base and may be made from veal, calves' feet or mutton shank bones, or if these are not available, use water.
To make savoury jelly (Aspic), put 900 ml veal stock (or other clear stock) into a saucepan. Add 1 chopped celery stick, 1 carrot and 1 small chopped onion to the pan, then pour in 125 ml (½ cup) sherry, 150 ml vinegar and add 2 tablespoons powdered gelatine. Add the finely grated zest and juice of 1 lemon, 2 cloves, 1 thyme sprig, 1 handful chopped parsley, 1 bay leaf and 1 blade mace. Bring to a near boil and add 2 stiffly beaten egg whites and the washed and crushed egg shells, and beat for a while. Allow the mixture to boil until it rises. Strain twice through a jelly bag (always pour boiling water through your jelly bag and then squeeze it dry before adding the liquid to be strained), and use jelly as required.

Aberdeen Sausage

Put 500 g steak, 250 g bacon slices and the meat of 1 little sausage through a mincer until ground. Add 200 g (2 cups) dry breadcrumbs and mix together. Moisten with 1 egg, well beaten. Form into a long roll, place in a piece of muslin dusted with plain flour and boil for 2 hours. Roll in extra breadcrumbs when cooked and eat cold.

Australian Goose

Take 2 or 3 flaps of mutton (according to size of family), put in bottom of large stewing pan or broiler and add 1 onion, 1 carrot, 3 cloves, 3 peppercorns, 1 celery sprig, salt and pepper. Simmer slowly in enough water to just cover the flaps. When quite tender, take out and bone, press between two dishes and leave until next day. Save the liquor.

When quite cold and firm, trim nicely. Roll in egg and breadcrumbs and grill slowly until golden brown. Make a sauce from the liquor and flavour with a little cayenne pepper, lemon and a tablespoon of sherry, if available.

Bacon and Liver Rolls

Wash and cut 500 g sheep or lamb's liver into thin pieces, then wipe dry. Cut rind from 250 g bacon rashers and lay a piece of bacon on a slice of liver, roll up and tie with strong kitchen string, or use a toothpick. Season 2 tablespoons plain flour with salt and pepper, then dust the liver rolls in the flour. Place in a pan and cook in bacon fat or vegetable oil (bacon fat preferred) until brown. Transfer to a casserole dish with 300 ml beef stock, 1 chopped onion and some parsley, and cook gently for 1½ hours. Remove the rolls to a serving plate, and thicken the gravy in dish. Pour over the liver and serve.

Bacon and Sausage Toasts

Put 2 sausages into a saucepan of cold water, bring to a simmer and cook slowly for 5 minutes. Cool slightly, remove the skins and chop the sausage meat. Remove the rind from 6 bacon slices and cut them in half. Divide the sausage meat between the bacon halves and roll up to enclose the sausage. Stick them on a skewer and grill until cooked. Lightly beat 2 eggs and mix them with 2 tablespoons milk, seasoning with salt and pepper. Melt 1½ tablespoons butter in a frying pan and stir in the egg mixture, and cook gently until it thickens; keep it stirred. Serve it on 6 oblongs of buttered toast, and garnish each with the rolls of bacon.

Bacon and Tomato Macaroni

Cook 155 g (1 cup) macaroni in a saucepan with plenty of boiling salted water, then drain. Skin 4 tomatoes and thinly slice. Remove the rind from 6 bacon slices. Put a layer of macaroni in a greased baking dish, then a layer of tomatoes and season with salt and pepper. Add a layer of bacon rashers, more macaroni and tomatoes, and a layer of bacon on top. Bake in a 150°C oven for about 30 minutes. Serve immediately.

Bacon Meatloaf

Put 750 g minced beef in a bowl with 2 beaten eggs and mix well. Add 100 g (1 cup) breadcrumbs and 250 ml (1 cup) milk. Season with salt and pepper, to taste. Remove the rind from 250 g bacon slices. Line a baking dish with half of the bacon slices and fill with the meat mixture. Cover with bacon and bake for 45 minutes in a 180°C oven. Turn out onto a large serving plate and garnish with tomatoes or vegetables.

Baked Ham

Soak 1 ham for at least 12 hours if necessary. Wipe it dry, trim away any discoloured parts underneath, and cover all over with a crust made of flour and water. Take great care that this is of sufficient thickness all over to keep in the gravy. Place the ham in a baking dish in a 200°C oven and bake for nearly 4 hours. Take off the crust and skin, cover with browned breadcrumbs, the same as for boiled ham (see page 155). When cooked the internal temperature of a ham should be 80°C. Measure by inserting the point of a cooking thermometer into the centre of the ham and leaving it there while cooking proceeds.

Baked Ham in Mustard Crust

Take a 7.5 cm thick middle cut of cold boiled smoked ham. Sprinkle over 1 tablespoon sugar and ½ teaspoon ground cloves. Mix 150 g (1 cup) plain flour and 1 tablespoon mustard powder into a paste with cold water. Cover the ham with the paste. Bake for 20 minutes in a 180°C oven; decorate with whole cloves. Serve on a bed of Savoury Jelly (Aspic) (see recipe, page 149).

To Cook a Ham

Soak the ham overnight in cold water. Next morning place in fresh water. Bring to the boil for 20 minutes. Have ready bags and old blankets to cover. Take off the fire, stand the pot on a bag, cover all over with the bags. Let stand for 12 hours — the ham will be cooked to perfection. Leave until cold before removing the skin, then loosen the edges with your fingers, pull towards the knuckle and the skin will pull off cleanly.

Baked Lamb

Place a 2–2.25 kg leg or shoulder joint of lamb in an ungreased baking tray. Add 1 tablespoon red currant jelly, ½ cup black coffee and 1 tablespoon of cream. Bake in a 180°C oven, basting every 15 minutes with the liquid. More coffee or water may be added to maintain the volume of the basting liquid. When the lamb is cooked, remove to a serving plate and season the pan juices with salt and pepper to make a gravy. Pour into a jug on the side to serve.

Baked Loin of Lamb

A loin of lamb is a good baking joint and a change from a leg or shoulder. Put a 2 kg lamb loin into a baking tray and cook in a 220°C oven for about 1 hour 15 minutes, lessening the heat as required. When cooked, transfer to a warmed serving plate. Serve the lamb with slightly thickened gravy made by adding a little flour to the pan juices after pouring off the dripping. Add a little water, seasoning and browning if required, and boil up, then strain and serve on the side.

Baked Stuffed Lamb Flaps

Get two flaps of lamb, weighing about 500 g each, and have the butcher bone them. Score them on the outside with a fork and then prepare a stuffing by mixing 100 g (1 cup) dry breadcrumbs, 1 egg, a pinch of mixed dried herbs and 1 finely chopped white onion. Season with salt and pepper, to taste. Spread the stuffing on the inside of the flaps and roll tightly, tying with three separate pieces of kitchen string — a piece tied lengthways keeps the meat flat and makes it easier to cut. Bake in a 150°C oven for about 1 hour 30 minutes. Flaps cooked this way are delicious either hot or cold and also make a tasty sandwich filling.

Beef Stroganoff

Cut 625 g topside or round steak in shreds and squeeze over the juice of 1 lemon. Set aside for 30 minutes. Lightly dust the steak in flour. Melt 1 tablespoon butter in a frying pan and add 2 finely chopped onions and 90 g (1 cup) finely chopped mushrooms and cook until golden. Remove the onion and mushroom and set aside. Heat a little butter in a saucepan and cook the meat for about 5 minutes, stirring constantly. Return the onion and mushroom to the pan and cook for 3 minutes further. Pour in 250 g (1 cup) sour cream and stir through. Serve immediately with rice.

Beef Olives

To make the veal forcemeat for the filling, mix together 125 g minced veal, 2 tablespoons breadcrumbs, 1 tablespoon chopped parsley, ½ tablespoon butter and the grated zest of 1 lemon. Season with, salt, cayenne pepper and a pinch of ground nutmeg. Stir in 1 beaten egg and combine well. Cut 450 g steak into 10 cm square pieces about 1 cm thick. Place a little roll of forcemeat in each, roll up, tie with kitchen string and roll to coat in flour. Heat 1½ tablespoons oil in a frying pan and cook the beef until brown. Add 300 ml water or stock, bring to the boil, then reduce the heat and simmer slowly for about 2 hours. Remove the meat from the pan and serve. Strain the pan juices and pour a little around each beef olive.

Variation Mix finely chopped olives into the forcemeat before cooking and add 12 whole olives to the stock and serve in the gravy.

Beef Roll

Finely chop 225 g cooked meat (such as leftover roast) and mix with 115 g (1½ cups) dry breadcrumbs, 30 g chopped suet or butter, ½ teaspoon salt, ¼ teaspoon beaten egg, and sufficient stock or gravy to make it moist enough to work into a roll. Sprinkle some flour on a clean work surface and turn out the meat mixture, working it into a neat roll. Brush the roll with a little egg wash. Place the roll in a greased baking tray, sprinkle with fresh or browned breadcrumbs, and bake for about 20 minutes. Serve with brown sauce or tomato sauce.

Beef with Fried Pineapple

Take the required number of fillets, about 1 cm thick. When purchasing beef fillets ask the butcher for the 'eye' of the fillet. It costs a little more, but there is not as much waste as there is with fillet steak. Remove all the fat and sinew and place the fillets in a large shallow container. Pour olive oil over the steaks and toss to coat. Set aside, turning occasionally, until you are ready to cook them. Place under a hot grill for 10 minutes, turning halfway. Take care they do not get too hard and dry on the outside.

Tinned or fresh pineapple may be used. If fresh it must be cooked in sugar and water until tender. Drain the juice from the tinned sliced pineapple. Melt a little butter in a frying pan and cook the pineapple slices on both sides. Season with salt and pepper and serve with the beef fillets and mashed potatoes. Garnish with sliced stuffed olives.

Boeuf Bourguignon

Melt 150 g butter in a saucepan and add 1.6 kg beef chopped into 1 cm cubes. Cook slowly for a few minutes, then add 150 g (1 cup) plain flour. Season with ½ teaspoon salt and 1 teaspoon pepper and cook for 3 minutes, stirring well. Add 1.2 litres boiling water, 1 cup tomato sauce and 600 ml red wine. Cook in a 200°C oven and add 36 pickled onions. Cook for 1½ hours or until the meat is tender.

Boiled Ham

Soak the ham in cold water for 6 hours before cooking. Scrape and put it in a saucepan and cover with water. Add a bunch of herbs, if liked, and a little mace. Cook very slowly for 5 hours (or the rule is for boiled salt meats, 25 minutes for every 450 g, and then 25 minutes over). Remove from the heat. (If the ham is to be served cold, leave in the cooking liquid until the ham is cold.) Skin the ham and cover in a layer of dry breadcrumbs, or glaze the ham and fasten a paper frill around the knuckle.

Variation When the ham is cooked, strain the liquid and pour 2 bottles of marsala over the ham. Simmer for just a short time. This improves the flavour greatly, but is rather extravagant.

Boiled Leg Of Lamb

Wrap a 2.25 kg leg of lamb in muslin and boil it very slowly for 1 hour 45 minutes. When cooked, dish it up and garnish with a border of boiled carrots and turnips cut into thick slices and also sprigs of cauliflower. Put a paper frill on the shank bone, and pour some Parsley Sauce (see recipe, page 109) over the lamb. Baked potatoes also go very nicely with this joint.

Boned Leg of Mutton

Buy a leg of mutton already boned or bone it with a very sharp knife, keeping the blade very close to the bone all the time. Make a stuffing by mincing 115 g cooked bacon or ham. Add 1 beaten egg, 100 g (1¼ cups) breadcrumbs, ¼ teaspoon ground nutmeg, ¼ teaspoon dried thyme, grated zest of ½ lemon, salt and pepper. Stuff the cavity. Fasten the leg together neatly, put into a baking tray, brush with melted butter and roast in a 180°C oven for nearly 2 hours, according to the size of the joint.

Brains and Potato Pie

Boil and mash 900 g potatoes. Beat 1 egg and stir into the mashed potato to bind it. Grease a casserole dish and line it with a thick layer of mashed potatoes — reserving some potato to use for a topping. Chop 2 sets lamb's brains and mix together with 450 ml White Sauce (see recipe, page 118) and 1 teaspoon chopped parsley. Pour this into the lined dish. Cover with the remaining potato, giving it a roughened appearance by scoring or pricking with a fork. Glaze with egg wash and bake in a 180°C oven until lightly browned. Serve hot as a luncheon or dinner dish.

Braised Beef Fillet

Use fat bacon only for larding. Cut the lardons (long strips of streaky bacon) all the same thickness and length. Thread larding needle with strips, lard the meat carefully across the top of the fillet, which has been rolled, keeping the lardons in evenly arranged places in a straight line.

Place the beef in a deep roasting tin over some rough-cut vegetables and two or three bones to make a bed on which to lay the joint. Pour in enough stock (or water) to just cover the lower edge. Put lid on closely and cook very gently until tender.

Remove the beef and vegetables. Strain the pan juices into a saucepan and boil until reduced by half. Remove half the stock to use as a gravy and boil the remainder to a whole glaze. Brush the joint with this before sending it to the table, also brush croutons with it and garnish with green peas.

Braised Beef with Mushrooms

Melt a little butter in a saucepan and add 900 g round beef steak chopped into small pieces. Brown very quickly, then remove the beef from the pan and set aside. Pour in 1 tablespoon brandy, then add 90 g (1 cup) button mushrooms and cook for a few minutes. Add 3 tablespoons plain flour, pour in 500 ml (2 cups) stock and stir until the liquid boils. Add 125 ml (½ cup) red wine and 1 tablespoon red currant jelly. Return the meat to the pan and cook slowly until tender. Arrange in a shallow dish, pour over the gravy and cover the top with 3 sliced tomatoes. Grate cheese over the top and surround the whole with mashed potatoes. Place the dish under a hot grill until the cheese and potatoes are nicely browned.

Braised Ox Tail with Walnuts

Joint 1 oxtail (about 1.5–1.75 kg), removing any surplus fat. Wash, dry and coat each joint in seasoned flour. Heat 1 tablespoon butter in a large saucepan; fry the joints until browned. Add 750 ml (3 cups) stock or water, and when boiling, add 3 peppercorns, 3 cloves and 2 blades mace. Simmer for about 3 hours. Chop 1 onion, 2 celery sticks, 1 carrot and 1 turnip and add to the stew. Simmer for 1 hour longer or until the vegetables are tender. Skim any fat that rises to the surface. Remove the meat and vegetables and keep warm. Strain the cooking juices into a small saucepan. Mix together 1 teaspoon plain flour and a little cold water to make a paste. Add this to the stock and simmer for 5 minutes, stirring often, until it boils and thickens. Cut 3–4 pickled walnuts in half and add to the stock with 1 tablespoon walnut vinegar. Season with salt and simmer for 10 minutes. Serve hot.

Brawn

Put 1 pig's cheek, 1 pig's ear, 3 large trotters and 2 pig's tongues into a large saucepan. Pour in enough water to cover and bring to the boil. Reduce the heat and simmer for 3½ hours, skimming off any scum that rises to the surface. Remove the bones, cut the meat into small pieces and leave it in the cooking liquid until cold, then take off the fat. Add to the meat a good seasoning of salt and pepper, a good pinch ground mace and a dash of cayenne pepper, if liked. Boil slowly for 8 minutes. Put into a mould and allow to set overnight. Turn out when set and serve.

Cambridge Sausage

Mix together 450 g minced beef, 80 g (1 cup) breadcrumbs, 115 g finely chopped streaky bacon, 1 egg, 1 tablespoon tomato sauce, 1 teaspoon salt and ½ teaspoon pepper. Stir until well combined then spread the mixture into the centre of a large piece of floured muslin. Roll up to form a sausage shape and tie securely at the ends. Cook in a saucepan of simmering water for 2 hours.

Cold Beef Cutlets

Cook crumbed cutlets in the usual way and let them become cold. Put on each cutlet a ring of cooked egg white and decorate with a teaspoon of Mint Jelly (see recipe, page 112) and a sprig of parsley. Place each cutlet on a crisp lettuce leaf with some jellied green peas and your favourite sauce.

Corned Beef

Wash 1.8–2.25 kg corned beef (silverside) in plenty of water. Put into a saucepan with 1 knuckle of veal, 1 bunch herbs, 2 bay leaves, 2 teaspoons vinegar. Cover with water and bring slowly to the boil, then reduce the heat and simmer gently until tender, or until the bones (if any) can be easily removed. Skim frequently to remove any fat that rises to the surface. Remove the corned beef and discard the other ingredients. Press into a round cake tin, place weights on top and refrigerate overnight. Turn the corned beef out of the tin and garnish with parsley or lettuce.

If the meat is to be served hot, boil the vegetables (carrots, white turnips, and parsnips) whole in the pan with the meat. Drain the vegetables well and serve with the corned beef and a mustard sauce.

Cornish Pasties

Prepare the filling first. Finely chop 450 g skirt steak finely, put into a bowl and season with salt and pepper. Chop 1 onion, 1 large potato and 1 turnip into small dice and stir through the meat until thoroughly combined.

To make the pastry, sift 350 g (2⅓ cups) plain flour, ¾ teaspoon baking powder and ½ teaspoon salt into a bowl. Rub in 225 g dripping or butter until it looks like breadcrumbs, then add 185 ml (¾ cup) water, gradually binding into a stiff dough. Turn onto a floured board and knead gently. Divide the dough into six portions and roll each out into a 5 mm thick round. Divide the meat filling among the pastry circles and place in the centre. Moisten the edges with water, fold the pastry in half to form a half–moon shape and crimp the edges to seal. Prick with a fork and brush over with egg wash and milk. Cook in a 220°C oven for 10 minutes. Reduce the heat to 180°C and continue cooking for 40 minutes.

Cutlets à la Macédoine

Trim 9 lamb cutlets, leaving cutlets 7.5 cm long, and trim cutlets into a pear shape, leaving about 4 cm of bare bone at the end. Pound the cutlets to flatten and season with salt and pepper. Dip first in egg wash, then in breadcrumbs to coat and fry them in a frying pan with about 3 tablespoons oil. Serve with steamed rice and vegetables, with brown sauce on the side.

Crème de Veau

Combine 450 g minced veal and 115 g minced ham and season with white pepper, cayenne pepper, salt and a pinch of ground mace. Melt 55 g butter and mix into the meat. Add 2 beaten eggs and 300 ml whipped cream. Beat these into the meat until all are thoroughly mixed, then turn the mixture into a mould and steam for 20 minutes. Turn out and serve with parsley or a lemon sauce. You can use half milk and half cream if a less expensive dish is required.

Devilled Kidney

Mix together 1 tablespoon butter, 2 tablespoons mustard, ½ teaspoon cayenne pepper, a squeeze of lemon juice and a little Worcestershire sauce. If using this mixture on cooked meats or chicken, thinly slice the meat and butter both sides with the mixture. Heat and grease a pan and score the meat first, then cook for about 4 minutes on each side. If using the mixture to devil kidneys, cut out the fat and remove the skin, cook for 8 minutes, and serve on fried toasted bread that has a slice of grilled bacon on it.

The correct accompaniments to serve with meat dishes

- **BOILED BACON**: with cabbage, haricot beans and parsley sauce. To make parsley sauce, put 1 1/2 cups finely chopped nice green parsley into a small saucepan with enough water to cover and bring to the boil for 10 minutes, then drain the water from it. Take 60 g anchovy fillets with 125 g butter. Mix all thoroughly together and pass through a fine sieve.
- **BOILED PORK**: with pease pudding, carrots, parsnips, plain White Sauce (see recipe, page 118) or meat liquor served plain.
- **BOILED RABBIT**: with pickled pork or bacon, onion sauce and seasoning.
- **CORNED BEEF**: with boiled old or new potatoes, glazed carrots, cabbage, buttered beets, turnips, parsnips, boiled onions and piccalilli, Dijon mustard, horseradish sauce or onion sauce.
- **FLANK STEAK**: with potatoes au gratin or mashed potatoes, grilled tomatoes, beans, melted butter sauce. Garnish with bacon curls and parsley. To make melted butter sauce, melt 1–2 tablespoons butter in a saucepan over low heat and add the juice of 1 good lemon and some chopped parsley, making sure not to boil. This sauce is very tasty and easily prepared.
- **FOWL**: may be stuffed with breadcrumbs, butter and oyster seasoning and served with thin brown gravy or bread sauce.
- **GRILLED MEATS**: with potato straw chips, grilled tomatoes, corn fritters, fried bananas, apple rings, broiled mushrooms, fried pineapple and natural meat juices or worcestershire sauce. Garnish with grilled cocktail sausages and bacon.
- **HAM**: with raisin sauce.
- **HAMBURGER STEAK**: minced with beef suet, then moulded into cakes (60 g suet to 500 g meat, a clove and onion juice). Serve with cream potatoes or baked potatoes, buttered carrots, stewed tomatoes or fried onions or tomato sauce. Garnish with parsley.
- **HARE**: with potatoes, green vegetables and red currant jelly, forcemeat balls, brown or port wine sauce.
- **LAMB CASSEROLE**: with mashed potatoes or new boiled potatoes, carrots, peas, mashed turnips, parsnips, boiled onions and natural gravy or caper sauce.
- **LAMB CHOPS**: with potato balls, asparagus tips, buttered peas, buttered lima beans, Brussels sprouts, cauliflower, seasoning butter. Arrange on a bed of watercress. To make seasoning butter, cream the butter with a little salt, allowing 1 tablespoon for each person — place on both sides of the meat and serve.

- **MUTTON CHOPS**: with potato croquettes, creamed turnips, buttered beets, spinach on toast, stuffed onions, seasoning butter. Garnish with grilled kidneys, bacon and watercress.
- **PIES AND PUDDINGS**: with boiled, mashed or creamed potatoes, rice, turnips, boiled onions, parsnips, string beans, cabbage, stewed celery and natural gravy or tomato sauce.
- **PORK CHOPS**: with fried sweet potato, plain boiled potatoes, Brussels sprouts, cauliflower, croquettes, creamed cabbage, apple sauce, seasoning, butter. Garnish with baked apple rings.
- **ROAST BEEF**: with Yorkshire pudding, sautéed corn, green peas, string beans, cabbage, cauliflower, baked pumpkin, baked potatoes and brown gravy, mushroom or horseradish sauce.
- **ROAST DUCK**: with thin brown gravy or Apple Sauce (see recipe, page 105).
- **ROAST LAMB**: with cauliflower, glazed carrots, green peas, onions, beans, baked potatoes and brown gravy, mint sauce or mint jelly, or onion seasoning.
- **ROAST MUTTON**: with baked potatoes, pumpkin, green vegetables and red currant jelly or thin gravy.
- **ROAST PIGEON**: with watercress on toast, potato chips or straws, green vegetables and thickened gravy.
- **ROAST PORK**: with baked potatoes, baked sweet potatoes, spinach, mashed turnips, creamed cabbage, corn, baked apples, brown gravy and apple sauce. Garnish with raisins or spiced apple rings, bacon, sage or onion seasoning.
- **ROAST RABBIT**: with potatoes, green vegetables, veal seasoning and forcemeat balls, thickened gravy or tomato sauce. Garnish with bacon curls.
- **ROAST TURKEY**: with thin gravy or cranberry sauce.
- **ROAST VEAL**: with baked potatoes, creamed celery, spinach, baked stuffed tomatoes, Brussels sprouts, string or broad beans and gravy, sauce piquant. Garnish with glazed tart apples, ham or bacon, cut lemon and seasoning.
- **ROUND STEAK**: with potato croquettes or sweet potato glace, macaroni and cheese, grilled or fried tomatoes in slices or creamed parsnips. Garnish with parsley.
- **SQUAB PIGEON**: with sweet potatoes and rich seasoned gravy.
- **QUAIL**: with lemon, mushrooms, sherry or port added.
- **WILD DUCK**: with Orange Sauce (see recipe, page 114) or salad, gravy, watercress, port wine sauce, cut lemon, green peas, seasoning; wild ducks may be stuffed.

Devilled Sheep's Tongues

Boil 300 ml stock in a saucepan and add 2 teaspoons mustard, 1 tablespoon flour, 100 g (⅓ cup) Indian Chutney (see recipes, pages 193–4) or Piccalilli (see recipe, page 197) and 1 tablespoon vinegar. Season with salt and pepper. Trim 4 sheep's tongues, cut each in half lengthways and add to the pan. Simmer until tender.

Drover's Dream

Roll 6 lamb shoulder or neck chops in seasoned flour to coat and place in a casserole dish. Fry 1 sliced onion in butter and add to the dish with 12 small sliced turnips. Add enough water to cover. Bake in a 180°C oven for about 1 hour, or until the chops are tender. Remove the lid during the final 15 minutes of cooking. Serve with small new potatoes sprinkled with chopped parsley and melted butter.

Egg and Bacon Pie

Make a good Shortcrust Pastry (see recipe, page 287) and line a baking dish with the pastry. Sprinkle lightly with flour. Cut strips of bacon and cover the bottom of the dish. Break in as many eggs as required, then season with salt and pepper, to taste. Cover with pastry and bake in moderate oven for 45 minutes. Serve hot for lunch or can be eaten cold and makes wonderful picnic food.

French Beefsteak

Place a thick rump steak in a roasting tin and dust to coat in plain flour seasoned with salt and pepper. Fill with water to almost cover and roast in the oven for 20 minutes. Cover with sliced onions, salt and pepper, then return to the oven for 30 minutes. Cover with a layer of sliced tomatoes, then return to the oven for a further 20 minutes. Finally, sprinkle grated cheese over the top and roast for 10 minutes longer, then serve immediately.

French Cutlets

Trim 7 lamb cutlets, leaving 5 cm of the bone bare. Grease a chargrill pan and grill the cutlets for 7–10 minutes. Turn frequently while cooking. Remove rind from bacon slices and cut into thin strips. Roll up the bacon, thread on a skewer, and grill until the fat is clear. Place chip potatoes in the centre of a hot dish. Stand the cutlets, which have been masked with a little Green Butter (see recipe, page 119), and place the rolls of bacon between the cutlets. Serve very hot.

Fricassée of Lamb

Cut up 625–900 g lamb shoulder or neck chops, removing any fat. Put in a saucepan, cover with water and bring to the boil. Reduce the heat and simmer for 30 minutes. Skim any scum that rises to the surface, then add 2 large sliced onions, 2–3 mint sprigs and 1 thyme sprig. Simmer gently for a further 30 minutes, then add 900 g (6 cups) shelled peas. Cook until the peas are cooked through, then add 250 ml (1 cup) milk. Bring back the boil and add 1 teaspoon cornflour that has been mixed to a paste with a little water. Stir until the sauce thickens. Serve with boiled new potatoes this makes a delicious dish.

Galantine of Veal

Bone 1.5 kg thick end breast of veal and remove any gristle. Cut 225 g gammon of bacon into small cubes and mix it with 450 g pork sausage meat. Boil 3 eggs for 10 minutes and allow them to cool. Take the bones from the veal and put them in a saucepan with 3.6 litres water, a small teaspoon of salt, a sprig each of parsley, thyme and marjoram, and 8 peppercorns. Bring to the boil. Put the boned meat on a board, skin downwards, and spread over half of the sausage meat mixture, then the halved eggs, then the remaining sausage mixture. Roll it up and tie it in a piece of muslin with kitchen string. Place the veal in the boiling stock (leave the bones in the saucepan – they prevent the roll sticking to the bottom). Boil gently for 4 hours. Take out the veal roll out and tighten the cloth again. Place a dish over the veal, with a weight on it to press it down. Glaze when cold, if liked.

Grilled Bacon and Bread Fritters

Sift 55 g (⅓ cup) flour into a bowl with a pinch of salt. Make a hole in the centre. Add 2 teaspoons melted butter and stir until smooth, gradually adding 80 ml (⅓ cup) water and stirring through. Beat 1 egg white to stiff peaks and fold through. Dip 4 round stale pieces of bread in milk, then into the batter. Deep-fry until golden brown. Drain on paper towel. Meanwhile roll up 8 bacon slices into logs and secure with a toothpick. Cook under a hot grill and serve with the bread fritters.

Grilled Loin Chops

Pin the tail to make a pinwheel and fasten with a toothpick. Grease and heat a chargrill pan and cook for 8–10 minutes, turning every 3 minutes using kitchen tongs. Remove the toothpicks and serve the chops on a serving dish topped with a little butter and seasoned with salt and cayenne pepper.

Sauce to Serve with Grilled or Fried Chops

Heat the juice of 1 lemon in a saucepan with 2 teaspoons butter and a little chopped parsley. Once melted and combined, pour over the chops and serve immediately.

Ham Shoulder with Sweet Potatoes

Wash and scrape a ham shoulder well, place in a saucepan and cover with cold water. Add some chopped onion and celery to the pan and bring to the boil, then reduce the heat and simmer until tender. When cooked, remove to a casserole dish, cover with brown sugar and a few cloves. Boil 4–6 medium sized sweet potatoes until nearly done, remove the skins and place in a saucepan with 3 tablespoons butter, 3 tablespoons sugar and 3 tablespoons water. Cook slowly, turning occasionally until the vegetables look clear, then place the potatoes around the ham, pour the cooking syrup over and cook in the oven for 30 minutes.

Irish Stew

Coat 450 g lamb neck chops in 2 teaspoons seasoned flour and lay flat in the bottom of a saucepan. Sprinkle in any flour that remains, cover with 450 ml water and simmer gently for about 15 minutes. Arrange 2 sliced onions in a flat layer on top of the meat, then arrange a layer of 900 g small even-sized whole potatoes over them. Cook for 1½–2 hours, simmering gently. Serve with vegetables in a circle and meat and gravy in centre. Small dumplings are nice served with Irish stew.

Light Dumplings to Serve with Stews

Put 450 g (3 cups) flour, 1 heaped teaspoon baking powder and ½ teaspoon salt through a sieve, then form a stiff dough with milk and water. Roll out lightly, form into dumplings and either put them in the stew for 1 hour, or steam the dumplings separately and then serve on the side. To keep them dry and light, put a piece of greased baking paper at the bottom of the steamer before adding the dumplings. Add 55 g finely grated suet to the dumpling dough if suet dumplings are required.

Lamb Cutlets and Bananas

Lightly flour 6 lamb cutlets and rub them over with 1½ tablespoons melted butter. Grill the cutlets until cooked. Peel and cut 3 bananas into quarters lengthways and fry them in 1½ tablespoons butter until just heated through. Whip 2 tablespoons cream; dust with white pepper and a pinch of salt, and stir in a sprig of finely chopped mint leaves. Put the cutlets on a hot dish, surround them with bananas, decorate with the mint cream and serve immediately.

Lamb Cutlets and Spaghetti

Cook 115 g dried spaghetti in a saucepan of salted boiling water for 8–10 minutes. Meanwhile, dip 4–5 lamb cutlets in egg wash and coat with breadcrumbs. Fry in shallow oil until cooked through and evenly browned, turning the cutlets once during cooking. When the spaghetti is cooked, drain it. Return to the saucepan with 1 tablespoon butter, 2 large tablespoons tomato sauce and salt and pepper, to taste. Stir until heated through. Pile in the centre of a hot dish. Boil and mash a couple of potatoes with milk, butter and seasoning. Place spoonfuls of mashed potatoes on a greased baking tray and use the back of two forks to work the potato into mounds. Bake in a 220°C oven for 10–15 minutes. Serve the cutlets on mounds of spaghetti and garnish with potato rounds.

Lamb's Fry and Bacon

Wash 1 lamb or calf's liver in warm water and dry well. Remove the rind from 125 g streaky bacon slices and cut each slice into thirds. Roll the bacon pieces up and thread on a skewer to garnish the dish. Cut liver downwards from the thin end, creating strips about 5 mm thick. Dip each piece of liver into seasoned flour to coat. Heat 40 g butter in a frying pan. Cook the liver for 5 minutes on each side, shaking the pan regularly to prevent the liver from burning and hardening. Remove to a plate when cooked. Drain all but 1 tablespoon of the cooking fat and add a little flour, salt and pepper from the plate; stir to make a smooth brown paste; add 300 ml water and 2 teaspoons tomato sauce. Bring to the boil and stir until the mixture thickens. Return the liver to the pan and simmer 7–8 minutes. Garnish with the bacon and sprinkle with finely chopped parsley.

A paper bag tied on the mouth of the mincer will prevent crumbs scattering when putting stale bread through.

Madras Steak

Place 450 g round steak in a baking dish, cover with 1 tablespoon vinegar, 3–4 sliced onions and season with salt and pepper. Mix 1 tablespoon plain flour with 2 teaspoons curry powder and stir in 500 ml (2 cups) water. Pour over the meat and onions in the dish and bake slowly until tender. Thicken the gravy once the meat is cooked and serve with steamed rice on the side.

Melton Mowbray Pie

To make the pastry, put 140 g lard and 85 g butter into a saucepan with 300 ml boiling water. Stir until dissolved, then remove from the heat. Sift 625 g (4 cups) plain flour into a bowl and add the melted butter and lard. Knead into shape while warm, otherwise it will crack if it gets too cold.

To make the filling, chop 1–1.3 kg lean pork and place in a baking dish in layers with streaky bacon. Slice a few hard-boiled eggs into rings and pack in alternate layers until the dish is filled. Cover and decorate with the pastry. Put the skin from a joint of pork and a pig trotter in a saucepan with enough water to just cover and simmer. When the pie is cooked, fill with the gravy from the pork, which will jelly when cold. Bake in a 220°C oven for a start, and slow down to 180°C and bake for about 1½ hours. This can be made into one or more pies.

Mixed Grill

Trim 1 lamb cutlet. Remove the rind from 1 bacon slice, cut in half and make into 2 rolls, securing with a toothpick. Skin 1 sheep's kidney and cut in half. Cut 1 tomato in half. Trim 1 small piece beef steak. Place the cutlet, bacon rolls, kidney, tomato and steak under a hot grill. Turn frequently. As each item is cooked, remove from the grill and keep hot until all are ready to serve. Sprinkle with butter, salt and cayenne pepper, before serving.

Mock Wild Duck

Cut steak into thin squares. Make a stuffing of breadcrumbs seasoned with chopped onions, butter or dripping, salt and pepper, and a little sage. Chop 1–6 sheep's kidneys finely, spread evenly over the steak, then cover with the stuffing. Place thin bacon strips on top. Roll up each steak and tie securely with kitchen string. Roll in seasoned flour and cook in a frying pan until brown. Transfer to a casserole dish, cover with thinly sliced apple and breadcrumbs, and grill until cooked through.

Moulded Lamb in Mint Jelly

Soak 1 tablespoon gelatine powder in 60 ml (¼ cup) water. Heat 185 ml (¾ cup) stock in a saucepan with 125 ml (½ cup) vinegar. Stir through the gelatine. When dissolved, add a little green food colouring. When partly thickened, add 3 cups cold, cooked diced lamb and ½ cup finely chopped mint leaves. Pour in a mould to set. If preferred, a small leg of lamb can be used; set in mint jelly, using extra gelatine, stock, vinegar and mint.

Mutton Steak

Melt 1 tablespoon of butter in a saucepan. Take 2.5 cm thick mutton steaks and dip each piece into the butter, then place in chargrill pan and grill for 10 minutes, turning often. Serve hot with butter.

Mutton and Rice (Economical)

Use 3 mutton shanks or 2 neck chops. Put the meat in a saucepan with 1 onion, a pinch of salt and ground nutmeg and cover with water. Bring to the boil, then reduce the heat and simmer for about 1 hour 15 minutes. Remove the meat from the bones and set aside with the onion. Cool the stock and remove any fat that rises to the surface, then bring back to the boil. Stir some water into a little rice flour to make a paste and add to the stock. When the sauce has reduced and thickened, return the meat and onions to the pan and heat through. Serve sprinkled with chopped parsley.

One-Pot Pie

Cut 450 g topside steak into small pieces. Finely chop 1 onion, 1 turnip and 1 carrot into small dice. Season the meat with the salt and pepper and roll to coat in flour. Place the steaks in a saucepan with the vegetables, layering as you go. Pour over 375 ml (1½ cups) water and simmer gently for 30 minutes. Make 115 g Suet Pastry (see recipe, page 287) and roll into a round shape the same size as the lid of the saucepan. Press the pastry into the saucepan to cover the meat. Cover with a lid and simmer slowly for a further 1 hour 30 minutes. To serve, cut the pastry into six triangular pieces. Place meat and vegetables in a hot dish and replace the pastry on the top.

Ox Heart

Select a nice, fresh ox heart; trim any tubes or other tough pieces, wash well and soak for 2 hours in warm water. Dry well with a cloth. Mix together 120 g (1½) cups stale breadcrumbs, 1 large finely chopped onion, 1 tablespoon chopped sage leaves and 2 tablespoons softened butter. Season with salt and pepper, to taste. Stir in 1 beaten egg or a little milk. Press the stuffing into the centre of the heart and stitch the openings with coarse thread to close. Wrap in greased baking paper, tie securely with kitchen string and bake in a 180°C oven, basting frequently. A large heart takes about 1 hour 30 minutes to cook. Serve with gravy.

Ox Tail

Wash an ox tail and cut it into joints. Wash, peel and slice 2 carrots and 1 onion. Roll the ox tail in 50 g (⅓ cup) flour to coat. Melt 55 g butter in a saucepan. Fry the meat until browned on all sides. Place the meat in a casserole dish. Fry the vegetables and add them to the dish. Stir the remaining flour into the hot dripping in the pan. Gradually add 875 ml (3½ cups) stock, stirring constantly. Bring to the boil. Add 1 tablespoon tomato sauce, ½ teaspoon celery salt and season with salt and pepper. Pour the stock into the dish, cover and cook in a 180°C oven. Bring to the boil, then reduce the temperature and simmer for 2½–3 hours. Skim off any fat that rises before serving.

Ox Tongue

Soak the ox tongue in cold water for a few hours. Wash it well in fresh water and trim the root. Place in a saucepan with a bunch of herbs, cover with water and bring to the boil, removing any scum that rises to the surface. Simmer gently for 3–4 hours, or until the tongue is tender — the time it takes will depend on the size of the meat. Skin the tongue while hot; trim the root, removing any small bones. If to be eaten hot, brush it over with glaze. Serve on a hot dish with cooked vegetables or slices of lemon and sprigs of parsley. To serve this dish cold, roll the tongue into a snake and place in a cake tin with a weight over the top and refrigerate overnight.

Variation You can make this dish using sheep's tongue instead. Proceed in the same manner as for the ox tongue, but allow a shorter time for cooking. When tender, remove the skin, cut in halves lengthways, arrange in a meat press or round, plain mould with weights on top.

Pickled Leg of Pork

Mix together 15 g powdered saltpetre (these days you can substitute pure crystalline ascorbic acid at a rate of 1 g for every 2 kg meat), 625 g (2 cups) salt and 110 g (½ cup) sugar. Rub this mixture into the leg of pork and turn it daily for 14 days, when it will be ready for use. If the weather is hot, instead of rubbing it dry, make a pickle of salt and water that is strong enough to float an egg on the surface, and pour it over the pork. When you require it for boiling, wash the pork with cold water and put it in a saucepan with as much water as will cover it. When it boils, skim any scum that rises to the surface. Reduce the heat and boil slowly but constantly for 2 hours or longer, according to the size of the joint. Serve with green vegetables.

Pork Brawn

Buy a 900 g pork fillet. Rub salt and pepper all over the pork and fry lightly in butter on both sides in order to close the pores and keep the meat juicy. Add a chopped onion and chopped mint to the pan and continue frying for a while. Add 600 ml water or stock and stew until cooked. Remove the meat from the pan and add a little extra water to the cooking juices. Set aside to cool.

When the stock is quite cold, remove the fat carefully and pour the liquid through a muslin cloth. There should be about 600 ml liquid. Put in a saucepan and add a little wine vinegar or lemon juice, with salt to taste. Dissolve 1 tablespoon gelatine in a little hot water and add to the liquid. Pour a little of the liquid into a mould and allow it to almost set. Place slices of hard-boiled egg and cucumber into the base, then a layer of thickly sliced pork. Continue this layering to build up the brawn. When the shape is almost full, pour in the liquid — it should cover the other ingredients. Turn out after about 20 minutes and serve with a cold tomato sauce and potato flakes.

Pork Rissoles with Apples

Roughly chop 225 g stale bread and 625 g cold roast pork. Grind a small blade of mace and finely grate the zest of ½ lemon. Mix the meat and bread in a bowl with 1 teaspoon chopped parsley, 3 finely chopped sage leaves and a pinch of ground nutmeg. Stir through 2 teaspoons tomato sauce and then combine in a food processor. Mash 115 g cold boiled potatoes and mix them with the mince. Moisten with 2 tablespoons gravy and set aside for 1 hour. Form the meat mixture into rissoles and fry on both sides until golden brown. Drain well on paper towel. Arrange the rissoles on a plate with the mashed potatoes and serve with fried or baked apples.

Baked Apple Rings

Wipe and core 4 apples, then cut into thick slices.
Place in a buttered baking dish. Put 110 g (½ cup) sugar in a saucepan
with 125 ml (½ cup) water, ½ cinnamon stick and 1 teaspoon cloves
and bring to the boil. Reduce the heat and simmer for 5 minutes.
Stir in 1 tablespoon lemon juice and strain the hot syrup over the apples.
Bake until tender, basting occasionally. These apple rings are delicious,
served with cold pork or ham.

Glazing Cold Meats

Cold Meat Glaze

Put 875 ml (3½ cups) stock in a saucepan with 1 teaspoon powdered gelatine which has been pre-soaked in a little cold water. Boil briskly until reduced to half quantity, add a few drops of brown food colouring, and when finished place in a jar. When needed, stand jar in basin of hot water to liquefy. Brush the glaze over the cold joint you wish to serve and leave it to set. If the stock is or has jellied it would not need gelatine. Rich meat stock should be a jelly and would only need the colouring.

Once glazed, cold meats make an appealing dish to serve with a few simple garnishes:

- **COLD MUTTON**: is greatly improved by glazing. Brush meat with glaze and let it set, then decorate with finely chopped aspic jelly and sprigs of parsley.
- **COLD CORNED BEEF**: can be garnished with boiled carrots and parsnips that have been cut into fancy shapes or alternate mounds of carrots and turnips cut into dice. Add fringe of parsley.
- **COLD PORK**: can be garnished with slices of beetroot and little white pickled onions or little mounds of apple jelly and the little onions placed alternately round.
- **COLD ROAST VEAL**: can be garnished after glazing it and surround it with slices of ham and forcemeat balls of veal seasoning.
- **COLD CUTLETS**: can be garnished with a frill on each and arranged in the centre of a dish, just overlapping each other. Surround with a border of cold boiled peas tossed in mayonnaise.
- **COLD ROAST POULTRY AND GAME**: is greatly improved by a coating of glaze. Garnish with watercress and beetroot. Sprinkle chopped aspic jelly on the glaze and pipe savoury cream in a neat design. To make savoury cream, put ½ cup of cream in a bowl with a pinch of salt and a sprinkle of white pepper. Whip until thick. Use it by filling an icing syringe and piping a pattern on the set glaze. Butter beaten to a cream and seasoned may be used if preferred.
- **COLD OX TONGUE**: can be glazed and left to set. Fill a syringe with savoury cream (see above) and design a lattice work of cream on the tongue. Decorate with diamonds of aspic jelly and finish with a frilled paper collar.

Pork Sausages and Apples

Peel, core and slice 225 g apples. Mix a little salt and pepper with 2 tablespoons flour on a plate. Roll 625 g pork sausages in the flour to coat. Heat 1½ tablespoons oil in a saucepan and fry 1 sliced onion until lightly browned. Remove and place it in a casserole dish. Fry the sausages until browned. Add half the sliced apples over the onion in the dish and layer with the chopped sausages. Add the remaining apples. Season each layer with salt and pepper. Pour in 375 ml (1½ cups) stock and gravy browning (Gravox). Cover and cook in 180°C oven for about 1 hour.

Potato Meat Pie

Finely chop some cooked beef or lamb. Add gravy, finely chopped onion, salt and cayenne pepper and mix well. Put into a greased pie dish. Mash some potato with a little butter, milk, salt, and cayenne pepper. Spoon the potato over the meat. Place in a 220°C oven to heat through and brown the potato. Serve at once.

Pot Roast of Beef

Coat 1.8 kg round or topside beef with 40 g (¼ cup) plain flour. Melt 3 tablespoons butter in a frying pan and brown the meat on all sides. Season with salt and pepper. Transfer to a large saucepan with any juices and add 250 ml (1 cup) water. Cover and gently simmer over low heat, replacing the water as necessary. Serve with brown gravy and vegetables.

Porterhouse Steak

Brush 450 g steak on both sides with olive oil. Grill in the usual way. Place on a hot serving plate and sprinkle with salt and cayenne pepper. Serve immediately with horseradish sauce.

Roast Lamb

Lay the meat in a baking dish in a 200°C oven, and baste plentifully from the time it is being warmed through until ready to send to the table. Allow for 2–2½ hours for 4.5 kg of meat. Scatter a little flour over the meat 20 minutes before taking it out of the oven to brown it nicely.

Roast Lamb, Spanish-Style

Take a leg of lamb; pierce the meat with a skewer and insert small bits of garlic (using not more than 1 clove of garlic to 1.8 kg meat). Mix some finely chopped mint leaves with 3 tablespoons olive oil, 1 tablespoon vinegar or lemon juice, a little Worcestershire sauce, salt, pepper and 2 teaspoons sugar. Stir together and add enough flour to make a paste, then cover the meat all over. Put it in a baking tray with 2 tablespoons oil and cook in a 240°C oven until a crust is formed, then lower the heat. Baste for about 2 hours, or until cooked.

Roast Leg of Pork

Choose a small leg of fine young pork, cut a slit in the knuckle with a sharp knife and fill with a little chopped sage and onion; season. When half cooked, score the skin of the pork in slices, but do not cut deeper that the outer rind. Apple sauce and potatoes should be served with it. The gravy is to be made the same way as for beef roast and adding a spoonful of flour stirred with enough water to make the right consistency.

Roast Mutton, French-Style

Bone and trim 1 small leg of mutton and season. Scatter over some chopped parsley and French shallots. Tie up with kitchen string and place in a roasting tin with slices of carrot and onion and 55 g butter. Place in a 220°C oven for 20 minutes, basting regularly. Reduce the temperature and finish roasting in a slightly cooler oven until tender. Pour off the fat and make gravy in the usual way. Add a ¼ teaspoon of Worcestershire sauce to the gravy. Mutton cooked in this way is delicious.

Roast Stuffed Crown of Lamb

Trim 2 whole loins of lamb (with bones in) into neat cutlets — the bones should be uniform in height, keeping each loin in one piece. Form into a crown shape, with the ribs turned out and the cutlet bones upwards. Tie securely in position with kitchen string. Wrap each bone in foil to prevent them from burning. Lift into baking dish. Melt a little butter in a frying pan and lightly sauté 1 tablespoon chopped shallots and 12 button mushrooms. Remove from the heat and place in a bowl. Add 300 g (3 cups) dry breadcrumbs, 1 teaspoon thyme and 1 tablespoon butter. Season to taste with salt and cayenne pepper. Add 2 egg yolks and 3 tablespoons milk or cream and mix to form a thick purée. Whisk 2 egg whites to stiff peaks and fold in lightly. Pour into the crown of lamb. Spread the outer surface of the bones with 115 g melted butter. Cover with baking paper and bake for 1–1½ hours, according to size, basting frequently. Remove the paper 5 minutes before serving. Lift onto a serving dish, remove the foil and replace with cutlet frills. Serve with green peas, roast potato balls and gravy.

When cooking rice, add a few drops of lemon juice — it will improve the flavour and the grains will keep separate.

Roast Suckling Pig

Add 1 finely chopped apple to a sage and onion stuffing and when cooked, add 2 potatoes that have been mashed. Fill the body of the pig with stuffing and sew up. Put in kneeling position in baking tray, the front feet bent under, the hind legs forward. Brush all over with olive oil or melted butter. Place a nicely peeled raw potato in the mouth. Place in a 220°C oven for 10 minutes, then reduce the heat to 180°C and cook slowly 3–3½ hours, basting frequently. Serve with vegetables, gravy and Apple Sauce (see recipe, page 105).

Roast Veal

Lay 1.3–1.8 kg boned shoulder of veal, skin side down, on a clean work surface. Pound the meat to flatten and set aside while making the stuffing. Mix together 115 g suet or 50 g butter with 225 g (2¼ cups) dry breadcrumbs, then stir in 1 tablespoon chopped parsley, the grated zest of 1 lemon and 1 well-beaten egg. Season with salt and pepper and add a little milk to moisten if needed. Spread the stuffing over the flattened veal and roll into a neat log. Secure with kitchen string. Dredge with flour and put the roll into a baking dish with a little oil. Cook for 1 hour 30 minutes, basting frequently. To serve, place on a hot dish, remove the string and pour over parsley sauce or thick brown gravy.

Rolled Mutton Flap

Take a boned flap of mutton, spread sausage meat over the inner side of the flap and season with salt and pepper. Roll the flap as you would a roly poly, wrap it in several layers of muslin, tie securely at 5 cm intervals, put into boiling water and boil hard for a few minutes, then gently for about 3 hours. When the muslin is taken off the meat is in a solid roll. It is nice served cold with salads.

Rolled Steak and Yorkshire Pudding Puffs

Rub 1 teaspoon butter into 100 g (1 cup) dry breadcrumbs. Add 1 small finely chopped onion, a little thyme and salt and pepper, to taste. Spread over 900 g lean steak fillets. Roll each steak up and secure with a skewer. Dust with a little flour and a pinch of sugar (the sugar imparts a delicious flavour and will make a nice brown gravy). Place the rolled meat in a baking dish and roast in a 180°C oven for 30–40 minutes. While the steak is roasting, make a Yorkshire Pudding batter by combining 1 egg yolk with 300 ml milk and 150 g (1 cup) self-raising flour. Season with a pinch of salt and stir until smooth. About 20 minutes before the steak is cooked, pour 2 teaspoons of batter into the dish at a time, leaving a space between each. When cooked, place the steak on individual plates with a few Yorkshire Pudding puffs and serve with brown gravy.

Rolls of Meat and Potato

For this recipe you need to use mince and scraps of cold meat from a ham or fowl — the greater the variety of meat used the better the result. Season the meats with salt, pepper, curry powder, tomato sauce or any flavouring you wish, including some green herbs. Make a crust with cold potatoes, mashed with a little milk, and thickened with a little flour. Roll out the potato on a floured board and cut into squares. Put a spoonful of the mince, moistened with a little gravy or milk, in the centre of each potato square. Roll up and bake in a 200°C oven for 30 minutes.

Savoury Round of Beef

Take 1.3–1.8 kg topside beef that is rolled into a neat compact joint — ask your butcher to do this. Take 225 g streaky bacon and, with a pair of scissors, cut it into strips about 5 mm wide and 10 cm long. Pierce a hole in a lean portion of the beef with a sharp-pointed wooden skewer and fill with a strip of bacon. Make holes in this way all over the beef and use up the bacon. Season the meat and roast in the usual way, basting frequently.

Sheep's Tongue in Jelly

Boil 3 sheep's tongues until tender, then skin them and cut each into two or more slices. Arrange in a mould. Dissolve 1 tablespoon gelatine in 600 ml stock and season with salt and pepper. Pour over the tongues and allow to set. Slice and serve.

Spiced Mutton Casserole

Take a small leg of mutton and bone it. Mix together ½ teaspoon ground nutmeg and ½ teaspoon cinnamon and dust the meat. Slice 1 onion. Lay half of the onion slices in the bottom of a casserole dish, put in the meat, and cover with the remaining onion, 1 crushed bay leaf, 1 garlic clove and a few cloves. Take 185 g (1 cup) brown sugar, add it to 250 ml (1 cup) vinegar and pour over the meat. Set aside overnight, turning occasionally. The next day, add a little water and cook in a 150°C oven for 2 hours or until tender. There should be just enough pan juices to make a gravy. Serve with potato dumplings.

Spiced Roast Lamb

Wipe 1.8 kg shoulder of lamb clean with a damp cloth. Rub with salt, pepper and flour, then put into a baking dish with 6 cloves, 12 allspice berries, 3 tablespoons sugar, 80 ml (⅓ cup) vinegar and 80 ml (⅓ cup) water and place in 220°C oven for 15 minutes to brown. Cover and cook until tender, adding more water as needed. Chop onions, carrots and potatoes into cubes and cook in boiling salted water until tender, but not soft. Drain carefully. Heat 125 ml (½ cup) olive oil in a frying pan and sauté the vegetables for 10 minutes until golden. Serve with the lamb and garnish with chopped parsley.

Steak and Kidney Pudding

Make 225 g Suet Pastry in the usual way (see recipe, page 287). Roll out and line a round baking dish with two-thirds of the pastry, pressing into the base and side. Cut 625 g steak and 2 sheep's kidneys into small cubes. Finely chop 1 onion and mix together with 1 tablespoon chopped parsley. Rub 1 tablespoon flour over the meat, season with salt and pepper and mix together with the onion and parsley. Add 225 ml water, stirring well to combine. Spoon into the pastry case. Roll out the remaining pastry and cover the pie, pressing the edges to seal. Steam in a steamer for 2½ hours or until cooked.

Savoury Steak Casserole

Place 625–900 g rump steak in a casserole dish. In a separate bowl, mix together 1 tablespoon chopped onion, 1 teaspoon mixed dried herbs, 1 teaspoon chopped capers, 1 teaspoon sugar, 1 teaspoon melted butter, 2 tablespoon vinegar, 2 tablespoons Worcestershire sauce and 2 tablespoons tomato sauce. Season with salt and pepper and stir through. Pour this over the steak and allow to stand for 1 hour for the flavours to develop. Cover and cook slowly in a 180°C oven for about 45 minutes, or until the steak is tender. Remove all traces of fat from the meat and the gravy. Cut 1 whole gherkin into slices and garnish the casserole with the gherkin and a few capers.

Shoulder of Mutton with Kidney Stuffing

Bone 1 shoulder of mutton. To make the stuffing, finely chop 3 sheep's kidneys, 1 slice of bacon and 1 onion. Mix in a bowl with 100 g (1 cup) breadcrumbs, a little parsley and thyme and season with salt and cayenne pepper. Stir in 1 egg and mix thoroughly. Place the stuffing in the cavity where the bone was removed, roll up and tie with kitchen string. Bake in a 200°C oven and allow 15 minutes for every 450 g meat, with 10 minutes over if necessary. Serve with gravy. When mushrooms are in season, serve some stewed, adding some of the juice to the gravy.

Steak Diane

With a meat mallet pound the steaks carefully until they are 5 mm thick. Rub with garlic cloves and lightly flour each steak. Cook in a thick-bottomed frying pan in butter, quickly browning on each side. Allow for 2 teaspoons lemon juice and 1 teaspoon Worcestershire sauce per person. Add to the pan and cook slowly for 2 minutes on each side. Serve immediately, drizzled with the juice from the pan. If desired, a little brandy or wine may be added to the sauce.

Steak Stuffed with Apples

Peel, core and slice 2 apples and add to a bowl with 2 teaspoons brown sugar and a little butter. Season with salt and pepper. Take 625 g steak and make a pocket in each steak; fill with the apple mixture. Melt 55 g butter, rub well into steak and roll to coat in breadcrumbs. Put in small baking dish, cover with baking paper and cook in a 180°C oven for 1 hour 30 minutes. Remove the paper and cook until brown. Served with diced carrots fried in butter, mashed potatoes and green peas. This makes a tasty dinner.

Stewed Steak

Trim 225 g thick steak and leave it whole or cut into pieces about 10 cm square. Finely chop ¼ apple and 1 onion and cut 1 small carrot into dice. Heat 15 g dripping in a frying pan and cook the steak until brown. Remove the steak from the pan and add the onion, apples and carrot. Dust with 2 teaspoons flour and toss to coat. Pour in 225 ml water and bring to the boil. Return the steak to the pan, reduce the heat to low and simmer for 2 hours. Garnish with chopped parsley, season to taste, and serve.

Surprise Meat Balls

For every 450 g of minced beef or any other kind of leftover meat, mix in 185 g (1½ cups) grated cheese, juice of 1 lemon, 2 tablespoons of chopped gherkins or olives, 100 g (1 cup) breadcrumbs, 1 lightly beaten egg. Season the mixture with salt and pepper and stir in 125 ml (½ cup) milk.

Use your hands to thoroughly combine the ingredients, then shape into balls and bake in a 180°C oven for 30 minutes, or until cooked through. Serve hot or cold.

Tripe and Onions

Peel 5–6 onions. Wash 900 g tripe, place it in a saucepan, cover with cold water and bring to the boil. Drain away the water. Repeat this blanching process. Return the tripe to the saucepan and cover with 1.8 litres cold water. Add the onions to the pan and season with salt and pepper. Cover and bring to the boil, then reduce the heat and simmer for about 3 hours, or until the tripe is tender. Strain and reserve 250 ml (1 cup) of the cooking liquid. Chop the tripe into pieces about 4 cm square. Roughly chop the onions. Melt 55 g butter in a saucepan. Add 50 g (1/3 cup) flour and stir to a paste. Remove from the heat and gradually stir in 600 ml milk and the reserved cooking liquid. Return to the heat and stir until the mixture boils. Add the tripe and onions and simmer for 15 minutes. Serve immediately.

Veal and Ham Pie

Dust 900 g veal fillets with plain flour to coat and season with salt and pepper. Cut 3–4 hard-boiled eggs into slices. Layer 225 g sliced ham or bacon into a round baking dish with the egg slices and veal fillets, sprinkling a little chopped parsley between each layer. Continue layering until the dish is full. Sprinkle a little flour over the top and pour in 300 ml stock or water and a squeeze of lemon juice to make a gravy in the pie. Cover with 225 g Puff Pastry (see recipe, page 286). Bake in a 200°C oven until the pastry is cooked. Remove from the oven and sit on top of the oven over high heat to finish cooking the meat at a gentle simmer.

Veal Birds with Raisin Stuffing

Put 600 g (1/2 cup) raisins in a bowl with 1/2 teaspoon salt, 1/4 teaspoon pepper and 1 beaten egg yolk. Add 200 g (2 cups) stale day-old breadcrumbs and mix to combine. Melt 2 tablespoons butter in 60 ml (1/4 cup) hot water and pour over the mixture in the bowl, stirring well. Cut 450 g veal escallopes into 5–6 square pieces and put a spoonful of stuffing in the centre of each; roll up and tie with kitchen string, season with salt and pepper and place in a baking tray. Put a piece of butter on top of each 'bird', add hot water to cover the bottom of the dish and roast until tender.

Veal Cutlets

Mix some chopped parsley and a little grated lemon zest into 3 tablespoons breadcrumbs. Cut 450 g veal cutlets into rounds and pound to flatten the meat. Roll each piece of meat in 1 tablespoon flour to coat, then dip in egg wash and roll to coat in the seasoned breadcrumbs. Heat 2 tablespoons oil in a frying pan and cook the cutlets for about 10–15 minutes, or until tender, turning frequently. Remove the rind from 2 bacon slices, cut into 5 cm pieces, thread onto a skewer, and grill or bake in the oven until cooked. Serve the cutlets on a bed of mashed potatoes, garnish with the rolls of bacon and Brown Sauce (see recipe, page 106).

Veal Goulash

Chop 625 g veal fillets into pieces. Heat a little hot butter in a frying pan and cook the veal until brown. Remove from the pan. Add 2 chopped onions, 2 chopped carrots, 1 chopped celery stick and 1 finely chopped garlic clove. Season with 1 tablespoon paprika and cook slowly for 5 minutes. Finely chop 1 red and 1 green capsicum and add to the pan with 3 tablespoons flour and 500 ml (2 cups) stock. Bring to the boil and season with salt and pepper. Reduce the heat, return the veal to the pan and cook slowly until tender. Allow the liquid to reduce until slightly thickened, then add 250 g (1 cup) sour cream and serve.

Veal Hawaiian

Chop 625 g veal fillets into pieces. Heat a little butter in a frying pan and cook the veal until brown. Transfer the veal to a casserole dish. Add 2 tablespoons flour to the butter in the pan and stir to make a paste. Add 250 ml (1 cup) dry white wine to the pan and enough water to make a thin sauce. Season with salt and pepper and pour over veal. Chop 4 slices pineapple into small pieces. Heat a little butter in a clean pan and cook the pineapple with 6 sliced mushrooms until tender. Add to the veal in the dish. Cook the casserole in a 180°C oven for about 1½ hours, or until tender and cooked through. Just before serving, add 125 g (½ cup) sour cream and stir through. Serve with steamed rice.

Sweetbreads and Brains

Brain Fritters

Cook 1–2 sets sheep or calf brains by dropping them into boiling salted water and simmering for 5 minutes. Drain them and allow to cool, and later cut them into pieces the size of walnuts. To make the batter, separate 1 egg. Mix the yolk into 150 g (1 cup) self-raising flour and 1/2 teaspoon salt, then beat in 125 ml (1/2 cup) milk and 125 ml (1/2 cup) water (add a little more if too thick). Add 1 spoonful of hot oil, and carefully stir in the stiffly beaten egg white. Drain on paper towel and serve.

Crumbed Sweetbreads

Wash and skin of 2 sets sweetbreads. Put into a saucepan; cover with cold water and bring to the boil; drain, cover with 750 ml (3 cups) strained seasoned stock and simmer until tender. Drain and press the sweetbreads between two plates, with a heavy weight on top; leave until cold and firm. Trim and cut into neat pieces. Dip in seasoned flour, beaten egg and toss in dry breadcrumbs. Cook in hot oil until golden brown. Drain on paper towel and serve hot with tomato sauce.

Fricassée of Brains

Wash 4 sets of sheep's brains well and skin. Put in a saucepan, cover with cold water and simmer until cooked. Mix 1 tablespoon flour with 1 tablespoon butter, add to 600 ml boiling milk, and cook for a few minutes after adding salt and pepper, to taste. Remove the brains from the water, pour sauce over, garnish with shredded parsley and serve hot.

Kidney Toast

Soak 3 sheep's kidneys in water for 30 minutes, then skin and split them open and remove the core. Chop into small pieces, sprinkle with salt and pepper. Melt a little butter in a aucepan, and when hot, put in the chopped kidney and the juice of 1 lemon; cook gently for about 5 minutes, then stir in 1 well-beaten egg. Remove from the heat to set. Serve on buttered toast. Cayenne pepper, a dash, may be added.

Stewed Tripe and Onions

Cut 450 g thick tripe into pieces, wash in warm water, then place into a saucepan of cold water and bring to the boil; blanch the tripe. Pour this water off and place fresh cold water on the tripe, enough just to cover it, then let it cook gently and add 1 peeled, whole onion. Let this cook 1 hour, then take out the onion and chop it up and return it to the pan with a little milk. Moisten the flour with a little of the milk and thicken the stew with it, adding a little parsley and 30 g butter. If tripe is not tender, longer cooking is necessary; some of the stock may be poured off before adding to the milk.

International Cookery

Chicken and Almond Stir-fry

Heat a little oil in a frying pan and add 225 g whole blanched almonds and a pinch of salt. Lightly fry the almonds until golden and drain on paper towel. Dice 500 g chicken meat. Remove the stems from 225 g mushrooms and cut into slices. Cut 2 celery sticks into small pieces. Mix the diced chicken with 1 tablespoon soy sauce, 2 teaspoons brandy, 2 teaspoons cornflour and a pinch of salt. Stir well to coat the chicken. Heat 2 teaspoons oil in a frying pan and add 1 finely chopped garlic clove. Cook for 3–4 minutes. Add the chicken and stir briskly. When almost cooked, add the mushrooms, celery and almonds; cook for 5 minutes. Add 125 ml (½ cup) water and stir through.

Chinese One-pot Meal

Cut 450 g blade steak into 1 cm cubes. Finely chop 2 onions and 1 celery stick. Heat 2 tablespoons butter in a saucepan and cook the onion and celery until transparent. Add the steak and cook until the meat has browned. Add 110 g (½ cup) short-grain rice, 250 ml (1 cup) chicken stock, 310 ml (1¼ cups) tinned condensed cream of mushroom soup, 1 tablespoon soy sauce and 250 ml (1 cup) water. Bring to the boil. Reduce the heat, cover, and simmer for 45 minutes, or until tender, stirring often. Serve hot.

Fried Rice

Place 2 tablespoons oil in a saucepan and add 225 g shredded pork, cooking until brown. Add 925 g (5 cups) cooked short-grain rice and season with salt. Cook for 10 minutes, stirring constantly, then add 115 g peeled, cleaned prawns and mix well. Make a well in centre of the rice and drop in 1 whole egg. When nearly cooked, stir it into the rice. Mix 2 teaspoons soy sauce and 2 teaspoons water and add to rice with 45 g (¼ cup) finely chopped spring onion. Garnish with finely chopped ham.

Boiled Rice

Put 8 cups of water in a saucepan with 2 teaspoons salt and bring to the boil. Sprinkle in 220 g (1 cup) white short-grain rice. Keep boiling rapidly for 15 minutes, with the lid off. Tip the rice and any remaining water into a sieve over the sink. Do not rinse or stir the rice, simply shake the sieve and allow the rice to dry naturally. Makes 3 cups of cooked rice.

Prawn and Almond Stir-fry

Heat a little oil in a frying pan and fry 115 g (¾ cup) whole blanched almonds with a little salt. Set aside. Peel and clean 450 g raw king prawns, leaving the tails intact. Place 1 teaspoon grated ginger and 2 teaspoons cornflour in a bowl and add 1 teaspoon soy sauce, 1 teaspoon dry sherry and 125 ml (½ cup) water. Stir until smooth and combined and set aside. Fry the prawns in hot oil for 2 minutes, sprinkle with pepper, then add 1 finely chopped celery stick and stir for 3 minutes. Add the almonds, then pour over the sauce and bring to the boil. Serve immediately.

Prawn Cutlets

Peel and clean 450 g raw king prawns, leaving the tails intact. Butterfly each prawn so it can lie flat. Beat 1 egg in a bowl and place 100 g (1 cup) dry breadcrumbs in another bowl. Sprinkle the prawns with salt and dip them first into the egg wash and then roll to coat in the breadcrumbs. Deep-fry until crisp. Drain on paper towel.

Prawn, Lobster, Crab or Chicken Omelette

Wipe clean 55 g mushrooms and remove the stems, then slice into thin strips. Beat 3 eggs well, than add 185 ml (¾ cup) milk and a little salt, stirring well. Peel and clean 115 g prawns and remove the tails. Heat 2 teaspoons oil in a large frying pan and lightly fry the prawns, mushrooms and 3 tablespoons chopped tinned bamboo shoots. Add 45 g (¼ cup) finely chopped spring onion to the egg, season with pepper and pour into the pan. Fold in the usual way and serve. You can use lobster, crab or chicken instead of the prawns.

Spiced Beef

Cut 625 g skirt steak into 4 cm squares and season with salt. Place in a bowl and add 1 tablespoon soy sauce, 1 tablespoon brandy and 8 star anise. Place in a saucepan with enough water to just cover the meat and simmer for 3 hours, replacing the water as needed. Stir in 2 teaspoons cornflour to thicken the sauce, and serve.

Sweet and Sour Chicken or Pork

If using chicken, bone and shred the chicken, dip into a bowl of beaten egg, then roll in cornflour to coat. If using pork, cut 350 g pork fillet into 2.5 cm cubes, then dip in egg wash and roll to coat in cornflour. Cook in hot oil, and when cooked, add Sweet and Sour Sauce (see recipe, below) and stir well.

Sweet and Sour Fish

To make the sauce, heat a little oil in a frying pan and add 1 teaspoon grated ginger. In a bowl, mix together 2 tablespoons vinegar, 1½ tablespoons sugar, 2 teaspoons tomato sauce, 2 teaspoons cornflour and 1 teaspoon brandy. Stir until smooth, then add to the frying pan with 250 ml (1 cup) water and stir well. Meanwhile, slice 450 g skinless, boneless fish fillets into thin pieces. Beat 2 eggs in a bowl. Put 125 g (1 cup) cornflour on a plate. Dip the fish pieces first in the egg and then roll in the cornflour to coat. Heat 1 tablespoon oil in a frying pan and add the fish, stirring well for 4 minutes. Add sauce and stir for 2 minutes, then serve immediately.

Sweet and Sour Sauce

Dice 1 cup tinned, drained pineapple pieces. Mix together 2 tablespoons vinegar, 2 tablespoons sugar, 2 teaspoons tomato sauce, 2 teaspoons soy sauce and 2 teaspoons brandy with 1½ tablespoons cornflour and add 1 litre (4 cups) water, stirring well. Heat 1 teaspoon oil in a frying pan and add 2 teaspoons grated ginger and the pickles. Cook for 2 minutes, then add the vinegar mixture, stirring well. Bring to the boil, then add some finely chopped spring onion. The sauce is now ready for use.

Curries

The most delicious curries are made with fresh meat, but it is also one of the best ways of reheating cold meat and poultry. Here are some helpful tips before you start:

- Buy the best curry powder and paste for your curries — they are the cheapest in the end, and good curry cannot be made with poor or stale powder and paste.
- Curries made of fresh meat need very slow cooking; the meat must be tender and thoroughly impregnated with the curry flavour.
- Cooked meat should be put in the sauce and allowed to remain in it for not less than 1 hour.
- French shallots are used in curries in preference to onions. They are first fried in a little butter or fat, but be sparing with the fat, as a greasy curry is a spoilt one.
- Some enjoy a little garlic in curry, but it should be a very small quantity. It is so powerful that a scrap too much may spoil a whole dish. The safest way to use it is to just rub the casserole inside with a piece of cut garlic.
- All curries should contain a sweet and a sour element. This is accomplished by the blending of such things as lemon juice or vinegar with a sweet chutney or red currant jelly.
- The best utensil in which to make curry is a glazed earthenware pot or casserole.
- Coconut milk is a great improvement in curry, but when you see this ingredient mentioned in a recipe do not confound it with the liquid drawn from a coconut. It is an infusion that can be purchased in tins or made by scraping some of the white part of a coconut into a cup or basin, according to the quantity you require. Only just cover it with boiling water and leave in to soak for an hour, then squeeze the juice through muslin. Stir it into the curry just before serving.

Cold Meat Curry

Cut 625 g meat into small pieces, removing any skin or gristle. Finely chop 2 spring onions and fry them until golden brown in 55 g butter. Stir in 2 teaspoons curry powder, 1 teaspoon curry paste and 2 teaspoons rice flour and cook 5 minutes longer. Stir in 450 ml stock and simmer for 45 minutes. Stir in 1 teaspoon freshly squeezed lemon juice or vinegar, 2 teaspoons chutney and 150 ml coconut milk. Remove from the heat, put in the meat and let it remain in the curry for 1 hour, then make it very hot over gentle heat but on no account must it boil. Serve with a border of boiled rice.

Madras Curry

Melt 40 g butter in a frying pan and add 450 g cubed topside steak. Cook until brown all over, the add 1 chopped onion and fry until brown. Sprinkle in 1 tablespoon curry powder and 1 tablespoon flour, fry a little longer. Add 2 tablespoons desiccated coconut, 1 chopped apple, 1 chopped banana, 2 teaspoons chutney and 1 tablespoon sultanas, then stir in 300 ml milk or water. Stir until boiling, cover, then reduce the heat and simmer until the meat is tender. Add a little lemon juice and salt to taste. Serve with boiled rice and chutney.

To Boil Rice For Curry

Wash rice thoroughly until all cloudiness has disappeared. Drop into boiling salted water and boil rapidly, uncovered for about 15 minutes or until the rice is soft. Drain well in a strainer and pour cold water through the rice to separate the grains. Return to the saucepan in which it was cooked, and place on a warm part of the stove to reheat until ready to serve.

Curry Sauce

Peel 1 onion and 1 apple and cut into dice. Cut 1 banana into rounds. Heat 2 teaspoons oil in a saucepan and add the onion, apple and banana. Stir-fry for a few minutes, then add 2 teaspoons flour and 1 tablespoon curry powder, mixing well to combine. Add 500 ml (2 cups) water, stock or milk and stir until the mixture boils and thickens. Simmer for about 20 minutes. Add a pinch of salt, a dash of lemon juice, 1 tablespoon desiccated coconut, 2 teaspoons sugar and 1 tablespoon chutney. Add the cooked meat of your choice. Thoroughly reheat and serve. The sauce can be strained, if liked, before adding the meat. The sauce is best made with milk if fish, prawns or lobster are used.

Curried Bananas

Put 45 g (1/2 cup) desiccated coconut in a bowl and pour over 300 ml milk; set aside for 1 hour to soak. Put in a saucepan with 2 tablespoons curry powder, 1 teaspoon sweet chutney, 1 teaspoon sugar and enough cayenne pepper and salt, to taste. Peel and slice 6 green bananas and add to the curry. Simmer for 10–15 minutes and, just before serving, add 1 well-beaten egg and stir in. Serve hot with boiled rice.

Curried Chops

Remove any fat and gristle from 4–5 lamb neck chops. Heat 1 teaspoon oil in a frying pan and brown the chops on both sides. Remove from the pan. Add 1 small chopped onion to the pan with 1 small chopped apple and stir-fry until brown. Add 1 tablespoon flour, 1 tablespoon curry powder, 1 teaspoon salt, 1 teaspoon sugar and 1/2 teaspoon mustard; stir until well browned. Add 375 ml (1 1/2 cups) water and bring to the boil. Return the chops to the saucepan, simmer in the sauce until tender. Serve on a hot dish with a border of cooked rice. Garnish with lemon and hard-boiled egg yolk, rubbed through a sieve.

Curried Eggs

Hard-boil 3 eggs. Heat 2 teaspoons butter in a frying pan and fry a little chopped onion until brown. Add 2 teaspoons curry powder and 2 teaspoons flour, and cook for a few minutes, stirring all the time. Add 2 teaspoons desiccated coconut, 300 ml milk and a pinch of salt. Bring to the boil, the reduce the heat and simmer for 30 minutes. Shell the eggs, cut each in quarters and add to the curry sauce to heat through. Serve in a hot dish with a border of boiled rice.

Singapore Fruit Curry

Melt 225 g butter in a saucepan and add 150 g (1 cup) flour, mixing to form a paste. Add 2–3 drops Tabasco sauce and 2 tablespoons tomato purée. Mix in 2 tablespoons curry powder and 2 tablespoons chutney. Depending on which fruits you are using, add the strained juice of tinned pineapples, apricots, peaches, pears or cherries and stir to achieve a creamy consistency. Chop the fruit into cubes and add to the pan. Serve with rice, desiccated coconut, chopped almonds and poppadams.

Pickles and Chutneys

Apple Chutney

2.7 kg apples, 1 large onion, 1 small chopped garlic clove, 750 ml vinegar,
900 g (4 cups) brown sugar, 450 g (3²/₃ cups) raisins,
450 g (3 cups) currants, 115 g salt, 2 teaspoons ground ginger,
2 teaspoons allspice, 1 teaspoon black pepper, 1 teaspoon white pepper,
1 teaspoon cayenne pepper, 1 teaspoon cloves

Core and chop the apples and peel and chop the onion. Put the apples and onion in a saucepan with a little water and boil until soft. Add the remaining ingredients, reduce the heat and simmer for 1½ hours. Pour into sterilised jars and seal securely when cool. Will keep indefinitely.

Apricot Chutney 1

12 cm piece (115 g) young ginger, 1 seeded red chilli, 3 garlic cloves,
900 g (2³/₄ cups) apricot jam, 225 g (1 cup) sugar,
3 teaspoons salt, 1.2 litres vinegar

Pound the ginger, chilli and garlic in a mortar using a pestle, to create a paste. Put the jam, sugar and salt in a saucepan, then stir in the paste and vinegar. Bring to the boil, then reduce the heat and simmer for 15 minutes. Pour into sterilised jars and seal securely when cool.

Apricot Chutney 2

1.8 kg apricots, 1.8 kg (8 cups) sugar, 450 g (3²/₃ cups) sultanas,
6 garlic cloves, 4 cm piece (30 g) young ginger, 3 teaspoons cayenne pepper,
3 cloves, 250 ml (1 cup) vinegar, 1 tablespoon salt

Stone the apricots and place in a saucepan with the sugar, sultanas, finely chopped garlic, grated ginger, cayenne pepper and cloves. Boil to a jam, then add the vinegar and salt and boil for 10 minutes. Add more vinegar if the chutney is too thick. Pour into sterilised jars and seal securely when cool.

Brandy Plums

Plums, sugar, brandy

Choose choice fruit and not too ripe. Prick the plums with a knife and cook in boiling water until soft. Refresh the plums in a bowl of cold water. Drain and prepare a syrup. Put the water and sugar in a saucepan over medium heat — allow 350 g (1½ cups) sugar for every 600 ml water (you can reserve and measure the water used from cooking the plums). Cook until bubbles appear on the surface. Add the fruit and bring to the boil. Remove from the heat and add 150 ml brandy for each 600 ml of syrup. Put the fruit into sterilised bottles and pour the syrup over. Seal securely when cool.

Dried Fruit Chutney

450 g (2½ cups) dried peaches, 450 g (2½ cups) dried apricots,
450 g (2½ cups) pitted dates, 450 g (3²/₃ cups) raisins, 1.5 litres (6 cups) vinegar,
440 g (2 cups) sugar, 1½ teaspoons salt, ½ teaspoon cayenne pepper,
½ teaspoon ground ginger, ½ teaspoon cloves (in a muslin bag), ½ garlic clove

Soak the dried peaches and apricots in cold water for 6 hours, drain, then chop. Chop the dates and halve the raisins. Put the peaches and apricots with the soaking liquid into a saucepan and add the remaining ingredients. Bring to the boil, then reduce the heat and simmer for 2–2½ hours, stirring occasionally to prevent burning. Pour into sterilised jars and seal securely when cool.

Dried Peach Chutney

900 g (5 cups) dried peaches, 1 onion, 350 g (1½ cups) sugar,
6 garlic cloves, 1 tablespoon peppercorns, 1 tablespoon cinnamon,
1 nutmeg, 1.2 litres vinegar, 1 clove, 225 g (1¾ cups) raisins, 3 small chillies

Soak the peaches overnight, drain and finely chop. Peel and slice the onion. Put the onion, sugar, chopped garlic, spices and 1½ teaspoons salt in an enamel saucepan with the nutmeg and bring to a simmer for 12 minutes. Add the peaches, raisins and shredded chillies; boil gently until the consistency of thick cream. Pour into sterilised jars and seal securely when cool.

Fruit Chutney

900 g tomatoes, 225 g apples, 225 g quinces, 225 g onions, 625 g sugar,
115 g (1 cup) sultanas, 115 g (¾ cup) currants, 1 teaspoon cayenne pepper,
1 tablespoon salt, 1 tablespoon cloves, 250 ml (1 cup) vinegar

Scald the tomatoes, peel them and roughly chop the flesh. Core the apples and quinces and peel and chop the onions. Put all the ingredients in a large saucepan with the enough vinegar to just cover. Bring to the boil. Reduce the heat and continue to simmer until the chutney is a nice reddish colour. Pour into sterilised jars and seal securely when cool.

Green Fig Preserve

625 g green figs, 440 g (2 cups) sugar, finely grated zest of ½ lemon,
125 ml (½ cup) port wine, ginger

Wash and dry the figs and set aside. Make a syrup by boiling the sugar with 125 ml (½ cup) water, the lemon zest and port wine; remove any scum that rises to the surface. Add the figs, reduce the heat and simmer until tender; drop in a few pieces of ginger and simmer until the figs are a dark colour, but not broken. Gently remove the figs, increase the heat and boil the syrup for 5 minutes, or until thickened slightly. Pour the syrup and figs into sterilised jars and seal securely when cool.

Green Tomato Chutney

450 g green tomatoes, 3 large apples, 3 large onions,
600 ml vinegar, 450 g (2 cups) sugar, ½ teaspoon cayenne pepper,
1 teaspoon ground cloves, 1 teaspoon cinnamon

Slice the tomatoes and sprinkle salt; let stand overnight. Next morning, boil in the juice that formed during the night. Add the sliced apples, onions, vinegar, sugar and spices and cook until tender. Pour into sterilised jars and seal securely when cool.

Green Tomato Pickles

3.6 kg green tomatoes, 2 teaspoons allspice berries,
2 teaspoons peppercorns, 2 teaspoons cloves, 1.2 litres vinegar,
1 tablespoon treacle, 1 tablespoon mustard powder, 2 teaspoons ground ginger,
2 teaspoons curry powder, 460 g (2 cups) brown sugar, 75 g (½ cup) plain flour,
1 tablespoon turmeric, extra vinegar

Slice the green tomatoes and sprinkle with salt. Set aside for 12 hours, then drain. Wrap the allspice, peppercorns and cloves in a piece of muslin and tie securely. Boil the vinegar and treacle in a saucepan with the tomatoes and add the spices. Mix the mustard, ginger, curry powder, sugar, flour and turmeric in a bowl. Add a little extra vinegar mixture to make a paste, then pour into the pan and cook for 20 minutes. Pour into sterilised jars and seal securely when cool. Cauliflower can be made up in the same way.

Indian Chutney 1

4.5 kg green apples, 2 pineapples, 115 g salt, 175 g (1 cup) preserved ginger,
1 tablespoon cinnamon, 1 tablespoon ground cloves, 450 g (3⅔ cups) sultanas,
1.3 kg (5⅔ cups) brown sugar, 1 litre brown vinegar

Core and roughly chop the apples and put in a saucepan with 1.8 litres water. Bring to the boil, then reduce the heat and simmer until the apples are half cooked. Add all the other ingredients, last of all put in the vinegar. Boil until the apples fall apart and the mixture is thickened. Pour into sterilised jars and seal securely when cool.

Indian Chutney 2

625 g green apples, 175 g (³/4 cup) brown sugar, 600 ml vinegar,
3 chopped garlic cloves, ¹/2 finely chopped onion, 12 cm piece (115 g) ginger,
1 dried red chilli, 115 g (1 cup) raisins, 55 g (¹/4 cup) mustard seeds

Peel, core and chop the apples and put them in an earthenware jar. Dissolve the sugar in 2 tablespoons of boiling water and add it to the apples, then pour the vinegar over. Stand the jar in a 180°C (350°F/Gas 4) oven and cook until the apples are soft. Allow to cool. Peel, finely chop and pound the ginger then add to the apples with the garlic, onion, ginger, chilli, raisins, mustard seeds and 115 g salt; mix well. Pour into sterilised jars and seal securely when cool. Leave for 1 month before use.

Indian Chutney 3

12 large apples, 450 g (2¹/2 cups) pitted dates, 115 g onions,
115 g (1 cup) raisins, 450 g (2 cups) sugar, 1.2 litres vinegar, 3 tablespoons
ground ginger, 1 tablespoon cayenne pepper, 1 teaspoon mustard powder

This recipe is credited with being over 100 years old and has a delicious flavour. Chop the apples, dates, onions, and raisins very fine. Put all the ingredients in a saucepan with 115 g salt and bring to a boil. Reduce the heat and simmer until soft. Pour into sterilised jars and seal securely when cool.

Lemon Chutney

4 large lemons, 225 g onions, 450 ml malt vinegar, 450 g (2 cups) sugar,
115 g (1 cup) raisins, 2 tablespoons mustard seeds,
1 teaspoon ground ginger, 1 teaspoon cayenne pepper

Wash and slice lemons, removing the pips. Peel and chop the onions and put into a dish with the lemons; sprinkle with 2 tablespoons salt and leave for 24 hours. Transfer to a saucepan with the remaining ingredients, bring to the boil, then reduce the heat and simmer until quite tender. Pour into sterilised jars and seal securely when cool.

Melon Chutney 1

1.8 kg melon, 225 g (1¾ cups) raisins, 6 chopped garlic cloves,
6 cm piece chopped young ginger, 2–3 chillies or ½ teaspoon cayenne pepper,
500 ml (2 cups) vinegar, 625 g (2¾ cups) brown sugar

Remove the melon rind and dice the flesh. Put the melon, raisins, garlic, ginger, chillies and 1 tablespoon salt in a saucepan. Add just enough of the vinegar to cover and boil until the melon is soft and tender. Add the sugar and boil until thick and clear. Pour into sterilised jars and seal securely when cool.

Melon Chutney 2

4 kg melon, 450 g apples, 450 g (2⅓ cups) preserved ginger,
450 g (3⅔ cups) raisins, 1.8 kg (8 cups) sugar, 1.5 litres vinegar,
1 tablespoon dried chilli, 115 g salt, 3–4 tablespoons ground ginger

Remove the melon rind and cut the melon lengthways into thin fingers, about 7.5 cm long. Put in a saucepan with the remaining ingredients and bring to the boil. Reduce the heat and simmer for about 2½ hours. Pour into sterilised jars and seal securely when cool.

Melon Pickles

3.6 kg melon, 1.8 kg onion, 1.2 litres vinegar, 900 g sugar, 600 ml treacle,
2 tablespoons salt, 2 tablespoons mustard powder,
2 tablespoons curry powder, 2 tablespoons allspice, 1 tablespoon cloves,
1 tablespoon peppercorns, 75 g (½ cup) plain flour

Remove the melon rind and dice the flesh. Put the melon, onions, vinegar, sugar, treacle, salt, mustard and curry powder in a stockpot and bring to the boil. Wrap the allspice, cloves and peppercorns in a piece of muslin and tie securely with kitchen string. Add to the pot and boil until the melon is tender, then add the flour and cook for 20 minutes longer. Pour into sterilised jars and seal securely when cool.

Mint Chutney

1 handful fresh mint, 1 handful sultanas, 2 tablespoons sugar,
1 red chilli, 2 tablespoons vinegar

Pound the mint, sultanas, sugar, chilli and a little salt in a mortar using a pestle until soft and juicy. Transfer to a small serving bowl and stir in the vinegar. This is quickly made and nice to serve with cold meat, especially lamb or mutton.

Paw Paw Chutney

1.8 kg paw paw, lime water, 4 cm piece (30 g) ginger,
115 g (1/2 cup) sugar, 1 tablespoon cornflour, 3 small red chillies,
2 teaspoons tumeric, 1 teaspoon mustard powder, 1.2 litres vinegar

Cut the paw paw into strips and peel. Cover with weak lime water, leave for 12 hours, drain well. Put into a preserving pan, barely covering with cold water. Boil gently for 10 minutes then drain again. Bruise the ginger and place in a separate saucepan with the remaining ingredients and 3 tablespoons salt. Bring to the boil and as soon as it boils, stir in the paw paw and boil for 20 minutes. Pour into sterilised jars and seal securely when cool.

Peach Chutney

1.8 kg peaches, 450 g (3²/₃ cups) raisins, 450 g (2 cups) sugar,
1 seeded red chilli, 12 cm piece (115 g) green ginger,
1/2 finely chopped onion, 1.2 litres vinegar

Peel and slice the peaches and put in a saucepan with the raisins. Cook the fruit a little before adding the sugar to the pan, then bring to a boil, reduce the heat and simmer until a jam forms. Pass the chillies, ginger and onion through a mincer and add to the cooled jam with the vinegar and 2 tablespoons salt. Bring to the boil for a short time, stirring constantly when nearly cooked, to prevent sticking. Pour into sterilised jars and seal securely when cool.

Piccalilli

Small onions, French shallots, little green tomatoes, small runner and French beans, cauliflower, marrow, cucumbers, nasturtium seeds (in fact any vegetable can be used). To every 150 ml vinegar, allow 2 tablespoons turmeric, 1 teaspoon mixed whole spice, 60 g (¼ cup) caster sugar, 2 tablespoons mustard powder, 1 teaspoon cornflour

Peel the onions and French shallots, string the beans, stalk the tomatoes and remove the seeds, peel the cucumbers. Cut all the vegetables into small pieces and put them into a bowl, sprinkle with salt (about 1 tablespoon to every 125 g of vegetables), and leave them for 24 hours. Allow 2 tablespoons turmeric for every 150 ml vinegar and add to a preserving pan. Wrap the spices in a piece of muslin and tie securely with kitchen string. Add to the pan with the sugar and mustard. Add the strained vegetables and boil gently for 10 minutes. Mix the cornflour with a little extra vinegar to make a thin paste, add to the vegetables and cook a little, then remove the spices and boil for 4 minutes, stirring all the time. Turn into sterilised jars, and seal securely when cool.

Pickled Cucumbers

1 seeded red chilli, tinned vine leaves, cucumbers

Make a brine allowing for 350 g (2 cups) salt to 1.5 litres water. Stir the salt until it dissolves. Skim and discard the sediment. Wash the bird's-eye chillies, wrap them in a piece of muslin and tie securely with kitchen string. Put a layer of vine leaves on the bottom of a sterilized jar, then the chillies, and continue alternating layers of cucumbers and vine leaves until the jar is comfortably filled, leaving plenty of room for the cucumbers to swell and move about without bruising them. The cucumbers must always be kept covered with the brine. After 5–6 days it will be necessary to skim off the fermentation and adjust the quantity of brine. By this method cucumbers take 4 weeks to pickle.

Pickled Gherkins

Gherkins, vinegar, peppercorns, cloves, blade of mace

Cover the gherkins with salted water and let them remain in the brine for 3 days. Drain the gherkins and pack them into a sterilised jar. Boil sufficient vinegar to cover them — allow peppercorns, 4 cloves and 2 blades of mace to each 1.2 litres of vinegar. Boil the vinegar and spices for 10 minutes, then pour the liquid over the gherkins and let stand until next day. Drain the liquid off, boil it again and pour over the gherkins, leaving them until the following day. This process must be repeated until the gherkins are sufficiently green; the gherkins and vinegar should then be poured into sterilised jars and sealed securely when cool.

Pickled Onions

Onions, 2.4 litres white vinegar, 1 tablespoon peppercorns,
1 tablespoon cloves, 1 tablespoon ground mace, 1 tablespoon ground allspice

Place the onions in warm water for 10 minutes, then skin the onions and place them in a stockpot. Cover with water and a generous amount of salt and stand for 12 hours. Drain and place the onions in sterilised jars to cool. Put the vinegar in a saucepan with the peppercorns, cloves, mace, allspice and a little salt. Bring to the boil, then reduce the heat and simmer for 1 hour. Pour over the onions while hot. Seal securely when cool.

Plum Chutney

900 g plums, 6 garlic cloves, 225 g (1 cup) brown sugar, 600 ml vinegar,
2 tablespoons ground ginger, 450 g (3²/₃ cups) raisins

Stone the plums and peel and chop the garlic. Put the plums into a saucepan with the sugar and vinegar and simmer until tender. Add the garlic, ginger, raisins, 30 g (¼ cup) salt and 2 tablespoons pepper and continue cooking till the mixture thickens. Pour into sterilised jars and seal securely when cool.

Quince Chutney

1.3 kg quinces, 450 g (3²/₃ cups) raisins, 450 g (2¹/₂ cups) pitted dates,
6 red chillies, 9 cm piece (85 g) green ginger or 3 tablespoons ground ginger,
225 g (1³/₄ cups) salt, 1 tablespoon cayenne pepper, 1 tablespoon mustard,
1.2 litres vinegar, 450 g (2 cups) brown sugar

Core the quinces and finely chop with the raisins and dates. Chop the chillies and grate the ginger. Put all in a saucepan with the chilli, ginger, cayenne pepper, mustard, 600 ml of the vinegar and 225 g (1³/₄ cups) salt. Bring to the boil, then reduce the heat and simmer until it is a soft pulp. Boil the sugar in the remaining vinegar until clear. Let all get cold, then mix everything together. Pour into sterilised jars and seal securely. Set in the sun for 2–3 weeks. Mangoes, green apples or pears may also be used instead of quinces.

Red Cabbage Pickle

1 red cabbage, vinegar, peppercorns

Strip off the outer leaves of the cabbage and cut the head into quarters. Remove the hard stalk, shredding the remainder of the vegetable rather finely. Spread on a large flat dish and let it stand for 24 hours. Drain in a colander, dry with a clean tea towel, and place in large sterilised jars. Boil up the vinegar, adding 2 tablespoons whole black peppercorns for each 1.2 litres vinegar. Fill the jars, taking care that the cabbage is well covered. This pickle can be eaten in a day or two, and, in any case, should not be kept very long, as it quickly deteriorates.

Spiced Red Tomatoes

10 kg ripe red tomatoes, 2.5 litres (10 cups) vinegar,
3.6 kg (15¹/₂ cups) brown sugar, 4 tablespoons ground cinnamon,
4 tablespoons ground allspice, 2 tablespoons ground cloves

Scald the tomatoes, peel the skin and roughly chop the flesh. Place in a large stockpot over high heat and add the remaining ingredients. Bring to a boil, then reduce the heat and simmer until reduced and thickened. Fill hot, sterilised jars, and seal.

Sweet Green Tomato Pickles

4.5 kg green tomatoes, 450 g onions, 2.5 litres (10 cups) vinegar,
900 g–1.8kg (4–7³/4 cups) brown sugar, 2 teaspoons cloves,
2 teaspoons peppercorns, 1 cinnamon stick, 4–6 seeded red chillies

Slice the tomatoes and onions, sprinkle with salt and leave overnight. Drain off excess liquid into a saucepan and add the vinegar, sugar, cloves, peppercorns and cinnamon. Bring to the boil and add the chillies and strained tomatoes and onions. Simmer until tender. Pour into sterilised jars and seal securely when cool.

Sweet Pickled Plums

1.8 kg ripe plums, 600 ml white vinegar, 350 g sugar, 1 egg white,
2 teaspoons ground cinnamon, 2 teaspoons cloves

Wipe the fruit and prick it all over. Put it into a large jar. Boil the vinegar and sugar for 15 minutes. Beat the egg white and allow it to boil in the syrup for a few minutes, then strain. Pour the boiling syrup over the fruit and stand until next day. Pour off the syrup and boil again. Pour over the fruit and stand until next day. The third day, wrap the cinnamon and cloves in a piece of muslin. Boil the syrup and add the spices; cook for a 3 minutes, remove the spices and pour the syrup over the fruit. Seal securely when cool.

Sweet Pineapple Pickles

3.6 kg pineapple, 3 cinnamon sticks, 1¹/2 tablespoons cloves,
¹/4 cup allspice berries, 2¹/2 tablespoons peppercorns, 1.2 litres vinegar,
1.8 kg (7³/4 cups) brown sugar

Chop the pineapple flesh. Wrap the spices in a piece of muslin and tie with kitchen string. Add to a stockpot with the pineapple, vinegar and sugar. Boil until soft. Remove the fruit and boil down the syrup, then pour over fruit. Next morning, drain the syrup and boil down well with more spices loose in the syrup. Pour the syrup, fruit and loose and wrapped spices into sterilised jars and seal securely when cool.

Tomato Chutney

2.7 kg ripe tomatoes, 12 cm piece (115 g) ginger, 1.3 kg dates,
2 tablespoons cayenne pepper, 16 garlic cloves, 115 g onions,
450 g (2 cups) brown sugar, 3 litres vinegar

Scald the tomatoes, peel them and roughly chop the flesh. Bruise the ginger, wrap it in a piece of muslin and tie securely with kitchen string. Put in a saucepan with the remaining ingredients and 55 g (½ cup) salt and bring to the boil. Reduce the heat and simmer for 5 hours. Pour into sterilised jars and seal securely when cool.

Tomato Quetta

2.25 kg tomatoes, 6 garlic cloves, 4 cm piece (30 g) green ginger,
1 small red chilli, 450 g (2 cups) sugar, 115 g (1 cup) sultanas,
250 ml (1 cup) vinegar, 55 g (½ cup) salt, 2 tablespoons plain flour

Peel and chop the tomatoes. Peel and slice the garlic and ginger, then finely slice the chillies. Put in a saucepan with the sugar, sultanas, vinegar and salt. Boil till quite thick. Stir well. Mix together the flour with a little of the vinegar mixture to form a paste, then stir through the chutney. Pour into sterilised jars and seal securely when cool.

Tomato Relish

2.7 kg tomatoes, 900 g sliced onions, vinegar, 450 g (2 cups) sugar,
2 tablespoons curry powder, 1 tablespoon mustard powder,
3 tablespoons cornflour, 1 teaspoon ground mace, 1 teaspoon ground cloves,
1 teaspoon cinnamon, 1 teaspoon nutmeg, 1 teaspoon ground ginger

Scald the tomatoes, peel, and roughly chop the flesh. Put in a bowl with the onion and 65 g (½ cup) salt and cover with water. Stand overnight. Pour off the brine, transfer the pulp to a saucepan and almost cover with vinegar. Boil, then add the sugar, stirring well. Mix the curry powder, mustard and cornflour with a little cold vinegar to make a smooth paste. Stir into the pan, boiling for about 45 minutes, or until the mixture thickens. Stir in the spices. Pour into sterilised jars and seal securely when cool.

UNTRY **W**OMENS **A**SSOCIATIO

CWA of New South Wales First Land Cookery Competition, 1951.

BAKING

Breads and Buns

Yeasts

The gas generated by the action of yeast is important as it causes the sponge to rise. There are several kinds of yeast that can be made at home. Liquid yeast is made from a mixture of potatoes, sugar, water and hops. Compressed yeast is made from hops and potatoes and pressed into cakes. A distillers' yeast can also be made from fermented rye. Never mix salt with your yeast. Salt is a deterrent to fermentation. A cup of hops yeast is equal to 1 cake of compressed yeast. However, many women are using with great success the different brands of compressed or dried yeast, which are supplied by most of the country stores.

- ACID YEAST: makes beautiful bread. To make acid yeast, boil 1 potato in water, then mash well and allow to cool. Add 1½ tablespoons sugar, ½ teaspoon citric or tartaric acid, 2 teaspoons plain flour and 250 ml (1 cup) water. Stir well to combine and pour into a sterilised jar and seal securely. Set aside in a warm place for 24 hours before using.

- HOPS YEAST: is made in the following way. Boil 1 large potato in 600 ml water and add 1 teaspoon hops while the water is boiling. Boil for 20 minutes, then strain and reserve the cooking liquid. Add 1 tablespoon plain flour and 1 tablespoon of sugar and stir to combine. The hops yeast then needs to be poured into a sterilised jar and sealed securely when cool. The yeast should work in a few hours if the bottle has been used previously. If using a new bottle, set aside in a warm place for 24 hours before using. A preserved fig or raisin will help to make yeast work.

A stale loaf of bread can be made quite fresh by being dipped quickly into hot milk and then baked dry in a quick oven. Bread may be sprinkled on the outside with cold water and placed in oven and will be quite fresh.

- LEMON YEAST: mix together the juice of ½ lemon, 1 tablespoon plain flour, 2 tablespoons sugar and 600 ml water. Stir well, pour into a sterilised jar and seal securely. Very good to use in hot weather.

Flours

Wheat yields the best flour for baking bread and in the past have been classified into the following categories: • Strong flour contains gluten cells are strong and dry, and absorb water well. Strong flour is best for baking bread. • New flour absorbs less water. A sure way to test 'newness' is to squeeze some of the flour in your hand, and if it holds its shape it is new. • Weak flour is deficient in gluten and doesn't have the capacity to retain the gases produced by the yeast. • Fine flour is soft and elastic, not spongy or puffy. Its gluten is plentiful and it is fine and nutty. Fine flour is best for baking Christmas cakes, pasties and shortbread.

Looking Back in Time...

CLEANING A WHITE SHEEPSKIN RUG

If the rug is lined, take out the lining and shake the skin well to free it from dust. Prepare a tub full of water and pour in enough good-quality hair shampoo to make a good lather. If the rug is greasy, add ammonia to the water (2 teaspoons to every 1.2 litres). Wash the rug thoroughly in this lather and afterwards rinse well in several waters. Don't leave a particle of soap in the fur or else it will be matted and sticky. Add a little blue to the last rinsing water, and if possible, pass the rug though a wringer; hang in the open to dry. During the process of drying it is important to shake the rug frequently. A fine comb will remove any slight matting or knotty patch.

Bath Buns

Sift 350 g (2⅓ cups) plain flour into a bowl. Rub in 85 g butter. Mix 1 tablespoon compressed yeast with 75 g (¾ cup) sugar, 125 ml (½ cup) warm milk and 2 well-beaten eggs. Stir well to combine. Make a well in the flour, pour in the yeast mixture and stir to thoroughly combine. Set aside in a warm place for about 1 hour, or until the dough doubles in size. Turn the dough onto a floured work surface and knead in the finely grated zest of 1 lemon. Divide the dough into small rounds, place on a greased baking tray and set aside to rise. Brush over with milk, sprinkle with a little sugar and bake in a 180°C oven for about 20 minutes.

Bretzel

Sift 450 g (3 cups) plain flour and 1 teaspoon salt into a bowl. Mix 1½ tablespoons yeast (or 2½ teaspoons instant dried yeast) and 2 tablespoons sugar together. Add 55 g butter, melted, and 300 ml lukewarm milk. Stir in 1 well-beaten egg. Mix into the flour to combine well, then cover and leave to rise in a warm place for about 40 minutes. Turn out onto a lightly floured work surface and knead well. Roll into a thin sheet. Mix together 4 tablespoons butter, 4 tablespoons brown sugar, 4 tablespoons raisins and a pinch of mixed spice and ground cinnamon. Spread this mixture over the dough mixture. Roll up the dough and cut lengthways into two or four lengths. Twist each length into a rope. Coil the ropes into the base of a greased cake tin; allow to rise to the top of the tin. Bake in 200°C oven for 45 minutes–1 hour. When cooked, glaze with a syrup made from equal quantities of sugar and water, boiled together.

Brown Bread

Sift 225 g (1½ cups) plain flour and 225 g (1½ cups) wholemeal flour into a bowl; add 1 teaspoon salt and ½ teaspoon sugar and make a well in the centre. Mix 2½ tablespoons instant dried yeast in 300 ml water and pour into the flour. Stir to form a moist dough. Cover and set aside in a warm place until the dough doubles in size. Knead the dough until smooth and elastic. Shape into loaves, place into greased tins and set aside in a warm place until the dough rises. Cook in a 220°C oven for 30 minutes and transfer to the bottom of the oven for a further 10 minutes.

Cream Buns

Mix together 1½ tablespoons compressed yeast or 3 teaspoons instant dried yeast and 300 ml tepid milk with 1 tablespoon sugar and 2 tablespoons flour. Set aside for 15 minutes, or until foamy. Sift 450 g (3 cups) flour and 1 teaspoon salt into a bowl. Rub in 55 g butter and add 55 g (¼ cup) sugar and 60 g (½ cup) sultanas. Add 1 beaten egg to the yeast mixture and then stir into the flour mixture to make a soft dough. Set aside in a warm place for 40 minutes, or until doubled in size. Turn out onto a floured work surface and knead until smooth and elastic. Cut into about 24 even-sized pieces. Knead each piece into a round; place on a greased baking tray, keeping the buns close together. Set aside in a warm place for 10–15 minutes. Bake in a 200°C oven for 15–20 minutes. When cooked, brush with a glaze made of equal quantities of sugar and water (about 1 tablespoon of each heated together). When cold, split the buns open and fill with sweetened whipped cream.

A Valuable Hint

To avoid waste in making homemade bread: after the dough has been mixed, place in a bowl and cover with plastic wrap before setting aside to rise. This way, there will not be any hard dough crust to waste or throw away.

Hot Cross Buns

Place 1½ tablespoons fresh compressed yeast or 3 teaspoons instant dried yeast in a bowl and add 300 ml milk, 1 teaspoon flour and 1 teaspoon sugar. Mix together and stand for 20 minutes. Sift 450 g (3 cups) plain flour into another bowl and rub in 55 g butter. Add a pinch of salt, 55 g (¼ cup) sugar and 60 g (½ cup) sultanas. Beat 1 egg well and add to the milk and yeast. Stir this into the dry ingredients and mix into a fairly soft dough. Leave in the bowl, cover with a clean cloth and place in a warm place to rise for 35–40 minutes. Turn out onto a lightly floured surface and knead well. Cut into about 16–18 even-sized portions. Form each into a bun shape and place on a greased baking tray, evenly spaced and rather close together. Cover and set aside in a warm place to rise for 10 minutes. Mark a cross on top with a knife. Make a glaze by mixing 1 heaped teaspoon icing sugar and 1 tablespoon boiling water. Brush over the buns and bake in a 220°C oven for 15 minutes.

Pulled Bread Take the crust off a fresh loaf of bread while
it is still warm, and use a fork to pull off the soft part in long strips.
Lay in a baking dish in a hot oven until crisp and golden brown.

Salad Rolls

Mix together 2 tablespoons sugar with 2 teaspoons salt, 60 g (¼ cup) melted butter
and 60 ml (¼ cup) lukewarm milk. Add 3 teaspoons instant dried yeast, then mix in
450 g (3 cups) sifted plain flour. Beat thoroughly, cover, and set aside until well risen.
Turn out onto a floured work surface and knead in 300 g (2 cups) plain flour or
enough to make a soft dough. Set aside to rise again; turn out onto a floured surface
and knead well a second time. Roll out to 5 mm thickness. Cut out large rounds with
a pastry cutter and make a deep crease in the middle of each with the floured handle
of a wooden spoon. Press the edges of each round together to form a half-circle. Set
aside to rise. Brush with milk and bake in a 220°c oven for 15 minutes.

Walnut Buns

Mix 1½ teaspoons instant dried yeast and ½ teaspoon sugar. Melt 30 g butter
and a little milk in a saucepan. Mix with the yeast and then pour into a bowl with
175 g (1 heaped cup) sifted plain flour. Combine to form a light dough, adding extra
warm milk as necessary. Set aside in a warm place until the dough has doubled in
size. Turn out onto a lightly floured work surface and knead the dough until smooth
and elastic. Shape into a rectangle and spread with raspberry jam. Sprinkle over 40 g
(⅓ cup) sultanas and 2 tablespoons finely chopped mixed peel. Roll up lengthways
and cut into 2.5 cm thick pieces. Set aside for 10 minutes to rise. Brush with egg wash
and bake in 220°C oven for about 15 minutes. When cool, cover with an icing made
with 115 g icing sugar and 1 tablespoon warm water. Sprinkle with chopped walnuts.

White Bread

Sift 450 g (3 cups) plain flour in a bowl; add 2 teaspoons sugar and make a well in
the centre. Mix 2 tablespoons yeast in 450 ml water and pour into the flour. Stir to
form a moist dough. Cover and set aside in a warm place until the dough doubles
in size. Turn onto a board and knead in another 225 g (1½ cups) plain flour and

1 teaspoon salt. Continue to knead the dough until smooth and elastic — the dough should not stick to the hand. Only use as much extra flour as you need to make the dough workable. Shape the dough into loaves, place into greased tins and set aside in a warm place until the dough rises. Cook in a 220°C oven for 30 minutes and transfer to the bottom of the oven for a further 10 minutes. When finished the bread should give a hollow sound when tapped on the bottom.

Wholemeal Bread

Sift 900 g (6 cups) wholemeal flour and 450 g (3 cups) plain flour into a bowl. Rub in 115 g softened butter. Put 3 tablespoons fresh compressed yeast or 3 teaspoons instant dried yeast in a jug with ½ teaspoon sugar. Add 250 ml (1 cup) milk and 125 ml (½ cup) water to the jug and stir well. Make a hollow in the centre and pour in the yeast. Sprinkle 1 tablespoon salt around the hollow. Stir with a wooden spoon, adding more warm water as necessary to form a soft dough. Cover with a clean tea towel and set aside for about 1 hour in a warm place until doubled in size. Turn onto a lightly floured surface and knead until smooth and elastic. Shape into two loaves and place into greased bread tins or on a tray. Set aside in a warm place for 10 minutes, then bake in a 200°C oven for 20 minutes. Reduce the heat to 180°C and cook for a further 45 minutes. Remove from the tin and cool on a wire rack.

Wreath Cake

Sift 450 g (3 cups) plain flour into a bowl. Put 2 teaspoons sugar in a bowl and add 3 tablespoons fresh compressed yeast or 3 teaspoon instant dried yeast, stirring together until moisture forms. Melt 40 g butter in saucepan and add 250 ml (1 cup) milk, stirring until the butter has melted. Beat 1 egg, add to the milk and butter, and then mix in the yeast. Pour this into the warm flour, and mix into a dough. Turn onto a lightly floured work surface and knead well. Roll out into a sheet and set aside. Mix together 110 g (½ cup) sugar, 115 g butter, ½ teaspoon cinnamon and ½ teaspoon mixed spice. Stir in 215 g (1¾ cups) raisins and 95 g (½ cup) chopped mixed fruit peel. Spread this over the dough. Roll up into a log shape, cut at regular intervals without cutting all the way through, then form into a round, or wreath, to slightly open the cuts and expose the filling. Place in a greased tin and set aside, covered, in a warm place, until the dough rises. Bake in a 220°C oven for 25 minutes. Turn out and brush the top of the dough with a glaze made by boiling together 2 tablespoons sugar and 2 tablespoons water.

Scones, Pikelets and Tea Cakes

Basic Loaf

You can make variations to this loaf by adding your choice of chopped nuts and dates, cinnamon, and dates, sultanas or mixed peel. It is also delicious made without the additions as a plain scone loaf.

Sift together 450 g (3 cups) plain flour, 3 teaspoons baking powder and ½ teaspoon salt in a bowl. Rub in 1 tablespoon butter and add 230 g (1 cup) brown sugar. Add 1 beaten egg and gradually add 250 ml (1 cup) milk to make a moist batter (moister than for scones). Fill three greased Cerebos salt tins (see glossary) or date roll tins to three-quarters capacity and cover with the lids. Bake for about 30–45 minutes (stand tins up for about 10 minutes, and then put them down, keep turning until cooked).

Belgian Tea Cake

Cream 1 tablespoon butter and 2 tablespoons of sugar in a bowl. Add 1 beaten egg, 125 ml (½ cup) milk and 150 g (1 cup) self-raising flour. Pour into a round cake tin and place thin slices of apple on top. Sprinkle with sugar and ground nutmeg. Bake in a 180°C oven for 30 minutes. Serve hot with butter.

If eggs are placed in cold water 2 hours before using they will beat more easily and make cakes lighter.

Cheese Loaf

Sift together 300 g (2 cups) plain flour and 2 teaspoons baking powder in a bowl. Rub in 1 tablespoon butter, then add 125 g (1 cup) grated cheese and 1 beaten egg. Stir in 170 ml (²/3 cup) milk to make a wet mixture. Place in a loaf tin and bake in a 220°C oven until cooked. Cut into slices and serve with butter.

Cheese Scones

Sift together 300 g (2 cups) self-raising flour and a pinch each of salt, cayenne pepper and mustard powder. Rub in 1 tablespoon butter, then stir through 60 g (½ cup) grated cheese. Add 1 beaten egg and 125 ml (½ cup) milk to form a soft dough. Turn out onto a lightly floured work surface and roll out. Cut into scone shapes, place on a greased baking tray and glaze with milk. Cook in a 220°C oven for 10 minutes.

Cinnamon Tea Cake

Cream 1 tablespoon butter and 110 g (½ cup) sugar in a bowl. Add 1 beaten egg, 125 ml (½ cup) milk, a few drops vanilla essence and a pinch of salt, stirring to combine. Sift in 150 g (1 cup) plain flour with 1 teaspoon baking powder. Mix to combine, then place in a greased round cake tin and cook in a 180°C oven, until a skewer inserted into the centre of the cake comes out clean. Once cooked, turn out onto a wire rack and spread the top with butter. Sprinkle over a mixture of 1 teaspoon ground cinnamon, 1 teaspoon sugar and 1 teaspoon desiccated coconut.

Coffee Roll

Cream 2 tablespoons butter and 1 tablespoon sugar in a bowl. Add 1 beaten egg, then stir in 250 ml (1 cup) milk. Sift in 375 g (2½ cups) plain flour, 1 teaspoon bicarbonate of soda and 2 teaspoons cream of tartar. Stir well to combine. Roll out thinly and cut into circles with a pastry cutter. Cook in a 200°C oven.

Homemade Baking Powder

Mix together 225 g cream of tartar, 200 g (1 cup) bicarbonate of soda and 55 g tartaric acid in a bowl. Pass through a sieve three times. Use 2 teaspoons of this mixture in place of baking powder for every 450 g (3 cups) flour.

Condensed Bread

Sift 150 g (1 cup) plain flour and 1 teaspoon baking powder into a bowl. Add 2 teaspoons sugar, 2 tablespoons butter and a pinch of salt. Add enough milk to form a soft dough. Turn out onto a lightly floured surface and knead well. Spoon into a loaf tin with a close-fitting lid and cook in a 180°C oven for 25–30 minutes.

Cream Scones

Sift 300 g (2 cups) plain flour into a bowl with 2 teaspoons baking powder and a pinch of salt. Add 1 tablespoon sugar and stir to combine. Add 1 beaten egg, 125 ml (1/2 cup) cream and enough milk to make a soft dough. Turn out onto a lightly floured work surface and knead the dough. Roll out and cut into squares with a sharp knife. Place on a greased baking tray, glaze with egg wash, and bake in a 220°C oven for 12–15 minutes. Cool slightly on a wire rack and serve hot with butter.

Damper

Put 450 g (3 cups) self-raising flour in a bowl with 1 teaspoon salt, 310 ml (1 1/4 cups) milk. Mix together with a knife to form a good dough — it should leave the side of the bowl clean. Bake in a 220°C oven for 30 minutes on the bottom shelf of the oven. Always cut across the dough before putting on the baking tray or prick the top before putting in the oven.

Tips for Making Scones

• Dough too dry produces tough-looking scones. • Dough too wet causes scones to spread. • Liquid added slowly and not mixed evenly causes scones to become leathery. • Beware of baking too slowly (tough) or too quickly (inside soggy). • Place scones on cake cooler immediately after cooking. • Do not cut with a knife, as this makes scones doughy. • Do not pack scones in a container while hot or they'll become doughy.

Drop Scones or Flap Jacks

Combine 1 beaten egg in a bowl with 125 ml (½ cup) milk. Add 120 g (¾ cup) self-raising flour, 2 heaped tablespoons sugar and a pinch of salt. Bake in a heavy-based frying pan (cast iron if you have one), using about 2 teaspoons for each scone. Pile onto a dish when cooked and keep warm until all are cooked.

Gem Scones

Cream 1 tablespoon butter and 1½ tablespoons sugar in a bowl. Add 1 beaten egg and a pinch of salt and mix together. Stir in 225 g (1½ cups) plain flour and gradually pour in 250 ml (1 cup) milk to form a soft dough — the mixture should not be too runny and should drop firmly off the spoon. Have the gem irons thoroughly hot and buttered. Put on the middle shelf and bake in a 220°C oven for 5–8 minutes.

Gundowringa Scones

Sift together 300 g (2 cups) plain flour in a bowl with 2 teaspoons baking powder. Add 125 g (½ cup) sour cream and 250 ml (1 cup) milk. Mix to form a dough, then turn out onto a lightly floured work surface. Press out with the palm of your hand and cut into scone shapes. Bake in a 220°C oven.

Iced Pineapple Buns

Sift together 225 g (1½ cups) plain flour, 1 teaspoon baking powder and a pinch of salt. Rub in 55 g butter, then add 55 g (¼ cup) sugar and a little finely chopped glacé pineapple. Stir in 1 beaten egg and 3 tablespoons milk, making a stiff batter. Turn out onto a lightly floured work surface and divide into 12 even-sized portions. Shape into rounds, place on a greased baking tray and bake in a 180°C oven for 15 minutes.

To make the chocolate icing, mix together 115 g sifted icing sugar, 1 tablespoon cocoa powder, 15 g chocolate, melted, and 1 tablespoon hot water in a bowl until smooth. Ice the cake and decorate with pieces of glacé pineapple.

Put lemon peel and sugar through mincer and when making a cake add to the butter and sugar before creaming. This dissolves the sugar on the peel and gives the cake a good flavour.

Jumping Johnnies

Whisk together 3 eggs and 2 tablespoons sugar in a bowl. Add the grated zest of 1 lemon, 125 ml (½ cup) milk and 375 g (2½ cups) self-raising flour. Deep-fry teaspoons of the mixture in hot oil, in batches. Drain on paper towels and roll in icing sugar. Serve hot or cold. Johnnies will turn themselves over when cooked on one side if there is enough oil in the pan.

Lemon Pikelets

Sift together 4 tablespoon self-raising flour and a pinch of salt into a bowl. Add 2 tablespoons sugar and stir well. Add 1 beaten egg, 125 ml (1/2 cup) milk, the juice of 1/2 lemon and the finely grated zest of 1 lemon. Beat well and make into a smooth batter. When ready to cook, heat a heavy-based frying pan. Drop teaspoons of the mixture into the greased pan and cook until bubbles appear on the surface and the underside is golden. Then turn and cook the other side until golden and the pikelets are cooked through.

London Tea Buns

Cream 1 tablespoon butter and 2 tablespoons sugar in a bowl. Add 1 beaten egg, 125 ml (1/2 cup) milk, stirring well. Sift in 300 g (2 cups) self-raising flour and 1/4 teaspoon salt and stir well to combine. Turn out onto a lightly floured work surface and roll out. Cut into small bun shapes and place on a greased baking tray. Bake in a 180°C oven for 15 minutes. When cooked, cool on a wire rack. When cool, ice each bun with Lemon Icing (see recipe, page 269) and sprinkle with crushed walnuts, to serve.

Nut Bread

Cream 1 tablespoon butter and 110 g (1/2 cup) sugar in a bowl. Sift together 300 g (2 cups) plain flour, 2 teaspoons baking powder and a pinch of salt in a separate bowl. Add 125 g (1 cup) chopped walnuts. Add the butter and sugar to the dry ingredients and stir in 1 beaten egg and 250 ml (1 cup) milk. Spoon the batter into a round cake tin and bake in a 180°C oven for 45 minutes. When cooked, cut into slices and serve with butter.

Variation You can use dates instead of walnuts. Substitute 160 g (1 cup) chopped dates instead.

Nut Loaf

Cream 1½ tablespoons butter and 1 tablespoon sugar in a bowl. Add 1 beaten egg, 1 tablespoon golden syrup and 250 ml (1 cup) milk. Lightly stir in 300 g (2 cups) plain flour and 90 g (¾ cup) finely chopped walnuts. Place into two greased loaf tins and bake in a 180°C oven for 40–50 minutes.

Orange Tea Cake

Cream 1 tablespoon butter and 110 g (½ cup) sugar in a bowl. Stir in 1 beaten egg and mix well to combine. Add the grated zest of 1 orange and 2 drops of lemon essence. Sift in 150 g (1 cup) plain flour, 1 teaspoon cream of tartar and ½ teaspoon bicarbonate of soda. Stir in 125 ml (½ cup) milk until all combined. Place in a cake tin and bake in a 180°C oven for 15–20 minutes.

Pikelets

Sift 120 g (¾ cup) plain flour into a bowl and add 2 tablespoons sugar. Combine 1 beaten egg with 4–5 tablespoons milk and stir into the dry ingredients with 2 teaspoons melted butter. Stir to form a thick smooth batter and let stand for 1 hour or more. When ready to cook, heat a heavy-based frying pan. Mix 1 teaspoon cream of tartar and ½ teaspoon bicarbonate of soda in a small bowl, then add to batter and stir in well. Drop teaspoons of the mixture into the greased pan and cook until bubbles appear on the surface and the underside is golden. Then turn and cook the other side until golden and the pikelets are cooked through.

Plain Scones

Sift together 450 g (3 cups) plain flour, 2 teaspoons baking powder and a pinch of salt. Rub in 1 tablespoon butter and gradually add 150 ml milk and 150 ml water. Stir together lightly with a knife, to make a smooth dough. Roll out 1 cm thick, cut into scone shapes and bake in a 220°C oven 7–10 minutes.

Potato Cakes

Put 450 g cold mashed potatoes in a large bowl. Sift in 50 g (1/3 cup) flour and a pinch of salt. Stir in 30 g softened butter with just enough milk to make a smooth thick paste. Roll out to 2 cm thick, cut into circles and bake on a greased baking tray for about 15 minutes. Split open, butter, and serve hot.

Variation You can make apple cakes using the above mixture. Simply roll out to about 5 mm thick, then put 3–4 very thinly sliced apple over half the cake mixture. Sprinkle with sugar, wet the edges and cover with the other half, pressing the edges to seal. Bake on a greased baking tray for 30 minutes. Split open and butter before serving.

Potato Tea Cake

A delicious potato tea cake can be made from the remains of cold mashed potato. Rub into it into an equal quantity of plain flour, a quarter as much butter and a pinch each of salt and baking powder. Mix this to a rather stiff paste with 1–2 beaten eggs. Roll out to 2.5 cm thick, cut into rounds or triangles, brush over with egg wash and milk, and bake in a 180°C oven until cooked.

Prize-Winning Scones

Sift 450 g (3 cups) plain flour into a bowl with 60 g (1/2 cup) icing sugar, 1/2 teaspoon of salt, 2 tablespoons cream of tartar and 1 tablespoon bicarbonate of soda. Sift the dry ingredients another two times, then rub in 55 g butter and stir in 1 beaten egg and 375 ml (1 1/2 cups) milk. The mixture should be handled as lightly as possible and patted into shape with the hands. Cut into scone shapes as desired and brush over with a little milk. Bake on a hot floured baking tray in a 220°C oven until a rich golden brown.

Pufftaloons

Sift together 300 g (2 cups) plain flour and 2 teaspoons baking powder. Rub in 2 teaspoons butter, then add 250 ml (1 cup) milk, stirring to make a dough. Roll out thinly and cut into rounds. Have ready plenty of boiling vegetable oil and fry, in batches, until golden brown. Drain on paper towel and serve very hot with golden syrup or jam.

Pumpkin Scones

Cream 1 tablespoon butter and 110 g (½ cup) sugar in a bowl. Add 1 cup of cold mashed pumpkin and 1 beaten egg, stirring well to combine. Sift in 450 g (3 cups) self-raising flour, stirring to make a soft dough. If the dough is too stiff, add a little milk. Turn out onto a lightly floured work surface and roll out. Cut into scone shapes and bake in a 200°C oven. If plain flour is used, add 1½ tablespoons baking powder.

Soda Loaf

Sift 675 g (4½ cups) plain flour and ¼ teaspoon salt into a bowl. Combine 1 teaspoon bicarbonate of soda with 250 ml (1 cup) milk and 1 teaspoon freshly squeezed lemon juice. Add to the dry ingredients, mixing to form a soft dough. Turn out onto a lightly floured work surface and knead well. Divide into two even-sized portions and shape into loaves. Place in floured loaf tins and bake in a moderate oven for 30–40 minutes. Turn out onto a wire rack to cool.

Sweet Scones

Beat 2 tablespoons cream and 2 tablespoons sugar in a bowl until light. Add 250 ml (1 cup) milk and stir well, then add 450 g (3 cups) plain flour, 2 teaspoons cream of tartar, 1 teaspoon bicarbonate of soda, 1/4 teaspoon salt and 125 g (1 cup) sultanas. Roll out the dough, cut into scone shapes and bake for 8–10 minutes. Brush a little milk over them before baking in a 200°C oven.

Variation You can use 160 g (1 cup) chopped pitted dates instead of sultanas.

When making scones put the milk and butter in the saucepan over the fire until the butter is melted, then add to the flour.

Tea Cake

Rub a good lump of butter into 225 g (1½ cups) self-raising flour. Stir in a pinch of salt, 110 g (½ cup) sugar and a few dates or walnuts. Add enough milk to make a firm dough. Use floured hands to press into a greased loaf tin. Sprinkle sugar and walnuts over the top and brush with milk. Bake in a 180°C oven for 25–30 minutes.

Wheatmeal Loaf

Cream 2 tablespoons butter and 2 teaspoons sugar in a bowl. Stir in about 1 tablespoon of boiling water. Combine 300 g (2 cups) wholemeal flour, 1 teaspoon baking powder and a pinch of salt in a separate bowl. Add the butter mixture and stir well. Add 1 beaten egg and 125 ml (½ cup) cold water. Mix well, then place the dough in a loaf tin and bake in a 180°C oven for 30 minutes. Serve hot.

Cakes and Sponges

Tips for Making Cakes

Cake making is an art and can be successfully accomplished if the following instructions are carried out:

- Remember that practice makes perfect!
- Choose reliable recipes and follow them carefully.
- Sift flour before adding baking powder, and sift again when added.
- Level spoonfuls should be used, smoothing off the full spoon with a knife.
- When a recipe calls for butter and sugar to be beaten to a cream (as in butter sponge) it should be thoroughly beaten until the sugar and butter are blended to a cream, so that when rubbed on the side of the bowl with the back of spoon there is no gritty feeling in the cream. If eggs are to be added one at a time, unbeaten, each egg must be very well beaten in. If this mixture curdles it proves that each egg has not been sufficiently beaten in before the next egg is added, or the mixture is too hot. (Some mixtures add only the yolk to the beaten sugar and butter, and have the beaten egg white added after the flour has been added.)

Common Baking Measurements

When baking, measuring correctly is absolutely necessary.
When using solids, butter, or other shortening, use a knife to even off superfluous amounts. An even cup means to the brim.
A brimming, or heaped cup means a cup running over. A scant cupful means about 1 centimetre off the top of the measure.

- When making sponge cakes add flour gradually, stirring lightly and slowly.
- Cake mixture should be kept at an even, cool temperature.
- Packets of cleaned mixed fruit (mixed peel) are a present-day convenience and greatly to be recommended to the busy housewife.
- If a cake is cooking too quickly, a piece of greased baking paper placed over the cake will prevent it from burning.
- Sugar, flour, salt, bicarbonate of soda and powdered spices should be tossed about before measuring.

Baking Times

Recipes generally state the times for baking and the temperature
of the oven, and this needs careful attention.
Do not look at your oven too often. • Layer cakes take about
20 minutes to cook. • Large plain cakes take about 1 hour
15 minutes to cook. • Large pound cakes take from anywhere
between 1 hour 15 minutes–4 hours, according to size,
and require a very slow oven.

- Grease cake tins carefully, using butter for sponge cakes. Dredge flour over the greased surface and sides of the tins. Always prepare tins before you begin to make the cake.
- Rich cakes need a paper lining, using greased baking paper; also be sure to butter the tins before lining with paper.
- Where a spoon is necessary, a wooden one is best and easier on the hand.
- To whisk egg white, beat quickly and add a pinch of salt.
- When making cakes in hot weather, place eggs in cold water for a few minutes before using.
- Yolks of eggs not used in cakes are useful for salad dressings.
- A cup of strong coffee can take the place of brandy in a rich cake.

Homemade Self-raising Flour

To make your own self-raising flour, mix together 3.6 kg plain
flour with 115 g (heaped ½ cup) cream of tartar and 55 g (¼ cup)
bicarbonate of soda. Sift together three or four times before
adding to the cake.

Small Cakes

Apple Spice Cakes

Cream 2 tablespoons butter and 2 scant tablespoons sugar in a bowl. Add 2 eggs and beat well. Sift together 150 g (1 cup) plain flour, ½ teaspoon baking powder and 1 teaspoon mixed spice and stir into the butter mixture. Spread 1 teaspoon of mixture into a greased patty tin, place ½ teaspoon of cooked apple in the centre and cover with a little of the cake mixture. Repeat until all the mixture is used — you should use about 2 cooked apples for the filling. Bake in a 230°C oven for 30 minutes. When cool, cover with pink icing and decorate with chopped almonds.

Babas

Put 4 eggs and 230 g (1 cup) sugar together in a heatproof bowl. Stand the bowl in a saucepan of boiling water and whisk the the eggs for 15 minutes. Sift together 190 g (1¼ cups) plain flour and ½ teaspoon baking powder, and stir them in as gently as possible with a wooden spoon. Grease some dariole moulds with butter. Sift together a little flour and white sugar — equal parts of each — and shake it round the insides of the moulds until well coated. Fill each mould rather more than half full with the cake mixture. Bake in a 180°C oven until nicely browned. Press each with your finger. If the mark of the finger fades out at once, the cake is done. Let them cool on a wire rack. When cool, trickle rum on them from a spoon until they are nicely soaked, but not wet enough to make ponds in which they can stand. Just before serving, whip up some cream and put a small dollop on each cake. The cream and the rum are the distinctive marks of a real baba, but the little cakes alone, or with just a dab of jam on each by way of a finish, are also excellent.

Butterfly Cakes

Beat the yolks of 3 eggs with 2 teaspoons lemon juice until very light. Whip the whites of the eggs until very stiff and then add 110 g (½ cup) sugar to the whites and whip well again. Add the yolks to the whites, then add 75 g (½ cup) sifted plain flour with 1 teaspoon baking powder. Season with salt, to taste. Line patty tins with paper cases and bake in a 150°C oven. Cut a round out of the centre of each little sponge, fill the centre with whipped cream, and use the cut-out circle, cut in half, to decorate the top to look like wings, placing the browned side facing out. Sprinkle the cream with coloured (pink) sugar.

Cherry Bars

Cream 115 g butter and 110 g (½ cup) sugar in a bowl. Add 2 eggs and a little milk. Add 240 g (1 cup) chopped cherries and 160 g (1 cup) chopped dates and stir through. Then add 125 g (1 cup) chopped walnuts. Finally, stir through 300 g (2 cups) self-raising flour and 2 teaspoons cocoa powder. Bake in square or rectangular cake tin. When cool, ice with Caramel Icing (see recipe, page 268), cut into squares and decorate with a glacé cherries or walnuts.

Cherry Vanities

Make jelly using 1 packet of jelly crystals. Set aside. Cream together 2 tablespoons butter and 165 g (¾ cup) sugar. Add 2 eggs and beat thoroughly. Sift 300 g (2 cups) self-raising flour and a pinch of salt and add to the butter mixture. Lastly, add 250 ml (1 cup) milk and stir to combine. Spoon into a greased muffin tin and cook in a 220°C oven. When cool, scoop out the centres of the cakes and fill with jelly. Place a small quantity of whipped cream on top and decorate with small fresh cherries.

Cream Pyramids

Roll a sheet of sweet shortcrust pastry out thinly and cut into rounds with an 8 cm fluted pastry cutter. Bake in a 180°C oven and leave until cold. Lightly whip 80 ml (⅓ cup) cream and place in a bowl. Sift in 115 g (1 scant cup) icing sugar and add 12 drops almond extract. Beat 1 egg white until stiff peaks form, then add just enough to the cream mixture to form a stiff paste. Place a little mound of the cream on each pastry round. Cut a sponge cake into thin fingers and arrange three sponge fingers around the edge to join at the top like a pyramid. Pipe a rosette of extra whipped cream where they join at the top and decorate with glacé cherries.

Fairy Cakes

Cream 115 g butter and 110 g (½ cup) sugar in a bowl. Add 2 eggs and beat well. Add a little milk. Mix 2 small teaspoons baking powder with 120 g (¾ cup) plain flour and 115 g cornflour, and add to other ingredients with 1 teaspoon vanilla essence. Fill a patty tin lined with paper cases and bake in a 180°C oven for 10 minutes.

Foundation for Small Cakes

Cream 115 g butter with 220 g (1 cup) sugar in a bowl. Add 3 eggs, one at a time, beating well after each addition. Add 125 ml (½ cup) milk and then stir in 270 g (1¾ cups) plain flour, 1 teaspoon bicarbonate of soda and 2 teaspoons cream of tartar. Put in patty tins and bake for 10 minutes in a 180°C oven. This is an excellent recipe and makes quite a lot of small cakes. Fill the paper cases with plain mixture, then put half a date on some, raisins or sultanas on others, and sometimes add a little cocoa powder to some of the mixture.

A little flour placed in the oven to brown is a good guide to temperature. The correct heat to bake a cake is when the flour is slightly browned.

Honey Jumbles

Put 115 g butter and 450 g (1¼ cups) honey in a saucepan and bring to the boil. Remove from the heat and allow to stand for 10 minutes. Add 60 ml (¼ cup) honey, 450 g (3 cups) plain flour and 1 teaspoon bicarbonate of soda and mix well to combine. Set aside for 2 hours. Turn the mixture out onto a lightly floured work surface and shape into oblongs. Place on baking trays lined with baking paper and bake for 10–15 minutes. Leave to cool on the trays. Ice with pink and white icing.

Jelly Blocks

Beat 3 eggs and 165 g (¾ cup) sugar in a bowl for 20 minutes. Sift in 120 g (¾ cup) self-raising flour. Dissolve 2 teaspoons butter in 3 tablespoons boiling water and lightly mix through. Pour into a greased square cake tin and bake in a 180°C oven for 20 minutes. Cool on a wire rack and cut into 5 cm squares. Make a jelly of raspberry or port wine jelly, by following the manufacturer's instructions. When the jelly is just beginning to set, use two forks to dip the cake squares into it. Roll in desiccated coconut before serving.

Lamingtons

Cream 140 g butter and 140 g (⅔ cup) sugar in a bowl. Add 2 beaten eggs with 4 tablespoons milk and a few drops of vanilla essence. Finally, stir in 270 g (1¾ cups) sifted plain flour. Grease a rectangular cake tin and pour the mixture into it. Bake in a 180°C oven for 30 minutes. Turn out onto a wire rack to cool and leave until the next day. Cut into squares. To make the icing, cream together 85 g butter and 215 g (1¾ cups) icing sugar. Mix together 1 tablespoon cocoa powder with a little hot water and add to the butter mixture. Stir in a few drop of vanilla essence. Ice the cake squares all over, then roll them in desiccated coconut, or browned coconut. To brown the coconut, spread coconut on a shallow plate or baking tin and place in a 150°C oven for a few minutes.

Mushrooms

Sift 225 g (1½ cups) self-raising flour into a bowl with 110 g (½ cup) sugar. Rub in 115 g butter. Add 1 well-beaten egg and lastly fold through ½ teaspoon vanilla essence. Roll the dough out to very thin and cut rounds with a pastry cutter, reserving some for the stems. Place into patty tins and bake in a 180°C oven for 10–15 minutes.

To make the stems, mix together some raspberry jam, cream and grated chocolate or cocoa powder. Roll several small pieces of the mixture and bake for the stems. Attach the stems to the 'mushroom' cap.

Napoleons

Make 115 g Puff Pastry (see recipe, page 286) and roll out as thinly as possible. Cut into strips 6 cm long and and 4 cm wide. Bake in a 180°C oven for 5 minutes. Make a Foundation Mixture (see recipe, page 237) and flavour with vanilla essence. Bake in a square cake tin so that it will be about 2.5 cm deep when cooked. Lay an oblong strip of pastry on top of the cake and cut out an oblong of cake, using the pastry as a guide. Spread the cake with apricot jam and sandwich the cake between two oblongs of pastry. Ice the top of the pastry with Royal Icing (see recipe, page 271) and sprinkle with chopped almonds or lightly browned coconut. Repeat the process of cutting out cake, using pastry oblongs as a pattern, until all used.

Ningadus

Beat 2 eggs and 210 g (1 scant cup) sugar until thick. Sift in 150 g (1 cup) self-raising flour, then add ¼ teaspoon bicarbonate of soda dissolved in 3 tablespoons milk. Bake in heated gem irons. When cool, ice with Chocolate Icing of your choice (see recipes, pages 268–9) and roll in coconut. Split in half, fill with whipped cream and join again.

Nougat Baskets

Melt 115 g (½ cup) caster sugar in a saucepan. When it is a golden colour, mix in 135 g (1½ cups) flaked almonds — this forms a soft paste, which hardens when cold. Grease some hot patty tins with butter, put some of the mixture into them, and with the handle of a greased spoon spread thinly around the moulds. Leave until cold, then turn out. Fill the baskets with 300 ml whipped cream that has been sweetened with ½ teaspoon vanilla essence. Make a handle for each basket using thin strips of angelica.

Rock Cakes

Rub 175 g butter into a bowl with 450 g (3 cups) plain flour, 2 teaspoons baking powder, 220 g (1 cup) sugar, 110 g (³/4 cup) currents or sultanas, the finely grated zest of 1 lemon and a pinch of ground nutmeg. Add 3 well-beaten eggs and a little milk, if desired. Drop onto a baking tray in small pieces. Bake in 180°C oven.

Rout Cakes

Cream 55 g butter and 80 g (¹/3 cup) caster sugar in a bowl. Add 115 g (1 heaped cup) ground almonds and 75 g (¹/2 cup) plain flour. When all are thoroughly blended, add 3 well-beaten eggs. Pipe the mixture in fancy shapes onto a greased baking tray and bake in a 180°C oven. Decorate with cherries and icing.

Snowball Cakes

Break 2 eggs into a bowl and beat with 210 g (1 small cup) sugar until thick. Sift in 150 g (1 cup) self-raising flour and add 3 tablespoons milk. Bake in preheated greased gem irons for 10 minutes. For the icing, mix together 1 tablespoon butter, 165 g (1¹/4 cups) icing sugar, vanilla essence and a little hot water. Roll in coconut, split the snowballs when cold, and fill with cream.

Sponge Rollettes

Lightly grease the bottom and sides of two Swiss roll tins. Cover evenly with greased baking paper. Separate the whites and yolks of 3 eggs. Beat the whites stiffly, then add the yolks and 110 g (¹/2 cup) sugar; beat until stiff and frothy. Add 120 g (³/4 cup) self-raising flour and stir in lightly. Lastly, add 3 tablespoons warm water. Pour into the prepared tins and bake in a 180°C oven for 10–15 minutes. When cooked, turn out onto a damp cloth, remove the paper and roll up while still warm. Unroll, lift onto a piece of paper sprinkled with icing sugar, spread with jam and roll up until it joins completely, then slice into smaller rollettes. Repeat with the other roll. Allow to cool. The rolling must be done quickly, or the rolls are hard to handle.

Other Cakes

Apple Cake

To make the apple purée, put 4 peeled and cored Granny Smith apples in a saucepan with 1 tablespoon water, a little cinnamon and cloves, and 2–3 drops lemon essence. Cook until the apples are tender and mash with a fork to a purée. Cream 115 g butter and 350 g (1²/₃ cups) sugar in a bowl. Add 1 well-beaten egg and 2 tablespoons cold water and stir to combine. Lastly, sift in 225 g (1½ cups) plain flour combined with ½ teaspoon bicarbonate of soda and 1 teaspoon cream of tartar. Divide the mixture into two equal portions. Roll out half the mixture, spread the apple on it. Roll out other half and put it on top of the fruit. Pinch the edges together to seal. Bake in a 180°C oven for 25 minutes. Pile with whipped cream, to serve.

Apple Walnut Cake

Cream 250 g butter and 220 g (1 cup) sugar in a bowl. Add 200 g (1 cup) stewed unsweetened apples or tinned apple purée and beat again to combine. Sift in 300 g (2 cups) plain flour with a pinch of salt, 1½ teaspoons ground cinnamon and 2 teaspoons cocoa powder. Add 125 g (1 cup) finely chopped walnuts and 125 g (1 cup) raisins. Dissolve 1 teaspoon bicarbonate of soda in 60 ml (¼ cup) milk and add to the cake batter, stirring well. Spoon into a greased cake tin and bake in a 150°C oven for 45 minutes–1 hour. When cold, ice the cake with Chocolate Icing (see recipes, pages 268–9) and decorate with walnuts.

If you happen to run short of eggs when making a cake, a mixture of warm milk and golden syrup will serve the same purpose. Use 1 tablespoon of syrup to every 300 ml of milk, which is equivalent to 3 eggs.

Banana Cake

Cream 2 tablespoons butter and 220 g (1 cup) sugar in a bowl. Add 1 beaten egg, and then add 3 whole mashed very ripe bananas, one at a time, beating well. Mix in 225 g (1½ cups) plain flour, 1 teaspoon bicarbonate of soda and 1 teaspoon baking powder. Add 2 tablespoons milk. Spoon into a greased cake tin and bake in a 180°C oven for 35–45 minutes. Make an icing by melting 2 teaspoons butter and stirring in 1 tablespoon of cocoa powder, 1 tablespoon of strong coffee and ½ teaspoon vanilla essence. Add enough icing sugar to make a smooth, even spread. Decorate with walnuts.

Banana Nut Cake

Cream 185 g butter and 330 g (1½ cups) sugar in a bowl. Separate 3 eggs and beat the whites until stiff peaks form. Add the yolks to the butter mixture and mix well. Sift 450 g (3 cups) plain flour into a separate bowl with 4 teaspoons baking powder. Sift another two times, then add to the butter mixture, alternately with 250 ml (1 cup) milk, beating well. Add 1 teaspoon vanilla essence and fold in the egg whites. Pour into in two greased sandwich tins. Bake in a 180°C oven for 30 minutes. To make the icing, put 345 g (1½ cups) soft brown sugar and 125 ml (½ cup) water in a saucepan and bring to the boil until it forms thin threads. Remove from the heat and add 2 stiffly beaten egg whites and 1 teaspoon vanilla essence; beat to a cream. Slice some bananas and arrange over one of the cakes, then pour over some icing. Put second cake on top and cover with bananas. Add 60 g (½ cup) chopped walnuts to the remaining icing before spreading over the upper cake layer.

Blowaway Sponge

Beat 4 eggs in a bowl for 10 minutes, then add 165 g (¾ cup) sugar and beat for 10 minutes. Sift together 75 g (½ cup) arrowroot, 1 teaspoon plain flour, 1 teaspoon cream of tarter and ½ teaspoon bicarbonate of soda, three times. Add a few drops of vanilla essence to the egg mixture and carefully fold through the dry ingredients to just combine. Grease and line cake tins with baking paper. Spoon into the tins and bake in a 180°C oven for about 12 minutes, being careful as it burns easily. This cake is too light to ice; spread a little whipped cream on top and sprinkle with coconut.

Blush Cake

Cream 115 g butter and 110 g (½ cup) sugar in a bowl. Add 2 eggs, one at a time, beating well after each addition. Stir in 60 ml (¼ cup milk), 1 teaspoon pink food colouring, 2½ tablespoons glacé cherries, 2½ tablespoons preserved ginger and 2½ tablespoons finely chopped almonds. Sift in 175 g plain flour (1 heaped cup) and 1 teaspoon baking powder, stirring well to combine. Pour into a greased loaf tin and bake in a 180°C oven for 45 minutes. Ice when cool with an icing made from 1 tablespoon butter, 4 tablespoons icing sugar, a little almond essence and a few drops of pink food colouring. Decorate with glacé cherries.

Bowra Brownie

Sift 450 g (3 cups) plain flour in a bowl with 110 g (½ cup) sugar, 2 teaspoons baking powder, 2 teaspoons cinnamon and a pinch of salt. Rub in 1 tablespoon butter. Mix together 1 beaten egg, 250 ml (1 cup) milk and 1 tablespoon treacle. Stir into the dry ingredients and then add 115 g (1 scant cup) sultanas. Mix to combine, then spoon into a greased cake tin. Bake in 180°C oven for 50–60 minutes. This is nicest when not too fresh, cut in slices and buttered.

Brownie (Has taken many prizes at Dubbo Show)

Cream 250 g butter and 230 g (1 cup) soft brown sugar in a bowl. Add 2 eggs, one at a time, beating well after each addition. Sift together 150 g (1 cup) flour in a bowl with 1 teaspoon ground nutmeg and 1 teaspoon cinnamon. Gradually add to the butter mixture, alternately with 250 ml (1 cup) milk, stirring until combined. Lastly, add 150 g (1 cup) currants and 125 g (1 cup) sultanas. A little chopped mixed peel may also be added. Spoon into a greased sandwich tin and bake in a 220°C oven for 1 hour 15 minutes.

Brunswick Cake

Cream 115 g butter and 165 g (³/4 cup) sugar in a bowl. Add 2 well-beaten eggs and 250 ml (1 cup) buttermilk, mixing well. Sift together 300 g (2 cups) plain flour, 2 teaspoons baking powder, 1 teaspoon ground cinnamon and 1 teaspoon allspice. Gradually add to the cake, stirring. Bake in a 180°C oven for 30 minutes.

Bushmen's Brownie

Sift 600 g (4 cups) flour in a bowl with 1 teaspoon bicarbonate of soda, 1 teaspoon cream of tartar, 1 teaspoon mixed spice and 1 teaspoon ground cinnamon. Rub in 250 g butter then add 220 g (1 cup) sugar, 150 g (1 cup) currants and 125 g (1 cup) raisins. Stir in just enough milk to make a dough slightly stiffer that that of a fruit cake. Place in a greased cake tin and bake in a 180°C oven for 1 hour.

Buttermilk Raisin Cake (Without Eggs)

Cream 125 g butter and 220 g (1 cup) sugar in a bowl. Add 250 ml (1 cup) buttermilk, 2 teaspoons ground cinnamon and ¹/2 teaspoon each of mixed spice, nutmeg and cloves. Add 225 g (1¹/2 cups) plain flour sifted with 1 teaspoon bicarbonate of soda, to make a nice firm batter. Stir in 125 g (1 cup) raisins and 150 g (1 cup) currants. Spoon into a greased cake tin and bake in a 180°C oven for 45 minutes.

Caramel Cake

Cream 2 tablespoons butter and 85 g sugar. Add 1 beaten egg, then 1 tablespoon golden syrup. Sift in 140 g (scant 1 cup) flour and finally ¹/4 teaspoon bicarbonate of soda and 125 ml (¹/2 cup) milk. Spoon into a greased loaf tin. Bake in a 180°C oven for about 30 minutes. Make a caramel icing by putting 230 g (1 cup) brown sugar, 2 tablespoons milk and 1 tablespoon butter in a saucepan. Bring to the boil and boil very slowly for 7 minutes. Beat until thickened, then pour over the cake.

Caramel Layer Cake

Cream 125 g butter and 115 g (½ cup) caster sugar in a bowl. Sift together 270 g (1¾ cups) plain flour, 3 teaspoons baking powder and 1 teaspoon ground ginger together. Separate 2 eggs and beat the whites until stiff peaks form. In a separate bowl, beat the yolks and stir in 125 ml (½ cup) milk. Add to the butter mixture, alternately with the flour mixture, until all incorporated. Gently fold in the stiffly beaten egg white. Grease two sandwich tins and spoon the mixture evenly between both. Bake in an 180°C oven for about 30 minutes, or until cooked. Meanwhile, make the caramel icing. Melt 1 teaspoon butter in a saucepan and add 345 g (1½ cups) caster sugar and 125 ml (½ cup) milk. Bring to the boil, stirring constantly to dissolve the sugar. Add 40 g (¼ cup) chopped dark chocolate and a pinch of ground cinnamon. Continue boiling, without stirring, for 13 minutes. Remove from the heat and beat to a spreadable consistency. Add vanilla and use immediately. Spread over one of the cooled cakes and place the other one on top.

Centenary Cake

Sift together 150 g (1 cup) self-raising flour, 150 g (1 cup) plain flour, ½ teaspoon salt and 2 tablespoons cocoa powder into a bowl. Add 110 g (¾ cup) currants, 115 g (1 scant cup) raisins, 115 g (1 scant cup) sultanas and the finely grated zest of ½ orange. Cream 175 g butter and 230 g (1 cup) soft brown sugar in a bowl. Add 3 eggs, one at a time, beating well after each addition. Add the flour mixture to the butter mixture alternately with 60 ml (¼ cup) milk. Add the freshly squeezed juice from ½ orange and beat until smooth. Spoon the mixture into a greased deep cake tin and bake in a 180°C oven 1½ hours. When the cake is cold, ice with Chocolate Fruit Frosting (see recipe, page 268).

Chocolate Cake

Sift 150 g (1 cup) self-raising flour with 165 g (¾ cup) sugar and a pinch of salt. Melt 125 g butter and place in a standard 1-cup capacity container. Break 2 eggs into the cup, then add 1 tablespoon cocoa powder combined with a little hot water — if the cup is not full of liquid, add milk to make it so. Pour into the cake batter and beat well for 3 minutes. Bake in a 180°C oven for 35 minutes.

Chocolate Cake (Delicious)

Cream 100 g butter and 275 g (1¼ cups) sugar in a bowl. Add 3 eggs, one at a time, beating well after each addition. Sift together 300 g (2 cups) self-raising flour with 1 teaspoon cream of tartar, ½ teaspoon bicarbonate of soda and 1 teaspoon salt. Fold into the butter mixture with 1 teaspoon vanilla essence. Mix together 60 g (½ cup) cocoa powder with 125 ml (½ cup) hot water, stirring well. Add to the cake mixture with 125 ml (½ cup) milk. Spoon into a flat baking dish or large cake tin. Bake in a 220°C oven for 20–25 minutes. When cool, decorate with a cream or chocolate icing and top with chopped almonds or preserved ginger.

Chocolate Coconut Cake

Cream 115 g butter and 110 g (½ cup) sugar in a bowl. Add 2 beaten eggs, then stir in 125 ml (½ cup) milk and 2 teaspoons cocoa powder. Sift in 175 g flour and 1½ teaspoons baking powder, then add 115 g (1¼ cups) desiccated coconut. Pour into a greased cake tin and cook in a 180°C oven for 40 minutes. Turn on to a wire rack and ice the cake when cool. To make the icing, cream 2 tablespoons butter and 3 tablespoons icing sugar in a bowl. Add 3 tablespoons coconut and 2 teaspoons cocoa powder, which has been mixed with just enough hot water to make a paste. Spread over the cake when cold and sprinkle with coconut.

Chocolate Layer Cake

Cream 90 g butter and 220 g (1 cup) sugar in a bowl. Add 1 beaten egg and slowly pour in 250 ml (1 cup) milk; mix well. Sift in 190 g (1¼ cups) plain flour with ¼ teaspoon salt and 4 small teaspoons baking powder. Mix in 1 teaspoon vanilla essence. Spoon into three round greased cake tins of equal size. Bake in a 180°C oven for 15–20 minutes. Turn out onto wire racks to cool. To make the chocolate filling, mix together 375 g (3 cups) icing sugar, 2 tablespoons cocoa powder, 1 teaspoon vanilla essence, ½ teaspoon finely grated orange peel and enough boiling water to make a smooth paste. Put between layers and ice all over top and sides.

Chocolate Ring Cake

Cream 115 g butter and 115 g (½ cup) caster sugar in a bowl. Add 1 egg and beat well. Sift together 165 g (1 heaped cup) self-raising flour and 4 teaspoons cocoa powder and add to the butter mixture alternately with 125 ml (½ cup) milk, stirring lightly. Add ½ teaspoon vanilla essence. Pour into a ring tin and bake in a 180°C oven for about 30 minutes.

Chocolate Sandwich

Separate 3 eggs and beat the whites until stiff peaks form. Add the yolks, then 210 g (1 scant cup) sugar, beating well until thick and creamy. Sift in 150 g (1 cup) self-raising flour. Dissolve 1 teaspoon butter dissolved in 4 tablespoons boiling water and stir through the cake mixture. Spoon into two greased sandwich tins — one 15 cm square and one 20 cm square. Bake in an 180°C oven for 20 minutes.

To make the icing, melt some chocolate in a double saucepan, and pour over the cake after having joined it together with fresh cream. Pipe freshly whipped cream around the edges, to serve. This makes a very attractive afternoon tea cake.

Christmas Cake

Cream 2½ breakfast cups butter and 2½ breakfast cups sugar in a bowl. Add 10 eggs, one at a time, beating well after each addition. Sift together 5 breakfast cups flour, a pinch of salt, ½ teaspoon mixed spice and 1 teaspoon cinnamon. Mix half of the flour into the butter mixture. In a separate bowl mix together 3 cups chopped mixed dried fruit, ½ cup preserved lemon peel and 115 g (¾ cup) blanched almonds. Add half of the fruit mixture to the cake batter. Once combined add the remaining flour and fruit, and then lastly add the freshly squeezed juice of 1 lemon. Beat well. Line two cake tins with baking paper. Spoon the mixture into the tins and bake in a 180°C oven for 3 hours. Ice with Royal Icing (see recipe, page 271).

Christmas Cake (Uncommon)

Cream 250 g butter and 345 g (1½ cups) brown sugar in a bowl. Separate 4 eggs and add the yolks to the butter mixture, beating for 2 minutes. Beat the egg whites until stiffly peaking and set aside. Sift together 300 g (2 cups) plain flour, 2 teaspoons ground cinnamon, 2 teaspoons allspice, 1 teaspoon ground cloves, 2 teaspoons salt and 1 teaspoon baking powder. In a separate bowl put 315 g (1½ cups) glacé cherries, 275 g (1½ cups) chopped dried figs, 330 g (1½ cups) chopped glacé pineapple, 125 g (1 cup) raisins, 280 g (2 cups) chopped mixed nuts and ½ cup mixed peel. Stir through 1 cup of the flour mixture to dust the fruit. Add the flour to the bowl, alternately with 250 ml pineapple juice, mixing well before incorporating more, then fold through the fruit and nuts with the remaining flour. Fold through the stiffly beaten egg whites. Grease and line a cake tin and pour in the cake mixture. Cook in a papered tin and bake in a 150°C (300°F/Gas 2) oven for 3–4 hours. These quantities make a very large and deliciously flavoured cake which keeps moist for a long time.

Cinnamon Roll

Cream 2 tablespoons butter and 2 tablespoons sugar in a bowl. Add 1 egg, stirring well. Sift in 300 g (2 cups) self-raising flour alternately with 250 ml (1 cup) milk, stirring to make a soft batter. Spoon into cake tins and bake in an 180°C oven for 1 hour. When cooked, butter all over and roll in ground cinnamon and icing sugar. Sultanas or preserved ginger may be added to the cake before baking.

Coffee Cake

Cream 225 g butter and 220 g (1 cup) sugar in a bowl. Add 4 eggs, one at a time, beating well after each addition. Sift together 350 g (2⅓ cups) plain flour and 2 teaspoons baking powder. Add the flour to the butter mixture with 125 ml (½ cup) milk. Spoon into a greased cake tin. In a separate bowl, mix together 2 tablespoons sugar, 30 g butter, 2½ tablespoons plain flour and good pinch each of nutmeg and cinnamon. Rub well with your fingertips until it resembles breadcrumbs. Push through a sieve over the uncooked cake to coat evenly. Bake in a 180°C oven for 1 hour. Cherries or fruit may be added to the cake.

Cream Cake

Beat 2 eggs in a bowl and add 250 ml (1 cup) cream and 220 g (1 cup) sugar, and heat well over a saucepan of simmering water. Sift together 225 g (1½ cups) plain flour, ½ teaspoon bicarbonate of soda, 1 teaspoon cream of tartar and 1 teaspoon salt; stir into the cream mixture. Spoon into a greased round cake tin and bake in an 180°C oven for about 40 minutes.

Cream Sandwich

Beat together 220 g (1 cup) sugar and 2 eggs in a bowl for 10 minutes. Add 2 tablespoons thick cream and beat for 5 minutes, then lightly sift in 225 g (1½ cups) self-raising flour. Add about 60 ml (¼ cup) milk. Spoon into two sandwich tins and bake in a 180°C oven for about 10 minutes. To make the filling, whip 250 ml (1 cup) cream with 1 teaspoon icing sugar. Add a few drops of vanilla essence and pink food colouring or 60 g (½ cup) chopped walnuts. Spread over the one of the cooled cakes and sit the other on top.

Date and Walnut Cake

Dissolve ¼ teaspoon bicarbonate of soda in 185 ml (¾ cup) milk. Pour the milk over 180 g (1 cup) chopped pitted dates in a bowl and leave to soak for 2 hours. Cream 225 g butter and 220 g (1 cup) sugar in a bowl. Add 3 eggs, one at a time, beating well after each addition. Stir in the dates, milk and 90 g (¾ cup) chopped walnuts. Sift together 300 g (2 cups) plain flour with 1½ teaspoons baking powder and a pinch of salt. Stir into the cake mixture until combined. Pour into a shallow cake tin. Bake in a 180°C oven for 50–60 minutes. When cold, ice with mocha icing (see recipes, page 270).

Foundation Cake Mixture

Cream 250 g butter and 330 g (1½ cups) sugar in a bowl. Add 4 eggs, one at a time, beating well after each addition. Add 250 ml (1 cup) milk, and then sift in 450 g (3 cups) plain flour and 1 teaspoon baking powder. Add a few drops of vanilla essence, to taste and pour into two greased rectangular or square cake tins. Fruit can be added for fruit cake or you can lemon zest to a plain cake.

Fruit Cake

Cream 225 g butter and 225 g (1 cup) sugar in a bowl. Add 4 eggs, one at a time, beating well after each addition. Chop 225 g (1¼ cups) pitted dates and combine with 225 g (1¾ cups) sultanas and 1 tablespoon plain flour. Add to the butter mixture with 225 g (1½ cups) plain flour, a pinch of grated nutmeg, 50 g (½ cup) rolled oats and the juice and finely grated zest of 1 lemon. You can stir in a few chopped nuts if you wish. Line the tin with a couple of layers of baking paper and spoon into the tin. Bake in a 180°C oven for 3 hours, or longer, until cooked.

Variation You can make a dark moist fruit cake by using the following ingredients: 450 g butter, 450 g (2 cups) soft brown sugar, 8 eggs, 450 g (3⅔ cup) sultanas, 450 g (3 cups) currants and 450 g (3⅔ cups) raisins, 225 g (1¼ cups) mixed peel, 450 g (3 cups) plain flour, 115 g (⅔ cup) cornflour, 1 teaspoon bicarbonate of soda, 1 teaspoon ground cinnamon, 2 teaspoons mixed spice, 125 ml (½ cup) brandy, 115 g (¾ cup) almonds, ¼ teaspoon salt.

Fruit Cake (Boiled)

Cream 3 eggs and 220 g (1 cup) sugar in a bowl. Put 180 g (1 cup) pitted dates in a saucepan with 125 g (1 cup) sultanas, 125 g (1 cup) raisins, 60 g (½ cup) chopped walnuts and 1 tablespoon mixed peel. Add 500 ml (2 cups) water, bring to the boil and boil for 10 minutes. Add 115 g chopped butter; remove from the heat. Sift 300 g (2 cups) plain flour into the bowl with the creamed sugar, then add 1 teaspoon mixed spice, ½ teaspoon ground nutmeg, 1 teaspoon ground cinnamon, 2 teaspoons cream of tartar and 1 teaspoon bicarbonate of soda. Add the boiled fruit and mix well. Spoon into a tin and bake in a 180°C oven for 30–45 minutes. Ice and sprinkle with walnuts.

Fruit Cake (Rich Christmas Cake)

Cream 450 g butter and 450 g (2 cups) sugar in a bowl. Add 10 well-beaten eggs and stir well to combine. In a separate bowl put 450 g (3²/₃ cups) sultanas, 450 g (3 cups) currants, 450 g (3²/₃ cups) raisins, 125 g (²/₃ cup) mixed peel, 115 g (²/₃ cup) chopped pitted dates, 115 g (½ cup) glacé cherries, 45 g (¼ cup) chopped preserved ginger, 45 g (¼ cup) chopped dried figs, 55 g (¼ cup) chopped pitted prunes, 55 g (⅓ cup) blanched almonds, 1 tablespoon finely grated orange zest and ¼ teaspoon grated ginger. Sift together 550 g (3²/₃ cups) plain flour with 1 teaspoon bicarbonate of soda, 1 teaspoon mixed spice, 1 teaspoon ground cinnamon, ¼ teaspoon ground nutmeg, ¼ teaspoon curry powder and a pinch of salt. Add the fruits to the butter mixture alternately with the flour, mixing well before adding more. Add 125 ml (½ cup) rum and 1 teaspoon each of vanilla, almond and lemon essences. Spoon into a greased tin and bake for 5 hours. Pour over 250 ml (1 cup) rum, and cool in the tin.

German Coffee Cake

Melt 350 g butter and mix in a bowl with 110 g (½ cup) sugar. Add 1 teaspoon lemon essence, 2 beaten eggs and 600 ml warm milk. Sift together 1.125 kg (7½ cups) flour, 1 teaspoon salt and a little ground nutmeg. Stir through the wet ingredients and finally add 185 ml (¾ cup) homemade yeast. Turn onto a greased oven tray. Dip your hands frequently into melted butter while gradually pressing the mixture out until it covers the tray and is 2 cm thick. Set aside in a warm place to rise. To make the streusel topping, mix together 80 g (½ cup) blanched chopped almonds in a bowl with 2 tablespoons sugar and 1 tablespoon plain flour. Rub in 1 tablespoon butter, then spread evenly over the cake. Bake in a 180°C oven for 20 minutes.

German Pound Cake

Cream 225 g butter and 225 g (1 cup) sugar in a bowl. Add 4 beaten eggs, mixing thoroughly. Gradually sift in 350 g (2⅓ cups) plain flour and ½ teaspoon baking powder, beating constantly. Fold through 125 g (²/₃ cup) mixed peel, 125 g (1 cup) sultanas and a few drops of lemon essence. You can also add 115 g (¾ cup) chopped almonds, if liked. Pour into a greased cake tin and bake in a 180°C oven for 1 hour. Ice the cake when cool.

Ginger Fluff Sandwich

Beat for 20 minutes 4 eggs with 165 g (³/₄ cup) sugar. Sift together 60 g (½ cup) arrowroot or cornflour, 1 tablespoon plain flour, 2 teaspoons ground ginger, 2 teaspoons cinnamon, 1 teaspoon cocoa, 1 teaspoon cream of tartar and ½ teaspoon bicarbonate of soda. Mix all together, and lastly add 2 teaspoons golden syrup. Pour into large sandwich tins and bake in a 180°C oven for 15–20 minutes. Filled with cream this makes a delightful sponge. If a revolving egg-beater is used the mixture seems much greater and lighter, and takes less than 2 minutes to beat.

Ginger Sandwich

Cream 1 tablespoon butter and 55 g (¼ cup) sugar in a bowl. Add 1 lightly beaten egg, stirring well. Add 175 g (½ cup) golden syrup, 125 ml (½ cup) milk, 150 g (1 cup) flour and 1 teaspoon ground cinnamon. Lastly, mix 1 teaspoon of bicarbonate of soda in a little boiling water and stir until dissolved. Add to the cake mixture and mix well. Spoon into two small greased sandwich tins and bake in a 180°C oven for 20 minutes. To make the filling, cream 4 tablespoons butter with 4 tablespoons of icing sugar in a bowl. Add 1 tablespoonful sherry or whisky and continue beating until smooth and spreadable. Spread over one cooled cake and place the other on top.

Ice Box Cake

Put 675 g (4½ cups) chopped chocolate in a bowl with with 2½ tablespoons of water. Sit over a saucepan of simmering water, making sure the bowl doesn't touch the water and stir until melted. Remove from the heat and continue beating until cold. Separate 4 eggs and beat the egg whites until stiffly peaking. Beat the egg yolks, one at a time, into the chocolate. Beat in 2 tablespoons of icing sugar, then the stiffly beaten egg whites. Add a dash of vanilla essence. Line a deep cake tin with baking paper. Cut a pre-bought sponge cake into three pieces horizontally to create three layers. Place one layer in the base. Pour half of the chocolate mixture on top, then sit another layer of cake on top. Add the rest of the chocolate mixture, and top with a layer of cake. Cover with the baking paper and place in the refrigerator overnight. Just before serving, cover the cake with whipped cream sweetened with a little vanilla essence. This cake will keep in the refrigerator for several days.

Jewish Cake

Cream 115 g butter and 210 g (1 scant cup) sugar in a bowl. Add 3 eggs, one at a time, beating well after each addition. Add 2 tablespoons milk, then stir in 150 g (1 cup) sifted plain flour, 2 heaped teaspoon cinnamon, 1 heaped teaspoon cream of tartar and ½ teaspoon bicarbonate of soda. Spoon into a rectangular cake tin lined with baking paper and cook in a 180°C oven for 15 minutes. Cut in half and spread with raspberry jam, then sandwich together. Sprinkle the top of the cake with icing sugar.

Madeira Cake

Cream 115 g butter and 110 g (½ cup) sugar in bowl. Add 4 eggs, one by one, beating well after each addition. Sift in 140 g (1 scant cup) plain flour and stir briefly to combine, but do not overmix. Add madeira liqueur according to taste. Spoon into a greased cake tin and bake in a 180°C oven for 30 minutes.

Marshmallow Cake

Whisk 4 egg whites in a clean bowl until stiffly peaking. Gradually incorporate 330 g (1½ cups) sugar one teaspoon at a time, then add a pinch of salt, 1 teaspoon vinegar and 1 teaspoon vanilla essence, and beat for about 20 minutes. Grease and line a sandwich tin with baking paper and cook in a 150°C oven. Spread a pre-bought sponge cake with jam and whipped cream and place the marshmallow cake on top.

'Oberon' Sponge Cake

Beat 4 eggs in a bowl with 110 g (½ cup) sugar until thick, adding a pinch of salt and 1 teaspoon bicarbonate of soda. Melt 1 teaspoon butter in a saucepan with 4 tablespoons milk and bring almost to the boil. Sift together 75 g (½ cup) plain flour, 60 g (½ cup) cornflour and 2 teaspoons cream of tartar. Add the milk to the flour alternately to the egg mixture. Lastly, stir through a little vanilla essence for flavouring. Spoon into a large greased cake tin and bake in an 180°C oven for 20–25 minutes.

Old English Sponge Cake

Grease a large cake tin. Sift together 2 teaspoons plain flour and 2 teaspoons icing sugar and sprinkle a little inside the greased tin to coat the base and side. (Keep the remainder for the top of the sponge.) Separate 8 eggs and whisk the whites until very stiff. Gradually add the beaten yolks and add 400 g (1¾ cups) caster sugar — whisk well for 10 minutes. Add 225 g (1½ cups) plain flour and stir through with a flat-bladed knife. Add the freshly squeezed juice of ½ lemon and stir to combine. Spoon into the prepared tin, but only fill to a little more than halfway. Use a small sieve and tap a little of the icing sugar and flour mixture over the top of the cake mixture like thick dust (this forms the crust). Bake in a 150°C oven for 1½–2 hours — do not open the door for at least 30 minutes and do not move the cake while baking.

One-Egg Sandwich

Cream 1 tablespoonful butter with 220 g (1 cup) sugar in a bowl and add 1 tablespoon of boiling water, stirring well. Add 1 well-beaten egg and mix in. Sift together 225 g (1½ cups) plain flour and 1 teaspoon cream of tartar, and add to the cake mixture. Stir ½ teaspoon bicarbonate of soda into 125 ml (½ cup) milk until dissolved and add to the cake mixture. Spoon into a greased cake tin and bake in a 180°C oven for 15–20 minutes.

One-Minute Cake

Sift 150 g (1 cup) plain flour into a bowl with 165 g (¾ cup) sugar, 3 eggs, 3 tablespoons milk and 1 tablespoon melted butter. Beat together briskly for 1 minute, then add 1 teaspoon cream of tartar and ½ teaspoon bicarbonate of soda. Mix lightly and spoon into a sandwich tin or small patty tins. Bake in a 180°C oven for 10–15 minutes. This recipe can be adapted to a variety of flavours and shapes.

Oriental Ginger Bread

Cream 125 g butter and 55 g (¼ cup) sugar in a bowl. Add 2 eggs, one at a time, beating well after each addition. Stir in 1 tablespoon golden syrup. Sift together 300 g (2 cups) self-raising flour, 1 teaspoon ground cinnamon and 1 teaspoon ground ginger. Sprinkle in 3 tablespoons desiccated coconut and add 125–185 ml water and thoroughly beat. Spoon into a greased cake tin and bake in a 180°C oven for 45 minutes.

Make an icing in the following manner. Cream 185 g (1½ cups) icing sugar and 2 teaspoons butter in a bowl. Add 1 teaspoon coffee essence and enough hot water to make a spreadable consistency. When the cake is cool, spread over the top and sprinkle with 45 g (½ cup) coconut.

Pineapple Sponge

Beat 5 eggs in a bowl and add 220 g (1 cup) sugar and beat for 20 minutes. Add 150 g (1 cup) plain flour and 1½ teaspoons baking powder. Lastly, stir through 1 tablespoon grated pineapple. Bake in sandwich tins in a 180°C oven for 20 minutes.

Make a filling by combining 1 tablespoon butter in a saucepan with 1 beaten egg, 110 g (½ cup) sugar, 2 tablespoons grated pineapple and 2 teaspoons arrowroot that has been moistened with a little warm water. Cook until the mixture thickens, stirring all the time. Allow to cool and spread between the sponge cakes.

Pineapple Wheel Cake

Melt 125 g butter. Pour into the bottom of a cake tin and cover evenly with 230 g (1 cup) brown sugar. Slice 1 tin pineapple rings into strips, leaving 1 whole ring intact. Place the pineapple ring in the middle of the cake tin over the sugar. Arrange the pineapple strips to radiate outwards — they should resemble the spokes of a wheel. Make a sponge cake mixture using 4 eggs and 220 g (1 cup) sugar, beaten for 10 minutes with a balloon whisk. Add 150 g (1 cup) self-raising flour and a little pineapple juice. Pour this mixture over the arranged pineapple wheel, place in 180°C oven and bake for 35–40 minutes, or until firm. Invert onto a plate to cool. Serve whipped cream on top, if liked.

A tablespoon of gelatine added to a cake will equal three eggs. Dissolve gelatine in a little cold water for a few minutes; then add enough boiling water to make a cupful. Whip mixture with an egg beater until it is light and add to the other ingredients.

Pound Cake

Put 450 g (3 cups) currants in a bowl with 450 g (3²/₃ cups) sultanas, 225 g (1½ cups) mixed peel and a few chopped almonds, if liked. Pour enough brandy over the fruit to coat and set aside overnight. Strain any liquid and reserve the fruit. Cream 450 g butter and 450 g (2 heaped cups) sugar in a bowl. Add 10 eggs one at a time, beating well after each addition. Add 1 tablespoon golden syrup, 1 teaspoon ground nutmeg and 1–2 drops each of vanilla essence and brandy. Add the fruit and mix through. Sift together 450 g (3 cups) plain flour and a pinch of salt, then stir through until thoroughly combined. Spoon into a cake tin and bake in a 150°C oven for 5 hours.

Prune Cake

Put 12 pitted prunes in a saucepan and add enough water to cover. Simmer for 20 minutes, or until the prunes are tender; strain the prunes and cut in half, reserving 4 tablespoons of the cooking liquid. Cream 115 g butter and 165 g (¾ cup) sugar. Add 2 eggs, one at a time, beating well after each addition. Sift in 160 g (1 heaped cup) self-raising flour, 1 teaspoon cocoa powder, ¼ teaspoon ground cloves, ¼ teaspoon cinnamon, ¼ teaspoon nutmeg. Stir into the butter mixture with the reserved prune juice and the prunes. Spoon into a greased and floured cake tin and bake in a 180°C oven for 45 minutes. For a change, cut the cake in half and put cream between.

Rainbow Cake

Cream 225 g butter and 165 g (¾ cup) sugar in a bowl. Separate 6 eggs. Add the egg yolks and beat well. Sift together 300 g (2 cups) plain flour, 1 teaspoon bicarbonate of soda and 2 teaspoons cream of tartar. Add to the butter mixture alternately with 250 ml (1 cup) milk. Whisk the egg whites until stiff peaks form then fold through. Divide the mixture into three parts; tint one yellow with yellow food colouring, colour one with 55 g (scant ½ cup) cocoa powder and one with 1 teaspoon red food colouring. Arrange the layers with chocolate at bottom, pink in the middle and yellow on top. Join with raspberry jam and ice with white icing. Sprinkle with coconut.

Raisin and Nut Cake

Cream 125 g butter in a bowl until white and creamy. Separate 2 eggs and beat the egg whites until stiff peaks form. Beat in 220 g (1 cup) sugar and the egg yolks. Dissolve ½ teaspoon bicarbonate of soda in 125 ml (½ cup) milk and stir into the butter mixture. Sift in 300 g (2 cups) plain flour and 1 teaspoon cream of tartar. Lastly, fold through the stiffly beaten egg whites, 125 g (1 cup) raisins and 125 g (1 cup) finely chopped walnuts. Spoon into a round cake tin and bake in a 180°C oven for 30–45 minutes. Allow to cool and ice the cake with your favourite icing.

Royal Cream Loaf Cake

Cream 125 g butter and 220 g (1 cup) sugar in a bowl. Separate 2 eggs and beat the whites to a stiff peak. Beat the egg yolks and a few drops of lemon essence in a separate bowl and add to the butter mixture. Sift together 150 g (1 cup) plain flour with 60 g ($\frac{1}{2}$ cup) cornflour and 1$\frac{1}{2}$ teaspoons baking powder. Gradually add to the cake mixture alternately with 125 ml ($\frac{1}{2}$ cup) milk. Fold in the stiffly beaten egg whites until combined. Spoon into a greased loaf tin and bake in a 180°C oven for 25–45 minutes. Ice.

Royal Strawberry Shortcake

Cream 4 tablespoons butter and 220 g (1 cup) sugar in a bowl. Add 1 beaten egg and mix well. Sift together 300 g (2 cups) plain flour, 1 tablespoon baking powder and a pinch of salt. Add to the butter mixture, alternately with 250 ml (1 cup) milk. Stir in 1 teaspoon vanilla essence and mix well. Pour into a greased square cake tin and bake in a 180°C oven for 30 minutes. When cool, halve the cake. Spread whipped cream over one half and topped with crushed sweetened strawberries. Sit the other cake half on top and spread with whipped cream. Decorate with whole strawberries.

Russian Nut Cake

Cream 3 tablespoons butter and 220 g (1 cup) sugar in a bowl, Add 3 eggs, one at a time, beating well after each addition. Sift together 225 g (1$\frac{1}{2}$ cups) plain flour, 2$\frac{1}{2}$ teaspoons baking powder, 1 teaspoon mixed spice, 1$\frac{1}{2}$ tablespoons cocoa powder and a few chopped almonds and walnuts. Stir in 185 ml ($\frac{3}{4}$ cup) milk and mix well. Bake in two sandwich tins. Fill with cream and ice with chocolate icing; sprinkle with extra chopped nuts to decorate.

Seed Cake

This cake was a prize-winner at Dubbo show. Cream 250 g butter and 220 g (1 cup) sugar in a bowl. Add 3 beaten eggs and a pinch of salt and beat well. Pour in 250 ml (1 cup) milk, then sift in 320 g (3 scant cups) plain flour with 1 teaspoon baking powder. Add 2 tablespoons caraway seeds and mix to combine. Spoon into a greased and lined round 18 cm cake tin. Bake in a 175°C oven for 1 hour.

Soda Cake (No Eggs)

In a bowl mix together 300 g (2 cups) plain flour, 2 tablespoons butter, 125 g (1 cup) raisins and 150 g (1 cup) currants and a little mixed peel. Stir in 220 g (1 cup) sugar, 1/2 teaspoon bicarbonate of soda, 1/2 teaspoon ground cloves and 1/2 teaspoon ground nutmeg. Add 2 teaspoons vinegar and 250 ml (1 cup) milk. Stir to form a rather stiff batter, spoon into a greased cake tin and bake in an 175°C oven for about 1 hour.

Soft Pound Cake

Cream 225 g butter and 440 g (2 cups) sugar in a bowl. Add 4 eggs one at a time, beating well after each addition. Add 250 ml (1 cup) milk, 1½ tablespoons caraway seeds and 1½ teaspoons vanilla essence. Lastly, add 550 g (3²/₃ cups) plain flour, 1 teaspoon bicarbonate of soda and 2 teaspoons cream of tartar. Grease and line a cake tin with baking paper. Bake in a 175°C oven for 1 hour.

Sour Cream Cake

Cream 175 g butter and 230 g (1 cup) soft brown sugar in a bowl. Add 2 eggs one at a time, beating well after each addition. Gradually add 250 g (1 cup) sour cream, beating well. Add 160 g (1 cup) chopped pitted dates or 125 g (1 cup) raisins and stir through. Sift together 270 g (1¾ cups) plain flour with 1 teaspoon bicarbonate of soda, 2 teaspoons ground cinnamon, 1 teaspoon ground nutmeg and a pinch of salt. Stir through the cake mixture, then spoon into a greased cake tin. Bake in an 180°C oven for 45 minutes.

Sour Cream Chocolate Cake

Beat 3 eggs well, then add 220 g (1 cup) sugar, and beat again. Stir 1 teaspoon bicarbonate of soda into 250 g (1 cup) sour cream, and beat into the egg and sugar mixture. Sift together 200 g (1⅓ cups) plain flour, ¼ teaspoon salt and 1 teaspoon baking powder. Fold the flour gradually into the wet mixture. Melt 55 g chocolate and stir through with 1 teaspoon vanilla essence. Pour into a greased loaf tin and bake in a 180°C oven for 45 minutes. Ice when cool.

To make the icing, cream 2 teaspoons butter and 185 g (1½ cups) icing sugar in a bowl. Add a few drops of vanilla essence and enough water to make a spreadable consistency. Spread over the cake to serve.

Speedway Cake

Put 115 g butter in a bowl with 165 g (¾ cup) sugar, 2 eggs, 1 breakfast cup self-raising flour, 3 tablespoons milk, a pinch of salt and the finely grated zest of 1 orange. Beat hard for 5 minutes, or until the mixture looks creamy and spongy. Bake in a 180°C oven for 30–45 minutes.

Sponge Roll

Separate 5 eggs and beat the whites until stiff peaks form. Add the yolks and 5 tablespoons sugar and beat until stiff. Sift together 5 tablespoons flour and 1 teaspoon baking powder and add to the egg mixture. Add a little vanilla essence, to flavour, and mix well. Spoon into a greased cake tin and bake in a 220°C oven for 10–15 minutes. Turn out onto a dry tea towel and roll up quickly into a log. Allow to cool, then unroll, spread with jam and re-roll as before.

Sponge Sandwich

Separate 3 eggs and beat the whites until stiff peaks form. Add the yolks, stirring well, then add 110 g (½ cup) sugar; beat until mixture is stiff and thick. Sift together 120 g (¾ cup) plain flour with ½ teaspoon cream of tartar and ¼ teaspoon bicarbonate of soda. Stir into the egg mixture. Melt 1 teaspoon butter in 3 tablespoons boiling water and mix in well. Spoon into two sandwich tins and bake in 180°C oven for 20–25 minutes. Join the sponges together with mock cream or any other filling of your choice.

Strawberry Shortcakes

Wash 250 g strawberries, remove the stems and cut into slices (reserve a few to use a garnish). Place in a bowl and add 165 g (¾ cup) sugar and the finely grated zest of 1 lemon. Set aside for about 1 hour — this will draw out the juice from the berries and dissolve the sugar. Sift together 300 g (2 cups) plain flour in a bowl with 2 teaspoons baking powder and ½ teaspoon salt. Add 120 g softened butter and rub in with your fingertips. Slowly add 125–185 ml milk until the mixture forms a ball that will leave the sides of the bowl. (It is difficult to give an exact amount of milk. It is best to begin by adding ½ cup and add more if needed). Place dough on a lightly floured work surface, press lightly into shape and roll out to about 1 cm thick. Cut into rounds with a 5 cm round pastry cutter. Brush the surface with melted butter, place one round over another and bake in a 200°C oven for 15–20 minutes. They will separate easily when baked. Arrange on individual plates. Place generous amounts of the macerated strawberries over the lower crust and top with the second biscuit. Cover with either cut strawberries or whipped cream.

Variation Instead of making individual shortcakes, you can make one large cake. Divide the dough in half and roll each piece out to about 1 cm thickness. Paint the surface of dough with melted butter, place one on top of the other and bake. Decorate in the same manner and serve on a platter.

Sultana Cake

Cream 225 g butter and 230 g (1 cup) caster sugar in a bowl. Add 3 eggs, one at a time, beating well after each addition. Sift together 350 g (2⅓ cups) plain flour, 1½ teaspoons baking powder and a pinch of salt. Sift three times in total. Dust 350 g (1¾ cups) sultanas with a little of the measured flour. Flavour 150 ml milk with a little vanilla essence. Add the flour, sultanas and milk alternately to the butter mixture until all incorporated. Grease and line a 20 cm square or round cake tin with baking paper and spoon the cake batter into the tin. Bake in a 180°C oven for 1 hour 15 minutes. Allow to cool in the tin before turning out.

Three Minute Sandwich

Sift together 150 g (1 cup) flour and 1 teaspoon cornflour. Place in a bowl with 220 g (1 cup) sugar, 3 tablespoons milk, 2 tablespoons melted butter and 3 well-beaten eggs. Beat all together for 3 minutes, then add 1 teaspoon baking powder. Spoon into sandwich tins and bake in a 180°C oven for 20 minutes.

Victoria Sandwich

Beat 220 g (1 cup) sugar and 3–4 eggs in a bowl for 10 minutes using an egg beater. Sift together 150 g (1 cup) plain flour and 1 teaspoon baking powder and add to the egg mixture. Melt 1 teaspoon butter in 4 tablespoon boiling water and stir into the cake mixture to combine. Spoon into greased sandwich tins and bake in a 180°C oven for about 20 minutes. Ice or fill as desired.

Biscuits and Slices

Afghan Biscuits

Cream 200 g butter and 110 g (½ cup) sugar in a bowl. Sift in 225 g (1½ cups) plain flour and a pinch of salt, then add 1 tablespoon cocoa powder and 1 tablespoon desiccated coconut, stirring well to combine. Lastly, add 55 g (1¾ cups) cornflakes and stir gently to combine. They must be crisped in the oven and then crushed. Bake in a 180°C oven. Ice with chocolate icing and decorate with chopped walnuts.

Almond Horseshoes

Cream 115 g butter and 115 g (½ cup) caster sugar in a bowl. Mix together 225 g (1½ cups) sifted self-raising flour, 115 g (⅔ cup) rice flour and 450 g (4½ cups) ground almonds. Mix together with the butter mixture. Bind with 2 egg yolks. Roll out thinly and cut into narrow strips, about 10 cm long and 2.5 cm wide. Shape into horseshoes (you should make about 40 biscuits in total) and stud each with an almond. Line a baking tray with baking paper and arrange the horseshoes on the tray. Bake in a 180°C oven for 20 minutes.

Belgian Shortbread

Cream 115 g butter and 110 g (½ cup) sugar in a bowl. Add 1 beaten egg yolk, then sift in 150 g (1 cup) self-raising flour and ¼ teaspoon salt. Roll out half the mixture to line a shallow square cake tin. Spread thinly with raspberry jam, then a layer of pitted dates. Place the remainder of the shortbread mixture on top. Bake in a 150°C oven for 35–40 minutes.

Bran Biscuits

Cream 115 g butter and 220 g (1 cup) sugar in a bowl. Add 1 beaten egg, stirring well. Sift in 190 g (1¼ cups) self-raising flour. Lastly, add 110 g (1½ cups) wheatbran. Roll out thinly, cut into strips, and bake in a 180°C oven until golden brown.

Brettles

Cream 125 g butter and 55 g (¼ cup) caster sugar in a bowl. Stir in 1 egg yolk, the finely grated zest of ½ orange and the finely grated zest of ½ lemon. Stir in ½ teaspoon vanilla essence. Beat well, then sift in 150 g (1 cup) plain flour and add 1 tablespoon freshly squeezed lemon juice; mix until the mixture is light. Cover the dough and stand in a cool place until firm. Roll into small balls, dip into beaten egg whites and roll to coat in finely chopped nuts. Top each with half a glacé cherry. Bake in a 180°C oven for 20–30 minutes.

Caramel Fingers

Cream 115 g butter with 115 g (½ cup) soft brown sugar in a bowl. Add 1 egg and beat well. Sift in 150 g (1 cup) self-raising flour and a pinch of salt, then add a little vanilla essence, to flavour. Add 120 g (¾ cup) finely chopped dates and 90 g (¾ cup) finely chopped walnuts. Spread thinly over a greased baking tray and bake in an 180°C oven for 45 minutes. Cut into short lengths and allow to cool on the tray.

Chocolate Biscuits

Melt 55 g milk chocolate in a bowl over a saucepan of simmering water. Stir in 60 g (½ cup) finely chopped walnuts and 75 g (2½ cups) rice bubbles. Place teaspoonfuls on a tray of baking paper and refrigerate to set.

Chocolate Macaroons 1

Mix 225 g (2¼ cups) ground almonds in a bowl with 115 g finely grated milk chocolate and 220 g (1 cup) sugar. Work into a firm paste with the 3–4 stiffly beaten egg whites. Drop mixture onto a greased baking tray and bake in a 180°C oven until firm.

Chocolate Macaroons 2

Carefully sift 225 g (1¾ cups) icing sugar in a bowl and add 60 g (½ cup) grated dark semi-sweet chocolate, 55 g (½ cup) ground almonds and ½ teaspoon vanilla essence. Mix in enough egg white to bind together (about 2 egg whites). Work into a piping bag with a rose-shaped nozzle, and squeeze out small fancy-shaped biscuits onto a lightly greased baking tray. Set aside for a few hours until dry and firm, then bake in a 150°C oven until crisp.

Chocolate Twists

Mix 200 g (1⅓ cups) plain flour with 60 g (½ cup) cocoa powder, 55 g (¼ cup) sugar and enough milk to make a not too firm dough. Break small pieces from the dough and roll into logs to make twists. Bake in a 180°C oven. When cool, ice with your choice of Chocolate Icing (see recipes, pages 268–9).

Coffee Creams

Cream 115 g butter and 110 g (½ cup) sugar in a bowl. Add 1 well-beaten egg, 1 tablespoon coffee essence and 1 teaspoon vanilla essence, beating well to combine. Sift together 300 g (2 cups) plain flour and 1 teaspoon bicarbonate of soda. Add to the butter mixture and stir to a nice stiff dough. Roll out very thinly and cut into shapes. Arrange on a greased baking tray and bake in 180°C oven for 10–15 minutes.

To make the icing, cream 125 g (1 cup) cup icing sugar and 1½ tablespoons butter in a bowl. Add enough coffee essence to flavour the icing and a little hot water if needed. Ice the cooled biscuits.

Variation You can make an Indian coffee cream using the following method. Cream 115 g butter and 110 g (½ cup) sugar in a bowl. Add 1 beaten egg and 1 tablespoon coffee essence and ½ teaspoon vanilla essence, beating well. Sift in 300 g (2 cups) self-raising flour and mix to a dough. Roll out the dough and cut into biscuits. Brush with an egg wash, cover with roughly chopped nuts and bake in a 180°C oven for 20 minutes. When cooled, join together with a filling made from 1 tablespoon butter, 125 g (1 cup) sifted icing sugar and a little coffee essence, to taste.

Cornflake Biscuits

Cream 250 g butter and 110 g (½ cup) sugar in a bowl. Add 1 well-beaten egg, 60 g (½ cup) chopped walnuts and 45 g (½ cup) desiccated coconut. Stir well to combine, then lightly fold in 150 g (5 cups) cornflakes. Spoon about 2 teaspoons into a patty tin lined with paper cases. Bake in a 150°C oven for 20 minutes. Store biscuits in an airtight tin.

Cornflake Kisses

Sift together 150 g (1 cup) plain flour, ½ teaspoon baking powder and a pinch of salt. Rub in 140 g butter, then add 220 g (1 cup) sugar, mixing well. Add 90 g (3 cups) cornflakes, 160 g (1 cup) chopped pitted dates and 70 g (½ cup) crushed peanuts. Mix in 2 beaten eggs and enough milk to make a stiff dough. Roll into balls and roll each ball in cornflakes, to coat. Place on a greased baking tray and bake slowly in a 150°C oven for 20–30 minutes.

Crisp Biscuits

Sift 550 g (3²/₃ cups) plain flour and a pinch of salt into a bowl and rub in 175 g butter until the mixture resembles fine breadcrumbs. Add 55 g (½ cup) ground almonds, then stir through a little milk or water to make a firm dough. Set aside for 30 minutes. Take small balls of dough and press into flattened rounds using the palm of your hand. Place on an ungreased tray. Bake in a 180°C oven for 15–20 minutes. This recipe makes 40–50 biscuits that are twice the size of a penny.

Date Biscuits

Put 450 g (2½ cups) pitted dates, 220 g (1 cup) sugar and 125 ml (½ cup) cold water in a saucepan. Bring to the boil, then reduce the heat and cook until the dates have softened. Cream 250 g butter and 230 g (1 cup) soft brown sugar in a bowl. Add 250 g (2½ cups) rolled oats and stir through. Sift in 375 (2½ cups) plain flour, 1 teaspoon bicarbonate of soda, then add 125 ml (½ cup) warm water. Knead the dough briefly, then divide in half. Roll out both halves, thinly, to the same size and shape. Spread the cooled date mixture over one half and cover with the other half. Cut into fingers, arrange on a greased baking tray and bake in a 180°C oven.

Date Dainties

Put 180 g (1 cup) pitted dates in a saucepan with 110 g (½ cup) sugar and the freshly squeezed juice of ½ lemon. Bring to a boil, cover, then cook over medium heat until the dates are soft. Remove from the heat and cool. To make the pastry, cream 30 g butter and 85 g (⅓ cup) sugar in a bowl. Add 1 egg and beat well to combine. Sift together 225 g (1½ cups) flour with 1 teaspoon baking powder and stir into the butter mixture to form a firm dough. Divide the dough into two portions and roll out to an even size and shape. Spread all of date mixture over one half and cover with the other sheet of dough. Bake in an 180°C oven for about 30 minutes. Cut into squares, to serve.

Date Slice

Sift together 175 g self-raising flour and a pinch of salt. Add 1 tablespoon caster sugar and rub in 85 g butter until the mixture resembles breadcrumbs. Beat 1 egg and stir through 3 tablespoons cold water and the freshly squeezed juice of 1 lemon. Add to the dough and stir with a flat-bladed knife to combine. Roll out the dough and divide into two portions. Place one half in the base of a 20 x 25 cm baking tin and cover with pitted dates. Cover with the other half of the dough and bake in the oven for 20 minutes. To make the icing, mix together 125 g (1 cup) icing sugar, 1 tablespoon melted butter, passionfruit pulp and enough hot water to make a spreadable consistency. When cool, spread the icing over the slice and cut into fingers to serve.

Elsie's Fingers

Cream 115 g butter and 3 tablespoons sugar in a bowl. Add 1 egg, beat again, then sift in 225 g (1½ cups) plain flour and 1 teaspoon baking powder. Break off small pieces, roll into log shapes between the palms of hands and dip in sugar, to coat. Bake in 180°C oven until pale brown.

Foundation Mixture

Put 450 g (3 cups) plain flour and 350 g (1½ cups) caster sugar in a bowl and rub in 225 g butter. Flavour with vanilla essence and the grated zest of 1 lemon. Add 3 well-beaten eggs, stirring well to combine. This should make a firm dough, which can be covered and left in a cool place for some time. When needed, roll out the dough and sprinkle over 1 teaspoon baking powder. Knead the dough, fold it over, and roll out again. Cut into shapes, lay on a greased baking tray and bake in a 200°C oven. When cooked, brush over with whipped egg whites and decorate.

Forcer Biscuits 1

Cream 115 g butter and 110 g (½ cup) sugar in a bowl. Beat in 1 egg, stirring well. Sift together 175 g flour, 60 g (⅓ cup) rice flour and 1 teaspoon baking powder. Fold through the butter mixture and add a few drops of vanilla essence, if liked. Roll out very thinly and cut with a pastry cutter. Bake in a 220°C oven for 8 minutes.

Forcer Biscuits 2

Melt 2 tablespoons butter in a saucepan and stir in 1 tablespoon honey until softened. Remove from the heat and place in a bowl. Add 1 egg and 110 g (½ cup) sugar, beating well. Sift together 300 g (2 cups) plain flour, 1 teaspoon cream of tartar, ½ teaspoon bicarbonate of soda and a pinch of salt. Add to the cake mixture to form a stiff dough. Half-fill a piping bag with the mixture and pipe 5 cm lengths onto a greased baking tray. Bake in a 180°C oven for about 10 minutes. When cold, sandwich the biscuits together with a cream filling made of icing sugar and butter.

French Biscuits

Sift 30 g (¼ cup) icing sugar in a bowl and add 85 g butter. Beat together until creamy, then sift in 75 g (½ cup) plain flour and stir until the mixture is soft and creamy. Add vanilla essence, to taste. Put the mixture into an piping bag with a rose-shaped nozzle and squeeze biscuits out onto a greased baking tray, leaving space for spreading. Leave them in a cool place to harden, then bake in a 200°C oven for 5–6 minutes. Garnish with crystallised rose petals, using a spot of jam to adhere.

French Coffee Creams

Cream 115 g butter and 110 g (½ cup) sugar in a bowl. Add 1 well-beaten egg, 1 tablespoon coffee essence and ½ teaspoon vanilla essence, stirring well to combine. Sift in 300 g (2 cups) self-raising flour. Roll out and cut into biscuits. Brush with a little egg wash, cover with chopped walnuts and bake in a 180°C oven for 20 minutes. To make the filling, cream 1 tablespoon butter and 125 g (1 cup) icing sugar in a bowl. Add a few drops of coffee essence and enough water to make a stiff paste. When cold, join together with the filling.

Fruit Slices

First make the fruit filling. Put 2 tablespoons arrowroot and ½ tablespoon water in a saucepan and stir to make a paste. Add 185 g (1½ cups) raisins or 185 g (1 cup) chopped pitted dates or 185 g (1 cup) mixed dried fruit. Add finely grated zest and juice of 1 orange and 1 lemon. Add 4 tablespoons soft brown sugar. Bring to the boil, then cook for 3 minutes. Remove from the heat and set aside to cool. To make the biscuit mixture, cream 115 g butter and 55 g (¼ cup) caster sugar in a bowl. Add 1 egg, stirring well to combine. Sift together 225 g (1½ cups) plain flour, 1½ teaspoons baking powder, ½ teaspoon ground nutmeg, ½ teaspoon ground ginger, ½ teaspoon allspice and ½ teaspoon ground cinnamon. Add to the butter mixture and stir to make a firm dough. Divide into two portions and roll each into an oblong sheet, about 5 mm thick. Place one sheet in the base of a greased rectangular cake tin. Cover with the cooled fruit mixture. Place the other biscuit sheet on top, glaze with water and sprinkle with sugar. Bake in a 180°C oven for 20 minutes. When nearly cooked, cut into fingers and return to the oven to dry.

Fruity Brittles

Sift 150 g (1 cup) self-raising flour into a bowl and rub in 140 g butter. Beat in 220 g (1 cup) sugar, 160 g (1 cup) chopped pitted dates and 40 g (^{1}/$_3$ cup) chopped walnuts. Beat 1 egg and stir in well. Roll small pieces of mixture in cornflakes to coat. Place on a hot greased baking tray and bake in a 220°C oven. The biscuits will rise quickly, then drop and have a 'bubbly' appearance. Watch them carefully during cooking, as they burn easily.

Lace Biscuits

Mix together 90 g (3 cups) cornflakes, 65 g (^{3}/$_4$ cup) desiccated coconut and 2 tablespoons melted butter in a bowl. Beat together 165 g (^{3}/$_4$ cup) sugar and 2 stiffly beaten eggs whites in another bowl. Add to the coconut mixture. Drop spoonfuls onto a greased baking tray and bake in a 180°C oven.

Lemon Biscuits

Cream 225 g butter and 220 g (1 cup) sugar in a bowl. Add 2 eggs and beat well to combine. Sift together 450 g (3 cups) plain flour and 2 teaspoons cream of tartar and add to the butter mixture with the finely grated zest of 1 lemon and a little lemon essence. Dissolve 1 teaspoon bicarbonate of soda in a little warm water and add to the mixture, stirring well. Roll out the dough and cut into the desired shapes. Arrange on a greased baking tray and bake in a 180°C oven for about 15–20 minutes.

Melting Moments

Cream 225 g butter and 2 tablespoons icing sugar in a bowl. Add 2 tablespoons cornflour, and then stir in 225 g (1½ cups) plain flour. Roll small pieces of the mixture into a ball, press flat with a fork and bake in greased baking tray in a 150°C oven until pale brown. Spread half of the biscuits together with jam or icing and top with the other halves. Press to join together.

Monte Carlos

Cream 115 g butter and 110 g (½ cup) sugar in a bowl. Add 1 well-beaten egg and beat well. Add 45 g (½ cup) desiccated coconut and 2 teaspoons golden syrup, mixing well. Sift in 300 g (2 cups) plain flour and ½ teaspoon bicarbonate of soda. Break off small pieces and arrange on a greased baking tray. Bake in a 180°C oven. When cooked, fasten two biscuits together with raspberry jam and icing.

Munchies

Sift 150 g (1 cup) flour into a bowl and add 90 g (1 cup) desiccated coconut and 200 g (2 cups) rolled oats. Put 250 g butter in a saucepan and melt with 2 tablespoons golden syrup. Dissolve 1 teaspoon bicarbonate of soda in 3 tablespoons boiling water and add to the butter mixture. Beat well to combine, then stir into the dry ingredients. Drop teaspoonfuls of the mixture onto a baking tray and bake in a 180°C oven until golden brown.

Oatmeal and Raisin Cookies

Put 175 g (1¾ cups) rolled oats through a food processor. Cream 125 g butter and 220 g (1 cup) sugar in a bowl. Add 1 well-beaten egg, beating well, then add 90 g (¾ cup) raisins and the rolled oats. Mix thoroughly to combine. Sift together 225 g (1½ cups) plain flour, 2 teaspoons baking powder, ½ teaspoon salt, ¾ teaspoon ground cinnamon, ½ teaspoon ground cloves and ½ teaspoon allspice. Add to the butter mixture alternately with 125 ml (½ cup) milk. Roll out on a lightly floured work surface, cut with a pastry cutter, and bake in a 180°C oven for 15–20 minutes. This makes about 30 cookies.

Oatmeal Shortbread

Melt 225 g butter in a saucepan. Transfer to a bowl with 150 g (1½ cups) oatmeal, 165 g (¾ cup) sugar, 150 g (1 cup) sifted plain flour and 1 teaspoon baking powder. Stir well to combine. Press the mixture into greased rectangular cake tins, flatten down with fingers or wooden spoon, and bake in a 150°C oven for 20 minutes. Cut into fingers or squares while still warm; do not remove from tin until quite cold.

Peanut Crisps

Melt 225 g butter and 2 teaspoons golden syrup in a saucepan. Sift together 225 g (1½ cups) plain flour and 1 teaspoon baking powder. Place in a bowl with 220 g (1 cup) sugar and 350 g (2 heaped cups) peanuts, then stir through the butter mixture. Lastly, stir through 1 well-beaten egg. Drop teaspoonfuls of the mixture onto a greased baking tray, leaving room for spreading. Bake in a 150°C oven.

Radio Biscuits

Cream 175 g butter and 60 g (½ cup) icing sugar in a bowl. Sift together 175 g flour and 60 g (½ cup) custard powder three times. Add to the butter and sugar. Roll into small balls and press with a fork. Bake in a 180°C oven for 15 minutes. When cooked, place together with jam or an icing sugar and butter filling.

Raspberry Cream Slices

Cream 115 g butter and 115 g (½ cup) caster sugar in a bowl. Add 2 tablespoons milk, then sift in 175 g self-raising flour, 2 tablespoons cornflour and a pinch of salt. Add a few drops of pink food colouring to make the mixture a pale pink colour. Divide the mixture into three portions and roll into logs. Cover in baking paper and chill in the refrigerator for 2 hours. Cut into slices with a knife and place on greased baking trays. Prick each biscuit with a fork. Bake in a 180°C oven for 10 minutes. To make the filling, cream 55 g butter and 140 g icing sugar in a bowl. Mix in 2 tablespoons jam and 1 teaspoon freshly squeezed lemon juice; join biscuits together.

Raspberry Crescents

Sift 225 g (1½ cups) plain flour into a bowl and rub in 140 g butter. Add 115 g (½ cup) caster sugar, 12 drops raspberry essence and a few drops of red food colouring to make a pretty pink colour. Mix to a firm paste with 1 well-beaten egg. Roll out to about 1 cm thickness and cut into biscuits with a crescent-shaped cutter. Bake in a 180°C oven for 10–15 minutes. Allow to cool.

To make the raspberry icing, sift 225 g (¾ cups) icing sugar through a fine sieve, and add 12 drops of raspberry essence, 3–4 drops red food colouring and enough whipped egg white to form a soft paste. Spread a coating of this on each biscuit, and leave them in a warm place to dry.

Raspberry Drops

Cream 120 g butter and 220 g (1 cup) sugar in a bowl. Add 2 well-beaten eggs, stirring well. Sift together 450 g (3 cups) plain flour and 2 teaspoons baking powder. Add to the butter mixture and stir to combine. Roll into small balls using your hands, dip into sugar to coat. Flatten slightly with the palm of your hand and make a small indent in the centre of each biscuits using your fingertips. Add a little raspberry jam into the centre of each and arrange on a greased baking tray. Bake in a 180°C oven for about 15 minutes.

Raspberry Rings

Sift 225 g (1½ cups) plain flour into a bowl with ½ teaspoon bicarbonate of soda and 1 teaspoon cream of tartar. Add 110 g (½ cup) sugar, then rub in 2 tablespoons butter. Add 1 well-beaten egg, and just enough milk to make a stiff dough. Roll out into a flat sheet, spread with raspberry jam, and roll up fairly tight like a jam roll. Cut into pieces about 1 cm thick, place on a greased baking tray and bake in a 180°C oven until a nice brown.

Raspberry Shortbread

Rub butter and sugar into flour and add beaten egg, no water to be used. This is a pastry base for biscuits. Roll mixture out thinly and line a flat and shallow tin, allowing paste to come up the sides neatly. Cut off square with edge of tin, spread with raspberry jam. Then add the following mixture spread over jam: 110 g (½ cup) sugar, 1 slightly beaten egg, 90 g (1 cup) coconut, and cook in a 180°C oven.

Ratafia Biscuits

Cream 85 g butter and 110 g (½ cup) sugar in a bowl. Add 1 egg and 14 drops of almond essence, beating well. Sift in 200 g (1⅓ cups) self-raising flour. Roll the mixture into balls, about the size of a marble, and arrange on a baking tray. Garnish each with half an almond or any kind of nut or crystallised cherry. Bake in a 180°C oven for about 15 minutes.

Rolled Oat Biscuits

Put 200 g (2 cups) rolled oats in a bowl with 230 g (1 cup) soft brown sugar, 1 teaspoon baking powder and a pinch of salt. Melt 125 g butter and mix in. Lastly, add 1 beaten egg. Stir well until thoroughly combined. Put teaspoonfuls of the mixture onto a greased baking tray. Bake in a 180°C oven for 15–20 minutes.

Variation If liked, you can use 150 g (1½ cups) rolled oats and 50 g (½ cup) desiccated coconut instead of 2 cups rolled oats.

Rosette Biscuits

Cream 225 g butter and 80 g (⅓ cup) caster sugar in a bowl. Stir in 225 g (1½ cups) sifted self-raising flour and 1 teaspoon vanilla essence. Put into a piping bag, using a rose-shaped nozzle. Pipe biscuits onto a greased baking tray and bake in a 180°C oven until light brown. When cold, dust lightly with caster sugar and serve with a little red jam in the centre of each biscuit.

Shortbread 1

Cream 225 g butter with 110 g (½ cup) sugar in a bowl. Add a pinch of salt and a few drops almond essence. Take 400 g (2⅔ cups) flour and remove 2 tablespoons of the flour; replace with 2 tablespoons arrowroot, then stir through the butter mixture. Roll out about 5 mm thick, cut into fancy shapes, prick with a fork, sprinkle with sugar and bake in a 150°C oven.

Shortbread 2

Cream 450 g butter and 220 g (1 cup) sugar in a bowl. Sift in 350 g (2⅓ cups) self-raising flour and 350 g (2 cups) rice flour. Mix into a dough, roll out to 1 cm thick and cut into squares. Pinch the edges, arrange on a greased baking tray and bake in a 180°C oven for 20 minutes.

Sugar Cookies

Cream 125 g butter and 220 g (1 cup) sugar in a bowl. Add 2 well-beaten eggs, stirring well to combine. Sift in 300 g (2 cups) plain flour, 2 teaspoons baking powder and ¼ teaspoon salt. Add to the butter mixture, stirring well. Add 1 teaspoon milk, the finely grated zest of 1 orange and 125 g (1 cup) chopped raisins. If dough is not stiff enough to roll, add more flour. Turn out onto a floured work surface and roll thinly. Cut into fancy shapes and bake in a 220°C oven for 10–15 minutes. Makes about 36 cookies.

Uncle Toby's Biscuits

Beat 2 eggs in a bowl with and 165 g (¾ cup) sugar for 5 minutes. Add 250 g (2½ cups) rolled oats, 1 teaspoon baking powder, and lastly 1 tablespoon melted butter. Drop teaspoonfuls onto a greased baking tray, allowing room for them to spread. Bake in a 180°C oven for 10–15 minutes. Remove the biscuits from the tray while hot.

Viennese Biscuits

Cream 225 g butter and 2 tablespoons icing sugar in a bowl. Sift in 300 g (2 cups) plain flour, 2 tablespoons cornflour, ½ teaspoon baking powder and a pinch of salt. Blend smoothly and put into a piping bag fitted with a rose-shaped nozzle. Pipe onto greased baking trays and bake in a 150°C oven until pale brown. Leave on trays to cool. Join together in pairs with mock cream, icing or jam. Decorate each top with a piece of crystallised cherry.

Wardell Cookies

Cream 175 g butter and 220 g (1 cup) sugar in a bowl. Add 1 egg, 70 g (½ cup) chopped walnuts or almonds and 160 g (1 cup) chopped dates. Lastly, add 300 g (2 cups) plain flour, ½ teaspoon bicarbonate of soda and 1 tablespoon boiling water. Take spoonfuls of the mixture and roll into balls. Roll cakes in cornflakes and press on lightly with hand. Place on baking trays lined with baking paper and press lightly with hands to flatten. Bake in a 180°C oven.

X.T.C. (Delicious)

Mix together 60 g (2 cups) cornflakes, 220 g (1 cup) sugar, 115 g (1¼ cups) desiccated coconut, 1 teaspoon baking powder, a pinch of salt and a few drops of almond essence. Add 1 cup melted butter. Press into a greased tin and bake in an 180°C oven for 15 minutes. Cut while hot, but leave in tin to cool.

Refrigerator Biscuits

Refrigerator biscuits are especially useful if a large quantity of the mixture is made at one time (say three times the recipe given). Portions of this can then be flavoured as desired, rolled in baking paper and stored in the refrigerator or freezer. When you desire fresh biscuits, simply cut off the required number and pop in the oven.

Refrigerator Biscuits Basic Recipe

Cream 125 g butter and 220 g (1 cup) sugar in a bowl. Add 1 egg yolk and beat well to combine. Add 1 tablespoon milk and $1/2$ teaspoon vanilla essence. Sift together 225 g ($1^1/2$ cups) plain flour, $1^1/2$ teaspoons baking powder and a pinch of salt. Add to the butter mixture and mix well. Divide into suitable portions and shape into a roll. Wrap in baking paper and chill in the refrigerator. When ready to use, cut thin slices and bake in a 180°C oven for 10–12 minutes, or until golden. Re-wrap ay leftover dough and store in the refrigerator or freezer until required.

Variations Biscuits may be glazed with egg white and sprinkled with any of the following: shredded coconut, chopped blanched almonds, chopped cherries, 2 teaspoons of cinnamon mixed with 2 teaspoons sugar. Chocolate Creams can be made by adding 1 tablespoon cocoa powder to one portion of the biscuit dough before chilling. When cooked and cooled, sandwich two biscuits together with cream and ice with chocolate icing. Coffee Walnut Biscuits can be made by adding 1 teaspoon coffee essence to half of the biscuit mixture and 2 tablespoons chopped walnuts to the other half before chilling. When cooked and cooled, ice with coffee icing and top with walnut halves.

Sherry Chocolate Slice

Crush 225 g plain biscuits finely and place in a bowl. Add 125 g (1 cup) sultanas or mixed fruit, 2 tablespoons cocoa powder and 4 tablespoons caster sugar. Melt 115 g butter in a saucepan and add to the dry ingredients with 1 beaten egg, stirring well. Press into a greased tin. Place in the refrigerator, until set. To make the icing, mix 1 heaped tablespoon butter with 125 g (1 cup) icing sugar and enough sherry to create a smooth paste (about 2 tablespoons). Colour with a few drops of pink food colouring. Decorate with glacé cherries and chopped nuts.

Coconut Wholemeal Slab

Crush 225 g wheatmeal biscuits. Add 4 tablespoons caster sugar and 90 g (1 cup) desiccated coconut, mixing well. Melt 115 g butter and add to the dry ingredients with 2 tablespoons sweet sherry and 1 beaten egg. Press into a greased tin and refrigerate until set. To make the icing, cream 1 tablespoon butter and 125 g (1 cup) icing sugar in a bowl. Add enough sherry to create a smooth paste and colour, if liked.

Looking Back in Time...

ANZAC BISCUITS

During World War I, the wives, mothers and daughters of Australian soldiers were concerned about the nutritional value of the food being supplied to their men at Gallipoli. They wanted to send the soldiers food from home, but were faced with problem of transporting it long distances on ships that had little, or no, refrigeration facilities.

A group of women came up with a solution — a biscuit that used ingredients that were readily available and would remain edible for over two months. Instead of using eggs as the binding agent, golden syrup or treacle was used, thus overcoming the problem of a general scarcity of eggs during the war. These biscuits were first called Soldier's Biscuits, but due to their increasing popularity, soon became known as Anzac biscuits.

As the war continued, many groups, such as the CWA, church groups, schools and other women's organisations devoted a great deal of time to making Anzac biscuits for the troops, which were packed in tins and sent abroad.

*150 g (1 cup) plain flour, 220 g (1 cup) sugar,
100 g (1 cup) rolled oats, 90 g (1 cup) desiccated coconut, 125 g butter,
1 tablespoon golden syrup or treacle, 2 tablespoons boiling water,
1 teaspoon bicarbonate of soda*

Preheat the oven to 180°C and lightly grease two baking trays. Combine the flour in a bowl with the sugar, rolled oats and coconut. Melt the butter in a saucepan with the golden syrup over medium heat. Combine the boiling water with the bicarbonate of soda and stir to dissolve. Add to the butter mixture and mix well, then stir into the dry ingredients until thoroughly combined. Drop teaspoons of the mixture onto the trays, allowing room for spreading. Bake for 10 minutes, or until golden brown. Allow to cool on the tray for a few minutes before transferring to a wire rack to cool completely.

Icings and Fillings

Icings for Cakes

To Ice a Christmas or Birthday Cake

The surface of the cake is the first consideration when it is to be iced, for if it is rough then, of course, the effect will be spoiled. Any rough pieces should be levelled off, and, if uneven on top, the cake should cut to create an even and level surface. If there are holes, then you will need to build them up and fill with Almond Icing (see recipes below) before smoothing the surface.

Almond Icing 1

225 g (2¹/₄ cups) ground almonds, 450 g (3²/₃ cups) icing sugar, 1 egg yolk, 2 tablespoons liquid (lemon juice, brandy, sherry)

Sift together the ground almonds and icing sugar into a bowl. Add the egg yolk and just enough liquid to make a stiff dough. Roll the icing into a ball and cut into two portions, one piece slightly larger for the sides of the cake. Put extra sifted icing sugar on a work surface and use your hands to knead into the shape and size required. Brush over with hands dipped in icing sugar. Put cake away to dry for a day or two before applying Royal Icing (see recipe, page 271). If there is not time to do this, put the cake into a slow oven with the door open so the almond icing can dry.

Variation Inexpensive almond icing may be made by substituting desiccated coconut for ground almonds and adding almond essence to taste, then follow recipe as above.

Almond Icing 2

350 g (3½ cups) ground almonds, 450 g (3⅔ cups) icing sugar,
2 tablespoons caster sugar, 3–4 egg whites, a little sherry

Sift together the ground almonds and icing sugar in a bowl and add the caster sugar. Add the egg whites, taking care not to add too much, and mix well, then add sherry (and if needed a little warm water). Mould to a firm paste, roll out to the shape required. If making almond icing for a Christmas cake, brush over the top and sides of cake with some egg white before putting on the almond icing.

Boiled Icing

220 g (1 cup) sugar, 1 egg white, 1 teaspoon lemon juice or other flavouring

Put 2 tablespoons water in a small saucepan and add the sugar, stirring with a wooden spoon until the sugar dissolves. Boil gently for 3 minutes, without stirring after the syrup boils. Whisk an egg white until stiff peaks form and gradually add the prepared syrup, whisking continually. Add the strained lemon juice, and continue whisking until thick enough to pour on the cake. The syrup must be boiled sufficiently, and the mixture whisked to the correct consistency before pouring over the cake. Over-cooking or whisking causes hard, brittle icing with a rough surface, while insufficiently boiled or whisked icing pours off the cake, leaving only a thin coating, which may not set firmly.

Butterscotch Icing

230 g (1 cup) soft brown sugar, 1 heaped tablespoon butter, 250 ml (1 cup) milk,
2 teaspoons plain flour, 2 well-beaten egg yolks, 1 teaspoon vanilla essence

Put the sugar in a saucepan with the butter and just enough milk to moisten and heat until the sugar dissolves. Mix together the flour, remaining milk and egg yolks. Add this to the sugar syrup and cook, stirring continuously, until thick, but do not boil. Remove from the heat and when cold, add the vanilla essence. This can be used on top of sponge cake, with cream, or on a tart.

Caramel Icing

460 g (2 cups) soft brown sugar, 125 ml (¹/2 cup) milk or cream,
2 teaspoons butter, a pinch of cream of tartar, ¹/2 teaspoon vanilla essence

Put the sugar, milk, butter and cream of tartar in a large saucepan, bring to the boil and boil for 10–12 minutes. Beat until thick and flavour with the vanilla essence.

Chocolate Cream Icing

55 g unsweetened cooking chocolate, 2 tablespoons butter,
60 g (¹/2 cup) icing sugar, 80 ml (¹/3 cup) cream

Melt the chocolate and butter in a heatproof bowl over a saucepan of simmering water. Add the icing sugar and cream, stirring for 1 minute, or until smooth and combined. Stir in the vanilla essence and beat until cool enough to spread.

Chocolate Fruit Frosting

2 tablespoons butter, 1 tablespoon cocoa powder,
¹/2 teaspoon vanilla essence, 250 g (2 cups) icing sugar,
2 tablespoons milk, 60 g (¹/2 cup) raisins

Beat the butter to a cream in a bowl. Dissolve the cocoa in sufficient boiling water to make a smooth paste and stir in the vanilla essence and a pinch of salt. Beat into the butter mixture. Sift in the icing sugar, alternately with the milk. Beat after each addition until smooth, adding more milk if required. Beat until the consistency of whipped cream. Finely chop most of the raisins, reserving a few for decoration. Fold the chopped raisins into the icing and mix well. Spread immediately over the cake and decorate with the reserved raisins.

Chocolate Honey Icing

250 g (2 cups) icing sugar, 2 teaspoons honey, 1 tablespoon cocoa powder,
1 tablespoon butter

Cream the butter and sugar in a bowl. Add the cocoa and honey, stirring well to combine. Mix with sufficient hot water to make a smooth icing. Spread over cake.

Fondant Icing

900 g (7½ cups) icing sugar mixture, 115 ml liquid glucose,
55 g white vegetable shortening, 2 egg whites, colouring, essence

Sift the icing mixture into a ceramic baking dish. Make a well in the centre and add the egg whites, glucose and shaved shortening. Knead until well mixed and smooth. Colour and flavour as required. Roll out to the correct size and mould onto the cake. This icing is recommended for Christmas or birthday cakes.

French Icing

165 g (1⅓ cups) icing sugar, vanilla essence

Sift the icing sugar into a small saucepan and gradually stir in 2 tablespoons boiling water and heat gently for 30 seconds, but do not boil. Add the essence for flavouring. Pour over cake and smooth with knife dipped in boiling water. Colour if preferred.

Fruit Icing

225 g icing sugar, 1 teaspoon melted butter, 2 tablespoons fruit juice (such as
lemon, orange, pineapple or passionfruit)

Add the melted butter to the sifted icing sugar and mix to a smooth pouring consistency, adding sufficient strained fruit juice as needed.

Liqueur Icing

115 g butter, 280 g (2¹/4 cups) icing sugar, 1 tablespoon liqueur
(such as maraschino, rum, Curaçao or brandy)

Cream the butter and sugar in a bowl. Add the liqueur and beat for about 10 minutes, or until the sugar is thoroughly dissolved and the mixture perfectly smooth. The icing may be spread on the cold cake, with a portion being reserved for piping decoration.

Marshmallow Icing

2 egg whites, 275 g (1¹/4 cups) sugar, 9 large marshmallows,
¹/4 teaspoon baking powder, ¹/2 teaspoon vanilla essence

Place egg whites and sugar and in top of a double boiler and add 4 tablespoons water. Place over boiling water and beat with an egg beater for about 10 minutes, or until thickened. Chop the marshmallows into smaller pieces and add to the pan, beating until smooth and thickened. Remove from the heat and add the vanilla essence. Beat until thick and nearly cold, then add the baking powder, and continue to beat until thick enough to spread on cake.

Mocha Icing

2 tablespoons butter, icing sugar, 1 egg yolk, 3 tablespoons espresso coffee,
¹/2 teaspoon vanilla essence

Cream the butter in a bowl with a little icing sugar and 1 well-beaten egg yolk. Stir in the coffee and vanilla essence. (Make sure you add enough icing sugar to make it spread easily.) Use smaller quantities of this icing for a butter sponge cake. Coffee essence could be also used and would not need so much icing sugar.

Orange Butter Icing

60 ml (¹/₄ cup) orange juice, 1 teaspoon butter, icing sugar

Place the orange juice and butter in a saucepan and heat gently until the butter has melted. Remove from the heat and add icing sugar, a little at a time, and beating well to form a delicate paste of easy spreading consistency.

Royal Icing

175–215 g (1¹/₂–1³/₄ cups) icing sugar, 1 egg,
a squeeze of lemon juice, food colouring

Sift the icing sugar into a bowl. Separate the egg and beat the white until stiff peaks form, discarding the yolk. Add 1 tablespoon of icing sugar at a time, to the egg white, stirring constantly with wooden spoon. Beat well until stiff. Add lemon juice and food colouring, if liked.

Soft Icing 1

550 g icing sugar, 1 teaspoon melted butter, 1 tablespoon sherry,
a few drops food colouring

Sift the icing sugar into a bowl. Add the melted butter, sherry and 4 tablespoons hot water to make a thick pouring consistency. Colour as required, and stir over a saucepan of hot water until the icing is slightly warm. Pour over the top and sides of the cake, and when firmly set, decorate with royal icing.

Soft Icing 2

225 g (1³/4 cups) icing sugar, 2 tablespoons fruit juice

Sift the icing sugar into a saucepan and add the liquid. Stir continuously over gentle heat until a smooth paste forms. Pour over the cake warm. To make chocolate icing, add 2 tablespoons of grated chocolate before heating.

Snowy Lemon Frosting

2 egg whites, 330 g (1¹/2 cups) sugar, 2 tablespoons lemon juice,
¹/4 teaspoon finely grated lemon zest

Put the egg whites, sugar and lemon juice in the top of a double boiler and add 3 tablespoons water. Beat well with a rotary egg beater. Place over boiling water, beating constantly until it stands in peaks. Remove from heat, add the lemon zest and beat until thick.

Toffee Icing

220 g (1 cup) caster sugar, chopped nuts

Put the sugar into a saucepan over a low heat and melt, without stirring. When a pale golden, remove from the heat and pour over the cake; sprinkle with nuts. If covering a sandwich cake, join together when toffee is cold. Alternatively, the toffee can be poured into a well-oiled tin and broken into shards to decorate.

Yolk Icing

1 egg yolk, icing sugar, 2 tablespoons hot milk, vanilla essence, ¹/2 teaspoon brandy

Beat the egg yolk in a bowl and add enough icing sugar to make a paste. Add the hot milk and flavour with vanilla and brandy; this makes a yellow icing.

Fillings for Cakes

Apricot Butter

120 g (²/₃ cup) dried apricots, 440 g (2 cups) sugar, 115 g butter, 4 eggs,
finely grated zest of 1 lemon, juice of 1 lemon

Place the dried apricots in a saucepan with just enough water to cover and heat until tender. Push the apricot pulp though a very fine sieve and set aside to cool. Add the sugar, butter, well beaten eggs, lemon juice and lemon zest to the top of a double boiler and mix all together, cook over a saucepan of simmering water until thick.

Apricot Filling

1 tablespoon freshly squeezed lemon juice, 115 g icing sugar,
55 g (¹/₂ cup) ground almonds, 3 tablespoons apricot jam

Mix all the ingredients together in a bowl for 5 minutes, or until well combined, then use as needed.

Banana Butter Filling

4 bananas, 220 g (1 cup) sugar, 60 g butter, 3 eggs

Mash the bananas with a fork. Put in a saucepan with the other ingredients and cook gently over low heat until the mixture thickens, stirring constantly. This makes a splendid cake filling.

Banana Filling

1 banana, 55 g butter, 115 g icing sugar, vanilla essence

Mash the banana and beat to a cream with the butter, icing sugar and vanilla. Spread between layers of cake and decorate the cake with banana slices.

Butter Cream Filling

55 g butter, 125 g (1 cup) sifted icing sugar, 1 teaspoon strained fruit juice or sherry, a few drops vanilla essence or other essence

Cream the butter in a bowl and gradually add the icing sugar. When well combined and smooth, add the fruit juice or sherry and add the vanilla essence, to taste. You can use 1 teaspoon hot water instead of the fruit juice, if liked.

Coconut Cream Filling

185 ml (³/4 cup) milk, 1 tablespoon sugar, 1 tablespoon desiccated coconut, 1 egg, 1 heaped tablespoon cornflour, vanilla essence

Put the milk, sugar and coconut into a saucepan over low heat. Once it is quite hot, remove from the heat and add the beaten egg, stirring well to combine. Mix the cornflour with a little extra milk and vanilla essence, then stir into the pan. Put back over heat for a minute, stirring well until smooth and combined.

CWA Filling

330 g (1½ cups) sugar, 1 tablespoon dark corn syrup, 2 egg whites,
1 teaspoon vanilla essence, 115 g (²/3 cup) chopped dried figs,
225 g (1¾ cups) raisins, 225 g (1¾ cups) chopped walnuts

Put the sugar and corn syrup into a saucepan with 170 ml (²/3 cup) boiling water and stir constantly until sugar has dissolved and the mixture boils. Cook until a little of the mixture dropped into cold water forms a soft ball. Beat the egg whites until stiff peaks form. Pour the syrup mixture over the egg whites, beating constantly, then add the vanilla. Beat until thick enough to spread. Add the fruits and nuts, stirring well to combine, and spread between layers of cake.

Date Filling

160 g (1 cup) chopped pitted dates, 1 tablespoon butter, 4 tablespoons milk,
1 tablespoon soft brown sugar

Put the dates and butter in a saucepan with the milk. Stir over low heat for 2–3 minutes, and then add the sugar. Beat for 1 minute and allow to cool before using.

Lemon Cheese Filling 1

2 eggs, 220 g (1 cup) sugar, 85 g butter, the juice of 1 lemon,
the finely grated zest of 1 lemon

Beat the eggs and place in a bowl with the sugar, butter, lemon juice and zest. Sit the bowl over a saucepan of hot water and stir the ingredients until they thicken. This filling will keep for 1 week.

Lemon Cheese Filling 2

440 g (2 cups) sugar, 6 eggs, 115 g chopped butter, juice of 6 lemons, finely grated zest of 2 lemons

Beat the eggs and sugar together in a bowl and add the butter and lemon juice, stirring well. Add the lemon zest. Place the bowl over a saucepan of simmering water and stir until thickened. Pour into a sterilised jar and seal securely when cool.

Lemon Cheese Filling (Uncooked)

210 g (²/₃ cup) sweetened condensed milk, juice of 1 lemon, icing sugar

Mix together the milk and lemon juice in a bowl. Add enough icing sugar to make a paste of spreadable consistency.

To make a good-quality butter, take 115 g butter and 150 ml milk. Warm the milk to blood heat (no hotter), add a little salt. Have the butter slightly warmed, but not melted. Beat the butter briskly, adding the milk gradually until the butter will not absorb any more milk. Let stand a few minutes. Result — 225 g of excellent butter.

Lemon Filling

juice of 1 lemon, finely grated zest of 1 lemon, 1 tablespoon butter,
165 g (³⁄4 cup) sugar, 1 tablespoon cornflour

Put all of the ingredients, except the cornflour, in a saucepan with 250 ml (1 cup) water and bring to the boil. Mix the cornflour with a little water and add to the pan. Stir for a few minutes after it thickens, then remove from heat. When cold, spread between cake layers.

Marshmallow Cream

1 tablespoon powdered gelatine, 440 g (2 cups) sugar,
1¹⁄2 teaspoons vanilla essence, 2 egg whites

Soak the gelatine in 125 ml (¹⁄2 cup) cold water. Put the sugar and 185 ml (³⁄4 cup) water in a saucepan and bring to the boil. Test the syrup; when a little of the syrup tested in cool water spins to a thread, then add soaked gelatine and set aside until cool. Add the vanilla essence and beat the mixture until white and thick. Whip the egg whites with a pinch of salt until stiff. Fold into the mixture. Put the marshmallow cream into sterilised jars and store in a cool place. This cream is excellent as a filling or an icing for cakes, also used for garnishing fruit salads, jellies and moulded desserts. It makes an excellent sauce for hot pudding and should then be slightly melted over hot water.

Mocha Filling

330 g (1¹⁄2 cups) sugar, 1¹⁄2 teaspoons butter, hot espresso coffee

Mix the ingredients together in a bowl with a pinch of salt, adding just enough coffee to moisten the paste and make a spreadable consistency.

Mock Cream 1

115 g butter, 280 g (2¼ cups) icing sugar, 1 tablespoon vanilla essence

Cream the butter and sugar in a bowl. Add the flavouring and stir to mix well.

Mock Cream 2

1 tablespoon butter, 1 tablespoon icing sugar, 1 cup unsweetened blanc mange

Cream the butter and icing sugar in a bowl and work in the cold blanc mange, until well combined and smooth. This can be used to coat small squares of cake called snowballs, which are similar to lamingtons.

Mulberry Butter Filling

115 g butter, 125 g (1 cup) mulberries, 350 g (1½ cups) caster sugar, 3 eggs

Melt the butter in a saucepan. Rub the mulberries through a sieve and add to the pan with the sugar, stirring over low heat until the sugar dissolves. Pour the mixture into a bowl with the well-beaten eggs, stirring well to combine. Return the mixture to the saucepan and stir over a low heat until it thickens.

Nut Filling

Add some finely chopped nuts to some sifted icing sugar and moisten with enough beaten egg white to form a paste of spreadable consistency. Another filling is to mix together some butter with a little finely chopped candied peel and raisins. You can also try mixing honey with some chopped nuts.

Orange Filling

55 g (¹/4 cup) sugar, ¹/2 tablespoon cornflour, 2 teaspoons finely grated orange zest,
60 ml (¹/4 cup) freshly squeezed orange juice, 2 teaspoons butter, 1 egg yolk,
1 teaspoon freshly squeezed lemon juice

Put the sugar, cornflour, orange zest and juice, butter and egg yolk into a jug. Add a pinch of salt. Stand the jug in a saucepan of simmering water and stir until smooth and thick. Remove from the heat and add the lemon juice, then use as needed.

Passionfruit Butter

225 g butter, 440 g (2 cups) sugar, 4 eggs, 12 passionfruit

Place the butter and sugar in an non-metallic saucepan over a low heat and slowly melt the butter. Beat the eggs and passionfruit pulp together and add to the butter and sugar. Simmer slowly until the mixture has the consistency of honey. Remove from the heat and when nearly cold, place in sterilised jars ready for use.

Pineapple Filling

2 egg whites, 125 g (1 cup) icing sugar, 1 tablespoon pineapple juice,
finely chopped pineapple

Whip the egg whites until stiff peaks form. Gradually beat in the icing sugar and add the pineapple juice. Stir in as much finely chopped pineapple as the icing will hold, adding a little more sugar if necessary. Put a thick layer between cakes.

Pineapple Filling for Tarts

1 pineapple or 440 g tinned pineapple pieces, 440 g (2 cups) sugar,
1 tablespoon cornflour, 3–4 egg yolks, 1 tablespoon butter

Peel, core and shred the fresh pineapple or drain the tinned pineapple pieces (reserving the juice) and place in a saucepan. Add the sugar and 125 ml (½ cup) water. Simmer for 20 minutes. Blend the cornflour with a little of the reserved pineapple juice to make a paste and stir into the pan. Cook for 3 minutes, then remove from the heat and cool slightly. Beat the egg yolks and add to the cooled pineapple. Beat in the butter. Pour into sterilised jars and seal securely when cool. Use the same as for lemon cheese.

Raisin Filling

125 g (1 cup) raisins, 140 g (1 cup) chopped mixed nuts, 220 g (1 cup) sugar,
freshly squeezed orange or lemon juice.

Put the raisins, nuts and sugar in a saucepan and cook slowly for 10 minutes, then stir in a dash of orange or lemon juice, to taste.

Raisin Nut Filling

55 g (¼ cup) soft brown sugar, 2 tablespoons butter, 125 g (1 cup) raisins,
90 g (¾ cup) chopped toasted walnuts, cream

Put the sugar and butter in a saucepan with 60 ml (¼ cup) water and cook until a little of the mixture forms a slightly firm ball when dropped into cold water. Remove from the heat and add the raisins and nuts until combined. Stir in enough cream to make a spreadable consistency.

Walnut Cream Filling

2 tablespoons butter, 6 tablespoons icing sugar, 2 teaspoons sherry,
1 tablespoon chopped walnuts

Cream the butter and icing sugar in a bowl. Beating constantly, add the sherry and the chopped nuts.

Fillings for Tarts or Biscuits

Mix together 3 tablespoons sultanas, ½ teaspoon mixed spice,
1 tablespoon sugar, 2 teaspoons warm water and a little vanilla
essence. You can also try mixing together 160 g (1 cup) chopped
pitted dates with 200 g (1 cup) stewed chopped or tinned apples,
60 g (½ cup) sultanas and a little mixed peel and mixed spice.
Both of these recipes make a delicious tart or biscuit filling.

CWA rest rooms at the Baby Show in Parkes, NSW.

PASTRIES
AND
PUDDINGS

Pies and Tarts

General Rules for Pastry

- See that the utensils and ingredients are cool. If the pastry becomes soft, wrap in baking paper and place in the refrigerator before rolling out.
- Use as little flour as possible when rolling out.
- Roll lightly and evenly. If a pastry board is used, it should be kept for pastry alone.
- Flour must be dry and well sifted.
- Water used in mixing must be very cold. Pastry should be just moist enough to handle without sticking to the hands.
- Mix pastry with a knife and follow with a little kneading with the hands.
- The oven must be quite hot when pastry is put in and the heat reduced later.
- When making short pastry, do not rub the shortening with the palms of the hand, use the tips of the fingers or cut shortening with a knife. When properly done it should run through the fingers, like grains of sand or fine breadcrumbs. Use about 300 ml of cold water to 450 g (3 cups) flour, but it is as well to use your discretion, as some mixtures need more or less water. The drier you make your short pastry the better it will be.
- To each 450 g flour allow 225 g fat (suet, dripping or butter), 1 teaspoon baking powder, a good pinch of salt (if you use dripping it may be sufficiently salted) and 300 ml water.
- Always sift flour, baking powder and salt together.
- Use as little flour as possible in making up, because where too much flour is used the pastry will be hard.
- On no account allow the oven to be opened for at least 5 minutes after pastry has been put in.
- To use butter alone makes a very rich pastry. Dripping alone may make the pastry too crumbly. Use butter and lard together or dripping and margarine together for best results.
- A little lemon juice added to the cold water to mix up pastry will improve it.
- If stewed fruit is to be used, have it perfectly cold before putting in or on pastry, otherwise it will soak and render the crust heavy.
- Never grease a pie plate; sprinkle it with flour. There is sufficient fat in the pastry and the pie or tart can be removed by inserting a flat edge lifter under it.
- Brush over the undercrust of a pie or tart with an egg white to prevent fruit juices or soft fillings from soaking into the crust.
- Use beaten egg yolk for glazing any savoury pastry. For sweet pastry, brush over with egg white and sprinkle sugar on top. When pastry is nearly cooked, remove from the oven and apply the above with a brush.

- When making savoury or meat pies the solids should be slightly raised above the level of the dish and the liquids should only come three parts of the way up the dish. The air space under the pastry facilitates cooking.
- Decorations should not be elaborate. An effective way is to make six or eight cuts on the pastry lid from the centre to the sides.

The Three Golden Rules for Success

- Pastry should never be overworked — handle as little as possible or it will become tough. It should be handled quickly and lightly so that the air may not be expelled. • Pasty should always be wrapped in plastic wrap and rested for at least 30 minutes after making, to relax the gluten and reduce the chance of shrinkage and toughening.
- Pastry should be cooked in a hot oven, so that the starch globules in the flour will burst at once and absorb the fat used in making it.

Flaky Pastry

Sift 225 g (1½ cups) flour into a bowl with 1 teaspoon baking powder and ¼ teaspoon salt. Add 150 ml ice cold water and 1 teaspoon lemon juice to make a dough. Turn out onto a lightly floured work surface and knead to a pliable dough. Roll the dough out square or oblong. Divide 175 g butter or shortening into three equal parts. Take one-third of this and dot all over the square of pastry, leaving about 2 cm all round the edges free of butter; sprinkle lightly with flour and fold the pastry in three. First, bring the top part over the middle and then the bottom part up over the top. It should be in the shape of a square. Turn the mixture around, the top to the right side, so that the open edges will be against and opposite to you. Leave the pastry in a cool place for 15–20 minutes, then roll out again and dot with the second portion of butter, sprinkle with flour and fold as explained for the first folding. Repeat this method with the third lot of butter, allowing to cool after each folding and rolling. At the fourth treatment do not add any butter, but fold the pastry in three and roll out again into the shape and size required for baking. Use for all kinds of meat pies, chicken pies, apple and most kinds of small pastry.

Note In making flaky pastry the chief thing is to have the fat and dough of the same consistency and be sure to knead the dough so that it will not stick to the board or hands. Be careful when using drippings, that they are not flavoured with any strong flavours such as onions, or seasonings. Lard and butter in equal proportions make a beautiful pastry.

Fleur Pastry

Sift 225 g (1½ cups) plain flour into a bowl with ½ teaspoon baking powder and a pinch of salt. Rub in 175 g butter until it resembles breadcrumbs, then add 2 teaspoons sugar. Beat 1 egg yolk in a bowl and add a squeeze of lemon juice and a little ice cold water. Stir into the dry ingredients to make a stiff dough. Turn out onto a floured board and roll out to the size and shape required. This recipe can be used for savoury and sweet pastries. If you have no 'fleur' ring, a small deep sandwich tin will be just as good.

Puff Pastry

Beat 1 egg yolk in a bowl with a squeeze of lemon juice and 150 ml ice cold water, mixing well. Sift 225 g (1½ cups) plain flour into a bowl and add the yolk mixture gradually, using just enough to make the dough the same consistency as the butter. (Some people use ⅛ teaspoon baking powder; it prevents toughness). Turn the dough out onto a lightly floured board and knead briefly until it will not stick to the hands.

Roll out a square about 5 mm thick. Press 225 g butter into a shape about half the size of the pastry; wet the pastry edge with a little egg yolk. Fold the dough over the butter, pinching around the edges to seal (this will prevent the butter from oozing through when rolled). Put the dough in the refrigerator for 20 minutes, then roll it out into an oblong shape. Fold in three, top to the centre and the bottom portion up over the top. Turn the dough around the top to the right side so that the open edges will be against and opposite to you. Put away to cool again, then fold and roll in this manner, leaving to cool between each rolling (six times). Roll as evenly as possible. Keep dough long and narrow, which when folded forms a square. (Roll with light strokes, not heavy and hard). Each time it is to be rolled out a little flour may be used, but it should be brushed away when beginning to roll into shape. At the last roll, shape it for desired dish you are making.

Puff pastry should be used for small things that are served whole. Use rough puff pastry or flaky pastry for pies and tarts, which are to be cut.

Raised Pie Crust

Blend 140 g lard and 140 g butter together and divide into four. Sift together 625 g plain flour and a pinch of salt into a bowl and then rub in one-quarter of the butter mixture. Put the other three portions of butter mixture on to boil with the water, then pour into the centre of the flour and mix to make an smooth dough. Turn out onto a board and cut one-third of the pastry off. Put this on a plate, cover, and stand it over boiling water until ready to use. Knead the large piece of dough, roll out and line the raised pie mould. Fill with mixture. Roll out smaller piece of dough, cover top of pie and decorate with pastry rose and leaves. Glaze. Bake in a 220°C oven.

Short Pastry

Sift 450 g (3 cups) plain flour into a bowl and add 1 tablespoon sugar and 225 g butter or dripping; mix in with knife or your fingertips. Combine 1 egg yolk in another bowl with 2 teaspoons lemon juice and 3 tablespoons ice cold water. Add to the flour mixture and combine, then knead lightly and roll up; only roll out once. Bake in a 180°C oven for 20–30 minutes.

Shortcrust for Pie Pastry

Sift 250 g (1²/₃ cups) flour and a pinch of salt into a bowl and add 2 tablespoons sugar. Rub in 115 g butter until the mixture resembles fine breadcrumbs. Mix with a little water, to form a dough, then roll out and use as required.

Suet Pastry

Sift 350 g (2¹/₃ cups) plain flour into a bowl and add 175 g shredded suet, mixing well to combine. Add ¼ teaspoon salt and 1 teaspoon baking powder, then stir in just enough ice cold water to make a fairly stiff dough. Knead lightly. Roll out and use for any pastry dish that must be eaten hot, such as meat pies and boiled puddings.

Three Minute Pastry

Melt 185 g butter in a little boiling water until it is a creamy consistency. Mix into a bowl with 300 g (2 cups) sifted flour, ½ teaspoon bicarbonate of soda, ½ teaspoon cream of tartar and ½ teaspoon salt to make a soft dough, adding a little more boiling water if necessary. Roll out and use as directed.

Vol-Au-Vent

For a vol-au-vent make a puff pastry case. Roll and cut as for a patty — 3 oval cutters are necessary, one for the patty, one for the centre, and one for the lid. The lid should be a size smaller than the patty. Bake in a 180°C oven for about 15 minutes, lift it out and take out the soft middle part. Put back in oven for a little while to dry and fill with stewed fruit and top with whipped cream. Put the pastry lid on top.

Almond Macaroon Tartlets

Make the pastry by rubbing 85 g butter into 175 g self-raising flour and a pinch of salt in a bowl. Add enough cold water to make a dough. Line a 12-hole tartlet tin with pastry. Put a little jam in the base of each tartlet. To make the filling, whip 2 egg whites until stiff peaks form, then add 1 teaspoon vanilla essence. Stir in 80 g (⅓ cup) caster sugar, 55 g (½ cup) ground almonds and 2 teaspoons rice flour, mixing well to combine. Put a spoonful of mixture into each tartlet and cook in a 220°C oven for 20 minutes.

Apple Pie

Cook 3 apples. Sift 150 g (1 cup) flour into a bowl with 55 g (¼ cup) sugar, 1 egg, 2 teaspoons cream of tartar and 1 teaspoon bicarbonate of soda. Rub in 125 g butter until it resembles breadcrumbs, then add 1 egg, mixing to combine. Put three-quarters of the mixture into a sandwich tin, then arrange the cooked apple on top. Cover with remainder of the mixture. Cook in a 180°C oven for 20–30 minutes.

Banana Cream Pie

Line a pie-plate or sandwich tin with thin layer of Shortcrust Pastry (see recipe, page 287) and fill with sliced bananas. Beat the yolk of 1 egg with ½ cup sugar, add 1 teaspoon of orange or vanilla extract, then add 1 cup cream or milk.

Put this over bananas and bake. Cover with meringue made of the whites of 3 eggs beaten stiff with 3 tablespoons of sugar.

A tablespoon of fine sugar sifted on the top of small pies before baking is an improvement.

Butterscotch Meringue Pie

Heat 250 ml (1 cup) milk with 230 g (1 cup) brown sugar in a double boiler. Mix 2 tablespoons cornflour with the 2½ tablespoons milk and 2 egg yolks. Gradually stir into the hot mixture. Cook until thick, stirring constantly for about 10 minutes. Add 2 tablespoons butter, then remove from the heat and when cool pour into a pre-baked Shortcrust Pastry shell (see recipe, page 287). Beat the egg whites with 2 tablespoons caster sugar until stiffly peaking. Put the meringue over the filling and brown in a 150°C oven.

Caramel Gramma Pie

Prepare the pie crust by beating 1 tablespoon butter and 110 g (½ cup) sugar to a cream in a bowl. Add 1 egg, 150 g (1 cup) flour, 1 teaspoon baking powder, and enough milk to make a thin dough (about 3 tablespoons). Roll out and line the base and side of a pie dish. Blind bake. To prepare the filling, put 4 cups cooked gramma pumpkin in a saucepan with 115 g (½ cup) soft brown sugar, 1 tablespoon golden syrup, 1 teaspoon cinnamon, ½ teaspoon ground nutmeg and the juice of 1 lemon. Simmer gently for 30 minutes. Spoon into the pastry case and bake in a 180°C oven until a golden brown. Remove from oven and sprinkle with red jelly crystals. Serve cold with whipped cream.

Cinnamon Apple Tart

Sift together 150 g (1 cup) plain flour, 1 teaspoon baking powder, ¼ teaspoon bicarbonate of soda, ¼ teaspoon mixed spice, ½ teaspoon ground cinnamon and ½ teaspoon ground ginger. Add 110 g (½ cup) sugar. Rub in 55 g butter and stir in 1 well-beaten egg to make a dough. Roll out three-quarters of the dough on a lightly floured work surface and line a deep sandwich tin. Fill with apple purée. Roll out the remaining pastry and cover the filling, pressing to seal the edges. Bake in a 180°C oven for about 25 minutes.

Custard Tart

To make the filling, cream 2 teaspoons butter and 2 tablespoons sugar in a bowl. Add 1–2 well-beaten eggs, stirring well to combine. Sift in 2 teaspoons plain flour, then add 250 ml (1 cup) boiling milk and a little vanilla essence. Arrange a few pitted dates in the base of a pre-cooked Shortcrust Pastry shell (see recipe, page 287) and fill with the custard mixture. Bake in a 150°C oven.

Date Cream Tart

Melt 2 tablespoons butter and 1 tablespoon plain flour in a saucepan. Gradually add 500 ml (2 cups) milk, 110 g (½ cup) sugar and 80 g (½ cup) chopped pitted dates. Simmer until the dates are soft, then add 2 egg yolks. Spoon into a pre-cooked pastry shell and bake. Make a meringue with 2 egg whites and sugar and place on top. Return to the oven and brown.

Fruit Flan

To make the pastry, sift 280 g (2⅓ cups) plain flour into a bowl and add 80 g (⅓ cup) sugar. Rub in 175 g butter until the mixture resembles breadcrumbs. Make a well in the centre of the flour and add half a beaten egg and 2 teaspoons ice cold water. Mix to a stiff dough and roll out to 5 mm thick. Line a deep sandwich tin with pastry and cover the base with baking paper. Fill with baking beads or rice. When cooked, remove the paper and beads and return to the oven to cook the bottom of the pastry. When the pastry is cold, fill the case with stewed fruit, draining it of juice before adding it to the crust, and arranging it as neatly as possible.

To make the glaze, put 110 g (½ cup) sugar into a saucepan with 125 ml (½ cup) fruit juice. Bring to the boil and stir until the sugar dissolves. Soften 1 teaspoon gelatine in a little cold water and add to the pan. Continue boiling the syrup until thickened. Allow the syrup to cool and when nearly cold, pour over the fruit in the flan, brushing to coat. Serve the flan with cream or custard.

Gramma Tart

Prepare 1 large piece gramma pumpkin (about 750 g). Cook until soft, then drain well and mash. Add to it 220 g (1 cup) sugar, some sultanas, currants, ½ teaspoon ground ginger, ½ teaspoon ground cinnamon and the juice and finely grated zest of 1 lemon. Mix well. Line a deep sandwich tin with Shortcrust Pastry (see recipe, page 287), fill with the gramma mixture, and cover with pastry. Ornament the edges, making sure they are well sealed. Glaze and sprinkle with sugar. Bake in an oven for 20–25 minutes. Serve either hot or cold.

Lemon Chiffon Pie

Separate 4 eggs and beat the egg yolks in the top of a double-boiler until thick. Add 125 ml (½ cup) freshly squeezed lemon juice, 110 g (½ cup) sugar and ½ teaspoon salt. Cook over gentle heat until thickened. Dissolve 2 teaspoons gelatine in 60 ml (¼ cup) cold water and add to the egg mixture. Add 1 teaspoon finely grated lemon zest and stir through, then cool until mixture begins to thicken. Beat 110 g (½ cup) sugar with the egg whites and fold into the gelatine mixture. Line a pie dish with a cooked pastry shell and pour the lemon mixture into the base. Refrigerate until set and serve cold.

Lemon Tart

To make the pastry, cream 1 tablespoon butter and 1 large tablespoon sugar in a bowl. Add 1 egg and beat in well, then sift in 150 g (1 cup) plain flour and 1 teaspoon baking powder. Roll out and line the base and side of a tartlet tin.

To make the filling, put 250 ml water in a saucepan and add 220 g (1 cup) sugar and the juice of 1 large lemon. Bring to the boil, then add 3 well-beaten egg yolks and 1 tablespoon cornflour mixed to a paste with a little water. Stir until thickened, then remove from the heat. Make meringues with the stiffly-beaten egg whites and 55 g (¼ cup) sugar and place on top of tart and bake a golden brown. Small meringues may be placed on top as a decoration as well.

Macaroon Tarts

Roll out Shortcrust Pastry (see recipe, page 287) and cut into rounds large enough to line deep patty tins, and place a little jam in the bottom of each. Mix together 115 g ground almonds and 110 g (½ cup) sugar, in a bowl. Add 2 beaten eggs, a little milk and vanilla essence. Mix well. Pour the mixture over the jam in the tartlets. Put strips of pastry on each to decorate. Bake in a 180°C oven for about 20 minutes.

Mince Pies

Line tartlet tins with 225 g rough pastry, puff pastry or short pastry, making extra rounds for the lids. To make the mince filling, chop 225 g shredded suet. Add 3–4 peeled, cored and chopped apples. Chop 215 g (1¾ cups) raisins and 125 g (¾ cup) mixed peel, and add them to the suet with 110 g (¾ cup) currants. Add 440 g (2 cups) sugar, the juice and finely grated zest of 1 lemon, 3 tablespoons brandy and 3 tablespoons sherry, and mix well. Fill the tartlet cases with the fruit mince. Place pastry lids on top, seal, and brush with a glaze. Bake in a 220°C oven for 15 minutes, or until golden.

Nougat Tart

Line the base and side of a pie dish with Short Pastry (see recipe, page 287) and spread raspberry or apricot jam lightly inside the base. Mix together 90 g (1 cup) desiccated coconut, 110 g (½ cup) sugar and 1 teaspoon baking powder in a bowl. Beat 1 egg in another bowl and add 1 tablespoon of milk, then add this to the dry ingredients. Spoon into the pastry case and bake in a 150°C oven for 45 minutes.

Pineapple Tart

Line a pie-plate with a thin layer of pastry. Put 425 g tinned crushed pineapple in a saucepan, add 2 tablespoons butter, 2 teaspoons sugar, 2 tablespoons plain flour, 1 egg yolk and a little milk and vanilla essence. Stir until it boils and thickens, then pour into the pastry case. Beat 2 egg whites with 2 tablespoons sugar until stiff, put on top of tart and bake in a 150°C oven.

Polo Tarts

Line patty tins with 225 g Shortcrust Pastry (see recipe, page 287). Place a little apricot jam in the bottom of each. Cream 85 g butter and 80 g ($\frac{1}{3}$ cup) sugar in a bowl. Add 1 egg, beating well, then stir in 2 tablespoons milk and 175 g self-raising flour. Put a little of the cake mixture into the tartlet cases and bake in a 180°C oven until pale brown. Cool the tartlets on wire racks and when cold, brush the filling with red currant jelly and sprinkle with some finely chopped nuts.

Pumpkin Pie

Line a pie dish with pastry, making sure you have enough to use as a lid. Mix together 1 large cup mashed pumpkin, 250 ml (1 cup) hot milk, $\frac{1}{4}$ teaspoon ground nutmeg, $\frac{1}{2}$ teaspoon ground cinnamon, $\frac{1}{2}$ teaspoon ground ginger, 115 g ($\frac{1}{2}$ cup) soft brown sugar and 1 lightly beaten egg. Mix together well, then spoon the mixture evenly into the pastry case. Cover with second piece of pastry, mark for slicing. Brush with egg white, sprinkle with sugar and bake in a 180°C oven for 30 minutes. Serve hot, with custard or cream.

Ratafia Tart

Line a sandwich tin or deep pie dish with 225 g Shortcrust Pastry (see recipe, page 287) and flute the edge. Spread a layer of apricot jam over the base. Beat 2 eggs in a bowl with 55 g ($\frac{1}{4}$ cup) caster sugar until frothy and creamy. Stir in 50 g ($\frac{1}{3}$ cup) plain flour and 60 g ($\frac{1}{2}$ cup) finely chopped walnuts. Melt 40 g butter and add to the mixture. Turn all into the prepared pastry case. Place in a 220°C oven and lower the temperature to 200°C. Cook until the pastry is set. Lower the temperature again to 180°C and cook slowly. It should take about 45 minutes altogether. Smear the base of 55 g ratafia or amaretti biscuits with jam and place them over the tart. Return to the oven for a few minutes.

Scotch Apple Tart

Line a greased pie dish with Shortcrust Pastry (see recipe, page 287). In the base arrange a layer of cooked apples that have been flavoured with grated lemon zest and sweetened to taste. Cover with a layer of sultanas, then more apples. Finally place a lid of pastry on top, and press the edges to seal. Bake in a 180°C oven for 20–30 minutes, or until the pastry is cooked. Serve with cream or custard.

St. Denis Tartlets

Cream 55 g butter and 55 g (¼ cup) caster sugar in a bowl. Add 2 egg yolks and beat thoroughly. Stir in 55 g (½ cup) ground almonds, 1 tablespoon cornflour and a few drops of vanilla essence. Lastly, beat the egg whites until stiff peaks form then fold into the filling mixture.

Line a 12-hole tartlet tin with pastry and spread a small teaspoon of raspberry jam in the bottom of each. Spoon in the filling and arrange two narrow strips of pastry across the top of each tartlet to decorate. Bake in a 180°C oven for 15–20 minutes.

St. Honoré Tart

Put 55 g butter in a saucepan with 300 ml water and bring to the boil. Take off the heat and stir in 120 g (¾ cup) sifted plain flour. Return to gentle heat and stir until it forms a ball and leaves the side of the pan. Turn into a bowl, and when cold, gradually add 3 well-beaten eggs. Spread half of the mixture into a greased sandwich tin; then use a piping bag to pipe balls of the mixture around the edge of the base. Bake in a 220°C oven for 25–30 minutes. Remove from the oven and cool.

To make the glacé syrup put 110 g (½ cup) sugar in a saucepan over low heat with 3 tablespoons water and stir until the sugar has dissolved. Bring to the boil and boil until the syrup reaches 150°C on a sugar thermometer. Remove from the heat and when cool pour the syrup gently over the tart and leave to set. Whip a little cream with some sugar and a few drops of vanilla essence. Pile the cream high in centre of the tart, and serve.

Strawberry Cream Tarts

Beat 1 egg and 1 egg yolk in a bowl with 3 tablespoons sugar. Sift in 3 tablespoons flour and mix until light and fluffy. Add 2 teaspoons gelatine and pour in 185 ml (3/4 cup) hot milk. Stir over medium heat until the mixture boils, then stir over ice until it partly cools. Mix in two stiffly beaten egg whites and 3 tablespoons whipped cream, then add a few drops of vanilla essence or a little rum. Fill small cooked tartlet shells with the mixture and then cover the top with the strawberries. Put 3 tablespoons red currant jelly in a saucepan with 2 teaspoons water and bring to the boil, then allow to cool and when warm, brush over the tart.

Strawberry Tarts

Line a 12-hole tartlet tin with a rich pastry; place baking paper in the uncooked tarts and fill with baking beads or rice. Cook in a 200°C oven. Empty out the beads and fill the tarts with small hulled strawberries. Push 150 g (1 cup) hulled strawberries through a sieve. Sweeten the strawberries with sugar and add 2 tablespoons of red currant jelly, stirring to combine. Place in a saucepan, bring to the boil, then strain. Pour into the tartlet cases and set aside to cool.

Summer Tart

Line a sandwich tin with Short Pastry (see recipe, page 287) and bake in a 180°C oven for 20–30 minutes. When cold, fill it with freshly hulled strawberries or raspberries, and sprinkle with caster sugar. Whip 300 ml chilled cream with 1 tablespoon icing sugar until it is stiff, then force it through a piping bag in little mounds on the fruit.

Vienna Apple Pie

Make a pastry using 3 tablespoons brown sugar, 50 g butter and 150 g (1 cup) self-raising flour and a little cold milk. Roll out to the size of a pie dish. Slice 3 large apples into the base of the pie dish and sprinkle with a little sugar and ground cinnamon. Lay the pastry on top and press to seal. Bake in a 180°C oven for 45 minutes.

Puddings

Puddings

There are three ways to make puddings: boiling, steaming and baking.

Boiled puddings are made with ingredients that take a very long time to cook, such as meat or plum puddings. Steamed puddings are for cooking light spongy puddings, such as fruit puddings. Baked puddings are chiefly to cook milk puddings, although milk puddings may also be steamed.

A pudding cannot be expected to turn out well if the water in which it has boiled ceases to boil, or if the steam in the steamer has cooled down, or if the baking oven is too cool or too scorchingly hot.

Boiling a Pudding

Butter a pudding basin (mould) and sprinkle thickly with sugar. If a cloth is being used, dip the cloth in boiling water and sift plain flour over an area in the centre sufficient to enclose the pudding, before securely tying. Drop the pudding into boiling water if it is in a cloth; if it is in a basin, place into a saucepan half filled with boiling water, so that water comes well up the side of basin. Steam will cook the top of the pudding. Do not lift the lid often, and keep a supply of boiling water handy to replace any water that has evaporated. Water must be kept boiling until the pudding is completely cooked.

Puddings that contain bread, breadcrumbs or flour must be allowed room to spread. Certain ingredients, such as syrup, sugar, butter and suet, become liquid when heated, and it is because of this that puddings sometimes break when turned out. They should be allowed to stand in the basin or cloth for 30 minutes or so before being turned out.

Very good boiled and steamed puddings can be made without eggs and should be given longer to cook. A little baking powder or egg powder (1 teaspoon to every 450 g flour) makes suet pudding or crust very much lighter and nicer, and less suet is required.

Steaming a Pudding

When steaming a pudding put it into a greased pudding basin (mould), stand it into a large deep saucepan with enough boiling water to come halfway up the side of the basin. It may be put in a 'steamer', but whichever way you do it, the water must be kept gently boiling all the time. Steam must be kept at a consistent level or the pudding will be heavy and uncooked.

When steaming a light pudding do not move the saucepan or remove the lid any more than necessary. If a bowl is used instead of a covered basin, the bowl should be covered with baking paper, greased on both sides and tied down.

A Standard Pudding Recipe

Sift 175 g flour, 2 teaspoons baking powder and a pinch of salt into a bowl. Clean the fruit that you will be adding — see options below. Cream 85 g butter and 80 g (1/3 cup) sugar in a bowl. Add 1 beaten egg, stirring well to combine. Add 150 ml milk to the butter mixture, then stir in the dry ingredients, mixing well. Add the fruit or flavouring (depending on which pudding is being made). Spoon into a pudding basin (mould), cover with the greased baking paper, greased side out, and steam gently but steadily for 1 hour 30 minutes.

You can make any of the following puddings by adjusting the standard recipe above with the flavourings listed below:

- DATE PUDDING: add 80 g (1/2 cup) chopped pitted dates. Serve with custard or ice cream.
- MIXED DRIED FRUIT PUDDING: add a total of 85 g (about 2/3 cup) sultanas, currants, raisins, figs and preserved ginger. Serve with custard.
- CHOCOLATE PUDDING: add 1–2 tablespoons of cocoa powder or grated chocolate sifted with the flour. Add vanilla essence. Serve with custard.
- GOLDEN PUDDING: add 2 tablespoons apricot jam onto the bottom of the mould before spooning in the pudding. Serve with apricot jam sauce.
- COLLEGE PUDDING: add 2 tablespoons raspberry jam to the pudding mould. Serve with raspberry jam sauce.
- PASSIONFRUIT PUDDING: add the pulp of 3–6 passionfruit to the pudding mixture. Instead of milk use a similar quantity of water. Serve with custard, cream or ice cream.
- HONITON SPONGE: add a little finely grated lemon zest and 60 g (1/4 cup) mixed peel. Serve with custard.
- CANARY PUDDING: add the finely grated zest of 1 lemon. Serve with custard.
- URNEY PUDDING: add 2 tablespoons of raspberry jam and 1 teaspoon of bicarbonate soda instead of the baking powder. Add the jam last. Use 2 tablespoons less milk when mixing the pudding. Serve with jam sauce.
- MARBLE PUDDING: divide the pudding mixture into 3 parts. Colour one portion with pink food colouring, add 1 teaspoon cocoa powder to another. Leave the third portion as is and spoon into the mould separately. Serve with custard.

Steamed Puddings

Apple Pudding

Roll out 225 g Suet Pastry (see recipe, page 287). Line a pudding basin (mould) with two-thirds of the pastry. Peel, core and chop 6 apples. Put half of the apples in the pastry-lined basin with 2 cloves, 1 tablespoon sugar, then add the remaining apples, 1 tablespoon sugar, 1 tablespoon marmalade and 55 g chopped butter. Wet the edges of pastry and cover with the remaining pastry, pinching the edges together to seal. Cover with greased baking paper and boil for 2 hours.

Apple Pudding with Sherry Sauce

Peel and cut 2 large apples into small pieces. Fry in a little hot butter until golden. Melt 3 tablespoons butter in a saucepan and stir in 3 tablespoons flour and 185 ml (³⁄₄ cup) hot milk. Stir until thick, but do not boil. Add 4 tablespoons sugar and 3 egg yolks and then the apples. Lastly, stir in 3 well-beaten egg whites. Place in covered pudding basin (mould) and steam for 30 minutes, or until firm. Allow to stand for 5 minutes before turning out.

To make the sauce, place 1 egg yolk and 1 whole egg in the top of a double boiler with 2 tablespoons sugar and 2 tablespoons sherry. Beat until stiff over simmering water, then pour over the pudding, to serve.

Billy Pudding

Mix together 125 g (1 cup) raisins, 150 g (1 cup) currants, 220 g (1 cup) sugar, 300 g (2 cups) plain flour and 2¹⁄₂ teaspoons finely chopped mixed peel. Stir in a little grated nutmeg and 1 large teaspoon baking powder. Melt 1 tablespoon butter or good dripping in 600 ml boiling water. Add to the pudding mixture and stir well to combine. Spoon the mixture into a 1.8 litre billycan, and leave overnight to rise. Next day, put the billycan in a saucepan of water and boil for 4 hours.

Caramel Pudding

Put 2 heaped tablespoons sugar, 1 tablespoon vinegar and 1 tablespoon water in a saucepan over medium heat, stirring until the sugar dissolves — let it stay over the heat until it caramelises. Make a custard by beating together 600 ml milk and 2 well-beaten eggs. Add 2 teaspoons sugar and a pinch of salt. Pour the sugar syrup into a wet pudding basin (mould) and allow it to cling to the sides of the basin. Pour in the custard, cover, and steam gently until set. Turn into a glass dish when cold.

Chocolate Pudding

Put 50 g (1/3 cup) chopped chocolate in a saucepan with 125 ml (1/2 cup) milk and heat gently until the chocolate has melted; cool. Cream 115 g butter and 140 g (2/3 cup) sugar in a bowl. Add 2 beaten egg yolks and 150 g (1 cup) self-raising flour. Add the chocolate mixture and a little vanilla essence. Beat 2 egg whites until stiff peaks form, and fold through the pudding mixture. Pour into a well-greased pudding basin (mould) and steam for about 1 hour 30 minutes. Serve with whipped cream.

Christmas Pudding

Put 900 g (7 1/4 cups) sultanas in a large bowl with 450 g (3 2/3 cups) raisins, 225 g (1 1/4 cups) mixed peel and 115 g (3/4 cup) blanched almonds. Pour over 300 ml of brandy or rum. Cover with plastic wrap and allow to stand at cool room temperature for 24 hours (or longer if preferred). Cream 450 g butter and 115 g (1/2 cup) soft brown sugar in a bowl. Add 8 eggs, one at a time, beating well after each addition. Sift in 120 g (3/4 cup) plain flour, 1 teaspoon mixed spice, 1 teaspoon ground ginger and 1 teaspoon ground nutmeg. Mix in 450 g (4 1/2 cups) breadcrumbs, mixing well, then add the soaked fruit and thoroughly combine. Spoon into 1 large or 2 small pudding basins (moulds) and boil for 4–5 hours.

Grated potatoes are an excellent substitute for suet in boiled puddings. Use 115 g to 225 g flour.

Coffee Pudding

Grease a pudding basin (mould) and decorate it with blanched almonds. Put 115 g butter in a saucepan over medium heat with 80 g (1/3 cup) soft brown sugar and 90 g (1/4 cup) golden syrup. When dissolved, remove from the heat and allow to cool. Add 1 beaten egg and 1 tablespoon coffee essence. Sift 225 g (1½ cups) self-raising flour into the mixture and beat well. Add 85 g (2/3 cup) sultanas and 1/4 teaspoon bicarbonate of soda dissolved in a little milk. Spoon into a pudding basin (mould), cover with baking paper, and steam for 2 hours.

Date Pudding

Sift 150 g (1 cup) plain flour and a pinch of salt into a bowl. Rub in 1 tablespoon butter. Add 225 g (1½ cups) chopped pitted dates, 2 tablespoons sugar and a little ground nutmeg and mixed spice. Boil 250 ml (1 cup) milk, and as it rises, stir in 1 teaspoon bicarbonate of soda and 1 tablespoon vinegar. While frothing, stir quickly into the dry ingredients. Steam for 2½–3 hours.

Ginger Dumplings

Sift 225 g (1½ cups) plain flour and a pinch of salt into a bowl. Rub in 55 g butter. Add 1½ teaspoons baking powder, 2 teaspoons ground ginger and 2 teaspoons sugar. Mix with enough cold water to form a soft dough. Put into a greased pudding basin (mould) and steam for 2 hours. Turn out and serve with syrup in a glass dish. This recipe is simple and inexpensive.

Golden Sponge

Cream 1 tablespoon butter and 110 g (½ cup) sugar in a bowl. Add 2 beaten eggs, stirring well to combine. Sift in 150 g (1 cup) plain flour and 1 teaspoon baking powder. Drizzle golden syrup into the bottom of a greased pudding basin (mould), then pour in the batter. Steam for 1 hour without raising the lid of the saucepan.

Golden Syrup Dumplings

Sift 450 g (3 cups) self-raising flour into a bowl. Rub in 1½ tablespoons butter and mix in just enough milk to make a rather stiff paste — it should resemble a thick batter. To make the syrup, put 750 ml (3 cups) boiling water in a saucepan with 220 g (1 cup) sugar, 2 tablespoons golden syrup and the juice of 1 lemon. Bring to the boil. Using a fork, immerse small lumps of the dumpling mixture (about the size of an egg) into the syrup. Boil for 20 minutes, but no longer. Do not lift the lid while the dumplings are in saucepan. Serve in a bowl with the syrup poured over.

Marguerite Pudding

Cream 1 tablespoon butter and 110 g (½ cup) sugar in a bowl. Add 1 egg and beat well. Stir in 150 g (1 cup) self-raising flour and 125 ml (½ cup) milk. Mix well. Grease a pudding basin (mould) and line it thickly with jam. Pour in the pudding mixture and steam for exactly 1½ hours.

Old English Plum Pudding

In a bowl mix together 225 g (1¾ cups) raisins, 225 g (1¾ cups) sultanas, 370 g (2 cups) chopped mixed peel and 115 g (⅔ cup) chopped dried figs. Add 225 g chopped beef suet. Sift 75 g (½ cup) plain flour in a separate bowl with ½ teaspoon ground cinnamon, ½ teaspoon ground mace, ¼ teaspoon ground ginger, ¼ teaspoon ground cloves and ½ teaspoon salt. Sprinkle the flour over 400 g (4 cups) dry breadcrumbs and add to the fruit and suet. Mix together 285 g (1¼ cups) soft brown sugar and 250 ml (1 cup) freshly squeezed orange juice or cider and add to the fruit, mixing well to combine. Add 6 well-beaten eggs and work together thoroughly; leave overnight in the bowl with brandy or rum poured over (covered). Spoon into a greased pudding basin (mould) and boil for 5 hours or steam for 5–6 hours.

Picton Pudding

Sift 225 g (1½ cups) plain flour into a bowl and rub in 1 tablespoon butter. Add ½ teaspoon bicarbonate of soda, 125 g (1 cup) sultanas and ½ cup chopped green apple, mixing well. Measure out 175 g (½ cup) golden syrup in a 1-cup measure and add enough milk to fill the cup, stirring well. Add this to the pudding mixture and stir well. Spoon into a greased pudding basin (mould) and steam for 3 hours.

Quince Dumplings

Peel 4 quinces and remove the core, but leave intact without breaking into quarters or halves. Fill the hollow left by the core with sugar. Make a short or Suet Pastry (see recipe, page 287) and divide the dough into four even-sized portions. Roll each portion out and use it to mould evenly around each quince. Sprinkle a piece of muslin lightly with flour, tie each dumpling separately in the cloth and drop into a saucepan of boiling water. Cook for about 2 hours, then lift out, remove the cloth and serve with sugar or honey.

Rich Christmas Pudding

In a large bowl mix together 80 g chopped beef suet, 150 g (1 cup) currants, 155 g (1 cup) chopped blanched almonds, 375 g (3 cups) raisins, 200 g (2 cups) breadcrumbs, 1 teaspoon ground cinnamon, 1 whole grated nutmeg, ½ teaspoon ground cloves, 155 g (2/3 cup) soft brown sugar, 95 g (½ cup) candied citron (cedro), 95 g (½ cup) candied lemon peel and 95 g (½ cup) candied orange peel. Cover with plastic wrap and let stand for 7–10 days. The day before Christmas add 4 well-beaten egg yolks, 250 ml (1 cup) warmed milk, 125 ml (½ cup) sherry and 125 ml (½ cup) brandy. Mix well and place in 1 large pudding basin (mould) — alternatively you can use 3 smaller basins. It is preferable to make small ones as there is less fear of the mixture being insufficiently cooked. Boil the puddings for 6 hours.

Rich Plum Pudding without Eggs

In a bowl mix together 300 g (2 cups) plain flour, 125 g (1 cup) raisins, 150 g (1 cup) currants, 125 g (1 cup) sultanas, 220 g (1 cup) sugar, 60 g (½ cup) finely grated lemon zest and 1 teaspoon mixed spice. Stir well to thoroughly combine. Melt 1 heaped teaspoon butter in 250 ml (1 cup) boiling water and add to the dry ingredients, stirring to combine. Cover and stand for 12 hours or overnight. Spoon into a greased pudding basin (mould) and boil for 4 hours. For a change, this can be made with less fruit, and other flavourings can be used as substitute.

Sago Plum Pudding

Soak 2 tablespoons of sago in 300 ml milk. Place in a bowl with 220 g (1 cup) sugar, 125 g (1 cup) sultanas, 110 g (1 brimming cup) breadcrumbs, 1 tablespoon melted butter, 1 teaspoon bicarbonate of soda and 1 beaten egg. Spoon into a greased pudding basin (mould) and steam for 3 hours. Serve with cream.

Steamed Apple Puff

Grease a deep pudding basin (mould) and place 3 peeled, cored and chopped apples in the bottom. Sift together 115 g flour, 1 teaspoon baking powder and a pinch of salt in a bowl. Rub in 2 teaspoons butter and add 1 tablespoon sugar. Mix into a very soft dough with 125 ml (½ cup) milk. Spoon into the basin over the apples, cover with greased baking paper, and steam for about 1½–2 hours. Turn out and serve with sauce or custard.

Steamed Banana Pudding

Mash 6 bananas in a bowl. Add 90 g (¾ cup) sultanas, 150 g (1½ cups) breadcrumbs, 110 g (½ cup) sugar, 125 ml (½ cup) lemon juice and a pinch of salt. Stir well to thoroughly combine. Spoon into a pudding basin (mould) and steam for 2½ hours.

Steamed Jam Pudding

Grease a pudding basin (mould). Make 225 g Shortcrust Pastry (see recipe, page 287). Roll out enough to line the pudding basin. Spread a layer of jam over the pastry, then roll out the remaining pastry and cut four rounds (more if liked), using graduated cutters, and keeping larger pieces of pastry to fit over the top of basin at the finish. Arrange alternate layers of jam and pastry in the basin until it is filled. Wet the edges and press together the lid and the side pastry to make it air and moisture proof. Cover with greased baking paper, or tie a cloth over the top, leaving enough room for the pastry to rise. Steam for 1½ –2 hours. Serve with sauce or custard.

Steamed Lemon Pudding

Cream 115 g butter and 110 g (½ cup) sugar in a bowl. Add 2 eggs, one at a time, beating well after each addition. Add 185 ml (¾ cup) milk and the finely grated zest of 1 lemon. Lastly, sift in 225 g (1½ cups) plain flour, 1 tablespoon baking powder and ½ teaspoon salt, mixing well to combine. Spoon into a greased pudding basin (mould) leaving plenty of room for the pudding to rise. Steam for 1 hour 15 minutes. Serve with cream or Lemon Sauce (see recipe, page 312).

Variation You can make an orange pudding by replacing the finely grated zest of 1 lemon with orange zest instead.

Steamed Pudding Without Eggs

Sift 150 g (1 cup) plain flour into a bowl with 1 teaspoon bicarbonate of soda. Rub in 1 tablespoon butter, then add 100 g (1 cup) breadcrumbs, 125 g (1 cup) sultanas, 1 cup chopped apples and 210 g (1 small cup) sugar. Gradually stir in 250 ml (1 cup) milk until all the ingredients are thoroughly combined (you may not need to use all the milk). Spoon into a greased pudding basin (mould) and steam for 2 hours.

Steamed Victoria Pudding

Sift 120 g (³/4 cup) plain flour into a bowl with a pinch of salt. Rub in 55 g suet or butter, then mix in ½ grated apple, some chopped glacé cherries and 1 tablespoon apricot jam. Stir in enough water to form a soft dough, then spoon into a greased pudding basin (mould) and steam for 1 hour.

Treacle Pudding

Sift 150 g (1 cup) flour into a bowl with 1 teaspoon salt, 1 teaspoon bicarbonate of soda and 1 large teaspoon ground ginger. Add 2 tablespoons sugar and then rub in 2 tablespoons butter until the mixture resembles fine breadcrumbs. Add 2 tablespoons treacle and mix well to combine. Lastly, add 250 ml (1 cup) milk. Spoon the mixture into a greased pudding basin (mould) and steam for 2 hours. This recipe is good made with fruit and a little mixed peel, omitting the treacle and ginger and adding a little more sugar, to taste.

Wagga Pudding

Put 2 large tablespoons butter in a bowl with 220 g (1 cup) sugar, 2 teaspoons bicarbonate of soda and a little ground nutmeg. Stir in 375 ml (1½ cups) boiling water until dissolved, then add 300 g (2 cups) sifted plain flour and 90 g (³/4 cup) mixed sultanas and currants. Stir in 1 beaten egg. Leave overnight; next day boil for 4 hours.

'Well' Plum Pudding (An Old Fashioned Recipe)

Sift 900 g (6 cups) plain flour into a bowl and rub in 240 g chopped suet or butter, 225 g (1½ cups) currants and a pinch of salt. Stir well, adding just enough water to make a stiff dough. Roll the dough out to about 2.5 cm. Grease a pudding basin (mould) and line the basin with pastry. Chop 350 g butter and put into the basin alternately with 1.1 kg (5 cups) sugar. Cover with the remaining dough. Boil the pudding for 6 hours. To serve, cut the top off the pudding and mix the butter and sugar together in the 'well'.

Milk Puddings

All milk puddings require slow and gentle cooking. Custard puddings need careful baking. Set the pudding basin in a large roasting tin of water. The pudding should be removed from the oven as soon as custard is set or it will go watery. Never allow a baked custard to come to the boil. Less rice and sago is needed with longer cooking.

Rules for Making Milk Puddings:
- For every 600 ml milk and 300 ml water allow 55 g grain, 1½ tablespoons sugar, flavouring and 2–3 eggs.
- The water is used for the grain and should be absorbed by it before the milk is added, rice is boiled for 10 minutes in the water and 20 minutes in the milk.
- Sago is soaked in water for 2 hours and boiled in milk until clear.
- Tapioca should be soaked overnight and cooked like sago.
- Semolina should be put into boiling milk and only half quantity of grain.
- When cooking milk puddings be careful that the mixture is cool before adding the eggs or the mixture will curdle; always stand the dish in a pan of cold water in the oven. It takes 20–30 minutes to bake a pudding.

Boiled Custard

Bring 500 ml (2 cups) milk just to the boil in the top of a double boiler. Beat together 2 eggs (or 4 egg yolks) in a bowl, then add 1–2 tablespoons sugar and a pinch of salt. Pour over the hot milk, stirring well. Return to the top of the boiler and cook over hot water, stirring constantly until the mixture coats the back of a spoon. Remove from the heat immediately and continue stirring for a few minutes. Flavour with vanilla essence, to taste.

Baked Custard Pudding

Beat 3 eggs in a bowl and add 600 ml milk and 75 g (⅓ cup) sugar and a few drops of vanilla essence. Stir well to combine. Pour into a greased pie dish. Lastly, add 1 tablespoon butter, breaking off little pieces and scattering on top. Sprinkle with ground nutmeg. Set the dish in a roasting tin with water and cook in a 150°C oven until set.

Bread and Butter Pudding

Using 3–4 slices of bread, fill a greased pie dish with alternate layers of bread and butter, scattering 50 g (1/3 cup) currants between the layers. Beat 1 egg in a small bowl and add 2 teaspoons sugar, stirring to combine. Mix together 2 tablespoons condensed milk with 300 ml water, then add to the egg mixture, stirring well. Pour over the bread and bake in a 180°C oven for about 30 minutes. Jam or marmalade may be used instead of currants.

Caramel Bread Custard

Butter 2 slices bread on both sides and place in the bottom of a greased pie dish. Make a caramel in a saucepan using cold water, sugar and a little lemon juice. When the caramel is thick, pour immediately over the bread and leave to cool (the more caramel, the better the pudding). Make a Boiled Custard (see recipe opposite), using yolks only. Pour over the caramel and bread and bake slowly. Make a meringue using egg whites, adding 2 small tablespoons sugar for each egg white. Put the meringue on the pudding and return to the oven until brown. Don't put too much sugar in the custard, as the caramel and meringue supply all of the sweetness. Serve cold.

Creamed Rice Pudding

Cover the bottom of a greased pie dish with 1 tablespoon rice. Pour in 600 ml milk, then add 2 teaspoons sugar and stir well. Grate a little nutmeg on top of the milk and add 3–4 knobs butter. Bake in a 150°C oven for 1 1/2–2 hours.

Golden syrup used in a pudding will serve the purpose of sugar, eggs and milk and will keep the pudding moist. This applies also to home use where there is no ice chest.

Baked Puddings

Apple Charlotte

Grease a pie dish with butter, then sprinkle with sugar. Line the pie dish with thin slices of bread or cake dipped in melted butter. Add sufficient apple purée to fill the pie dish. Cover the top with bread or cake crumbs. Sprinkle with sugar and mixed spice and scatter small pieces of butter on top. Bake in a 180°C oven for 30–45 minutes. Serve with Boiled Custard (see recipe, page 306) or whipped cream.

Apple Dumplings

Peel, core and halve as many apples as you wish to eat. Make a Short Pastry (see recipe, page 287) and cut into portions that will be large enough, when rolled, to enclose each apple half. Place the pastry-covered apples in a large baking dish and sprinkle 220 g (1 cup) sugar on top, then pour in enough milk to almost cover the dumplings. Bake for 1 hour, or a little longer if necessary. If the milk evaporates during cooking, add a little more. The sugar and milk will form a delicious creamy sauce to serve with the dumplings.

Sponge Topping for Apple Sponge Pudding

Cream 2 tablespoons butter and 2 tablespoons sugar in a bowl. Add 1 well-beaten egg, stirring to combine, then add 4 tablespoons boiling water. Lastly, sift in 150 g (1 cup) plain flour, 1 teaspoon baking powder and a pinch of salt. Pour evenly over hot fruit and bake for 30 minutes.

Baked Apples

Peel and core 6–8 apples and place them in a deep baking dish with a spoonful of water to prevent them from burning. Fill the centres with sugar, adding a little grated lemon zest to each. Bake slowly until quite soft (test them with a skewer). Whip 2 egg whites until stiff peaks form and add a little sugar and lemon juice to flavour the meringue. Drop a spoonful of the meringue on top of each apple and dot with tiny pieces of red currant jelly. Serve with Boiled Custard (see recipe, page 306), for which the 2 egg yolks may be used.

Baked Date Pudding

Cream 2 tablespoons butter and 165 g (¾ cup) soft brown sugar in a bowl. Add 1 egg, beating well to combine. Add 3 tablespoons milk, 270 g (1½ cups) pitted dates, 75 g (½ cup) plain flour, and mix well. Stir in another 3 tablespoons milk; lastly add another 75 g (½ cup) plain flour with ½ teaspoon bicarbonate of soda and 1 tablespoon cocoa powder. Mix well. Bake in a pie dish for 25–30 minutes in a 180°C oven. Serve with cream or custard.

Butterscotch Apples with Custard Sauce

Put 220 g (1 cup) caster sugar in a saucepan with 250 ml (1 cup) water. Stir over medium heat until the sugar dissolves, then bring to the boil and simmer for 10 minutes. Add 6 peeled and cored apples and simmer very slowly until tender. Remove the apples and set aside. Dissolve 1 teaspoon gelatine in the warm sugar syrup in the saucepan. In a separate saucepan put 230 g (1 cup) soft brown sugar, 60 ml (¼ cup) milk and 1 tablespoon butter. Cook over medium heat until the mixture forms a soft ball when a little is tested in cold water. Add 125 g (1 cup) chopped walnuts to the milk mixture. Stuff the cooked apples with the nut mixture and place in a serving dish. Pour the sugar syrup over the top and decorate with whipped cream. Serve with 450 ml pouring custard on the side.

Butterscotch Pudding

Put 2 tablespoons plain flour and 230 g (1 cup) soft brown sugar in a saucepan. Add 2 well-beaten egg yolks and gradually stir in 500 ml (2 cups) milk. Bring to the boil and stir continuously until thickened. Add 2 tablespoons butter and spoon into a greased pie dish. Beat 2 egg whites with 110 g (½ cup) sugar and spoon over the top of the pudding. Bake in the oven until the meringue is nicely brown.

Caramel Banana Pudding

Grease a shallow dish with butter and sprinkle brown sugar in the base. Line the dish with sliced bananas. Cream 1 tablespoon butter and 230 g (1 cup) soft brown sugar in a bowl. Add 1 egg, beating well to combine. Alternately stir in 125 ml (½ cup) milk and 150 g (1 cup) self-raising flour, mixing well. Spoon into the prepared dish over the bananas and bake in a 180°C oven for 30–40 minutes. Turn out onto a large plate and serve with custard or cream.

Chocolate Fudge Pudding

Sift 150 g (1 cup) self-raising flour into a bowl with ½ teaspoon salt and 1 tablespoon cocoa powder. Add 165 g (¾ cup) sugar. Melt 2 tablespoons butter in a saucepan with 125 ml (½ cup) milk and 1 teaspoon vanilla essence. Mix into the dry ingredients and stir until smooth. Add 60 g (½ cup) chopped walnuts and pour into a dish (larger than the mixture). Mix together 115 g (½ cup) soft brown sugar and 30 g (¼ cup) cocoa powder for the topping and sprinkle over the top of the pudding. Pour boiling water carefully over the back of a wooden spoon onto the pudding and bake in a 190°C oven for 50 minutes–1 hour. Serve with cream or custard.

Cleopatra Pudding

Put 600 ml milk and 1 teaspoon butter in a saucepan and heat over low heat. Add 2 tablespoons sugar, 90 g (1 cup) desiccated coconut and 125 g (1 cup) dry biscuit crumbs. Stir in 3 well-beaten egg yolks, beating well to combine. Spoon half of the mixture into a greased pie dish, then add 300 g (1½ cups) tinned apple purée over the top. Spoon the remaining pudding mixture on top and bake in a 180°C oven for about 30 minutes, or until set. Whip 3 egg whites with 2 tablespoons sugar, and place on top of the pudding. Return to the oven and brown. Serve cold.

Coconut Pudding

Melt 55 g butter with 110 g (½ cup) sugar in a saucepan over low heat. Bring to the boil and boil for 2 minutes, then remove from the heat and add 60 g (⅔ cup) desiccated coconut, 2 tablespoons finely chopped candied citron, the grated zest of ½ large lemon, 3 eggs and 25 g (¼ cup) breadcrumbs. When all these ingredients have been beaten together, add the strained juice of ½ lemon. Spoon the mixture into a greased pudding basin (mould) and bake in a 180°C oven for 45 minutes. Turn out and, if desired, cover with white icing and decorate with cherries and apricot jam. This can be served either hot or cold.

Cottage Pudding

Cream 2 tablespoons butter and 220 g (1 cup) sugar in a bowl. Add 2 well-beaten eggs add then gradually stir in 250 ml (1 cup) milk. Sift in 300 g (2 cups) plain flour, 2 teaspoons cream of tartar, 1 teaspoon bicarbonate of soda and ½ teaspoon salt, mixing well to combine. Spoon the mixture into a greased pie dish and bake for 45 minutes. Turn out and serve with jam, cream, or a sauce made by heating 175 g (½ cup) golden syrup in a saucepan with the juice of 1 lemon, a knob of butter and 2 tablespoons water.

Delicious Pudding

Cream 1 tablespoon butter and 220 g (1 cup) sugar in a bowl. Add the finely grated zest and juice of 1 lemon and 2 beaten egg yolks. Sift in 1 heaped tablespoon plain flour, then stir in 310 ml (1¼ cups) milk. Whip 2 egg whites until stiffly peaking and gently fold through. Spoon into a greased pudding basin (mould). Place in a roasting tin of water and bake in a 150°C oven for 30 minutes.

Dutch Apple Cake with Lemon Sauce

Sift 300 g (2 cups) plain flour into a bowl with 3 teaspoons baking powder and ½ teaspoon salt. Add 2 tablespoons sugar and rub in 3 tablespoons butter. Add 170 ml (²/₃ cup) milk and 1 well-beaten egg. Mix quickly with a flat-bladed knife until the dough is soft enough to spread into the base of a shallow baking dish. Peel and slice 4 tart apples and press them into the dough to create a design. Sprinkle with sugar and ground cinnamon and bake in a 200°C oven for 30 minutes. To make the lemon sauce put 220 g (1 cup) sugar in a saucepan with 2 tablespoons cornflour. Add 500 ml (2 cups) boiling water and stir continuously until the sugar has dissolved. Bring to the boil and boil for 10 minutes, then add finely grated lemon zest and butter, to taste. Serve warm with the pudding.

Peach Crisp

Drain the syrup from 440 g (2¼ cups) tinned sliced peaches, reserving the syrup. Arrange the peach slices over the base of a greased pie dish. Cream 55 g butter and 115 g (½ cup) soft brown sugar in a bowl and add ½ teaspoon finely grated lemon zest and a pinch of ground nutmeg. Add 1 well-beaten egg and mix well. Work in 60 g (2 cups) crushed cornflakes. Spread over the peaches in the dish. Bake in a 180°C oven for 20–25 minutes. Serve hot with ice cream.

Prune and Apricot Rice Bake

Put 110 g (½ cup) pitted prunes in a saucepan with 1 tablespoon sugar and 170 ml (²/₃ cup) water. Cover and cook for 15 minutes until the prunes are soft, then strain, reserving 125 ml (½ cup) of the cooking liquid. Put the prunes in the bottom of a deep glass pie dish. Mix together 1 tablespoon powdered milk with 250 ml (1 cup) water, stirring well to combine. Boil 1 cup uncooked rice to make 3 cups cooked rice, draining rice well. In a bowl, mix together the boiled rice, prune juice and milk. Add 1 well-beaten egg and 1 tablespoon sugar. Stir in 220 g (1 heaped cup) tinned apricot pie filling. Mix together to combine and pour over the prunes in the dish. Sprinkle 2 teaspoon desiccated coconut or cornflakes over the top. Sit in a roasting tin with hot water and bake in a 180°C oven for 30 minutes. During the last few minutes of cooking, brown the topping at a higher heat.

Queen Pudding

Boil 450 ml milk in a saucepan and add a small knob of butter. Put 80 g (1 cup) fresh breadcrumbs in a bowl and pour over the milk. When cool, add 1 beaten egg yolk and about 2 tablespoons sugar. Spoon the mixture into a greased pie dish and bake in a 180°C oven until firm. Spread 1½ tablespoons jam over the top. Make a meringue by whisking 1 egg white with 2 tablespoons sugar until stiffly peaking. Put this on top of the jam and bake in a 180°C oven until the meringue is light brown. If a lemon flavour is desired, add a little finely grated lemon zest to the crumbs before mixing with the milk.

Walden Chocolate Pudding

Cream 140 g butter and 80 g (⅓ cup) sugar in a bowl. Sift together 225 g (1½ cups) plain flour in a bowl with 85 g (⅔ cup) cocoa powder, ½ teaspoon salt and 2 teaspoons baking powder. Add 1 egg to the butter mixture with one-third of the dry ingredients, mixing well to combine. Add another 2 eggs, one at a time, beating well after each addition. Lastly, add 125 ml (½ cup) milk and the remaining dry ingredients. Stir in 80 g (¾ cup) ground almonds or other nuts and ½ teaspoon almond essence. Pour into a greased pie dish and bake in the oven at 190°C for 15 minutes, then reduce the heat to 180°C for 1 hour 45 minutes or until the pudding feels firm to the touch. Serve with Chocolate Sauce (see recipe, page 121).

Velvet Pudding

Beat 3 egg yolks in a bowl and add 55 g (¼ cup) sugar. Dissolve 2 tablespoons cornflour in enough milk to make a paste and add to the egg yolks. Pour this into a saucepan of 900 ml boiling milk and return to the boil, stirring until thickened. Remove from the heat and add a little vanilla essence to flavour. Pour the mixture into a greased pie dish and allow to cool. Beat 3 egg whites, then add 110 g (½ cup) sugar and 2 teaspoons lemon juice and beat until soft peaks form. Pour the meringue over the top of the pudding and bake in a 150°C oven until light brown. Serve with cream or fruit. Good when cold.

Cold Puddings

Angels' Food

Soak 3 tablespoons gelatine in a glass bowl with 400 ml milk. Sit the bowl over a saucepan of simmering water and stir until the gelatine dissolves. Put 800 ml milk in a saucepan and bring to the boil. Add the gelatine mixture and 110 g (½ cup) sugar. Heat just to a simmer then add 3–4 well-beaten egg yolks, stirring constantly and taking care it does not curdle. Pour into a bowl, then add the juice of 1 large or 2 small lemons, stirring occasionally until cool and beginning to set. Add 3–4 stiffly beaten egg whites and ½ teaspoon vanilla essence. It is an improvement to boil the thinly peeled zest of the lemons with the milk. Half this quantity is enough for a small mould. Refrigerate until set.

Apricot Trifle

Take a 20 cm day-old sponge cake and cut it into 2.5 cm cubes. Arrange in the bottom of a glass serving dish. Sprinkle with 2 tablespoons sherry. Add a layer of tinned apricots (a little sugar may be added to apricots if liked). Put 1 teaspoon cornflour in a saucepan with 300 ml milk and 2 teaspoons sugar. Stir over medium heat until boiling, then remove from heat and cool a little. Add 1 beaten egg yolk and stir over low heat for 2–3 minutes, but do not let it boil again. Cool, pour over the apricots and cake in the dish and set aside until cold. Dissolve 40 g (½ packet) lemon jelly in 250 ml (1 cup) hot water. When cold (but not set) pour over the custard. Set in the refrigerator. Before serving, decorate with whipped cream and toasted almonds.

When you have no lemons and wish to make a lemon sago, boil sago in water, add a packet of lemon jelly crystals, and a little lemon essence and sugar to taste. Serve with cream or custard.

Banana in Jelly

Stir water into 125 g (1½ packets) strawberry or blackcurrant jelly crystals until dissolved. Place a little jelly in the bottom of a mould and lay a circle of overlapping banana slices on top. Drop a little more jelly over the banana slices and let the jelly set to keep the bananas in place. Once set, add a 2.5 cm layer of jelly, and continue layering in this way until the mould is full. Vary it by using chopped pistachio nuts on the banana before adding the jelly, also jelly could be coloured a pale green instead of pink.

Butterscotch Sponge

Make a caramel by heating 90 g butter in a saucepan with 230 g (1 cup) soft brown sugar until the butter has melted. Add 500 ml (2 cups) hot milk and stir in 3 well-beaten egg yolks to make a smooth custard. Remove from the heat and cool. Put 1 tablespoon gelatine in a glass bowl with a little water. Sit the bowl over a saucepan of simmering water and stir until the gelatine dissolves. Add to the cool custard. Beat 3 egg whites until stiffly peaking and fold into the mixture. Spoon into a mould to set.

Caramel Cream

Stir 55 g butter and 165 g (¾ cup) soft brown sugar in a saucepan over low heat until the sugar dissolves. Bring to a boil and boil to a light caramel. Remove from the heat and set aside to cool. Separate 3 eggs. Beat the egg yolks and put in the top of a double boiler with 500 ml (2 cups) milk; stir until smoothly blended. Put 1 tablespoon gelatine in a glass bowl with some water. Sit the bowl over a saucepan of simmering water and stir until the gelatine dissolves. Add to the milk mixture. Gradually stir into the cooled caramel mixture. Whisk the egg whites until stiff peaks form and fold into the caramel with a little vanilla essence. Pour into small individual moulds or one large mould. Leave to cool until set. To serve, turn the caramel creams from the moulds onto serving dishes and garnish with whipped cream and a crystallised cherry.

Charlotte Russe

Line the bottom of a plain mould with red jelly 2.5 cm in thickness and allow to set. Trim 6–7 savoiaordi (sponge fingers) and line the sides of the mould with them, wedging them well together so that they to fit snugly around the side. Put 1 tablespoon gelatine in a glass bowl with 3 tablespoons water. Sit the bowl over a saucepan of simmering water and stir until the gelatine dissolves. Whip 300 ml cream and add 2 tablespoons caster sugar and 1 teaspoon vanilla essence. Gradually add the gelatine, beating lightly. When nearly set, pour into the centre of the mould. Refrigerate until firm, then trim the top of the sponge fingers and turn out onto a glass dish. Serve decorated with some extra chopped red jelly.

Chocolate Blanc Mange

Soak 1 tablespoon gelatine in a glass bowl with 2 tablespoons water. Sit the bowl over a saucepan of simmering water and stir until the sugar dissolves. Put 300 ml milk in a saucepan with 55 g (¼ cup) sugar and bring to the boil. Add the gelatine and stir together until dissolved. Grate 55 g dark chocolate and dissolve it in a little of the milk mixture, before returning it to the pan. Stir well and strain through a fine sieve. Pour into a wet mould, leave until cold, then turn out and decorate with whipped cream.

Coffee Cream

Put 2 well-beaten egg yolks and 450 ml milk in a saucepan over medium heat and stir until thickened; sweeten to taste. Remove from the heat. Mix together 2 tablespoons gelatine and 2 tablespoons hot strong black coffee and add to the milk mixture, stirring well to combine. When nearly cold, stir in 150 ml whipped cream. Pour into a mould and refrigerate until set.

Dainty Chocolate Mould

Line the base and sides of a mould with fingers of sponge cake, leaving 1 cm spaces between each. Heat 600 ml milk in a saucepan with 3 tablespoons sugar and bring to the boil. Mix 1 tablespoon cocoa powder with a little of the hot milk, then return to the pan and boil for 1 minute. Remove from the heat and set aside to cool. Put 1 tablespoon gelatine in a glass bowl with a little water. Sit the bowl over a saucepan of simmering water and stir until the gelatine dissolves. Stir into the chocolate mixture. Flavour with vanilla essence, to taste. When nearly cold, whisk the mixture for 5 minutes, then pour into the prepared mould over the cake and leave to set. Turn out onto a serving dish, decorate with whipped cream and a glacé cherry on top.

Exeter Pudding

Put 600 ml milk in a saucepan with 2 well-beaten eggs and stir over medium heat, without boiling, until thickened into a custard. Sweeten with sugar, remove from the heat and set aside to cool. Soak 1 tablespoon gelatine in a glass bowl with a little water. Sit the bowl over a saucepan of simmering water and stir until the gelatine dissolves. Stir through the cooled custard. Scoop the pulp from 12 passionfruit and strain to remove the seeds. Add the juice and pulp to the mixture and stir well to combine. Whisk 2 egg whites until stiffly peaking then fold through the custard to combine. Spoon into a mould and refrigerate until set.

Flummery

Put 1 tablespoon gelatine in a glass bowl with 3 tablespoons water. Sit the bowl over a saucepan of simmering water and stir until the gelatine dissolves. Put 250 ml (1 cup) water in a saucepan and bring to the boil. Mix 1 tablespoon flour with a little water to make a paste and then stir into the pan. Stir in the gelatine, then mix in the freshly squeezed juice of 4 oranges, 1/2 lemon, the pulp of 4 passionfruit and 165 g (3/4 cup) sugar. Bring to the boil, then remove from the heat and allow to cool. Beat the mixture for about 20 minutes. Place in dish ready for next day.

Ginger Blanc Mange

Take 115 g (¾ cup) preserved ginger in syrup and drain off the syrup to get 80 ml (⅓ cup); finely chop the ginger. Put 1 beaten egg in the top of a double boiler over medium heat with 300 ml milk and 2 tablespoons caster sugar until thick, making sure the mixture does not boil. Remove from the heat and cool. Put 1½ tablespoons gelatine in a glass bowl with 80 ml (⅓ cup) water. Sit the bowl over a saucepan of simmering water and stir until the gelatine dissolves. Add to the cooled custard with the ginger syrup, stirring until the mixture begins to set. Add the preserved ginger and mix well. Spoon into a wet mould and set. (If you would like to make the blanc mange with a spongier consistency, fold in 1–2 stiffly beaten egg whites before pouring into the mould.) Turn onto a serving dish and decorate with extra ginger pieces.

Lemon Pudding

Beat 4 egg yolks in a bowl and mix in 2 tablespoons sugar until well combined. Pour in the freshly squeezed juice of 2 lemons and a little of the finely grated zest. Add 2 tablespoons boiling water and cook in the top of a double boiler, stirring constantly until thickened. Beat 4 egg whites until stiffly peaking. Add 2 tablespoons sugar and beat again, then beat into the pudding mixture while still hot. Spoon into a mould and leave to set. Serve cold.

Marshmallow Cream

Take some marshmallows and cut up into small pieces and cover with sherry. Refrigerate all day. Whip some cream and fold through the marshmallows and sherry. Spoon into small serving dishes and pour over a little cherry brandy. Decorate with chopped burnt almonds and cherries.

Marshmallow Pineapple Pudding

Soak 1 heaped tablespoon gelatine in 125 ml (½ cup) water for 10 minutes, then fill the cup with boiling water. Add 1 tablespoon vanilla essence and a pinch of salt and allow to cool. Add 3 unbeaten egg whites and beat well. Gradually add 165 g (¾ cup) sugar, beating constantly until very thick, spongy and white. Arrange a few slices of tinned pineapple in a glass dish and place a crystallised cherry over each pineapple slice. Pour the marshmallow over the top and decorate with cherries. Allow to set.

Marshmallow Pudding (Children's Favourite)

Put 30 g gelatine in a bowl with 125 ml (½ cup) boiling water. Fill up the bowl with boiling water, add 1 teaspoon vanilla essence and a pinch of salt. Allow to cool. Add the unbeaten whites of 3 eggs and mix well together. Gradually add 165 g (¾ cup) sugar, and beat well — the mixture will turn white and be thick like snow. Pour into a wet mould and set for 2 hours. To make the sauce, caramelise 2 tablespoons sugar in a saucepan with a little water, then add 80 ml (⅓ cup) cream. Mix together and pour over the pudding before serving.

Orange Sponge

Soak 1 tablespoon gelatine in 250 ml (1 cup) water. Add 220 g (1 cup) sugar and stir well. Blend 1 tablespoon flour with 250 ml (1 cup) water and add 250 ml (1 cup) orange juice. Put all together in a saucepan and stir until it boils and thickens. Cook for a few minutes. Pour into a pudding basin and let it almost set, then whisk it for 10–15 minutes until light and frothy. Set in a mould.

Passionfruit Jelly

Put 2 teaspoons gelatine in a saucepan with the juice of ½ lemon, 250 ml (1 cup) water, 165 g (¾ cup) sugar and the pulp of 12 passionfruit. Stir until it just comes to the boil. Let stand a second, then strain and allow to cool. Beat 2 egg whites until stiffly peaking and fold through. Spoon into a mould and refrigerate until set.

Peach Cream Shape

Blend 2 teaspoons cornflour with a little milk to make a paste, then add to a saucepan with 435 ml (1¾ cups) milk and 1 tablespoon sugar. Stir until boiling, then reduce the heat and simmer for 3 minutes. Add 2 egg yolks and 1 teaspoon butter and stir over low heat for 1–2 minutes, making sure the mixture does not boil. Drain 330 g (1½ cups) tinned peaches, reserving 60 ml (¼ cup) syrup. Heat the peach slices in a separate saucepan with 1 tablespoon sugar and the reserved syrup. Soften 1 tablespoon gelatine in 2½ tablespoons water and add to the pan, stirring until dissolved. Mix the gelatine mixture into the custard and stir occasionally while cooling. When the mixture begins to thicken, fold in 2 stiffly beaten egg whites. Pour into a wet mould and place in the refrigerator until set. Turn out and serve with cream or custard.

Peach Delicious

Beat 2 egg whites until stiffly peaking, then gradually add 110 g (½ cup) sugar and beat well until the mixture holds its shape. Drain the syrup from 440 g (2¼ cups) tinned peaches and fold in half the peaches. Dissolve 3 teaspoons gelatine in 125 ml (½ cup) hot water; allow to cool but not set. Pour the gelatine slowly into the peach mixture, mixing lightly with a fork. Arrange the remaining peaches in the base of individual serving dishes. When the mixture is beginning to thicken, spoon over the peaches in the dishes. Sprinkle with chopped nuts and decorate with a cherry. Set in the refrigerator until just firm.

Pear Hedgehog

Drain the juice from 825 g tinned pear halves, reserving the syrup for serving. Whip 2 egg whites until stiffly peaking and slowly beat in 55 g (¼ cup) sugar until well combined. Stir in another 55 g (¼ cup) sugar until thoroughly mixed. Place the pear halves on a baking dish, cover each pear with the meringue mixture and insert sliced almonds to represent hedgehog prickles in the meringue. Bake in a 150°C oven for about 45 minutes, or until the meringue is stiff. Allow to cool and serve with the reserved syrup in a small jug on the side.

Looking Back in Time...

TANNING SHEEPSKINS

This method for tanning sheepskin was first included in the Coronation Cook Book during the Second World War, when the idea was conceived that servicemen in the line of duty could benefit from sheepskin vests. CWA members throughout country New South Wales took on the task of tanning and drying sheepskins, producing hundreds of vests, gloves and gauntlets — by the end of the war, more than 40,000 vests had been made and forwarded to Australian servicemen.

Take a freshly skinned sheepskin. Soak in a tub of warm water at 38°C with 2 tablespoons washing soda (sodium carbonate). Soap the wool well and leave to soak for 1 hour. Rinse in fresh, warm water without soda, until the wool is clean and white.

Rinse the soap out of the skin, stretch it on a table and, with a large knife that does not bend, scrape the flesh and fat from the skin, being careful not to damage it. Make a frame of four stout battens large enough to stretch a skin with six holes on the sides and four holes at the top and bottom. Tie pieces of string on the pelt by means of a marble or pebble in such a manner that the pebble is in a bag. Pass the ties through the holes in the batten and pull tightly.

TANNING (CHROME)
Mix together a solution of 450 g chrome tanning salt, 450 g common salt and 1.2 litres water. Place the sheep skin on trestles, skin side up. The solution is brushed on the skin and is kept wet for two days. Any surplus liquor not absorbed by the skin is then removed and the skin allowed to dry. It is then washed thoroughly to remove the chrome salt. Use no soap until the chrome salt is quite removed. For final washing use soap and rinse well.

ALUM TANNAGE
Mix together a solution of 450 g alum, 200 g salt and 1.2 litres water. Soak the sheep skin overnight after first scouring. Any surplus liquor not absorbed by the skin is then removed and the skin allowed to dry. It is then washed thoroughly to remove the chrome salt. Use no soap until the chrome salt is quite removed. For final washing use soap and rinse well.

Jams and Jellies

Jams

- Jam should be stirred carefully from time to time, skimming thoroughly. Use a stainless steel or wooden spoon.
- As jam cooks it is prone to burning so care must be taken that it is not left over too high a heat. A few sterilised silver coins in the bottom of the preserving pan will prevent the mixture burning.
- No hard and fast rule can be given about the time for cooking jam, as it depends on the kind of fruit used. When a little jam is poured on a saucer and it 'jellies' or sets in a few minutes, it is ready.

Blackberry Jam

450 g blackberries (include some not so ripe berries as well), 450 g sugar

Put the blackberries in a preserving pan and crush with a bottle. Boil for 30 minutes, stirring constantly. Heat the sugar on a baking tray in the oven and add to the pan. Boil for 10 minutes, or until jellied.

Cherry Jam

4.5 kg cherries, 4 kg sugar

Stone the cherries and put them in a preserving pan with 3 kg sugar. Boil for 20 minutes, or until the cherries are tender but unbroken. Add the rest of the sugar (heated in the oven on baking dishes), and boil fast for about 45 minutes, or until it jellies.

Choko Jam

10 large or 12 small chokos, 3 small lemons, 1.8 kg (8 cups) sugar,
45 g (¹/₄ cup) preserved ginger

Cut up the chokos very small or put through a mincing machine; cut the lemons into thin slices; put all into a non-metallic dish, in layers, sprinkling a little salt between each layer. Leave overnight and drain off the liquid in the morning. Put 375 ml (1¹/₂ cups) water in a preserving pan with the sugar; when it is coming to the boil, add the chokos, lemon and ginger. Boil slowly for 4–5 hours. Any other flavouring could be used instead of lemon – pineapple could be substituted, but in that case would not be cut up until ready for use.

Citron Marmalade

3 large citrons, 2 kg (9 cups) sugar

Cut the fruit into quarters lengthways. Remove the pulp, squeeze the juice, discarding any seeds and pulp. Refrigerate the juice. Finely chop the peel and put into a pan with 450 ml water and stand overnight. Next day, strain the peel. Return the peel to a clean pan and add 450 ml fresh water; allow to stand 24 hours, then add the citron juice and boil until tender. Allow to cool. Bring to the boil again and add the sugar. Continue to boil until cooked.

Cocktail Jam

Dried fruits (such as apricots, apples, figs and peaches),
sugar, 250 ml (1 cup) brandy or rum

Allow for 450 g (2 heaped cups) sugar for every 450 g (2¹/₂ cups) dried fruits. Wash the dried fruit and soak in water for 24 hours. Put all into the preserving pan and boil for 20 minutes, then add the sugar, stirring until dissolved. Boil for a further 20 minutes or until it jellies. Before removing from the heat, add 250 ml (1 cup) rum or brandy. Stir well.

Cumquat Marmalade

Cumquats, sugar

Slice the cumquats and place in a bowl. Add 1.2 litres water to every 450 g fruit. Set aside overnight. Next day, bring to the boil and cook until tender; set aside overnight. Next day, add 625 g sugar to every 450 g cooked fruit; boil for about 45 minutes, or until it jellies.

Dried Apricot and Apple Jam

450 g (2½ cups) dried apricots, 450 g Granny Smith apples,
2.25 kg (10¼ cups) sugar

Soak the apricots in 1.5 litres water overnight. Peel and slice the apples, then place in a saucepan with a little water and boil until they are soft and not watery. Put the apricots and water in a saucepan and bring to the boil. Boil for 30 minutes, then add the sugar and cooked apples and boil for 10 minutes further. Try a little on a cold saucer and if it forms a skin it is ready to bottle.

Dried Apricot Jam

900 g (5 cups) dried apricots, 3 litres water, 2.7 kg sugar,
80 g (½ cup) blanched almonds

Cut the apricots into quarters and put them into a bowl with 3 litres water; soak for 24 hours. Place in a preserving pan and add the sugar, then simmer slowly until the sugar dissolves. Bring to the boil and continue boiling until it jellies when tested. Chop the almonds and add them to the jam a few minutes before it has finished boiling.

English Marmalade

6 oranges, 6 lemons, sugar

Slice the oranges and lemons as thinly as possible, removing the pips. Weigh fruit and put into a large stainless steel or glass bowl. Add 1.5 litres cold water to every 450 g fruit; let stand for 24 hours. Boil until the peel is tender, then remove from the heat and allow to cool. Weigh the cold mixture and to every 450 g fruit add 625 g sugar. Boil over medium-high heat for 1 hour, being careful to remove all scum that forms — do not boil too hard or the peel will harden.

Fig Conserve

5.4 kg figs, 4.5 kg sugar, 450 g (5 cups) preserved ginger,
225 g (1½ cups) blanched almonds

Cut the figs into rather large pieces. Put the sugar in a saucepan with 1.5 litres (6 cups) water. Boil for 20 minutes, then add the figs and boil for a further 3 hours. After 2 hours cooking, add the ginger and almonds. Continue cooking until it jellies.

Gooseberry Jam

1.3 kg gooseberries, 2.7 kg (12¼ cups) sugar

Rinse the gooseberries and wipe clean. Put the sugar in a saucepan with 3 litres (12 cups) water and bring to the boil. Boil for 10 minutes, then add the fruit and boil for another 1 hour 30 minutes, or until it jellies.

Grapefruit Marmalade

Grapefruit, sugar

To every 450 g grapefruit allow 1.8 litres water. Cut the grapefruit very finely and soak in water for 24 hours. Bring just to the boil, then remove from the heat and strain the fruit, measuring the water carefully as you will need to replace it with the same quantity of fresh water. Stand again for 12 hours. Bring to the boil and cook steadily until the fruit and rind are quite tender. Measure the pulp and liquid, and to every 600 ml water allow 440 g (2 cups) sugar. Boil until it jellies.

Green Tomato Jam

1.3 kg Green tomatoes, 1.1 kg (5 cups) sugar, 3 lemons, ginger, cinnamon, cloves

Prick each tomato several times with a fork. Make a syrup using 300 ml water and the sugar; boil for a few minutes, then add the tomatoes and squeeze in the juice from the lemons. Wrap the ginger, cinnamon and cloves in muslin and secure with kitchen string; add to the pan. Boil for 3 hours, or until it jellies. Remove the spices before storing.

Lemon Jam

7 large lemons, 1 teaspoon bicarbonate of soda, 2.7 kg (12¼ cups) sugar

Slice the lemons and place in a saucepan with enough cold water to just cover the lemons. Bring to the boil. Add the bicarbonate of soda and boil for 15 minutes. Strain off water and discard. Put the lemons back in a clean pan and add 3.6 litres cold water; boil until the rind is tender, then add the sugar. Boil until it jellies.

Loganberry Jam

Loganberries, sugar

Allow 450 g sugar for every 450 g loganberries. Choose firm, not quite ripe loganberries and pick and wash them carefully. Put into a pan with a few spoons of water, bring to the boil and boil for about 15 minutes. Add the sugar and boil, stirring constantly, for about 10 minutes, or until it jellies.

Variation Using the same method, a mixture of strawberries and loganberries makes a delicious jam.

Mandarin Marmalade

Mandarins, sugar

Finely slice the mandarins. Allow for 500 ml (2 cups) water for 1 cup fruit. Put the mandarin slices in a bowl and cover with water. Allow to stand for 12 hours. Bring to the boil and cook for about 30 minutes, or until tender. Remove from the heat and allow to stand until the next day, then add 220 g (1 cup) sugar to every 1 cup fruit. Bring to the boil and cook for about 45 minutes, or until it jellies.

Marmalade Cooked in Pressure Cooker

900 g fruit (this may consist of 1 grapefruit, 2 oranges,
1 lemon, or 900 g cumquats or mature mandarins, 1 orange and 1 lemon),
1.3 kg (6 cups) sugar

Peel the fruit, removing any pith and reserving the peel. Halve and finely slice the fruit, removing and reserving any seeds and the ends of the fruit. Put the pith, seeds and ends of fruit in a muslin bag, tie and place in the pressure cooker with the sliced fruit and peel. Add the sugar, cover with the 900 ml hot water and cook for 20 minutes, or until it jellies.

Melon and Mandarin Jam

2.7 kg melons, 2.1 kg (9½ cups) sugar, 6 mandarins, citric acid

Cut the melons, place in a bowl, sprinkle with a little sugar and stand overnight. Next day, bring to the boil and 15 minutes later add the sugar. Slice 4 of the 6 mandarins. Remove the pulp from the remaining two mandarins and add to the pan with the sliced mandarins. When nearly ready to remove from the heat, add a little citric acid to prevent jam from crystallising. Boil until it jellies.

Melon Jam

4.5 kg pie melon, 2.7 kg (12¼ cups) sugar, 6 lemons

Cut the melon up into small pieces. Cover with a little sugar and leave overnight. Squeeze the juice from 6 lemons and remove the zest and finely chop. Put the melons in a saucepan and add the lemon juice and zest. Bring to the boil, then reduce the heat and simmer for 30 minutes. Add the sugar and stir through until dissolved.

Orange and Apple Jam

3 large oranges, 3 Granny Smith apples, 2.7 kg (12¼ cups) sugar

Cut the oranges and soak for 36 hours in 2.75 litres (11 cups) water. Put in a saucepan with the apples and boil until tender. Add the sugar and boil for about 30 minutes, or until it jellies.

Orange Conserve (Special)

8 oranges, 3.25 kg sugar

Cut the oranges into rounds that are thin enough to keep their shape, so that they will not break during cooking. Take out all the pips, add 4.8 litres of water, and let stand overnight in a bowl. Next day, boil the oranges and water until the liquid is reduced by half. (To do this, when it is in pan ready to boil place a stick in the pan and mark plainly how far the mixture comes up to on the stick, boil well until the mixture is about halfway — the orange rings should be soft and tender to the touch.) Do not stir. Add the sugar and boil until it jellies. Do not stir, but lift and move the jam carefully at times — this will prevent the jam burning.

Orange Jam

10 oranges, 2 lemons, 4 kg sugar

Cut up the oranges and lemons and place in a bowl. Cover with 3 litres (12 cups) water and a pinch of salt. Leave to soak overnight. Next day, bring to the boil and boil until the fruit is very tender. Add the sugar and boil for 1 hour further, or until it jellies.

Orange Marmalade (A Famous Recipe)

Oranges, sugar

Each fruit must be quartered and finely shredded with a very sharp knife. To each measure of shredded fruit allow 3 measures of water. Place in a preserving pan and set aside to soak for 24 hours. Set the preserving pan on the stove and let come to the boil, and boil for 10 minutes. Again, set in a cool place for 24 hours. Measure the mixture, and to every 1 cup pulp allow 220 g (1 cup) sugar, and at the last add 1 cup more of sugar. Put on the stove and cook until it jellies.

Variation Try this out with 1 orange, 1 lemon, the water, and sugar. It will make several glasses of delicious marmalade.

Passionfruit and Tomato Jam

36 passionfruit, 1.8 kg firm ripe tomatoes, sugar

Halve the passionfruit and scoop out the pulp. Put the skins in a preserving pan, cover with about 1.2 litres water and boil quickly for 1 hour; strain. Pour boiling water over the tomatoes, remove the skins and roughly chop. Put into a preserving pan, allowing 450 g sugar to every 450 g cooked tomatoes. Measure the passionfruit pulp and allow 450 g sugar for every 600 g pulp; add the pulp and sugar to the tomatoes. Boil together for 1½ hours or until it jellies.

Peach Jam

Peaches, sugar

Allow 350 g sugar for every 450 g peaches. Peel the peaches and cut into slices, discarding the stones. Put them into a large non-metallic bowl, sprinkle with half of the sugar and leave overnight. Next day, bring to the boil and boil until the peaches are tender. Add the sugar and boil rapidly until tested in the usual way.

Pear Honey

Mince 1.8 kg pears, being careful to save the juice. Put the pulp and juice in a saucepan with a little water and bring to the boil; cook for 1 hour. Add the juice of 4 lemons and 1.3 kg (6 cups) sugar. Cook until it jellies.

Pear Marmalade

4 oranges, 1 lemon, 2.7 kg pears, 2.7 kg sugar

Finely chop the unpeeled oranges and lemon. Put into bowl, cover with 750 ml (3 cups) water and leave overnight. Next day, peel the pears, cut finely and place in a bowl with the oranges and lemon. Add the sugar and let stand overnight. Next day, boil gently for 1–2 hours, or until it jellies.

Preserved Cumquats

Prick 450 g very ripe cumquats with a darning needle.
Put 550 g (2½ cups) sugar in a saucepan with enough water
to cover and bring to the boil. Boil until tender. Put sugar and
300 ml water in a saucepan and bring to the boil, stirring to dissolve
the sugar. Add the fruit and boil for 10 minutes.

Raisin Jam

Raisins, lemons

Soak raisins in water overnight. In the morning weigh the raisins. Allow the juice of 1 lemon for every 450 g soaked fruit. Boil the raisins and lemon juice together until the raisins are tender and clear.

Raspberry Jam

450 g raspberries, 450 g sugar

Boil the fruit for 5 minutes in a saucepan, then add the sugar and boil for a further 5 minutes, or until it jellies.

Rosella Jam

Rosella berries, sugar

Peel off the red leaves from around the berries. Put the berries in a saucepan and add just enough water to cover them; bring to the boil. Strain the berries and reserve the juice. Allow 450 g sugar for every 600 ml juices and 450 g leaves. Boil the leaves in the strained juice for 30 minutes, or until well cooked, then add the sugar. Boil until it jellies.

Shaddock Jam

2 kg shaddock or pomelo fruit, 10 kg sugar

Soak the whole fruit for several hours in a mixture of salt and water to just cover. Cut up the fruit into very thin slices and soak overnight in 14.5 litres water. Boil for 2–2½ hours. Add the sugar and boil for 1 hour. A lemon may be added.

Strawberry Jam

1.8 kg strawberries, the juice of 4 lemons, 1.6 kg (7¼ cups) sugar

Remove the stalks and hulls from the strawberries and rinse well. Put in a saucepan with the lemon juice and simmer for 30–45 minutes. Add the sugar and stir until dissolved. Test for setting frequently after 15 minutes boiling. Remove from the heat and stir occasionally, until it jellies.

When making jams and jellies, fruit that is even slightly bruised must be rejected; otherwise you will have jars of mouldy and badly-set preserve before the winter is half through.

Jellies

- When selecting fruit for jellying look for fruit that is nearly ripe – not fully so; at this time it possesses the gelatinous properties which make the jelly set so well.
- You will find that a coarse linen cloth tied to the legs of an upturned chair will make an excellent jelly bag. Place a big pudding basin underneath to catch the juice. Failing a jelly-bag, a strong, fine sieve will answer the purpose equally well, and is less trouble. Put the fruit and juice in the sieve, and let the liquid gradually drip through into a bowl; just move the fruit occasionally to quicken matters but do not press it at all or the jelly will be cloudy.
- Do not put cold sugar into the fruit juice. Warm it in the oven first, but do not let it melt or get in the least brown.

Guava Jelly

2.4 kg guavas, 1 quince, juice of 1 lemon, 2.25 litres (9 cups) cold water.

Cut up the guavas and boil for 3 hours. Strain overnight through a double layer of muslin. To every 600 ml syrup allow 400 g sugar. Place over the heat and stir until the sugar dissolves; boil slowly, skimming the surface frequently, for 1½ hours or until it jellies.

Lime Jelly

Limes, sugar

Put the limes in a non-metallic vessel, cover with boiling water and leave for a few hours. Pour the water off, then crush the limes, cover well with fresh water and boil to a pulp, strain and allow to stand overnight. Next day add 330 g (1½ cups) sugar to every 250 ml (1 cup) liquid and boil briskly for 40 minutes. Bottle while still warm, and when cold seal down. The wild limes which grow in parts of Queensland may be used for this jelly.

Parsley Honey

8 bunches parsley, 4 lemons, sugar

Wash the parsley well, put in a saucepan and cover with water. Bring to the boil and cook for about 2 hours, or until the parsley is light in colour. Strain the liquid into a bowl, add the lemon juice and 220 g (1 cup) sugar for every 250 ml (1 cup) liquid; boil until it jellies like honey.

Parsley Jelly

Parsley, sugar, gelatine, lemon essence, green food colouring

Wash any amount of parsley, cover with water and boil for 1 hour. Strain the liquid and measure. Add 450 g sugar for every 600 ml parsley juice. Using 2 teaspoons gelatine for every 600 ml parsley juice, soak the gelatine in the water. Boil the parsley juice for 30 minutes. Remove from the heat and stir in the gelatine, 1 teaspoon lemon essence and a few drops of green food colouring, stirring well.

Quince Jelly

Quinces, sugar

Wipe the quinces, peel and cut them into small pieces, discarding the cores. Put into a preserving pan, cover with cold water, and bring very gradually to simmering point. Cook gently until the quinces are reduced to a pulp and strain through a fine sieve — this will take a very long time — then boil the juice for 20 minutes. Add warm sugar, 450 g to every 600 ml, melt in by degrees, then boil for 20 minutes.

Rosella Jelly

Rosella berries, sugar

Allow 450 g sugar to every 600 ml rosella juice. Put the rosellas in a preserving pan. Cover with cold water and boil for 2–3 hours. Strain. Return to a clean pan and add the sugar. Boil for 1 hour.

Tomato Jelly

2.7 kg tomatoes, 3 large lemons, sugar

Cut up the tomatoes and put them into a preserving pan. Peel the lemons and remove any white pith from the zest, then chop. Add to the pan with the tomatoes, and heat gradually so that the juice runs out well. Simmer for a few minutes, then strain through a fine sieve. Boil up the juice and add 450 g sugar to every 600 ml juice. Add the juice of the lemons, and boil together until the jelly sets when tested.

Looking Back in Time...

PRESERVING BUTTER

Simmer butter gently in a saucepan until a sediment falls to the bottom. The oil is then poured off into bottles. The preserved butter will keep for months. Only use for cooking and use about three-quarters of the amount as you would for ordinary butter. Care must be taken that no sediment comes off with the oil.

ANSETT-ANA   KLM ROYAL DUTCH AIRLINES

DESSERTS

Fruit Desserts

Candied Plums

Cut a number of large ripe plums in half and remove the stones. Place the halved fruit in a baking tray, cut side up, a few centimetres apart, and sprinkle each half well with sugar. Put the plums into a 180°C oven for 15–20 minutes, or until they are warmed through and the sugar has melted. Remove the plums from the oven and allow to stand until the sugar begins to harden. When the glaze is almost set sprinkle well with more sugar. These make delicious dessert fruit, the full flavour of the plums being retained. Serve with whipped cream or ice cream.

Caramel Bananas

Slice 6 bananas lengthways. Melt 1 ½ tablespoons butter in the base of a heavy-based frying pan and arrange the banana slices in the base of the pan. Sprinkle 115 g (½ cup) soft brown sugar over the bananas and fry until just cooked — the sugar and butter will form a caramel sauce. If liked, rum or brandy can be poured over the bananas and set alight. Serve with very cold ice cream.

Grapefruit

If wanted in the shell, halve large fruit and allow half a grapefruit for each guest. With a sharp-pointed curved grapefruit knife, loosen the tough membrane around the inside of the skin, and cut in between the fruit segments. With a pair of kitchen scissors reach below the pulp and snip out the membrane core. Sprinkle each grapefruit half with 1 teaspoon caster sugar and ½ teaspoon lemon juice, then put in the refrigerator until ready to serve. Put each grapefruit half in a bowl and garnish the centre with a little chopped candied pineapple, ginger, a maraschino cherry or a black grape.

Pears Belle Helene

Drain 825g (3³/4 cups) tinned pear halves, reserving 175 ml (³/4 cup) of the syrup. Put 110 g (³/4 cup) chopped chocolate in the top of a double boiler with the syrup and heat until the chocolate has melted; keep hot. Place the pear halves in individual dishes, heap with ice cream and pour over the hot chocolate. Serve immediately.

Pineapple Fruit Melange

Choose a ripe pineapple, cut in half vertically, leaving the leaves intact. Remove the flesh, cutting it out in small pieces and taking care to collect the juices and to leave the skin intact. Hollow the halves to leave sturdy shells to hold your fruit. Cut up oranges, pears, apricots, passionfruit, bananas and cherries and mix with the chopped pineapple. Add a little kirsch or rum, if you wish, and sprinkle the fruit lightly with sugar. Refrigerate until cold. Put the fruit into the pineapple 'bowls' and garnish each end with a thin half-circle of lemon and some green grapes. This is a lovely dessert in very hot weather and tastes wonderful served with cream.

Pineapple Royal

Put 825 g tinned pineapple rings in the top of a double boiler with the syrup from the tin and boil for 10 minutes. Cut a sponge cake into circles the same size as the pineapple rings and about 2 cm thick. Spread the sponge circles with apricot jam. Flavour the heated syrup with rum and dip slices of sponge cake in syrup. Build a pineapple shape in the base of an ovenproof dish with alternating slices of pineapple and cake. Pour a little dissolved apricot jam over the pineapple and sponge. Beat together 3 egg whites until stiffly peaking, then add 115 g (¹/2 cup) caster sugar and continue beating until stiff. Cover the pineapple shape with small spiked meringue shapes, using a piping bag, to resemble the spikes of a pineapple. Bake in a 150°C oven to set the meringue. Decorate the top with real pineapple leaves.

Test the purity of milk with a steel knitting needle. If the liquid runs off the needle quickly, water has been added, but pure milk will cling to the needle, dropping off slowly.

Rhubarb Fool

Put 300 ml stewed rhubarb through a fine sieve to make a pulp. Stir in 150 ml Boiled Custard (see recipe, page 306), then fold in 150 ml lightly whipped cream. Serve in chilled tall glasses, decorate with whipped cream and maraschino cherries.

Rockmelon Fruit Basket
(Pretty supper dish for a children's party)

Choose 1 ripe rockmelon, and with a sharp knife cut it into a basket shape with a handle. Remove the seeds, cut the flesh from the portion of the melon not required for the basket, and cut into neat chunks. Mix this with 1 chopped pineapple, 3 sliced peaches, 1 sliced orange, the pulp of 4 passionfruit and 2 sliced bananas. Sprinkle with 3 tablespoons caster sugar. Chill and when ready to serve fill the rockmelon baskets. Serve with whipped cream.

Spanish Cream

Soak 3 tablespoons gelatine in 750 ml (3 cups) milk for 30 minutes. Put the soaked gelatine and milk in a saucepan over low heat and stir until the gelatine dissolves. Bring to the boil. Stir together 3 well-beaten egg yolks with 110 g (½ cup) sugar and add to the gelatine mixture, stirring well. Return to the boil, then add vanilla essence, to taste. Remove from the heat and fold in 3 stiffly beaten egg whites. Pour into a wet mould and set. When cold, turn out.

Strawberry Chantilly

Place a thin round piece of sponge cake in a dish and pour over it some tinned strawberry syrup. Cut some strawberries in half and arrange over the top. When well covered with fruit, sprinkle with sugar and cover with plenty of whipped cream. Place 6 small round meringues over the top of the dish, pressing them into the cream. Decorate between the meringues with whipped cream that has been pushed through a piping bag. The cream may be slightly coloured, if desired. Any tinned fruit may be used to replace the strawberries when they are not in season.

Tokay Rings

Arrange the leaves of scented geraniums on individual plates and place a tinned pineapple ring on each. Fill the hollow centre of each pineapple slice with diced orange that has been mixed with whipped cream. Arrange halved grapes in the centre, to serve.

Looking Back in Time...

KEEPING FLOWERS FRESH

A lump of sugar added to the water in which cut flowers are placed will keep them very much longer, as the sugar is an 'energy' feeder to them as it is to anything else. Sugar is splendid for freshening lettuce before making a salad by placing some in the water in which the lettuce is soaking. Three or four pennies in a vase will keep roses fresh. Alum in the water will prolong the life of flowers. Wilted violets may be restored by plunging, head down, in water.

Ice Creams and Sorbets

Baked Alaska

Fill a 24 cm round dome mould with vanilla ice cream and re-freeze. Beat 4 egg whites until stiff peaks form, then mix in 4 tablespoons caster sugar. Turn the frozen ice cream onto a 24 cm round pre-made sponge cake which has been placed on a board. Cover with meringue. Dust with icing sugar and place in a 220°C oven for 3 minutes, or until the meringue begins to brown. Serve at once. May also be served with sliced, brandied peaches or other fruit.

Banana Ice Cream

Beat 3 egg yolks and 110 g (½ cup) sugar in a heatproof bowl. Add 250 ml (1 cup) milk and slowly stir over a saucepan of simmering water until the custard coats the back of a spoon. Leave to cool for a few minutes then transfer to a bowl and refrigerate. Peel 6 ripe bananas and purée using a potato masher or press through a sieve. Mix the banana purée with a pinch of salt and 2 tablespoons orange juice. Add the banana purée, 125 ml (½ cup) lightly whipped cream and 1 tablespoon maraschino (or other liqueur) to the chilled custard. Mix thoroughly, transfer to a shallow metal tray and freeze, stirring occasionally.

Caramel Ice Cream (1)

To make the caramel, put 110 g (½ cup) sugar and 1 tablespoon water in a saucepan over medium heat without stirring until it caramelises. Make a custard with 3 egg yolks, 300 ml milk and 110 g (½ cup) sugar. Add the caramel and stir until combined, then add 1 teaspoon vanilla essence and 300 ml lightly whipped cream. Mix well, transfer to a shallow metal tray and freeze, stirring occasionally.

Caramel Ice Cream (2)

Slowly melt 110 g (½ cup) caster sugar in a saucepan over medium heat until it caramelises, then stir in 60 ml (¼ cup) boiling water and simmer until the caramel is smooth. Gently heat 500 ml (2 cups) milk in a separate saucepan, blend in 1 heaped teaspoon cornflour and simmer for 5 minutes. Add 55 g (¼ cup) sugar and gradually mix in the caramel. Leave to cool for a few minutes then transfer to a bowl and refrigerate. Beat 3 egg whites until stiff peaks form, add a pinch of salt and 55 g (¼ cup) sugar and mix until the sugar dissolves. Add the beaten egg white mixture, 250 ml (1 cup) lightly whipped cream and 2 teaspoons vanilla essence to the chilled caramel custard. Mix well, transfer to a shallow metal tray and freeze, stirring occasionally.

Cherry Ice Cream

Put 450 g pitted cherries in a large bowl with 165 g (¾ cup) sugar and 50 ml strained lemon juice. Cover and leave to stand for a few hours. Put the cherry mixture and 250 ml (1 cup) water in a large saucepan over medium heat and simmer until the fruit is quite tender. Purée in a food processor and refrigerate. Put 1 teaspoon gelatine in a glass bowl with 2 tablespoons water. Sit the bowl over a saucepan of simmering water and stir until the gelatine dissolves. Combine 55 g (¼ cup) sugar and 250 ml (1 cup) milk in a small saucepan and heat over medium heat, being careful not to boil. Transfer to a bowl and allow to cool, then add the dissolved gelatine and a few drops of pink food colouring. Lightly whip 250 ml (1 cup) cream, add to the milk mixture and freeze slightly in a shallow metal tray. When the mixture begins to thicken, add the chilled cherry purée, then continue to freeze, stirring occasionally.

Coffee Ice Cream

Make a custard with 3 egg yolks, 300 ml milk and 110 g (½ cup) sugar. Stir in 150 ml hot black coffee, 300 ml cream and 175 g sugar. Leave to cool. Strain into a bowl, transfer to a shallow metal tray and freeze, stirring occasionally.

Crème De Menthe Sorbet

Peel the zest of 2 lemons. Put 175 g caster sugar, 500 ml (2 cups) water and the lemon zest in a saucepan over medium heat and simmer for 10 minutes. Allow to cool, then add 200 ml freshly squeezed lemon juice. Beat 2 egg whites in a bowl until stiff peaks form and gradually add the strained sugar syrup. Transfer to a shallow metal tray and partially freeze. Turn into a bowl and beat in 2 tablespoons crème de menthe. Return to the freezer to finish freezing before serving in individual glass dishes.

Ginger Ice Cream

Dissolve 1 teaspoon gelatine in 250 ml (1 cup) hot water. Leave to cool. Lightly whip 370 ml (3 cups) cream in a large bowl, then stir in 1 tablespoon sugar, 220 g (1 cup) chopped preserved ginger, 80 ml (⅓ cup) ginger syrup and the dissolved gelatine. Transfer to a shallow metal tray and freeze, stirring occasionally.

Ice Cream Recipe 1

Gradually stir 300 ml milk and 900 ml cream together in a large bowl. Add ¼ teaspoon salt, 1 tablespoon vanilla essence and 230 g (1 cup) caster sugar, then stir until the sugar has dissolved. Transfer to a shallow metal tray and freeze. Or if you prefer, place the milk in the top of a double boiler, add the salt, vanilla essence and sugar, and when both are dissolved cool the milk. Mix in the cream, then transfer to a shallow metal tray and freeze, stirring occasionally.

Ice Cream Recipe 2

Combine 60 g caster sugar and 375 ml (1½ cups) milk in a saucepan over medium heat, then leave to cool. Dissolve 1 teaspoon gelatine in 1 tablespoon hot water, then add to the milk mixture. Lightly whip 300 ml cream and stir into the sugar and cream. Transfer to a shallow metal tray and freeze, stirring every 5 minutes, or until it is smooth.

Ice Cream (with Condensed Milk)

Combine 210 g (²/₃ cup) condensed milk with 300 ml water in a heatproof bowl. Combine ½ tablespoon cornflour with some water to make a smooth paste, then mix in 2 beaten egg yolks. Add to the milk mixture and stir over a saucepan of simmering water until the custard coats the back of a spoon. Leave to cool for a few minutes, stir in 1 teaspoon vanilla essence, then transfer to a bowl and refrigerate. When the mixture is chilled transfer to a shallow metal tray and freeze, stirring occasionally.

Water ices are made of equal quantities of syrup (allow for 600 ml water to 450 g sugar) and fruit pulp, boiled down. Lemon water ice needs no fruit pulp, but it has the whites of 2 beaten eggs added when half frozen (600 ml lemon juice to 600 ml water). Water ices are never completely frozen, and should be served before the roast meat course at dinner.

Lemon Water Ice

Peel the zest from 2 lemons and put in a saucepan over medium heat with 600 ml water and 175 g caster sugar and boil for 10 minutes. Allow to cool, then strain into a bowl. Beat 2 egg whites until stiff peaks form, then add to the sugar mixture with 200 ml freshly squeezed lemon juice. Transfer to a shallow metal tray and freeze, stirring occasionally. When almost frozen turn into a bowl and beat. Then return to the freezer to finish freezing.

Nut Ice Cream

Beat 2 eggs well, then add 220 g (1 cup) sugar. Beat. Add 500 ml (2 cups) cream, 375 ml (1½ cups) milk and 115 g (¾ cup) chopped nuts. Transfer to a shallow metal tray and freeze, stirring occasionally. Serve with hot chocolate or caramel sauce, if liked.

Orange Ice

Put 500 ml (2 cups) water and 220 g (1 cup) sugar in a saucepan over high heat and boil for 5 minutes, then allow to cool. Dissolve 1 teaspoon gelatine in 2 tablespoons hot water and add to the sugar syrup with 2 tablespoons lemon juice and 500 ml (2 cups) orange juice. Pour into shallow metal trays and freeze, stirring occasionally. When almost frozen turn into a bowl and beat. Return to the freezer to finish freezing.

Peach Melba

Place half a poached or tinned peach in each glass dish, fill centre with ice cream, pour over a little peach syrup, then pile whipped cream on top. Garnish with a maraschino cherry. Vary this by using raspberry syrup instead of peach syrup.

Pineapple Sherbert

Put 500 ml (2 cups) water and 220 g (1 cup) sugar in a saucepan over high heat and boil for 10 minutes. Allow to cool then add 250 ml (1 cup) pineapple juice and 60 ml (¼ cup) lemon juice. Transfer to a shallow metal tray and partially freeze. Pour into a chilled bowl and whisk until light and fluffy. Beat 1 egg white until stiff peaks form, then fold into the fruit mixture. Return to the tray to finish freezing.

Pineapple Water Ice

Finely chop 1 pineapple (or 825 g tinned pineapple rings) into a large bowl. Put 500 ml (2 cups) water and 450 g sugar in a saucepan over high heat and boil for 10 minutes. Pour the sugar syrup over the pineapple and leave to stand until quite cold. Add 1½ tablespoons lemon juice. Press through a sieve into shallow metal trays and freeze, stirring occasionally. When almost frozen turn into a bowl and beat. Return to the freezer to finish freezing.

Sherberts are economical to make, wholesome for both children and grown-ups, being similar in preparation to ices, with the addition of stiffly whisked egg white to the partially frozen mixture. Sherberts are lighter in texture and smoother than ices. Milk sherberts are made of rich milk, or a milk and cream mixture, sweetened, and flavoured with fruit juice, a little dissolved gelatine, and whisked egg white.

Praline Ice Cream

Put 115 g (½ cup) brown sugar and 2 teaspoons lemon juice in a small saucepan over medium heat and melt slowly, stirring until the sugar caramelises. Lightly toast 115 g (¾ cup) whole blanched almonds, and stir into the pan. Pour the mixture into a greased, flat cake tin and leave to stand. When cool and crisp, pound or roll the mixture to a powder. Beat 2 egg yolks and 110 g (½ cup) sugar in a heatproof bowl. Add 500 ml (2 cups) milk and stir over a saucepan of simmering water until the custard coats the back of a spoon. Dissolve 1 teaspoon gelatine in 2 tablespoons hot water and stir into the milk mixture. Add the powdered almond caramel, leave to cool for a few minutes, then add 2 tablespoons brandy or liqueur (or 2 teaspoons vanilla essence) and 250 ml (1 cup) cream. Transfer to a shallow metal tray and freeze, stirring occasionally.

Strawberry Ice Cream

Mix 400 g (2 cups) crushed strawberries with 220 g (1 cup) sugar and 125 ml (½ cup) orange juice in a bowl and refrigerate. Dissolve 1 teaspoon gelatine in 2 tablespoons hot water. Combine with 375 ml (1½ cups) milk and add to the berry mixture. Lightly whip 250 ml (1 cup cream) and stir through with enough red food colouring to make strawberries pink. Transfer to a shallow metal tray and freeze, stirring occasionally.

Soufflés

Apricot Soufflé

Tie a band of stiff paper around the outside of a soufflé tin so that it stands about 2 cm above the top. Beat 3 egg yolks and 85 g caster sugar in a heatproof bowl. Rub sufficient apricots through a fine strainer to fill 1 cup and add to the egg mixture. Put the bowl over a saucepan of simmering water and slowly stir until the mixture becomes hot, then leave to cool. Beat 3 egg whites until stiff peaks form. Dissolve 1½ tablespoons gelatine in 3 tablespoons hot water, add to the apricot mixture with 2 teaspoons lemon juice and then stir in 2 tablespoons of whipped cream and the beaten egg whites. Turn into a soufflé tin. Refrigerate until set.

Chocolate Soufflé

Melt 1 tablespoon butter in a saucepan over medium heat, add 1 tablespoon plain flour and mix well. Remove from the heat and stir in 85 g (²/₃ cup) grated chocolate and 150 ml milk. Return to the heat and stir until the mixture thickens. Remove from the heat and allow to cool. Transfer to a bowl and add three egg yolks, one at a time, beating well after each addition, then add 1 tablespoon caster sugar and flavour with vanilla essence, to taste. Beat 3 egg yolks until stiff peaks form and stir lightly into the butter mixture. Grease and lightly flour a soufflé tin with baking paper and pour in the mixture. Bake in a 180°C oven for 30 minutes or until the soufflé has risen.

Coffee Soufflé

Put 450 ml strong coffee in a heatproof bowl, add 125 ml (½ cup) milk, 3 tablespoons sugar and 1 tablespoon powdered gelatine, and heat over a saucepan of simmering water. Add 3 beaten egg yolks, 2 extra tablespoons sugar, and a pinch of salt. Stir until the mixture thickens, then remove from the heat and add ½ teaspoon vanilla essence. Beat 3 egg whites until stiff peaks form and fold into the coffee mixture. Set in a mould and refrigerate to set. Decorate with blanched almonds before serving.

Delicious Lemon Soufflé

Separate 3 eggs and beat the whites and yolks. Add 170 g (³/₄ cup) sugar and 50 ml lemon juice and beat until well combined. Dissolve 2 tablespoons gelatine in 2 tablespoons hot water, add to the egg yolk mixture, fold in the egg whites and add 150 ml hot water. Stir well and turn into a soufflé tin. Refrigerate until set.

Frozen Lemon Soufflé

Beat 4 egg yolks and 165 g (³/₄ cup) sugar in a heatproof bowl. Add the zest from 1 lemon, 125 ml (¹/₂ cup) water and pinch of salt and slowly stir over a saucepan of simmering water until the mixture thickens, then leave to cool. Dissolve 2 teaspoons powdered gelatine in 1 tablespoon hot water. Add to cool lemon mixture. Beat 4 egg whites until stiff peaks form and add to the lemon mixture. Beat until evenly mixed, add 1 tablespoon sweet sherry, pour into a shallow metal tray and freeze slightly. Lightly whip 150 ml cream and gradually mix into the chilled mixture, whisking until smooth. Freeze thoroughly before serving.

Fruit and Nut Soufflé

Melt 1 tablespoon butter in a saucepan, add 1 tablespoon plain flour, 1 tablespoon sugar, 300 ml cream, 1¹/₂ teaspoons vanilla essence, and stir until it thickens. Cool. Separate 3 eggs and beat the whites until stiff peaks form. Add the egg yolks to the milk mixture, one at a time, beating well after each addition, then add the egg whites. Place in a soufflé tin and bake in a 180°C oven for 20 minutes.

Lemon Soufflé

Separate the yolks and whites of 8 eggs and lightly beat. Combine the yolks in a bowl with 220 g (1 cup) sugar, zest from 2 lemons and 50 ml lemon juice. Fold through the stiffly beaten egg whites. Line the side of a soufflé tin with baking paper and pour in the mixture. Bake in a 180°C oven for 15 minutes or until the soufflé is risen. Serve immediately.

Parfaits

Parfaits are the richest of frozen desserts, and are made by beating a hot, boiled syrup into well whipped egg yolks, until the mixture is cool, then adding stiffly whisked egg whites, whipped cream and flavourings. The mixture is then poured into shallow metal trays to freeze smoothly, without further beating. No gelatine is added to parfaits.

Almond and Cherry Parfait

Slowly heat 220 g (1 cup) sugar in small saucepan over medium heat, stirring until thoroughly melted. Gradually stir in 125 ml ($^1/_2$ cup) hot water, and when combined, increase the heat to high and boil without stirring until the syrup spins a thread. Beat 2 egg yolks in a bowl then add the hot syrup, mixing thoroughly. Beat 2 egg whites until stiff peaks form, add to the sugar mixture and beat until cool. Pour the mixture into a shallow metal tray and refrigerate. Lightly whip 300 ml cream and pour in the chilled mixture. Beat thoroughly and add 80 g ($^1/_2$ cup) sugar-coated almonds and 100 g ($^1/_2$ cup) sliced, drained or glacé cherries. Pour into the tray and freeze.

Butterscotch Parfait

Put 95 g ($^1/_2$ cup) brown sugar and 1 tablespoon butter in a saucepan over low heat and stir until the butter has melted. Increase the temperature to high and boil for 1 minute. Add 125 ml ($^1/_2$ cup) water and stir until the butterscotch is smooth, then transfer to a heatproof bowl. Put 2 egg yolks and a pinch of salt in a bowl and lightly beat, then gradually add to the hot syrup. Slowly stir over a saucepan of simmering water until the custard coats the back of a spoon, remove from the heat, and allow to cool. Stir in 60 ml ($^1/_4$ cup) milk, then transfer to a shallow metal tray and refrigerate. Beat 2 egg whites until stiff peaks form and lightly whip 300 ml cream. Pour the chilled custard mixture gradually into the egg whites, add the whipped cream and 2 teaspoons vanilla essence, and stir until smooth. Pour the mixture into the tray and freeze without further stirring. Serve with wafers.

Milan Soufflé

Stir 4 beaten egg yolks and 2 tablespoons caster sugar in a saucepan over medium heat until creamy. Do not boil. Stir in the zest from 2 lemons and 150 ml freshly squeezed lemon juice, then allow to cool. Dissolve 1½ tablespoons gelatine in 2 tablespoon hot water. Lightly whip 300 ml cream, add the dissolved gelatine and stir in the egg mixture. Turn into a soufflé tin and refrigerate until set.

Passionfruit Soufflé

Dissolve 2 teaspoons gelatine in 2 tablespoons water. Beat 2 egg yolks and 2 tablespoons sugar in a heatproof bowl. Add 435 ml (1¾ cups) milk and the dissolved gelatine and slowly stir over a saucepan of simmering water until the mixture thickens. Allow to cool and, when almost set, add the pulp from 6 passionfruit. Beat 2 egg whites until stiff peaks form, fold into the passionfruit mixture, and turn into a soufflé tin. Refrigerate for 6 hours or overnight before serving.

Pineapple Soufflé

Melt 2 tablespoons butter in a saucepan over medium heat, add 2 tablespoons plain flour, 150 ml milk and 3 tablespoons pineapple syrup, and stir until it thickens. Transfer to a bowl and add 3 egg yolks, one at a time, beating well after each addition. Beat 3 egg whites until stiff peaks form and stir lightly into the butter mixture. Line the side of a soufflé tin with baking paper to let the soufflé rise and pour in the mixture. Bake for 30 minutes. Meanwhile, make a pineapple sauce by combining 125 ml (½ cup) pineapple syrup, 1 tablespoon sugar and 3 tablespoons sweet sherry in a saucepan over medium heat and simmer for a few minutes. Serve the soufflé immediately, drizzled in pineapple sauce.

Strawberry Soufflé

Tie a band of stiff paper around the outside of a soufflé tin so that it stands about 2 cm above the top. Chop 300 g strawberries. Beat 1 tablespoon butter to a cream in a bowl and mix in 3 tablespoons self-raising flour and 3 tablespoons caster sugar. Beat 2 egg yolks and combine with 250 ml (1 cup) milk. Mix in with the butter mixture and flavour with 1 teaspoon lemon juice. Transfer to a saucepan over low heat and slowly stir until it thickens. Remove from the heat and add the strawberry pieces. Beat 2 egg whites until stiff peaks form and add to the strawberry mixture. Pour into the soufflé tin. Bake in a 200°C oven until risen. Serve immediately.

Strawberry Soufflé (Cold)

Tie a band of stiff paper around the outside of a soufflé tin so that it stands about 2 cm above the top. Put enough strawberries in a food processor and blend well to make 600 ml purée. Beat 3 egg yolks and 3 tablespoons sugar in a heatproof bowl. Add the strawberry purée and slowly stir over a saucepan of simmering water until warm. Remove from the heat and add 80 ml (1/3 cup) milk. Dissolve 2 tablespoons gelatine in 3 tablespoons hot water and strain into the egg mixture with a few drops of lemon juice. Beat 3 egg whites until stiff peaks form. When the strawberry mixture begins to thicken fold in the egg whites. Pour into the soufflé tin and refrigerate until set.

Soufflé à la Milanese

Tie a band of stiff paper around the outside of a soufflé tin so that it stands about 2 cm above the top. Beat 3 egg yolks and 175 g caster sugar in a heatproof bowl. Add the zest from 2½ lemons and 125 ml (½ cup) freshly squeezed lemon juice and slowly stir over a saucepan of simmering water until the custard coats the back of a spoon. Strain into a bowl and allow to cool, then fold in 300 ml lightly whipped cream. Dissolve 2 tablespoons gelatine in 3 tablespoons hot water, then strain into the mixture. Beat 3 egg whites until stiff peaks form and fold into the mixture. Let the mixture set before pouring into the soufflé tin. Refrigerate until firm. Remove paper, shake crumbled ratafias or amaretti biscuits on top and serve.

Toffee Soufflés

Blanch 30 g almonds, then chop and dry-roast in a 180°C degree oven until golden. Melt 2 tablespoons butter in a saucepan over medium heat, stir in 1 tablespoon hot water and 115 g brown sugar and bring to the boil for a few minutes. Leave to cool. Melt 1 tablespoon butter in another saucepan, stir in 1 tablespoon plain flour, then add 300 ml milk and bring to the boil. Boil gently for a few minutes then leave to cool. Stir in 1 beaten egg yolk and return to the heat. Simmer gently then remove from the heat and slowly stir through the toffee mixture. Dissolve 1 tablespoon gelatine in 2 tablespoons hot water and strain it into the mixture, then add half of the roasted almonds. Beat 2 egg whites until stiff peaks form. When the egg yolk mixture begins to set fold in the egg whites then turn into small soufflé tins. Serve the toffee soufflés with the remainder of the nuts sprinkled on top.

Wine Soufflé

Melt 1 tablespoon butter in a saucepan over medium heat, add 1 tablespoon plain flour and stir for 1 minute. Add 125 ml milk and stir until it thickens. Allow to cool then transfer to a bowl and stir in 1 tablespoon sugar and 2 teaspoons sherry. Add three egg yolks, one at a time, beating well after each addition. Beat 3 egg whites with a pinch of salt until stiff peaks form and stir lightly into the butter mixture. Pour into prepared soufflé tin and bake for 35–45 minutes, or until risen. Serve immediately with wine sauce.

Vanilla Soufflé

Melt 1 tablespoon butter in a saucepan over medium heat, add 1 tablespoon plain flour and 1 tablespoon sugar. Stir in 300 ml milk and 1½ teaspoons vanilla essence, until the mixture thickens. Leave to cool. Beat 3 egg whites in a bowl until stiff peaks form. Add three egg yolks to the butter mixture one at a time, beating well after each addition, then add the egg whites. Line the side of a soufflé tin with baking paper to let the soufflé rise and pour in the mixture. Bake in a 180°C oven for 20 minutes, or until the soufflé is risen. Serve immediately.

Éclairs, Cream Puffs and Meringues

Éclairs and Cream Puffs

Petit Choux: Foundation Mixture

Put 335 g butter and 300 ml water in a saucepan and bring to the boil. Allow to boil a few minutes, then add 450 g plain flour and cook until it forms a ball. Remove from the heat and add 14 eggs, one at a time, beating well after each addition. The mixture should be quite stiff. Place small amounts of the dough at regular intervals in an ungreased baking tray, allowing room for them to rise, or put the mixture in a piping bag with a plain nozzle and force out the mixture in 5 cm lengths. Leave plenty of room for the dough to spread. Bake in a 425°C oven for 30 minutes, or until deep golden and crisp on the outside.

Chocolate Éclairs

Melt 2 tablespoons butter in a saucepan over medium heat, add 250 ml (1 cup) water and bring to the boil. Add 115 g plain flour and stir well until the mixture comes away from the side. Allow to cool, then add 3 eggs, one at a time, beating well after each addition. Pipe the dough in long narrow strips using a large plain nozzle onto a greased baking tin and bake in a 180°C oven for 30 minutes. Remove from the oven and when cool, fill with whipped cream and cover with chocolate icing.

Coffee Walnut Puffs

Prepare the Choux Pastry (see recipe, page 354) and bake as directed for foundation mixture, shaping the paste from a teaspoon according to the size required. Make an incision at the side of each cooked, cold pastry shell. Put 1 tablespoon caster sugar, ½ teaspoon vanilla essence and 300 ml cream in a bowl and whip lightly until thick. Do not over whip, which will curdle the cream. Fill the pastry shells with cream. Mix 225 g sifted icing sugar with 1 teaspoon melted butter, 1 tablespoon coffee essence and 1 tablespoon hot water to make the icing. Cover each filled puff with coffee icing, and top with a shelled walnut. If preferred, chop the shelled walnuts and sprinkle on top. In place of vanilla essence, a teaspoon of coffee essence may be added to the cream before whipping.

Cream Puffs

Melt 2 tablespoons butter in a saucepan over medium heat, add 2 tablespoons water and bring to the boil. Remove from the heat and stir in 2 tablespoons self-raising flour. Mix thoroughly then add 2 eggs, one at a time, beating well after each addition. Place spoonfuls of the mixture at regular intervals on an greased tray, and bake in a 220°C oven for 15–20 minutes. Remove from the oven and leave to stand. When cool fill with whipped cream.

Do not grate chocolate, it is far easier to stand in the oven for a few minutes — it will become quite soft, and can be easily beaten up with butter or eggs as needed.

Custard Puffs

Put 125 g butter in a saucepan with 250 ml (1 cup) water and heat until the butter melts. Add 150 g (1 cup) sifted plain flour and stir constantly until the mixture leaves the sides of the pan. Remove from the heat and cool slightly, then add ¼ teaspoon bicarbonate of soda. Pipe onto a greased baking tray and bake in a 180°C oven for 30 minutes. To make the custard filling, heat 250 ml (1 cup) milk in a saucepan with 1 egg and 110 g (½ cup) sugar, stirring until thickened. Flavour with vanilla essence to taste; remove from the heat and allow to cool. When puffs and cream are both cool, open the puffs a little on the side with a sharp knife. Fill with the custard filling.

Variation Press a hole in each puff and insert a little jam before baking – this is a variation from a recipe that is over 100 years old.

Strawberry Éclairs

Take some plain éclair cases, split them lengthways. Whip some cream until stiff, and add sugar. Then stir in some mashed strawberries. Fill the cases and coat the top with a dab of warm icing and decorate with whole strawberry.

Meringues

To achieve success in the making of meringues is the ambition of most women. They are delectable dainties that may be served for afternoon tea or used as decoration to many sweet dishes. They may be elaborate or simple, forced through a rose tube and made in fancy shapes and roses. Large meringues may be piled one on top of the other and joined with cream, flavoured to taste (passionfruit cream and strawberry cream are delicious). Milk puddings may be topped with meringue and decorated with cherries.

Meringues

Meringue

Put 3 egg whites in a large bowl, stir in 2 teaspoons caster sugar (this helps to break the egg whites up), and beat until stiff peaks form (so firm that if the bowl is held upside down the mixture will not fall out). Fold in 170 g (¾ cup) sifted caster sugar, one tablespoon at a time. Shape the meringues with a tablespoon onto a baking tray lined with baking paper. Some cooks use 2 spoons in shaping, others use the mixture through a piping bag. One of the commonest faults in meringue making is overcooking in the early stages. Meringues should be dried out rather than cooked, so place in 100°C oven for about 2 hours. Remove the meringues from the oven and leave to stand in a warm place to dry for several hours.

If the weather is warm it is a good plan to chill the whites before whipping. If a large number of whites are being whipped it is advisable to stand in front of a window to beat them. Meringues improve by keeping. Using an airtight container they should keep for weeks. Colourings may be added to meringues: use red fod colouring for pink and coffee essence for coffee meringue.

Be careful when adding the sugar, add a tablespoon at a time to the beaten egg whites, and beat slightly after each spoonful. Always fold the sugar in, lifting the egg white from the bottom of the bowl so that it is evenly blended. Do this as gently as possible, not rapidly stirring. Icing sugar may be dredged over the meringues before putting in the oven.

If you need the meringues plain just let them remain firm and turn them over to dry. If you need them hollow, turn them over when cooked on top and scoop out the soft part for filling with cream.

Coconut or almond meringues may be made by adding desiccated coconut or finely shredded blanched almonds to the mixture. Leave 2 cm or more space between each meringue. Meringues may be used in a variety of ways. They are delicious if filled with a mixture of crushed strawberries and cream or bananas and cream, while small ones make a very pretty decoration for a trifle and are also a tasty accompaniment to an ice cream of any flavour.

Cocoa Meringues

Put 2 egg whites in a bowl with a pinch of salt and beat until stiff peaks form. In another bowl mix together 1 tablespoon sugar, a pinch cinnamon and 2 teaspoons cocoa powder. Gradually fold in the egg whites, then fold in 80 g (½ cup) chopped, blanched almonds. Place the mixture in heaped tablespoons on a tray lined with greased and floured baking paper. Bake in a 100°C for 1–2 hours, or until light golden and completely dry. Remove from the oven and leave to cool before serving.

Meringue Cake, Fairy Pie or Pavlova

Beat 5 egg whites until stiff peaks form, then gradually add 220 g (1 cup) sugar, 1 teaspoon vanilla and 1 teaspoon vinegar. Place the mixture on a baking tray lined with baking paper and flatten slightly. Bake in a 100°C oven for 2½–3 hours. Leave on the tray until required, or in a cake tin. It will keep 2–3 days. Immediately before use, spread thickly with whipped cream and passionfruit, with juice of the passionfruit poured over the top.

Less egg can be used, taking 40 g sugar for each egg white, and flavouring in proportion. If doubtful of it being sufficiently cooked, it may go in a 100°C oven again for an hour or less.

Meringue (for Pudding)

Beat 2 egg whites until stiff peaks form, then gradually add 55 g (¼ cup) sugar, beating well. Spread a thin layer of the mixture over the pudding, and then place the remaining mixture in mounds on top. Bake in a 180°C oven for 25 minutes, or until crisp and golden. Shredded almonds may be sprinkled over the meringue before baking, or thin slices of orange or marmalade jam may be placed across top of each mound of meringue for decoration.

Meringue Gateau

Make meringue as described above. Cut a shape on baking paper 5 cm larger than size required for the meringue. Pencil the size you wish the meringue to be on the paper, place on a baking tray and spread the mixture to the pencil mark, about 1 centimetre thick. Fill a piping bag with some meringue mixture and pipe roses around the edge of the circle. A second row around may be added, leaving the centre plain to be filled with whipped cream. Bake in a 100°C oven for 2–3 hours, or until very dry.

A good plan is to make meringue at night after the dinner is over and then leave it in the oven after it is turned off to cool overnight.

Meringue Tarts

Sift 225 g self-raising flour and add 1 teaspoon sugar and ½ teaspoon salt. Rub 2 tablespoons butter and 2 tablespoons lard into the mixture until it resembles breadcrumbs. Add just enough water to make a very stiff dough. Roll out the dough and cut with a fluted pastry cutter to desired size. Place the dough in tins, prick the centre with a fork and glaze with water, milk, or egg and milk. Bake in a 230°C oven for 10 minutes, or until golden. Remove from the oven. Reduce the heat to 100°C. Fill the pastry with jam or lemon cheese, and place a teaspoon of meringue made from egg whites stiffly beaten with sugar on top. Place in the oven 2–3 minutes to brown.

Pavlova

Beat 4 egg whites until stiff, then gradually add 115 g (½ cup) caster sugar, beating constantly. Add another 115 g (½ cup) sugar with 1 teaspoon vinegar, 1 teaspoon cornflour and a pinch of cream of tartar. Cut a large circle of baking paper and place on a baking tray, then heap the mixture onto it, allowing it to spread to the edge. Bake in a 180°C oven for 3 minutes, then without opening the oven, turn the heat down to 130°C. Cook for 1 hour. When cool, turn the pavlova upside down and top with whipped cream and sweetened fruit. Strawberries or passionfruit are excellent.

Fritters, Pancakes, Doughnuts and Waffles

Fritter Batter

Sift 115 g plain flour into a bowl. Make a well in the centre and pour in 1 tablespoon melted butter or oil, then gradually whisk in 225 ml water. Whisk thoroughly to make a smooth batter then set aside for about 1/2 hour. Beat 2 egg whites until stiff peaks form and then fold into the batter just before cooking.

Apple Fritters

Peel and core 3–4 large green cooking apples and cut into 1 cm rounds. Dip the apple slices in the fritter batter and deep-fry until golden. When the apple rounds are golden lift out and drain on paper towel. Sprinkle with sugar before serving. (These are delicious, but be sure and use a saucepan of clean oil and have it boiling to blue heat and serve as soon as possible. Cook one piece at a time, or two if you are using a large saucepan.)

Banana Fritters

Cut 3–4 bananas in half lengthways. Dip in the fritter batter and deep-fry one or two slices at a time. When the banana slices are golden lift out and drain on paper towel. Sprinkle with sugar before serving.

Cheese and Mint Fritters

Put 1 tablespoon plain flour in a bowl and mix in 1 beaten egg and a pinch salt. Add 2 tablespoons milk and stir thoroughly to make a smooth batter. Set aside for 1 hour. Just before cooking, add 1 tablespoon grated cheese and 1 tablespoon finely chopped mint or parsley. Melt some butter in a frying pan over medium heat. Pour in 1 tablespoonful of the mixture and lightly brown on both sides. Drain on paper towel, sprinkle with paprika, and roll up. Repeat with the remaining batter. Serve hot with green vegetables or tomato sauce.

Doughnuts 1

Measure and sift 500 g (4 cups) plain flour into a bowl twice, then add 1 tablespoon baking powder, 1 teaspoon salt, ½ teaspoon cinnamon and ½ teaspoon nutmeg. In a separate bowl, lightly beat 2 eggs, one at a time, then add 220 g (1 cup) sugar and mix well. Combine 250 ml (1 cup) milk, 2 tablespoons melted butter and ½ teaspoon vanilla, and mix into the egg mixture gradually, alternating with the flour mixture. Turn out onto a lightly floured surface and sprinkle the top with a little flour. Roll the dough out to 1 cm thick and cut with a floured pastry cutter into doughnut rounds. Carefully drop the doughnuts into boiling oil, 180°C, and fry for 3 minutes until golden. Drain on paper towel and serve immediately.

Doughnuts 2

Dissolve 1 tablespoon instant dried yeast and 2 tablespoons sugar in water. Rub 1 tablespoon butter into 450 g sifted plain flour and combine with 290 ml water to make a smooth dough. Mix with the yeast, separate into small portions and place a little jam in the centre. Carefully drop the doughnuts into boiling oil, 180°C, and cook until golden. Drain on paper towels, roll in caster sugar and serve immediately.

French Pancakes

Combine 3 egg yolks, 1 teaspoon sugar and 125 ml (½ cup) milk in a bowl. Add 60 g (½ cup) sifted plain flour and ½ teaspoon of salt and mix until smooth. Gradually add an extra 125 ml (½ cup) milk to make a smooth batter. Beat 3 egg whites until stiff peaks form and fold into the batter. Cook mixture, in batches, in a large cast-iron frying pan, spreading the mixture to form large thin pancakes. Spread with tart fruit jelly, roll up and serve while hot.

Hotel Westminster Doughnuts

Rub 1 tablespoon butter into 175 g sifted plain flour, and combine with 55 g sugar, ½ teaspoon baking powder, 1 beaten egg and a little milk to make a stiff dough. Roll the dough out lightly, ½–1 cm thick and cut with a floured pastry cutter into rounds. Put a little jam in the centre, wet the edges, place a round of dough on top and pinch the edges together. Carefully drop the doughnuts into boiling fat, 180°C, and cook until golden. Drain on paper towels, dust with icing sugar and serve immediately. Can be made in single rounds without jam if preferred.

Indian Fritters

Sift 3 tablespoons plain flour into a bowl and mix with a little butter to make a stiff paste. Add 4 egg yolks, one at a time, beating well after each addition. Beat 2 egg whites until stiff peaks form and fold into the batter. Drop tablespoons of the mixture into boiling oil and deep-fry until the fritters are golden.

Muffins

Measure and sift 250 g (2 cups) plain flour into a bowl twice, then add 1 tablespoon baking powder, 55 g (¼ cup) and ¾ teaspoon salt. In a separate bowl mix 1 egg, 250 ml (1 cup) milk and 60 ml (¼ cup) melted butter until smooth, then combine with the flour mixture. Grease muffin tins and fill with the muffin batter. Bake in a 200°C oven for 15–20 minutes for small muffins, or 25–30 minutes for large muffins.

Variations For Plain Muffins

APPLE: add 1 cup finely chopped fresh apple to sifted ingredients.
BACON: cut 2 thin slices of bacon in small pieces, measure ¼ cup and
fry slightly. Use bacon and fat in place of butter in plain muffins.
CHEESE: add ½ cup grated cheese to sifted dry ingredients.
DATES: add ½ cup chopped dates to sifted dry ingredients.
PEANUT BUTTER: substitute ⅓ cup peanut butter for butter in
plain muffins. Cut the peanut butter into sifted dry ingredients.
WHOLE WHEAT: substitute 1 cup wholemeal flour and 1 cup plain
flour for 2 cups flour in sour-milk muffins. Brown sugar
improves the flavour.

Pancakes 1

To every egg allow 1 tablespoon sifted flour, 150 ml milk, ¼ teaspoon vegetable oil or butter and a pinch salt. Put the egg yolks in a bowl, add the flour, salt, oil and a little of the milk. Mix until smooth, then gradually add the rest of the milk to make a smooth batter. The mixture may be made to this stage up to a day in advance. Just before frying beat the egg whites to form stiff peaks and fold into the batter. Melt some butter in a small frying pan over medium heat, pour in some of the batter and let it spread evenly over the bottom of the pan as thinly as possible. Cook on both sides until golden, then sprinkle with lemon juice and sugar, roll up and serve immediately.

Pancakes 2

To every egg allow 1 tablespoon self-raising flour, 150 ml milk, ¼ teaspoon vegetable oil or butter and a pinch salt. Put the egg yolks in a bowl, add the flour, salt, oil and a little of the milk. Mix until smooth, then gradually add the rest of the milk to make a smooth batter. Set aside for at least 30 minutes. Just before frying beat the egg whites to form stiff peaks and fold into the batter. Melt a teaspoon butter in a small frying pan over medium heat, pour in some of the batter and let it spread evenly over the bottom of the pan as thinly as possible. Cook on one side until golden and the other side is set, then sprinkle with lemon juice and sugar, roll up and serve immediately.

Pancakes 3

Sift 125 g (1 cup) plain flour into a bowl with a pinch salt. Make a well in the centre and add 2 eggs, one at a time. Mix until smooth, then gradually add 375 ml (1½ cups) milk to make a smooth batter. Melt some butter in a small frying pan over medium heat, pour a little batter and let it spread evenly over the bottom of the pan as thinly as possible. Cook on both sides until golden and repeat with the remaining batter.

Pancakes Suzette

Sift 225 g plain flour into a bowl with a pinch salt. Make a well in the centre and add 5 egg yolks, one at a time, 80 g (⅓ cup) caster sugar and 300 ml milk. Mix until smooth, then gradually add another 300 ml milk to make a smooth batter. Set aside for at least 30 minutes. Just before frying, beat the egg whites to form stiff peaks and fold into the batter. Melt a teaspoon butter in a small frying pan over medium heat, pour in some of the batter and let it spread evenly over the bottom of the pan as thinly as possible. Cook on both sides until golden.

To make the filling, cream 3 tablespoons butter, 85 g (⅔ cup) icing sugar and a pinch of salt in a bowl. Add 3 egg yolks, one at a time, and mix until smooth. Drizzle 2 teaspoons over each pancake, dust with a little icing sugar and dash with Grand Marnier. Flame and serve immediately.

Savoury Muffins

Mix 2 tablespoons self-raising flour, 2 tablespoons breadcrumbs and ½ tablespoon chopped parsley in a bowl. Gradually stir in just enough milk to make a stiff dough. Stir in 1 well beaten egg, 2 tablespoons of chopped cooked ham and 1 diced cooked potato. If the mixture is too stiff add more milk, but it must not be thin. Drop tablespoons of the mixture into boiling fat and cook until the muffins are golden. Lift out and drain on paper towel, then serve immediately on a hot dish surrounded with boiled green peas.

Sweet Corn Fritters

Put 440 g drained tinned corn kernels into a bowl and add 155 g (1 1/4 cups) plain flour, 1 teaspoon baking powder, 1 teaspoon salt and 2 beaten egg yolks, one at a time. Beat 2 egg whites until stiff peaks form and fold into the batter. Drop tablespoons of the mixture into boiling oil and cook until the fritters are golden. Lift out and drain on paper towel and serve with maple syrup or honey.

How to Make Waffles

Waffle batter is easily made and should be of a consistency to pour on to a hot waffle iron. Using 2 tablespoons of batter is sufficient to make one waffle, and the waffle should be cooked 2 minutes on each side until golden. Grease the waffle iron before each new waffle is started. If the waffle sticks it may be that the iron was not heated sufficiently. Maple syrup is the ideal syrup for waffles. Golden syrup, cream and jam, or grated cheese may be used.

Waffles

Measure and sift 250 g (2 cups) plain flour into a bowl twice, then add 4 teaspoons baking powder and 3/4 teaspoons salt. In a separate bowl combine 375 ml (1 1/2 cups) milk, 4 tablespoons melted butter and 2 beaten egg yolks, then gradually add to the flour mixture, stirring until smooth. Beat 2 egg whites until stiff peaks form and fold into the batter. Cook until golden and serve with your favourite toppings.

Waffles (Brighton)

Measure and sift 185 g (1 1/2 cups) plain flour and 120 g (3/4 cup) wholemeal flour into a bowl twice, then add 1/2 teaspoon cinnamon, 1/2 teaspoon salt, 170 g (3/4 cup) caster sugar and 1 teaspoon baking powder. Mix in 2 beaten eggs, then add 125 ml (1/2 cup) melted butter, 125 (1/2 cup) to 185 ml (3/4 cup) milk and 1 teaspoon vanilla essence, and stir until smooth. Grease the waffle iron and when smoking hot, spread with batter. Cook for 2–3 minutes, or until golden. Serve with butter or with syrup or honey for breakfast or tea.

Homemade Sweets

Barley Sugar

450 g caster sugar, juice of ½ lemon,
strips of lemon zest from ½ lemon, pinch of cream of tartar

Put the sugar and 150 ml water in a saucepan over low heat and stir until the sugar has dissolved. Add the cream of tartar and strips of lemon zest. Boil the mixture until it reaches 115°C on a sugar thermometer. Remove from the heat, add the lemon juice, then bring to the boil. Remove the rind from the pan and pour into a lightly oiled tray. Cool slightly, then fold sides to middle, pull into strips and twist. Store in sterilised airtight jars.

Butterscotch

660 g (3 cups) sugar, 185 g butter, 1 cup boiling water, ½ teaspoon vanilla essence

Put the butter, sugar and 250 ml (1 cup) boiling water into a saucepan and bring to the boil until a little tried in cold water is brittle. This takes about 45 minutes. Add the vanilla and pour into a greased baking tray, making the mixture not more than 5 mm deep. When nearly cold, mark into small squares with a buttered knife. Cover the butterscotch if liked with some chopped nuts.

Candied Lemon or Orange Peel

Make a brine by boiling 600 ml water and 115 g salt. Cut 6 lemons or oranges in halves, pour the brine over the top and soak for 3 days. Lift out, drain and set aside for 24 hours. Make a syrup of 660 g (3 cups) sugar and 900 ml water and boil for 10 minutes. Remove pulp from the fruit and place the rind in the boiling syrup. Cook for 20 minutes, then lift out and drain for 4 days. Bring to the boil again for 20 minutes again using the same syrup. Allow to cool in the syrup, then lift out, drain for another 3–4 days and store in airtight containers. Excellent.

Caramel Cream (Fudge)

225 g butter, 220 g (1 cup) soft brown sugar,
420 g (1¹/₃ cups) sweetened condensed milk

Melt the butter in a saucepan. Add the sugar and condensed milk and bring to the boil, stirring constantly for 25 minutes. Pour into a greased dish to set and cut into squares, to serve.

Chocolate Roughs

85 g (²/₃ cup) icing sugar, 3 tablespoons cocoa powder,
90 g (1 cup) desiccated coconut, 85 g white vegetable shortening

Sift the icing sugar and cocoa into a bowl and add the coconut. Melt the shortening over gentle heat, then allow to cool. Gradually add to the dry ingredients, stirring well. Place in roughly shaped mounds on a baking tray lined with baking paper and stand in a cool place to set.

Coconut Ice 1

440 g (2 cups) sugar, 125 ml (¹/₂ cup) milk, 65 g (³/₄ cup) desiccated coconut,
¹/₂ teaspoon vanilla essence, pink food colouring

Put the sugar and milk in a saucepan and stir over low heat for 5 minutes, until the sugar dissolves. Bring to the boil and add the coconut; boil 1 minute longer. Remove from the heat and add the vanilla essence; beat until creamy. Divide into equal halves: colour one with pink food colouring. Press half into a greased a shallow tray or dish and press the other half over the top to form a layer. Slice in cubes or bars. Allow to cool and set.

Coconut Ice 2

450 g (3²/₃ cups) icing sugar, 225 g (2½ cups) desiccated coconut,
1 teaspoon vanilla essence, 2 lightly beaten egg whites,
115 g white vegetable shortening, pink food colouring

Sift the icing sugar into a bowl and add coconut, vanilla and egg whites. Melt the shortening over gentle heat. It should be barely warm, not hot. Pour into the bowl and mix thoroughly to combine. Press half of the mixture into the base of a 15 cm square shallow cake tin. Colour the remaining mixture a delicate pink and press over the white mixture. Stand in a cool place until set firm, then cut into blocks.

Variation To make a chocolate coconut ice, add 2 tablespoons cocoa powder with 1 tablespoon warm water or milk instead of the pink food colouring.

Coffee Walnuts

1 egg white, 1 tablespoon strong coffee, 280 g (2¼ cups) icing sugar,
halved walnuts

Put the egg white in a bowl and add the coffee, stirring well. Gradually add the icing sugar until firm enough to mould, then roll into a ball and press between walnut halves. Leave for a few hours to set.

Crystallised Cherries

330 g (1½ cup) sugar, 450 g cherries

Put 110 g (½ cup) of the sugar and 110 g (½ cup) sugar in a saucepan and bring to the boil for 10 minutes. Allow the syrup to stand overnight and boil it again before pouring it over the fruit. Repeat this process for three days, and on the fourth day add 220 g (1 cup) sugar to the syrup. Bring to the boil, add the cherries, and cook for 10 minutes. Drain the cherries in a sieve. When fairly dry, place them on brown paper. Sprinkle with coarse sugar and leave in the air until dry and firm. Rub in caster sugar and store in airtight jars until required.

Crystallised Figs

440 g (2 cups) sugar, 1.8 kg fresh figs

Boil the sugar and 600 ml water in a saucepan for 30 minutes. If using sugar figs, peel them and place in the pan and boil for about 30 minutes, or until transparent. If you use green figs (white Adriatic) or any dark fig, do not peel them, but boil them in the syrup for at least 1 hour. Turn out onto dishes and pour the syrup over the top. Put out in a warm place to dry, turning them each day for three days. Remove to clean dishes and dry for another three days. Roll each fig in caster sugar, to coat, and dry for one day more. Pack away in an airtight container until needed.

Crystallised Pineapple

450 g caster sugar, ½ teaspoon freshly squeezed lemon juice, 1 pineapple

Boil the sugar in 300 ml water for 10 minutes without stirring. Remove from heat and add the lemon juice. Peel the pineapple, remove any black specks, and cut the flesh into cubes. Take a cube on the end of a skewer and dip into the syrup. Place on a wire rack in a warm place and turn every day for four days. Roll in coarse sugar. Store in an airtight container.

Crystallised Violets

Boil the sugar in a little water to 138°C on a sugar thermometer, then throw in 440 g (2 cups) violets without the stems. Always use large violets. Place a few violets in, one at a time, then bring to the boil again and stir the syrup until it turns white. Allow the violets to drain on a piece of fine cloth, set on a sieve to dry in a warm oven, turning two or three times until cool.

Fondant Cream (Uncooked)

1 egg white, 225 g (1¾ cups) icing sugar, peppermint oil or peppermint essence

Put the egg white into a bowl and beat it lightly. Gradually sift in enough icing sugar to form a stiff paste and beat well. Sprinkle the board and rolling pin with icing sugar and roll the mixture out to a 5 mm thickness. Cut into rounds with a small pastry cutter and place the rounds on a sheet of baking paper. Leave them to firm. Add a few drops of peppermint oil if using — you will need more if peppermint essence is used. Work trimmings together and roll out, using all the mixture.

French Jellies

2 tablespoons gelatine, 900 g (4 cups) sugar, essence, colouring

Soak the gelatine in 2¼ cups water for 1 hour. Put the gelatine and sugar in a saucepan, bring to the boil, and continue cooking for 20 minutes, skimming frequently. Add the essence. Pour half into a wetted sandwich tin. Colour the remainder and pour into another tin. Leave for 24 hours. Cut into squares and dust in icing sugar. Store in an airtight container with icing sugar between the layers.

French Nougat

800 g (3⅔ cups) sugar, 450 g light corn syrup, 1 egg white,
55 g (⅓ cup) almonds, 55 g (¼ cup) glacé cherries, vanilla or almond essence

Put the sugar and corn syrup in a saucepan with 300 ml water. Stir over medium heat until the sugar and corn syrup dissolve. Cover and bring to the boil for a few minutes. Remove the lid and brush the saucepan sides with a brush dipped in cold water to prevent the sugar graining. Boil to 127°C on a sugar thermometer or until a little syrup forms a hard ball in cold water. Remove from the heat and pour into a bowl. Cool slightly. Beat the egg white until stiff peaks form and add to the syrup. Beat until white. Chop the almonds and cut the cherries into rings. Add to the nougat with the vanilla essence. Beat the mixture until smooth and very thick. Pour into a greased tray. Cut into neat bars or small blocks. Wrap each in wax tissue.

Fudge

660 g (3 cups) sugar, 250 ml (1 cup) milk, 1 tablespoon butter,
1 tablespoon cocoa powder, 1 teaspoon vanilla essence

Put the sugar, milk, butter and cocoa powder in a saucepan. Bring to the boil and boil for 15 minutes. Remove from the heat and add the vanilla, stirring until creamy. Pour into a greased dish and leave to set. Cut into squares, to serve.

Honeycomb Toffee

220 g (1 cup) sugar, 1 tablespoon vinegar, 1 tablespoon honey,
1/2 tablespoon butter, 1/2 teaspoon bicarbonate of soda

Put the sugar, vinegar, honey and butter into a non-metallic saucepan and bring to the boil. Boil until it reaches about 155°C on a sugar thermometer, or until it 'cracks'. Stir the bicarbonate or soda into the toffee and pour immediately into a greased dish.

Honey Toffee

440 g (2 cups) sugar, 450 g (1¼ cups) honey, 55–85 g butter

Put all the ingredients in a saucepan and bring to the together boil, stirring constantly. Do not stir once it comes to the boil. When a little hardens in cold water, take it from the fire and pour into greased baking trays.

JuJubes

3 tablespoons gelatine, 625 g sugar, lemon essence, red food colouring

Soak the gelatine in 250 ml (1 cup) water for 30 minutes. Put the sugar in a saucepan with 250 ml (1 cup) water and bring to the boil for 10 minutes, then add the gelatine and boil for another 10 minutes. Add the lemon essence, to taste. Butter two deep dishes and pour half the mixture into one dish. Colour the remainder with red food colouring and pour into the other dish. Leave until perfectly cold, then cut into squares and roll in sugar.

Marshmallows 1

3 tablespoons powdered gelatine, 330 g (1½ cups) sugar,
1 tablespoon glucose, chopped nuts, vanilla essence, raspberry essence,
red food colouring, cornflour

Soak the gelatine in a saucepan with 250 ml (1 cup) water. Add the sugar and glucose and boil for 10 minutes; then set aside. When almost cold, beat until white. Add the chopped nuts. Divide the mixture into two equal portions. Add the vanilla essence to one half and the raspberry essence and red food colouring to the other portion. Pour separately into two greased tins and leave overnight. Cut into squares with a pair of scissors and roll in cornflour, to dust. Store in an airtight tin.

Marshmallows 2

115 g gum Arabic, 1½ tablespoons gelatine, 215 g (1¾ cups) icing sugar,
3 egg whites, 300 ml water, flavouring and colouring

Soak the gum Arabic and gelatine in 300 ml water until soft, then heat gently in a saucepan until dissolved and strain through a fine muslin. Return to a clean pan and add the icing sugar, stirring until the sugar dissolves. Add the egg whites and whisk until the mixture is quite stiff. Flavour and colour, if liked. Spread out in a tin dipped in cold water and let it stand for 12 hours. Cut into small squares and dredge liberally with icing sugar.

Marzipan (Uncooked)

30 g (¹⁄₄ cup) icing sugar, 1 tablespoon grated chocolate, 1 egg white,
100 g (1 cup) ground almonds, vanilla essence, cocoa powder

Sift the icing sugar into a bowl and add the chocolate, mixing well. Whisk in the egg white until quite stiff, then add the chocolate mixture, almonds and essence. Knead until quite smooth. If not stiff enough, add a little more sugar. Allow to stand for a few hours. Roll into small balls and then dust all over in the cocoa.

Orange Creams

350 g (2³⁄₄ cups) icing sugar, ¹⁄₂ large orange, a pinch of cream of tartar

Finely grate the zest of the orange half into a bowl. Add the strained juice and stir in the cream of tartar. Add the icing sugar gradually until a stiff paste is formed, beating it constantly. Turn the mixture out onto a board and knead it until quite smooth. Then form it into balls or cubes, or fancy shapes.

Variation Lemon creams are made in the same way. Simply substitute a lemon for the orange. To make ginger creams, follow the same recipe, but substitute a few teaspoons ground ginger and add a few drops of lemon colouring.

Peanut Brittle

165 g (³⁄₄ cup) sugar, 115 g glucose, 2 teaspoons butter, 110 g (²⁄₃ cup) chopped
peanuts, 3 tablespoons bicarbonate of soda, ¹⁄₄ teaspoon salt

Boil sugar and glucose in a saucepan with water. Add the butter and peanuts and boil for about 10 minutes, stirring constantly, until the peanuts are cooked. Remove from the heat and add the bicarbonate of soda and salt dissolved in 1 teaspoon of water. Stir well, and then pour out on a large greased tray, making sure it is quite thin in the tray. Allow to set.

Peppermints

330 g (1½ cups) sugar, 6 drops peppermint essence

Put the sugar and 125 ml (½ cup) boiling water into a non-metallic saucepan and stir over low heat until the sugar has dissolved. Bring to the boil and boil for 10 minutes. Remove from the heat and stir in the peppermint until the right consistency. Drop from the tip of a spoon onto lightly buttered paper and set.

Russian Toffee

440 g (2 cups) sugar, 55 g butter, 1 tablespoon golden syrup,
1 tablespoon red currant jelly, 420 g (1⅓ cups) sweetened condensed milk

Rinse a saucepan with cold water. Put in the sugar, butter, golden syrup and red currant jelly. Stir until almost boiling, then add the condensed milk. Stir constantly until the toffee boils, then reduce the heat to low and simmer for about 15–20 minutes, or until the toffee is sticky when tested in cold water. Pour onto a greased tray. When nearly cold, turn out and cut into squares.

Snowballs

1 tablespoon gelatine, 440 g (2 cups) sugar, 2 teaspoons light corn syrup,
1 egg white, a few drops vanilla essence, 50 g (⅓ cup) chopped chocolate,
50 g (½ cup) desiccated coconut

Soak the gelatine in 150 ml water. Put the sugar, corn syrup and 300 ml water in a saucepan over medium heat, stirring until the sugar has dissolved. Cover and boil for a few minutes to steam the sides. Remove the lid. Wipe the sides of the pan with a brush dipped in cold water to prevent the sugar graining. Boil to 115°C. Stir in the dissolved gelatine, and boil again. Beat the egg white; add the strained syrup gradually with a few drops of vanilla essence, and beat until thick and stiff. Shape into small balls. Leave until firmly set before coating. Stir the chocolate in a heatproof bowl over a saucepan of simmering water until smooth. Add a few drops vanilla essence. Dip each ball separately in the melted chocolate and roll in coconut, to coat.

Toffee Apples

Small red apples, 350 g (1²/₃ cups) sugar, 225 g glucose,
1 tablespoons butter, cochineal

Wash the apples, dry them thoroughly and put each on a clean stick of wood. Make a toffee by boiling together the sugar, glucose, butter and 125 ml (½ cup) hot water, or until when tested in cold water it is brittle. A few drops of cochineal will ensure a bright, transparent red colour. Dip each apple in toffee, covering the fruit well, then allow to cool on a well-greased tray.

Turkish Delight

900 g (4 heaped cups) white sugar, 2 egg whites, 1 lemon, 115 g cornflour,
rose or lemon essence, icing sugar

Put the sugar and 1.5 litres water in a saucepan and stir over low heat until the sugar dissolves. Clear it with the juice of the lemon and the whites of the eggs. Dissolve the cornflour in 300 ml cold water, strain, and add it to the syrup when boiling. Boil until the mixture is stringy and thick, then flavour with rose or lemon. Have ready two dishes – one greased lightly with oil and the other covered with sifted icing sugar. Pour the mixture on the oiled dish, let it stand for a minute or two to cool, then turn it over onto the sugared one. Cut into squares and cover with sugar so that the squares will not stick together when stored.

Preserved Orange, Lemon, Mandarin or Grapefruit Peel

Soak the peel for 24 hours in a saucepan with 2 teaspoons salt and 1.2 litres water. Bring to the boil and drain. Repeat this another five times and on the sixth time continue boiling until tender. Make a syrup by boiling 900 g sugar in 450 ml water. Add the peel to the syrup and cook for 2 hours. Strain off the syrup and roll in sugar. Place on a wire rack to dry.

Stains and Their Removal

	WOOL AND SILK	LINEN AND COTTON	RAYON
ADHESIVE OR GUM	Rub gum with ice and scrape off alternately with carbon tetrachloride* and water	As for silk	As for silk
BLOOD	Sponge with cold water and wash.	Treat with ammonia and wash	As for silk
COFFEE OR TEA	Warm water. Rub lightly with glycerine. Stand ½ hour, rinse.	Boiling water. If stain is old rub first with glycerine, not soap.	As for silk
CHOCOLATE	Warm water and detergent. Grease caused by cream with carbon tetrachloride*.	Detergent and hot water. Bleach with peroxide if necessary. Rinse.	As for silk
FAT OR GREASE	Place blotting paper under spot. Cover with talcum or starch, then porous paper. Press with iron.	If washable, detergent and water; non washable, use carbon tetrachloride*	As for silk
FRUIT OR GRASS	Add a few drops ammonia to bowl of steaming water. Spread fabric over bowl. Add peroxide from dropper every 5 minutes. Rinse in warm water.	Pour boiling water through from height. If washable, wash; non-washable, sponge with lukewarm water	As for silk
INK	Saturate with glycerine. Sponge clean with water, oxalic acid or lemon juice. Rinse.	As for silk	As for silk
LIPSTICK	A colourless grease or cold cream. Apply and then sponge with carbon tetrachloride*.	As for silk	As for silk

	WOOL AND SILK	LINEN AND COTTON	RAYON
MILDEW	Wash in hot soap, then peroxide if white wool or silk.	White: Soak in weak solution chloride of lime (1 tsp. to 600 ml water) for about 5–10 minutes. For stubborn stains repeat. Rinse thoroughly.	If coloured, sponge with soap and water.
PAINT	Sponge with turpentine. Traces may be removed with carbon tetrachloride*.	Soak washables in equal parts of ammonia and turpentine. Wash in suds. Non-washables treat as for wool.	As for silk
PERSPIRATION	Soap and water. Then peroxide if necessary.	Soap and water. If coloured, damp with water, hold over fumes from open ammonia bottle.	Treat with soap and water
RUST	Moisten with lemon juice and salt. Dry in sun.	As for silk	As for silk
SOOT	Brush spot then cover with starch. Work over stain and brush away. Sponge washables with detergent and water.	As for silk	As for silk
TAR	Turpentine or carbon tetrachloride*.	As for silk	As for silk
WATER	Allow to dry, then rub with another portion of the material. Press under damp cloth. Wash entire garment if washable.	As for silk	As for silk
WAX	Scrape off loose wax, then place blotter above and beneath spot. Press with hot iron. Treat remaining stain with carbon tetrachloride*.	As for silk	As for silk

*Carbon tetrachloride was formerly used in a wide variety of applications beforeits carcinogenic hazard was well known.

Glossary

The following glossary is largely taken from the first editions, with some new additions to define a few of the older terms.

ASPIC Savoury jelly in which cold meats, poultry and fish can be served.

BABA A French yeast cake.

BASTE Pouring hot fat over joints while baking or roasting.

BAIN MARIE A roasting tin or similar, that is filled with boiling water, in which saucepans or baking dishes can be placed — the contents can be kept hot without actually boiling. Also used to cook certain delicate dishes such as baked custards to stop them cooking too quickly, curdling or burning.

BÉCHAMEL A white sauce made with flour and butter (roux) and milk.

BEIGNETS French fritters fried in deep fat.

BLANC MANGE A flavoured and sweetened milk pudding thickened with cornflour.

BLANCH When foods (usually tender vegetables but sometimes citrus zest or meat) are plunged briefly into boiling water then drained and quickly refreshed in cold water. The purpose is to pre-cook, lightly set colour or purge of impurities.

BOUILLON A clear soup, stronger than broth, yet not as strong as consommé.

BOUQUET GARNI Herbs of different kinds, usually put in a muslin bag to season stews, etc.

BOVRIL Meat extract product.

BRAISE Braising is a 'wet' method of cooking, akin to stewing, and is most appropriate for tougher cuts of meat such as shin, chuck steak, brisket etc. Long, slow, moist cooking is essential to break down tough fibres and connective tissues.

BROIL To grill.

CARAMEL Colouring for soup, gravy, sauce, etc.

CEREBOS SAL TIN Vintage salt tin. A loaf tin or similar can be used as a substitute.

CHARLOTTE RUSSE A sweet containing cream prepared in a mould that has been lined with sponge fingers and topped with jelly.

CHAUD-FROID A cold entrée sauce used for masking cold poultry or eggs.

CONSOMMÉ Strong clear gravy, obtained by stewing meat a long time, also used to mean making soup.

CROQUETTES Minced fish, fowl or meat that is seasoned, rolled in egg and breadcrumbs, and fried crisp.

CROUSTADES Fried forms of bread on which savouries are served.

ESPAGNOLE One of the 'mother' sauces in French cookery made using rich beef stock, browned vegetables, a bit of tomato paste and some browned roux.

FILLETS Pieces of meat or fish freed from bone.

FLAN A French custard or open fruit tart with jellied juice.

FONDANT Boiled sugar beaten to a cream paste.

FORCEMEAT Finely ground and highly spiced meat, fish or poultry that is served alone or used in stuffing.

FRICANDEAU Term for well-trimmed pieces of veal stewed in various ways.

FRICASSÉE A very pale stew in which meat is blanched first to rid it of impurities, then simmered in a pale, creamy, mild-flavoured sauce; usually chicken or veal fricassée.

GALANTINE A dish of boned duck, chicken, veal, or turkey, filled with forcemeat and poached. It is garnished and served cold.

GLAZE Brush over with liquid, such as milk, egg, or water and sugar.

GRANADILLA An exotic fruit belonging to the passionfruit family, granadillas are twice the size of passionfruit with a smooth, fragile orange skin and a mild sweet pulp inside.

GUM ARABIC Resin exuded by Acacia Senegal trees; acts as a thickening agent.

LARD The white solid or semi-solid rendered fat of a hog; suggest substituting with margarine, butter or oil.

MACE A spice with a web-like, reddish mass that occurs on the outside of a nutmeg — nutmeg is the only thing that resembles it in flavour.

PARISIAN ESSENCE A rich brown concentrate of burnt caramel or sugar which is almost flavourless. Used mostly as a gravy browning agent, it is also used to enhance the rich appearance of a Christmas cake or in microwave cooking.

PEASE PUDDING A pudding made with strained split peas mixed with egg.

POT AU FEU A country-style one-pot dish from regional France.

POTTED MEAT Meat preserved in a can or jar, such as Spam.

QUENELLE A ball or dumpling of finely chopped meat or seafood bound with eggs and poached in stock or water.

RATAFIA A liqueur or cordial, flavoured with peach or cherry kernels, bitter almonds, or other fruits; many different varieties are made. Also a type of biscuit similar to amaretti.

ROUX A mixture of butter and flour used to thicken soups and stews.

SUET Hard fat around the kidneys and loins in beef and mutton.

SWEETBREAD The culinary term for the thymus gland (in the throat) and the pancreas (near the stomach) in calves, lambs and pigs.

VELOUTÉ A rich, creamy white sauce made using stock (as opposed to milk, which is used in béchamel sauce).

VOL-AU-VENT A pastry case shaped like an oversized patty case, filled with fricassée of fish, poultry or stewed fruit.

Index